# RECENT

# SPEECHES

AND

# ADDRESSES.

BY

CHARLES SUMNER.

Such busy multitudes I fain would see
Stand upon Free Soil with a people free.
GOETHE'S FAUST.

Nihil autem gloriosius libertate, præter virtutem, si tamen libertas recte a virtute sejungitur. — JOHN OF SALISBURY.

BOSTON:
HIGGINS AND BRADLEY,
20 WASHINGTON STREET.
1856.

CAMBRIDGE:
STEREOTYPED AND PRINTED BY THURSTON AND TORRY.

# CONTENTS.

# ACCEPTANCE OF THE OFFICE OF SENATOR OF THE UNITED STATES.

LETTER TO THE LEGISLATURE OF MASSACHUSETTS, 14TH MAY, 1851.

Read in the Senate by Hon. Henry Wilson, President, and in the House of Representatives by Hon. N. P. Banks, Speaker.

---

FELLOW-CITIZENS OF THE SENATE AND HOUSE OF REPRESENTATIVES:

I HAVE received by the hands of the Secretary of the Commonwealth a certificate, that, by concurrent votes of the two branches of the Legislature, namely, by the Senate, on the 22d day of January, and by the House of Representatives, on the 24th day of April, I was duly elected, in conformity to the provisions of the Constitution and Laws of the United States, a Senator to represent the Commonwealth of Massachusetts, in the Senate of the United States, for the term of six years, commencing on the 4th day of March, 1851.

If I were to follow the customary course, I should receive this in silence. But the protracted and unprecedented contest which ended in my election,— the interest it awakened, — the importance universally conceded to it, — the ardor of opposition and the constancy of support which it aroused, — also the principles, which more than ever among us, it brought into discussion, seem to justify, what my own feelings irresistibly prompt, a departure from this rule. If, beyond these considerations, any apology may be needed for thus directly addressing the Legislature, I may find it in the example of an illustrious predecessor, whose clear and venerable name will be a sufficient authority.*

The trust conferred on me is one of the most weighty which a citizen can receive. It concerns the grandest interests of our own Commonwealth, and also of the Union whereof we are an indissoluble part. Like every post of eminent duty, it is a post of eminent honor. A personal ambition, such as I cannot confess, might be satisfied to possess it. But when I think what it requires, I am obliged to say, that its honors are all eclipsed in my sight by its duties.

Your appointment finds me in a private station, with which I am entirely content. But this is not all. For the first time in my life, I am now called to political office. With none of the experience so amply possessed by others, to smooth the way of labor, I might well hesitate. But I am cheered by the generous confidence, which, throughout a lengthened contest, persevered in sustaining me, and by the conviction that, amidst all seeming differences of party, the sentiments, of which I am the known advo-

* John Quincy Adams.

cate, and which led to my original selection as a candidate, are dear to the hearts of a large majority of the people of this Commonwealth. I derive, also, a most grateful consciousness of personal independence from the circumstance, which I deem it frank and proper thus publicly to declare and place on record, that this office comes to me, unsought and undesired.

Acknowledging the right of my country to the service of her sons wherever she chooses to place them, and with a heart full of gratitude that a sacred cause has been permitted to triumph through me, I now accept the post of Senator.

I accept it as the servant of Massachusetts; mindful of the sentiments solemnly uttered by her successive Legislatures; of the genius which inspires her history; and of the men, her perpetual pride and ornament, who breathed into her that breath of Liberty, which early made her an example to her sister States. In such a service, the way, though new to my footsteps, will be illumined by lights which cannot be missed.

I accept it as the servant of the Union; bound to study and maintain, with equal patriotic care, the interests of all parts of our country; to discountenance every effort to loosen any of those ties by which our fellowship of States is held in fraternal company; and to oppose all *sectionalism*, whether it appear in unconstitutional efforts by the North to carry so great a boon as Freedom into the slave States, or in unconstitutional efforts by the South, aided by Northern allies, to carry the *sectional* evil of Slavery into the free States; or in whatsoever efforts it may make to extend the *sectional* domination of Slavery over the National Government. — With me the Union is twice-blessed; first, as the powerful guardian of the repose and happiness of thirty-one sovereign States, clasped by the endearing name of country; and next, as the model and beginning of that all-embracing Federation of States, by which unity, peace and concord will finally be organized among the nations. Nor do I believe it possible, whatever may be the delusion of the hour, that any part thereof can be permanently lost from its well-compacted bulk. *E Pluribus Unum* is stamped upon the national coin, the national territory, and the national heart. Though composed of many parts united into one, the Union is separable only by a crash which shall destroy the whole.

Entering now upon the public service, I venture to bespeak for what I may do or say that candid judgment, which I trust always to extend to others, but which I am well aware the prejudices of party too rarely concede. I may fail in ability; but not in sincere efforts to promote the general weal. In the conflicts of opinion, natural to the atmosphere of liberal institutions, I may err; but I trust never to forget the prudence which should temper firmness, or the modesty which becomes the consciousness of right. If I decline to recognize as my guides any of the men of to-day, I shall feel safe, while I follow the master principles which the Union was established to secure, and lean for support on the great triumvirate of American Freedom — Washington, Franklin and Jefferson. And since true politics are simply morals applied to public affairs, I shall find constant assistance from those everlasting rules of right and wrong, which are a law alike to individuals and communities: nay, which constrain the omnipotent God in self-imposed bonds.

Let me borrow, in conclusion, the language of another: "I see my duty; that of standing up for the liberties of my country; and whatever difficulties and discouragements lie in my way, I dare not shrink from it; and I rely on that Being, who has not left to us the choice of duties, that whilst I shall conscientiously discharge mine, I shall not finally lose my reward." These are the words of Washington, uttered in the early darkness of the American Revolution. The rule of duty is the same for the lowly and the great; and I hope it may not seem presumptuous in one so humble as myself to adopt his determination, and to avow his confidence.

I have the honor to be, fellow-citizens,
With sincere regard,
Your faithful friend and servant,
CHARLES SUMNER.

BOSTON, May 14, 1851.

## WELCOME TO KOSSUTH.

SPEECH IN THE SENATE OF THE UNITED STATES 10TH DEC. 1851.

---

MR. SEWARD, of New York, brought forward in the Senate the following joint resolution:

"*Be it Resolved, &c.*, That Congress, in the name and behalf of the people of the United States, give to Louis Kossuth a cordial welcome to the capital and to the country, and that a copy of this resolution be transmitted to him by the President of the United States."

December 9th, Mr. BERRIEN, of Georgia, addressed the Senate at length in opposition to any action by Congress, and, in closing his speech, moved the following amendment:

"*And be it further Resolved*, That the welcome thus afforded to Louis Kossuth be extended to his associates who have landed on our shores; but while welcoming these Hungarian patriots to an asylum in our country, and to the protection which our laws do and always will afford to them, it is due to candor to declare that it is not the purpose of Congress to depart from the settled policy of this Government, which forbids all interference with the domestic concerns of other nations."

December 10th, on motion of Mr. SEWARD, the Senate proceeded to the consideration of the special order, being his resolution of welcome to Kossuth.

MR. SUMNER then addressed the Senate as follows:

*Mr. President:* — Words are sometimes things; and I cannot disguise from myself that the resolution in honor of Louis Kossuth, now pending before the Senate, when finally passed, will be an act of no small significance in the history of our country. The Senator from Georgia [Mr. Berrien] was right when he said that it was no unmeaning compliment. Beyond its immediate welcome to an illustrious stranger, it will help to combine and direct the sentiments of our own people everywhere; it will inspire all in other lands who are engaged in the contest for freedom; it will challenge the disturbed attention of despots; and it will become a precedent whose importance will grow, in the thick-coming events of the future, with the growing might of the Republic. In this view, it becomes us to consider well what we do, and to understand the grounds of our conduct.

For myself, I am prepared to vote for it without amendment or condition of any kind, and on reasons which seem to me at once obvious and conclusive. In assigning these I shall be brief; and let me say that, novice as I am in this hall, and, indeed, in all legislative halls, nothing but my strong interest in the question as now presented, and a hope to say something directly upon it, could prompt me thus early to mingle in these debates.

The case seems to require a statement, rather than an argument. As I understand, the last Congress requested the President to authorize the employment of one of our public vessels to receive and convey Louis Kossuth to the United States. That honorable service was performed, under the express direction of the President, and in pursuance of the vote of Congress, by one of the best-appointed ships of our navy — the steam-frigate Mississippi. Far away from our country, in foreign waters, in the currents of the Bosphorus, the Hungarian chief, passing from his Turkish exile, first pressed the deck of this gallant vessel; first came under the protection of our national flag, and, for the first time in his life, rested beneath the ensign of an unquestioned Republic. From that moment he became our guest. The Republic — which, thus far, he had seen only in delighted dream or vision — was now his host; and though this relation was interrupted for a few weeks by his wise and brilliant visit to England, yet its duties and its pleasures, as I confidently submit, are not yet ended. The liberated exile is now at our gates. Sir, we cannot do things by halves; and the hospitality thus, under the auspices of Congress, begun, must, under the auspices of Congress, be continued. The hearts of the people are already open to receive him; Congress cannot turn its back upon him.

But I would join in this welcome, not merely because it is essential to complete and crown the work of the last Congress, but because our guest deserves it at our hands. The distinction is great, I know; but it is not so great as his deserts. He deserves it as the early, constant, and incorruptible champion of the Liberal Cause in Hungary, who, while yet young, with unconscious power, girded himself for the contest, and by a series of masterly labors, with voice and pen, in parliamentary debates, and in the discussions of the press, breathed into his country the breath of life. He deserves it by the great principles of true democracy which he caused to be recognized — representation of the people without distinction of rank or birth, and *equality before the law.* He deserves it by the trials he has undergone, in prison and in exile. He deserves it by the precious truth, which he now so eloquently proclaims, of the Fraternity of Nations.

As I regard his course, I am filled with reverence and awe. I see in him, more than in any other living man, the power which may be exerted by a single, earnest, honest soul, in a noble cause. In himself he is more than a whole cabinet — more than a whole army. I watch him in Hungary, while, like Carnot in France, he "organizes victory;" I follow him in exile to distant Asiatic Turkey, and there find him, with only a scanty band of attendants, in weakness and confinement, still the dread of despots; I sympathize with him in his happy release; and now, as he comes more within the sphere of our immediate observation, amazement fills us all in the contemplation of his career, while he proceeds from land to land, from city to city, and, with words of matchless power, seems at times the fiery sword of freedom, and then the trumpet of resurrection to the nations — *Tuba mirum spargens sonum.*

I know not how others have been impressed; but I can call to mind no incident in history — no event of peace or war — certainly none of war — more strongly calculated — better adapted — to touch and exalt the imagination and the heart than his recent visit to England. He landed on the southern coast, not far from where William of Normandy, nearly eight centuries ago, had landed; not far from where, nineteen centuries ago, Julius Cæsar had landed also; but William on the field of Hastings, and Cæsar, in his adventurous expedition, made no conquest comparable in grandeur to that achieved by the unarmed and unattended Hungarian. A multitudinous people, outnumbering far the armies of those earlier times, was subdued by his wisdom and eloquence; and this exile,—proceeding from place to place, — traversing the country, — at last, in the very heart of the Kingdom, threw down the gauntlet of the Republic. Without equivocation, amidst the supporters of monarchy, in the shadow of a lofty throne, he proclaimed himself a republican, and proclaimed the republic as his cherished aspiration for Hungary. And yet, amidst the excitements of this unparalleled scene, with that discretion which I pray may ever attend him, as a good angel — the ancient poet aptly tells us that no Divinity is absent where Prudence is present — he forbore all suggestion of interference with the existing institutions of the country whose guest he was, recognizing that vital principle of self-government, by virtue of which every State chooses for itself the institutions and rulers which it prefers.

Such a character, thus grandly historic — a living Wallace — a living Tell — I had almost said a living Washington — deserves our homage. Nor am I tempted to ask if there be any precedent for the resolution now under consideration. There is a time for all things; and the time has come for us to make a precedent in harmony with his unprecedented career. The occasion is fit; the hero is near; let us speak our welcome. It is true that, unlike Lafayette, he has never directly served our country; but I cannot admit that on this account he is less worthy. Like Lafayette, he perilled life and all; like Lafayette, he has done penance in an Austrian dungeon; like Lafayette, he has served the cause of freedom; and whosoever serves this cause, wheresoever he may be, in whatever land, is entitled, according to his works, to the gratitude of every true American bosom — of every true lover of mankind.

The resolution before us commends itself by its simplicity and completeness. In this respect, it seems to me preferable to that of the Senator from Illinois [Mr. Shields]; nor is it obnoxious to objections urged against that of the Senator from Mississippi [Mr. Foote]; nor do I see that it can give any just umbrage, in our diplomatic relations, even to the sensitive representative of the house of Austria. Though we have the high authority of the President, in his message, for styling our guest "Governor" — a title which seems to imply the *de facto* independence of Hungary at the very time when our Government declined to acknowledge it — the resolution avoids this difficulty, and speaks of him without title of any kind — simply as a private citizen. As such, it offers him a welcome to the capital and to the country.

The comity of nations I respect. To the behests of the law of nations I profoundly bow. As in our domestic affairs, all acts are brought to the Constitution, as to a touchstone, so in our foreign affairs, all acts are brought to the touchstone of the law of nations — that supreme law, the world's collected will, which overarches the Grand Commonwealth of Christian States. What that forbids, I forbear to do. But no text of this voluminous code, no commentary, no gloss, can be found which forbids us to welcome any exile of freedom.

Looking at this resolution in its various lights — as a carrying out of the act of the last Congress; as justly due to the exalted character of our guest; and as proper in form and consistent with the law of nations — it seems impossible to avoid the conclusion in its favor. On its merits it would naturally be adopted. And here I might stop.

But an appeal has been made against the resolution, on grounds which seem to me extraneous and irrelevant. It has been attempted to involve it with the critical question of intervention by our country in European affairs; and recent speeches in England and New York have been adduced to show that such intervention is sought by our guest. It is sufficient to say in reply to this suggestion, introduced by the Senator from Georgia [Mr. Berrien] with a skill which all might envy — and also by the Senator from New Jersey [Mr. Miller] — *that no such intervention is promised or implied by the resolution.* It does not appear on the face of the resolution; it is not in any way suggested by the resolution, directly or indirectly. It can only be found in the imagination, the anxieties, or the fears of Senators! It is a mere ghost, and not a reality. As such we may dismiss it. But I feel strongly on this point, and desire to go further. Here, again, I shall be brief; for the occasion allows me to state conclusions only, and not arguments.

While thus warmly — with my heart in my hand — joining in this tribute, I wish to be understood as in no respect encouraging any idea of belligerent intervention in European affairs. Such a system would have in it no element of just self-defence, and it would open phials of perplexities and ills which I trust our country will never be called to affront. But I inculcate no frigid isolation. God forbid that we should ever close our ears to the cry of distress, or cease to swell with indignation at the steps of tyranny! In the wisdom of Washington we may find perpetual counsel. Like Washington, in his eloquent words to the Minister of the French Directory, I would offer sympathy and God-speed to all, in every land, who struggle for Human Rights; but, sternly as Washington on another occasion, against every pressure, against all popular appeals, against all solicitations, against all blandishments, I would uphold with steady hand the peaceful neutrality of the country. Could I now approach our mighty guest, I would say to him, with the respectful frankness of a friend, "Be content with the outgushing sympathy which you now so marvellously inspire everywhere throughout this wide-spread land, and may it strengthen your soul! Trust in God, in the inspiration of your cause, and in the Great Future, pregnant with freedom for all mankind. But respect our ideas, as we respect yours. Do not seek to reverse our traditional, established policy of peace. *Do not, under the too plausible sophism of upholding non-intervention, provoke American intervention on distant European soil.* Leave us to tread where Washington points the way."

And yet, with these convictions, Mr. President, which I now most sincerely express, I trust the Senator from Georgia [Mr. Berrien] will pardon me when I say I cannot join in his proposed amendment; and for this specific reason. It attaches to an act of courtesy and welcome a condition which, however just as an independent proposition, is most ungracious in such connection. It is out of place, and everything out of place is, to a certain extent, offensive. If adopted, it would impair, if not destroy, the value of our act. A generous hospitality will not make terms or conditions with a guest; and such hospitality, I trust, Congress will tender to Louis Kossuth.

## JUSTICE TO THE LAND STATES AND POLICY OF ROADS.

SPEECHES IN THE SENATE OF THE UNITED STATES ON THE IOWA RAILROAD BILL, 27TH JAN., 17TH FEB., AND 16TH MARCH, 1852.

---

In the Senate, *January* 27, 1852. The Senate having under consideration the special order, being the "bill granting the right of way, and making a grant of land to the State of Iowa, in aid of the construction of certain railroads in said State," —

Mr. Sumner said: —

This bill is important by itself, inasmuch as it promises to secure the building of a railroad at large cost, for a long distance, through a country not thickly settled, in a remote corner of the land. It is more important still as a precedent for a series of similar appropriations in other States. In this discussion, then, we have before us, at the same time, the special interests of the State of Iowa, traversed by this projected road, and also the great question of the administration of the public lands.

I have no inclination to go into these matters at length, even if I were able; but entertaining no doubt as to the requirements of policy and of justice in the present case, and in all like cases, seeing my way clearly before me by lights that cannot deceive, I hope in a few words to exhibit these requirements and to make this way manifest to others. And I am especially moved to do so by the tone of remarks often heard out of the Senate, and sometimes even here, begrudging these appropriations, and charging the particular States for which they are made with an undue absorption of the property of the Union. It is sometimes said — not in this body, I know — that "the West is stealing the public lands;" and the Senator from Virginia [Mr. Hunter], who expresses himself with a frankness and a moderation of manner worthy of regard, in discussing this very measure, distinctly said that "we are squandering away the public lands;" and he complained that such appropriations were partial, "because very large amounts of land are distributed to those States in which they lie, while nothing is given to the old States." And the Senator from Kentucky [Mr. Underwood], taking up this strain, has dwelt at great length, and in every variety of expression, on the alleged partiality of the distribution.

Now, I know full well that the States in which these lands lie need no defender like myself. But, as a Senator from one of the old States, I desire thus early to declare distinctly my dissent from these views, and the reasons for my dissent. Beyond a general concern, that the public lands, of which the Union is now the almoner, the custodian and proprietor, should be administered freely, generously, bountifully, in such wise as most to promote their settlement, and to build upon them towns, cities, and States, the nurseries of future empire — beyond this concern which leads me to adopt gladly the proposition, in favor of actual settlers, brought forward by the Senator from Wisconsin

[Mr. Walker], I find a clear and special reason for supporting the measure now before the Senate, in an undeniable rule of justice to the States in which the lands lie.

Let me speak, then, for *justice* to the land States. And in doing so I wish to present an important, and, as it seems to me, decisive consideration — which has not been adduced thus far in this debate, nor do I know that it has been presented in any prior discussion — *founded on the exemption from taxation enjoyed by the National lands in the several States, and the unquestionable value of this franchise.* The subject naturally presents itself under two heads: *First*, the origin and nature of this franchise; and, *secondly*, its extent and value, after deducting therefrom all reservations and grants to the several States.

I. And now, in the *first* place, as to the origin and nature of the immunity enjoyed by the national domain in the several States.

The United States are the proprietors of large tracts of country within the municipal and legislative jurisdiction of States of the Union. These lands are not held directly by virtue of any original prerogative or eminent domain, by any right of conquest, occupancy, or discovery, but under acts of cession from the old States, in which the lands were situated, and from foreign countries, recognized and confirmed in the various statutes by which the different States have been constituted. The words determining this relation are found in the Ordinance of 1787. They are as follow: "The Legislatures of these districts or new States shall never interfere with *the primary disposal of the soil* by the United States in Congress assembled,

nor with any regulations Congress may find necessary for securing the title in such soil to *bona fide* purchasers." This provision has been incorporated, as an article of compact, in the subsequent statutes under which the new States have taken their place in the Union. It is the "primary disposal of the soil," without any incident of *sovereignty*, which is here secured.

Regarding the United States, then, as simple proprietors of these lands, under the jurisdiction of the States, would they not be liable, in the discretion of the States, to the burdens of other proprietors, unless especially exempted therefrom? This exemption has been conceded. In the ordinance of 1787, it is expressly declared that "no tax shall be imposed on land the property of the United States;" and this provision, like that already mentioned, is embodied in succeeding acts of Congress by which new States have been constituted. The fact that it was formally conceded and has been thus imbodied, seems to denote that such concession was regarded as necessary to secure the desired immunity. Indeed, from the principles recognized in our jurisprudence, and particularly by the Supreme Court, it is reasonable to infer that, without such express exemption, this whole amount of territory would be within the field of local taxation, liable, like the lands of other proprietors, to all customary burdens and incidents.

Thus, in an early case in Pennsylvania, it was decided that the purchase of land by the United States would not alone be sufficient to vest them with the jurisdiction, or to oust the jurisdiction of the State, without being accompanied or followed by the consent of the Legislature of the State. (See *Commonwealth of Pennsylvania* v. *Young*. 1 Kent's Comm. 431.) And it has been judicially declared by the late Mr. Justice Woodbury, in a well-considered case:

"Where the United States own land situated within the limits of any particular States, and over which they have no cession of jurisdiction, for objects either special or general, little doubt exists *that the rights and remedies in relation to it are usually such as apply to other landholders within the State*."

After setting forth certain rights of the United States, the learned judge proceeds:

"All these rights exist in the United States for constitutional purposes, and without a special cession of jurisdiction; though it is admitted that the powers over the property and persons on such lands will, of course, remain in the States till such cession is made. Nothing passes without such a cession, except what is an incident to the title and purposes of the General Government." — *United States* v. *Ames*, 1 Woodbury & Minot, R. 76.

The Supreme Court have given great eminence to the sovereign right of taxation in the States. They have said:

"Taxation is a sacred right, essential to the existence of Government — an incident of sovereignty. The right of legislation is co-extensive with the incident, to attach it upon all persons and property within the jurisdiction of a State." — *Dobbins* v. *Commissioners of Erie Co.*, 17 Peters, R. 447.

And again, the Court say in another case:

"However absolute the right of an individual may be, it is still in the nature of that right that it must bear a portion of the public burdens, and that portion must be determined by the Legislature." — *Providence Bank* v. *Pittman*, 4 Peters, R. 514.

And in the same case the Court, after declaring "that the taxing power is of vital importance; that it is essential to the existence of Government; that the relinquishment of such a power is never to be assumed," add, cautiously, that they will not say "that a State may not relinquish it — *that a consideration sufficiently valuable to induce a partial release of it may not exist.*"

While thus upholding the right of taxation as one of the precious attributes of sovereignty in the States, the Court, under the Constitution of the United States, have properly exempted from taxation the instruments and means of the Government; but they have limited the exemption to these instruments and means. Thus it has been expressly decided in a celebrated case, (*McCulloch* v. *Maryland*, 4 Wheaton, 316,) that, while the Bank of the United States, being one of the necessary *instruments and means* to execute the sovereign powers of the nation, was not liable to taxation, yet the real property of the Bank was thus liable in common with the other real property in a particular State.

Now, the lands held by the United States do not belong to the *instruments and means* necessary and proper to execute the sovereign powers of the nation. In this respect they clearly differ from fortifications, arsenals, and navy yards. They are strictly in the nature of *private property* of the nation, situated within the jurisdiction of States. In excusing them from taxation, our fathers acted unquestionably according to the suggestions of prudence, but also under the influence of precedent, derived *at that time* from the prerogatives of the British Crown. It was an early prerogative, transmitted from feudal days, when all taxes were in the nature of aids and subsidies to the monarch, that the property of the Crown, of every nature, should be exempt from taxation. *But mark the change.* This ancient feudal principle is not now the existing law of England. By the statute of 39 and 40 George III, cap. 38, passed twelve years after the Ordinance of 1787, the lands and tenements purchased by the Crown out of the privy purse or other moneys not appropriated to any public service, or which came to the King from his ancestors or private persons — in other words, lands and tenements in the nature of *private property* — are subjected to taxation, even while they belong to the Crown.

Thus the matter now stands. Lands belonging to the nation, which, it seems, even royal prerogative at this day, in England, cannot save from taxation, are in our country, under express provisions of compact, early established, exempted from this burden. Now, sir, I make no complaint of this; I do not suggest any change; nor do I hint any ground of legal title in the States. But I do confidently submit that in this peculiar, time-honored immunity, originally claimed by the nation, and conceded by the States within which the public lands lie, there is ample ground of equity, under which these States may now appeal to the nation for assistance out of these public lands.

When I listen to comparisons discrediting these States by the side of the old States; when I hear it charged that they have been constant recipients of the national bounty; and when I catch those sharper terms of condemnation, by which they are characterized as "plunderers" and "robbers" and "pirates," I am forced to inquire whether the nation has not already received from these States something more than it has ever bestowed, even in its most liberal moods; whether, at this moment, the nation is not *equitably* the debtor to these States, and not these States the debtors to the nation. The answer is clear.

In order to estimate the importance of this *equity* — for I will call it by no stronger term — we must endeavor to understand the extent and value of the franchise or immunity conceded by the States.

II. And I am now brought to the *second* head of this inquiry; that is, the extent and value of the immunity from taxation enjoyed by the national domain, after deducting therefrom all reservations and grants to the several States. Authentic documents and facts place these beyond question.

From the official returns of the Land Office in January, 1849, [Exec. Doc. 2d session, 30th Cong., H. R. No. 12, p. 225,] it appears that the areas of the twelve Land States — Ohio, Indiana, Illinois, Missouri, Alabama, Mississippi, Louisiana, Michigan, Arkansas, Wisconsin, Iowa, and Florida — embrace 392,579,200 acres. California was not at that time a State of the Union. Of this territory, only 289,961,954 acres had been, in pursuance of the laws of the United States, surveyed, proclaimed, and put into the market. In some of the recent States, more than a moiety of the whole domain had never been brought into this condition. It continued, at the date of these official returns, still unconscious of the surveyor's chain. Thus, in Wisconsin, out of a territory of more than thirty-four millions of acres, only a little more than thirteen millions had been proclaimed for sale; and in Iowa, the very State whose interests are now particularly in question, out of a territory of more than thirty-two millions of acres, only a little more than twelve millions had been proclaimed for sale. It is evident, therefore, that, in point of fact, the true extent of territory, belonging to the United States at any time, much exceeds the extent actually in the market; but since it may be said, that the lands not yet surveyed, proclaimed, and put into the market, though nominally under the jurisdiction of the State, must actually lie out of the sphere of their influence, so as not to derive any appreciable advantage from the local Governments, and, as I desire to hold this argument above every imputation of exaggeration — knowing full well that it can afford to be under-stated — I shall forbear to take the larger sum as the basis of my estimates, but shall found them upon the extent of territory actually proclaimed for sale, from the beginning down to January, 1849, amounting to 289,961,954 acres.

All these lands thus proclaimed have been exempt from taxation. But since they were proclaimed at different periods, and also sold at different periods, so far as the same have been sold, it is necessary, in order to arrive at the value of this immunity, to ascertain what is the average period during which the lands, after being put into the market, have been in the possession of the United States. This we are able to do from the official returns of the Land Office. Here is a table, now before me, from which it appears that of the lands offered for sale during a period of thirty years, large quantities — in some cases more than half — were, at the expiration of the period, still on hand. Of the fourteen millions offered in Ohio during this period, more than two millions remained; while, of the nineteen millions offered in Missouri, more than twelve millions remained. Of all the lands offered during this period of *thirty* years, more than half were still unsold. And out of the above aggregate of all the lands proclaimed from the beginning down to January, 1849, notwithstanding the advancing tread of our thick-coming population, only 100,209,656 acres had been sold. Now, without further pursuing these details, I shall assume what cannot be questioned, as it is most clearly within the truth, that the lands proclaimed are not all sold till after a period of fifty years. This estimate will make the average period during which the lands, after being surveyed and proclaimed, are actually in the possession of the United States, and free from taxation, twenty-five years.

According to this estimate, 289,961,954 acres proclaimed for sale, have been absolutely free from taxation, during the space of twenty-five years, and yet during this whole period have, without the ordinary consideration therefor, enjoyed the protection of the State, with the advantages and increased value from highways, bridges and school-houses, all of which are supported by the adjoining proprietors, under the laws of the State, without assistance of any kind from the United States.

Such is the extent of this immunity. But, in order to determine its precise value, it is necessary to advance a step further and ascertain one other element;

that is, the average annual tax on land in these States; for instance, on the land of other non-residents. There are no official documents within my knowledge by which this can be determined. But after inquiry of gentlemen, themselves landholders in these States, I have thought it might be placed, without chance of contradiction, at one cent an acre. Probably it is rather two or even three cents; but, desiring to keep within bounds, I call it merely one cent an acre. The annual tax on 289,761,954 acres, at the rate of one cent an acre, would be $2,809,619, and the sum total of this tax for twenty-five years would amount to $72,490,475, being the apparent value of this immunity from taxation already enjoyed by the United States; or, if we call the annual tax two cents an acre instead of one cent, we have the enormous sum of $144,980,950, of which the United States may now be regarded as trustees in *equity* for the benefit of the Land States.

But against this large sum I may be reminded of reservations and grants by the nation to the different States in question. These, however, when examined, do not materially interfere with the result. From the official returns of the Land Office in 1848, [Executive Doc., Thirtieth Congress, second session, H. R. No. 18,] we learn the precise extent of these reservations and grants down to that period. Here is the exhibit:

| | Acres. |
|---|---|
| Common schools | 10,807,958 |
| Universities | 823,950 |
| Seats of Government | 50,860 |
| Salines | 422,325 |
| Amount carried forward, | 12,105,093 |

| | | |
|---|---|---|
| Amount brought forward, | | 12,105,093 |
| Deaf and dumb asylums . . . . | | 45,440 |
| Internal improvements | By act Sept. 4, 1841, . | 4,169,439 |
| | Roads, rivers, and canals . | 4,305,034 |
| | | 20,625,006 |

This is all. In the whole aggregate, only a little more than twenty millions of acres have been granted to these States. The value of this sum total, if deducted from the estimated value of the franchise enjoyed by the nation, will still leave a very large balance to the credit of the Land States. Estimating the land at $1.25 an acre, all the reservations and grants will amount to no more than $25,788,257. Deducting this sum from $72,490,475, and we have $46,702,218 to be entered to the credit of the Land States; or, if we place the tax at two cents an acre, more than double this sum.

This result leaves the nation so largely in debt to the Land States, that it becomes of small importance to scan closely the character of these grants and reservations, in order to determine whether in large part they have not been already satisfied by specific considerations on the part of the States. But the stress that, in the course of this debate, has been laid upon this bounty, leads me to go further. It appears, from an examination of the acts of Congress by which the Land States were admitted into the Union, that a large portion of these reservations and grants was made on the express condition that the lands sold by the United States, under the jurisdiction of the States, *should remain exempt from any State tax for the space of five years after the sale.* This condition is particularly applicable to the appropriations for common schools, universities, seats of Government, and salines, amounting to 12,105,093 acres. It is also particularly applicable to another item, not mentioned before, which is known as the five per cent. fund, from the proceeds of the public lands, for the benefit of roads and canals, amounting in the whole to $5,242,069. These appropriations being made on specific considerations, faithfully performed by the States down to this day, may properly be excluded from our calculations. And this is a response to the Senator from Kentucky [Mr. Underwood], who dwelt so energetically on these appropriations, without seeming to be aware of the conditions on which they were granted.

That I may make this more intelligible, let me refer to the act for the admission of Indiana. After setting forth the five reservations and grants already mentioned, it proceeds :

"*And provided, always*, That the five foregoing provisions herein offered are on the condition that the convention of the said State shall provide by an ordinance, irrevocable without the consent of the United States, that every and each tract of land sold by the United States, from and after the 1st day of December next, shall be, and remain, exempt from any tax laid by order of any authority of the State, whether for State, county, or township, or any other purpose whatever, for the term of five years from and after the day of sale."

This clause does not stand by itself in the acts admitting the more recent States, but is mixed with other conditions. I will not believe, however, that any discrimination can be made between particular Land States, on the ground of a difference in their conditions which may properly be attributed to accidental circumstances. The provision just quoted is found substantially in the acts for the admission of Ohio, Missouri, Illinois and Arkansas. So far as these States are concerned, it is a complete consideration, in the nature of satisfaction, for the reservations and grants enjoyed by them. It also helps to illustrate the value of the *permanent immunity* from taxation belonging to the United States, by exhibiting the concessions made by the United States to assure this franchise to certain moderate quantities of land during the brief space of five years only.

After the constant charges of squandering the public lands and of partiality to the Land States, I think all will be astonished at the small amount to be entered on the debtor side, in the great account between the States and the National Government. This consists of grants for internal improvements, in the whole reaching to only 8,474,473 acres, which, at $1.25 an acre, will be $10,593,091. If this sum be deducted from the estimated value of the immunity from taxation already enjoyed by the United States, we shall still have *upwards of* $60,000,000 *surrendered by the Land States to the nation;* or, if we call the annual tax two cents an acre, more than double this sum.

In these estimates I have grouped together all the Land States. But, taking separate States, we shall find the same proportionate result. For instance, there is Ohio, with 16,770,984 acres proclaimed for sale down to January 1, 1849. Adopting the basis already employed, and assuming that these lands continued in the possession of the United States after being surveyed and proclaimed an average period of twenty-five years, and that the land tax was one cent an acre, we have $4,192,725 as the value of the immunity from taxation already enjoyed by the United States in Ohio. From this may be deducted the value of 1,181,134 acres, being grants to this State for internal improvements, at $1.25 per acre, equal to $1,476,367, leaving upwards of two millions — nearly three millions — of dollars yielded by this State to the nation.

Take another State — Missouri. It appears that, down to January, 1849, 39,685,609 acres had been proclaimed for sale in this State. Assuming again the basis already employed, and we have $9,908,900 as the value of the immunity from taxation already enjoyed by the United States in Missouri. From this may be deducted the value of 500,000 acres, granted to this State for internal improvements, which, at $1.25 an acre, will amount to $625,000, leaving upwards of nine millions of dollars thus yielded by this State to the nation.

I might in this way proceed with all the Land States individually; but enough has been done to repel the charges against them, and to elucidate their *peculiar equity* in the premises. On the one side, they have received little — very little — from the nation; while, on the other side, the nation, by strong considerations of equity, is largely indebted to them. This obligation of itself constitutes an equitable fund to which the Land States may properly resort for assistance in their works of internal improvement, and Congress will show an indifference to the reasonable demands of these States, should it fail to deal with them munificently — in some sort, according to the simple measure of advantage which the nation has already so largely enjoyed at their hands.

Against these clear and well-supported merits of the Land States, the old States can present small claims to consideration. They have waived no right of taxation over lands within their acknowledged jurisdiction; they have made no valuable concessions; they have yielded up no costly franchise. It remains, then, that, with candor and justice, they should recognize the superior — I will not say exclusive — claims of the States within whose borders and under the protection of whose laws the national domain is found.

Thus much for what I have to say in favor of this bill, on the ground of *justice* to the States in which the lands lie. If this argument did not seem sufficiently conclusive to render any further discussion superfluous, at least from me, I might go forward, and show that the true interests of the whole country — of every State in the Union, as of Iowa itself — are happily coincident with this claim of justice.

It will readily occur to all, that the whole country will gain by the increased value of the lands still retained and benefited by the proposed road. But this advantage, though not unimportant, is trivial by the side of the grander gains — commercially, politically, socially and morally — which will necessarily accrue from the opening of a new communication, by which the territory beyond the Mississippi will be brought into connection with the Atlantic seaboard, and by which the distant post of Council Bluffs will become a suburb of Washington. It would be difficult to exaggerate the influence of roads as means of civilization. This, at least, may be said: Where roads are not, civilization cannot be; and civilization advances as roads are extended. By roads, religion and knowledge are diffused; intercourse of all kinds is promoted; the producer, the manufacturer, and the consumer, are all brought nearer together; commerce is quickened; markets are opened; property, wherever touched by these lines, is changed, as by a magic rod, into new values; and the great current of travel, like that stream of classic fable, or one of the rivers of our own California, hurries in a channel of golden sand. The roads, together with the laws, of ancient Rome, are now better remembered than her victories. The Flaminian and Appian Ways — once trod by returning proconsuls and tributary kings — still remain as beneficent representatives of her departed grandeur. Under God, the road and the schoolmaster are the two chief agents of human improvement. The education begun by the schoolmaster is expanded, liberalized, and completed, by intercourse with the world; and this intercourse finds new opportunities and inducements in every road that is built.

Our country has already done much in this regard. Through a remarkable line of steam communications, chiefly by railroad, its whole population is now, or will be soon, brought close to the borders of Iowa. The cities of the Southern seaboard — Charleston, Savannah, and Mobile — are already stretching their lines in this direction, soon to be completed conductors; while the traveller from all the principal points of the Northern seaboard — from Portland, Boston, Providence, New York, Philadelphia, Baltimore, and Washington — now passes without impediment to this remote region, traversing a territory of unexampled resources — at once a magazine and a granary — the largest coal-field, and at the same time the largest corn-field, of the known globe — winding his way among churches and school-houses, among forests and gardens, by villages, towns, and cities, along the sea, along rivers and lakes, with a speed which may recall the gallop of the ghostly horseman in the ballad :

"Fled past on right and left how fast
Each forest, grove, and bower !
On right and left fled past how fast
Each city, town, and tower !

"Tramp ! tramp ! along the land they speed,
Splash ! splash ! along the sea."

On the banks of the Mississippi he is now arrested. The proposed road in Iowa will bear the adventurer yet further, to the banks of the Missouri; and this distant giant stream, mightiest of the earth, leaping from its sources in the Rocky Mountains, will be clasped with the Atlantic in the same iron bracelet. In all this I see not only further opportunities for commerce, but a new extension to civilization and increased strength to our National Union.

A heathen poet, while picturing the golden age, has perversely indicated the absence of long lines of road as creditable to that imaginary period in contrast with his own. "How well," exclaimed the youthful Tibullus,* "they lived while Saturn ruled — *before the earth was opened by long ways :*"

"Quam bene Saturno vivebant rege, priusquam
Tellus *in longas est patefacta vias.*"

* Opera, Lib. i. Eleg. 3, v. 35.

But the true Golden Age is before us, not behind us; and one of its tokens will be the completion of those *long ways*, by which villages, towns, counties, States, provinces, nations, are all to be associated and knit together in a fellowship that can never be broken.

The debate on the Iowa Railroad Bill was continued on successive days down to 17th February, when the speech of Mr. Sumner was particularly assailed by Mr. Hunter, of Virginia. To this he replied at once:

Mr. Sumner. One word, if you please, Mr. President. The Senator from Virginia [Mr. Hunter], who has just taken his seat, has very kindly given me notice that I am to expect a broadside from the Senator from Kentucky [Mr. Underwood]. For this information I am properly grateful. When, a few days ago, I undertook to discuss an important question in this body, I expressed certain views, deemed by me of weight. Those views I submitted to the candor and to the judgment of the Senate. I felt confidence in their essential justice, and nothing which I have heard since has impaired that confidence. I have listened with respect and attention to the address to-day from the Senator from Virginia, as it becomes me to listen to everything any Senator undertakes to put forth here. But I hope to be excused if I say, that in all that he has so eloquently uttered with reference to myself, he has not touched by a hair-breadth my argument. He has criticized — I am unwilling to say that he has cavilled at — my calculations; but he has not, by the ninth part of a hair, touched the conclusion which I drew. That still stands. And let me say, that it cannot be successfully assailed in the way attempted by him.

I said that injustice had been done to the Land States, out of this body and in this body, — out of this body, because I often heard them called "land stealers" and "land pirates;" in this body, by the Senator from Virginia, when he complained of the partial distribution of the public lands, and particularly pointed out the bill now before the Senate as an instance of this partiality. I said that this charge was without foundation. And why did I say so? and on what ground? Because there was an existing equity (I so called it — nothing more) on the part of the Land States as against the General Government. And on what was this founded? On a fact of record in the public acts of this country. That is, the exemption of the public domain from taxation by the States in which it is situated. The Senator from Virginia has not questioned this fact; of course he could not question it, for it is imbodied in the acts of Congress.

The next inquiry, then, was, as to the value of this immunity from taxation, which I called an equity on the part of the Land States. In order to illustrate this value, I went into calculations and estimates, which I presented, after some study of the subject — not, perhaps, such study as the Senator from Virginia has found time to give to it, or such as the Senator from Kentucky, in the plenitude of his researches, doubtless has given to it. On those calculations and estimates I attributed a certain value to the equity in question. My calculations and estimates may be overstated; they may be exaggerated. The Senator from

Virginia thinks them so. Other gentlemen with whom I have had the privilege of conversing, think them understated. But however this may be, it does not touch the argument. I may have done injustice to my argument by overstating them. I intended to understate them. I still think from all that I hear, that I have understated them. But, whether understated or overstated, the argument still stands, that these States have conceded to the General Government an immunity from taxation; that this immunity has a certain value — I think a very large value — and that this value constitutes an equity to which the Land States have a right to appeal for bountiful, ay, for munificent treatment from the General Government. Has the Senator from Virginia answered this argument? Can he answer it?

But I forbear to go into the subject at this time. I arose simply to state, that as the Senator from Virginia had kindly given me notice that I am to expect a broadside from the Senator from Kentucky, I am to regard what he said to-day, so far as I am concerned, simply as a signal gun. The Senator will pardon me if I say it is nothing more, for it has not reached me, or my argument. Meanwhile I await, with resignation and without anxiety, the broadside from Kentucky.

The debate was continued for many days, during which the speech of Mr. Sumner was attacked and defended. Finally, on the 16th March, immediately before the question was taken, he again returned to the subject:

Mr. Sumner. Much time has been consumed by this question. At several periods the debate has seemed about to stop, and then again it has taken a new spring, while the goal has constantly receded. I know not if it is now near the end. But I hope that I shall not seem to interfere with its natural course, or unduly occupy the time of the Senate, if I venture again for one moment to take part in it.

The argument which I submitted on a former occasion has not passed unregarded. And since it can owe little to my individual position, I accept the opposition it has encountered as a tribute to its intrinsic importance. It has been assailed by different Senators, on different days, and in different ways. It has been met by harmless pleasantry, and by equally harmless vituperation; by figures of rhetoric and figures of arithmetic; by minute criticism and extended discussion; also, by that sure resource of a weak cause, hard words and an imputation of personal motives. I do now propose to reply to all this array, least of all shall I retort the hard words or repel the personal imputations. On this head I content myself now with saying — and confidently, too, — that, had he known me better, the Senator from Kentucky [Mr. Underwood], who is usually so moderate and careful, would have hesitated long before uttering expressions which fell from him in this debate.

The position I took was regarded as natural, or excusable in a Senator from one of the Land States, acting under the vulgar spur of local interest; but it was pronounced unnatural and inexcusable in a Senator from Massachusetts. Now, sir, it is sufficient for me to say, in reply to this suggestion, that, while I know there are influences and biases incident to particular States or sections of the Union, I recognize no difference in the duties of Senators on this floor. Coming from different States and opposite sections, we are all Senators of the Union; and our constant duty is, without fear or favor, to introduce into the national legislation the principle of justice. In this spirit, while sustaining the bill now before the Senate, I spoke for justice to the Land States.

In sustaining this bill, I but followed the example of the Senators and Representatives of Massachusetts on kindred measures from their earliest introduction down to the present time. The first instance was in 1823, on the grant to the State of Ohio of land one hundred and twenty-five feet wide, with one mile on each side, for the construction of a road from the lower rapids of the Miami River to the western boundary of the Connecticut Reserve. On the final passage of this grant in the House, the Massachusetts delegation voted as follows: Yeas — Samuel C. Allen, Henry W. Dwight, Timothy Fuller, Jeremiah Nelson, John Reed, Jonathan Russell. Nay — Benjamin Gorham. In the Senate, the bill passed without a division. In 1828, a still greater unanimity occurred on the passage of the bill to aid the State of Ohio in extending the Miami canal from Dayton to Lake Erie; and this bill is the first instance of the grant of alternate sections, as in that now before the Senate. On this the Massachusetts delegation in the House voted as follows: Yeas — Isaac C. Bates, Benjamin W. Crowninshield, John Davis, Edward Everett, John Locke, John Reed, Joseph Richardson, John Varnum. Nays — none. In the Senate, Messrs. Silsbee and Webster both voted in the affirmative. I pass over the intermediate grants which, I am told, have been sustained by the Massachusetts delegations with substantial unanimity. The extensive grants at the last session of Congress to Illinois, Mississippi, and Alabama, in aid of a railroad from Chicago to Mobile, were sustained by all the Massachusetts votes in the House, except one.

Still further, in sustaining the present bill on grounds of justice to the Land States, I but followed the recorded instructions of the Legislature of Massachusetts, addressed to its Senators and Representatives here on a former occasion. The subject was presented in a special message to the Legislature in 1841, by the distinguished Governor at that time, who strongly urged "a liberal policy towards the actual settler, and *towards the new States*, for this is justly due to both." And he added: "Such States are entitled to a more liberal share of the proceeds of the public lands than the old States, as we owe to their enterprise much of the value this property has acquired. *It seems to me, therefore, that justice towards the States in which these lands lie, demands a liberal and generous policy towards them.*" In accordance with this recommendation, it was *resolved* by the Legislature, "That, in the disposition of the public lands, *this Commonwealth approves of making liberal provisions in favor of the new States;* and that she ever has been, and still is ready to co-operate with other portions of the Union in securing to those States such provisions." Thus a generous policy towards the Land States, with liberal provisions in their favor, was considered by Massachusetts the part of justice.

It was my purpose, before this debate closed, to consider again the argument I formerly submitted, and to vindicate its accuracy in all respects, both in principle and in detail. But this has already been so amply done by others so much abler than myself — by the Senator from Missouri [Mr. Geyer], both the Senators from Michigan [Mr. Felch and Mr. Cass], the Senator from Arkansas [Mr. Borland], the Senator from Iowa [Mr. Dodge], and the Senator from Louisiana [Mr. Downs], — all of whom, with different degrees of fulness, have urged the same grounds in favor of this bill, that I feel unwilling at this hour, and while the Senate actually waits to vote on the question, to occupy time by further dwelling upon it. Perhaps on some other occasion I may think proper to return to it.

But, while avoiding what seems superfluous discussion, I cannot forbear to ask your attention to the amendment of the Senator from Kentucky [Mr. Underwood].

This amendment, when addressed to the Senators of the favored States, is of a most plausible character. It proposes to give to the original thirteen States, together with Vermont, Maine, Tennessee, and Kentucky, for purposes of education and internal improvement, portions of the public domain, at the rate of one acre to each inhabitant according to the recent census. This is commended by the declared object — education and internal improvement. Still further, in its discrimination of the old States, it assumes a guise well calculated to tempt them into its support. It holds out the attraction of seeming, though unsubstantial, self-interest. It offers a lure, a bait to be unjust. I object to it on several grounds.

1. But I put it in the fore-front, as my first objection, its clear, indubitable, and radical injustice, written

on its very face. The amendment confines its donations to the old States, and, in so doing, makes an inequitable discrimination in their favor. It tacitly assumes that, by the bill in question, or in some other way, the Land States have received their proper distributive portion, so as to lose all title to share with the old States in the proposed distribution. But if there be any force in the argument, so much considered in this debate, that these railroad grants actually enhance the neighboring lands of the United States, and constitute a proper mode of bringing them into the market, or if there be any force in the other argument which I have presented, drawn from the equitable claims of the Land States, in comparison with the other States, to the bounty of the *great untaxed proprietor*,* then this assumption is unfounded. There is no basis for the discrimination made by the amendment. If the Iowa land bill be proper to be passed without this amendment, as I submit it is, then this amendment, introducing a new discrimination, is improper to be added to it. Nor do I well see how any one, prepared to sustain the original bill, can sustain this amendment. The Senator from Kentucky, who leads us to expect his vote for the bill, seems to confess the injustice of his attempted addition.

2. I object to it as out of place. The amendment proposes to ingraft upon a special railroad grant to a

* Mr. Webster in his greatest speech, the celebrated reply to Mr. Hayne, touched on this consideration. He said: "And, finally, have not these new States singularly strong claims, founded on the ground already stated, that the government is a great untaxed proprietor in the ownership of the soil?"—WEBSTER'S SPEECHES, Vol. III. p. 291.

single State a novel system of distribution of the national domain. Now, there is a place and a time for all things ; and nothing seems to me more important in legislation than to keep all things in their proper place, and to treat them at their proper time. The distribution of the public lands, is worthy of attention; and I am ready to meet this great question whenever it arises legitimately for our consideration; but I object to considering it merely as a rider to the Iowa land bill.

The amendment would be less objectionable, if proposed as a rider to a general system of railroad grants, as, for instance to a bill embracing grants to all the Land States; but it is specially objectionable as a graft upon a single bill. The Senator who introduced it doubtless assumed that other bills, already introduced, would pass ; but, if his amendment be founded on this assumption, it should await the action of Congress on all these bills.

3. If adopted, the amendment would endanger, if it did not occasion the defeat of, the Iowa land bill. This seems certain. Having this measure at heart, believing it founded in essential justice, I am unwilling to place it in this jeopardy.

4. It prepares the way for States of this Union to become landholders in other States, subject, of course, to the legislation of those States — an expedient which, though not strictly objectionable on grounds of law, or under the Constitution, is not agreeable to our national policy. It should not be promoted without strong and special reasons therefor. In the bill introduced by the Senator from Illinois [Mr. Shields], bestowing lands for the benefit of the insane in different States, this

objection has been partially obviated, by providing that the States in which there were no public lands should select their portion in the Territories of the United States, and not in other States. But, since in a short time these very Territories may become States, this objection is rather adjourned than entirely removed.

5. But the lands held under this amendment, though in the hands of States, will be liable to taxation, as the lands of other non-resident proprietors, and on this account will be comparatively valueless. For this reason, I said that the amendment held out the attraction of seeming, though unsubstantial, self-interest. That the lands will be liable to taxation, cannot be doubted. The amendment does not propose in any way to relieve them from this burden; nor am I aware that they can be relieved from it. The existing immunity is only so long as they belong to the United States. Now, there is reason to believe that, from lack of agencies and other means familiar to the United States, the lands distributed by this amendment would not find as prompt a market as those still in the hands of the Great Landholder. But howsoever this may be, it is entirely clear, from the recorded experience of the national domain, that these lands, if sold at the minimum price of the public lands, and only as rapidly as those of the United States, and if meanwhile they are subject to the same burdens as the lands of other non-residents, will, before the sales are closed, be eaten up by the taxes. The taxes will amount to more than the entire receipts from the sales of the lands; and thus the grant, while unjust to the Land States, will be worthless to the old States, the pretended beneficiaries. In

the Roman law, an insolvent inheritance was known by an expressive phrase as *damnosa hereditas.* A grant under this amendment would be *damnosa donatio.*

For such good and sufficient reasons, I am opposed to this amendment.

# CHEAP OCEAN POSTAGE

SPEECH IN THE SENATE OF THE UNITED STATES ON HIS RESOLUTION IN RELATION TO CHEAP OCEAN POSTAGE, 8TH MARCH, 1852.

[This proposition Mr. Sumner has renewed at each session of Congress.]

---

MR. SUMNER. I submit the following resolution. As it is one of inquiry, merely, I ask that it may be considered at this time :

*Resolved*, That the Committee on Naval Affairs, while considering the nature and extent of aid proper to be granted to the Ocean Steamers, be directed to inquire whether the present charges for letters carried by these steamers are not unnecessarily large and burdensome to foreign correspondence, and whether something may not be done, and, if so, what, to secure the great boon of Cheap Ocean Postage.

There being no objection, the question was stated to be on the adoption of the resolution.

MR. SUMNER. The Committee on Naval Affairs have the responsibility of shaping some measure by which the relations of our Government with the ocean steamers will be defined. And since one special inducement to these relations, involving the bounty now enjoyed and further solicited, is the carrying of the mails, I trust this Committee will be willing to inquire whether there cannot be a reduction on the postage of foreign correspondence. Under the postage act of 1851, the postmaster, by and with the advice of the President, has power to reduce, from time to time, the rates of postage on all mailable matter conveyed between the United States and any foreign country. But the existence of this power in the postmaster will not render it improper for the Committee, now drawn into connection with this question, to take it into careful consideration, with a view to some practical action, or, at least, recommendation thereon. The subject is of peculiar interest; nor do I know any measure so easily accomplished, which promises to be so beneficent as cheap ocean postage. The argument in its favor seems to me at once brief and unanswerable.

A letter can be sent three thousand miles in the United States for three cents, and the reasons for cheap postage on the land are equally applicable to the ocean.

In point of fact, the conveyance of letters can be effected in sailing or steam packets at less cost than by railway.

Besides, cheap ocean postage will tend to supersede the clandestine or illicit conveyance of letters, and to bring into the mails all mailable matter, which, under the present system, is carried in the pockets of passengers, or in the bales and boxes of merchants.

All new facilities for correspondence naturally give new expansion to human intercourse; and there is reason to believe that, through an increased number of letters, cheap ocean postage will be self-supporting.

Cheap postal communication with foreign countries will be of incalculable importance to the commerce of the United States.

By promoting the intercourse of families and friends, separated by the ocean, cheap postage will add to the sum of human happiness.

The present high rates of ocean postage — namely, twenty-four cents on half an ounce, forty-eight cents on an ounce, and ninety-six cents on a letter which weighs a fraction more than an ounce — are a severe tax upon all, particularly upon the poor, amounting, in many cases, to a complete prohibition of foreign correspondence. This should not be so.

It particularly becomes our country, by the removal of all unnecessary burdens upon foreign correspondence, to advance the comfort of European emigrants seeking a home among us, and to destroy as far as practicable, every barrier to free intercourse between the Old World and the New.

And, lastly, cheap ocean postage will be a bond of peace among the nations of the earth, and will extend good-will among men.

By such reasons this measure is commended. Much as I rejoice in the American steamers, which vindicate a peaceful supremacy of the seas, and help to weave a golden tissue between the two hemispheres, I cannot consider these, with all their unquestionable advantages, an equivalent for cheap ocean postage. But I trust that they are not inconsistent with each other, and that both may happily flourish together.

Objection was made to the resolution, as not being addressed to the proper Committee, and a brief debate ensued, in which Mr. Rusk, Mr. Gwin, Mr. Badger, Mr. Davis, Mr. Seward, Mr. Mason and Mr. Sumner, took part. It was urged by the latter, in reply to objections, that the Committee on Naval Affairs was the proper Committee, as at the present moment it is specially charged with a subject intimately connected with the inquiry into the importance and practicability of Cheap Ocean Postage. At the suggestion of Mr. Badger, the matter was allowed to lie over till the next day.

On Tuesday, 9th instant, the Senate proceeded to consider the resolution submitted by Mr. Sumner on the 8th inst., relative to Ocean Steamers and Cheap Ocean Postage. On motion of Mr. Sumner, it was amended, and finally adopted, without opposition, as follows:

*Resolved*, That the Committee on the Post Office and Post Roads be directed to inquire whether the present charges on letters carried by the Ocean Steamers are not unnecessarily large and burdensome to foreign correspondence, and whether something may not be done, and, if so, what, to secure the great boon of Cheap Ocean Postage.

# THE PARDONING POWER OF THE PRESIDENT.

ARGUMENT SUBMITTED TO THE PRESIDENT 14TH MAY, 1852, ON THE APPLICATION FOR THE PARDON OF DRAYTON AND SAYRES, DETAINED IN PRISON AT WASHINGTON FOR HELPING THE ESCAPE OF SLAVES.

---

This case excited peculiar interest. Messrs. Drayton and Sayres had already been in prison more than four years, when Mr. Sumner applied to President Fillmore for their pardon. To this application, which was sustained by petitions from other quarters, the President interposed doubts of his right to exercise the pardoning power in their case, but expressed a desire for light on this point. On his invitation, Mr. Sumner laid before him the following paper. Shortly afterwards the pardon was granted.

BY the laws of Maryland, 1737, chapter 2, section 4, it is provided that any person "who shall steal any negro or other slave," "or who shall counsel, hire, aid, abet, or command any person or persons" to do so, shall suffer death as a felon. The punishment has since been changed to imprisonment, for a term not less than seven, nor more than twenty years.

Fourteen years later, by the act of 1751, chapter 14, section 10, it was provided that "if any free person shall entice and persuade any slave within this province to run away, and who shall actually run away from the master, owner, or overseer, and be convicted thereof, by confession or verdict of a jury, upon an indictment or information, shall forfeit and pay the full value of such slave, to the master or owner of such slave, to be levied by execution on the goods, chattels, lands, or tenements of the offender, and, in case of inability to pay the same, shall suffer one year's imprisonment without bail or mainprise."

Still later, by the act of 1796, chapter 67, section 19, "the transporting of any slave or person, held to service" from the State, was made a distinct offence, for which the offender was made liable in an action of damages, and also by indictment.

By the act of Congress, organizing the District of Columbia, (Feb. 27, 1801,) it was declared that "the laws of the State of Maryland, as they now exist, shall be, and continue in force, in that part of the said District which was ceded by that State to the United States, and by them accepted as aforesaid." Under this provision, these ancient laws of Maryland are to this day of full force in the District of Columbia.

The facts to be considered are few. Messrs. Drayton and Sayres, on indictment and trial, under the act of 1737, for stealing slaves, were acquitted; the jury rendering a verdict of "not guilty." Resort was then had to the statute of 1796, chapter 67, section 19, as follows: —

"And be it enacted, that any person or persons who shall hereafter be convicted of giving a pass to any slave, or person held to service, or shall be found to assist, by advice, donation, or loan, or otherwise, the transporting of any slave, or any person held to service, from this State, or by any other unlawful means depriving the master or owner of the service of his slave, or person held to service, for every such offence the party aggrieved shall recover damages in an action on the case against such offender or offenders, and such offender or offenders also shall be liable, upon indictment and conviction upon verdict, confession or otherwise, in this State, in any county court where such offence shall happen, be fined a sum not exceeding two hundred dollars, at the discretion of the court, one half to the use of the master or owner of such slave, the other half to the county school, in case there be any, if no such school, to the use of the county."

Under this statute, proceedings were instituted by the attorney of the District of Columbia, against these parties, in seventy-four different indictments, each indictment being founded on the alleged "transporting" of a single slave. On conviction, Drayton was sentenced on each indictment to a fine of $140, and costs, in each case $19.49, amounting in the sum total to $11,802.26. On conviction, Sayres was sentenced on each indictment to a fine of $100 and costs, in each case $17.38, amounting in the sum total to $8,686.12. One half of the fine was, according to law, to the use of the masters or owners of the slaves transported; the other half to the county school; or, in case there be no such school, to the use of the county. Afterwards, on motion of the attorney for the District, they were "prayed in commitment," and committed until the fine and costs are payed. In pursuance of this sentence, and on this motion, they have been detained in prison, in the city of Washington, from April, 1848, and are still in prison, unable, from poverty, to pay these large fines. The question now occurs as to the power of the President to pardon them, *so at least as to relieve them from their imprisonment.*

The peculiar embarrassment in this case arises from the nature of the sentence. If it were simply a sentence of imprisonment, his power would be unquestionable. So, also, if it were a sentence of imprisonment, with fine superadded, payable to the United States, his power would be unquestionable; and the same power would extend to the case of a fine payable to the United States, with imprisonment as the alternative on non-payment of the fine.

But in the present case, the imprisonment is the alternative for non-payment of fines, which are not payable to the United States, but to other parties, viz.: the slave owners and the county. It is important, however, to bear in mind, that these fines are a mere donation to these parties, and not a compensation for services rendered. These parties were not informers, nor were the proceedings in the nature of a *qui tam* action.

It should be distinctly understood, at the outset, that the proceedings against Drayton and Sayres were not at the suit of any informer or private individual, but at the prosecution of the United States by indictment. They are, therefore, removed from the authority of the English cases, which protect the share of an informer after judgment from remission, by pardon from the crown.

The power of the President in the present case may be regarded, *first*, in the light of the common law;

*secondly*, under the statutes of Maryland, and *thirdly*, under the Constitution of the United States.

*First.* — As to the *common law*, it may be doubtful whether, according to early authorities, the pardoning power can be used so as to bar or divest any legal interest, benefit, or advantage, vested in a private individual. It is broadly stated by English writers, that it cannot be so used. (2 Hawkins, P. C. 392, cap. 37, sec. 34; 17 Viner's Abridgment; 39 Prerogative of King JJ., art. 7.) But this principle does not seem to be sustained by practical cases in the United States, except in the instances of informers and *qui tam* actions, while, on one occasion, in a leading case in Kentucky, it was rejected. (*Routt* v. *Flemster*, 7 J. J. Marshall, 132.)

But it is clearly established that, where the fine is allotted to a public body or a public officer, for a public purpose, it may be remitted by a pardon. This may be illustrated by several cases.

1. As where in Pennsylvania, the fine was for the benefit of the county. In this case, the court said, "Until the money is collected and paid into the treasury, the constitutional right of the Governor to pardon the offender, and remit the fine or forfeiture, remains in full force. They can have no more vested interest in the money than the Commonwealth, under the same circumstances, would have had; and it cannot be doubted that, until the money reaches the treasury, the Governor has the power to remit. In the case of costs, private persons are interested in them; but as to fines and forfeitures, they are imposed upon principles of public policy. The latter, therefore, are under the exclusive control of the Governor." (*Com-*

*monwealth* v. *Denniston*, 9 Watts, 142.) The same point is also illustrated by a case in Indiana. (*Holliday* v. *The People*, 5 Gilman, 214, 217.)

2. As where, in Georgia, the fine was to be paid to an inferior court, for county purposes. (*Johns* v. *Georgia*, 1 Kelly, 606, 610.)

3. As where, in South Carolina, the fine was to be paid to the Commissioners of Public Buildings, for public purposes. (*The State* v. *Simpson*, 1 Bailey, 378.) Or the Commissioners of Public Roads. (*The State* v. *Williams*, 1 Nott & McCord, 26. See also *Rowe* v. *State*, 2 Bay, 565.)

According to these authorities, the portion of the fine allotted to the county, or to the school, may be remitted. Of this there can be no doubt.

*Secondly.—The Statutes of Maryland*, anterior to the organization of the District of Columbia, may also be regarded as an independent source of light on this question, since these statutes have been made the law of the District. And here the conclusion seems to be easy.

By the Constitution of Maryland, adopted 14th August, 1776, it was declared—"The Governor may grant reprieves or pardons for any crime, except in such cases where the law shall otherwise direct." Notwithstanding these strong words of grant, which seem to be as broad as the common law, it was further declared, as if to remove all doubt, by the Legislature, in 1782, (chap. 42,) "That the Governor, with the advice of the Council, be authorized *to remit the whole or any part of any fine*, penalty, or forfeitures, heretofore imposed, or hereafter to be imposed, in any court of law." Here is no exception or limitation of any kind. By express words, the Governor is authorized to remit the whole or any part of any fine. Of course, under this clause he cannot remit a private debt; but he may remit *any fine*. The question is not whether the fine be payable to the United States or other parties, but whether it is *a fine*. If it be a fine, it is in the power of the Governor.

This view is strengthened by the circumstance that in Maryland, according to several statutes, fines were allotted to parties other than the government. The very statute of 1796, under which these proceedings were had, was passed subsequent to this provision respecting the remission of fines. It must be interpreted in harmony with the earlier statute; and since all these statutes are now the law of the District of Columbia, the power of the President, under these laws, to remit these fines, seems established without special reference to the common law or to the Constitution of the United States.

If this were not the case, two different hardships would ensue; first, the statute of 1782 would be despoiled of its natural efficacy; and, secondly, the minor offence of "transporting" a single slave would be punishable, on non-payment of the fine, with imprisonment for life, while the higher offence of "stealing" a slave is punishable with imprisonment for a specific term, and the other offence of "enticing" a slave is punishable with a fine larger than that for transporting a slave, and on non-payment thereof, imprisonment for one year only.

*Thirdly.* — Look at the case under the *Constitution of the United States.*

By the Constitution, the President has power "to grant reprieves and pardons for offences against the

United States, except in case of impeachment." According to a familiar rule of interpretation, the single specified exception leaves the power of the President applicable to all other cases. *Expressio unius exclusio est alterius.* Mr. Berrien, in one of his opinions as Attorney-General, recognizes "the pardoning power as co-extensive with the power to punish;" and he quotes with approbation the words of another writer, that "the power is general and unqualified, and that the remission of fines, penalties, and forfeitures, under the revenue laws, is included in it." (Opinions of Attorney-General, vol. ii. p. 756.)

On this power, Mr. Justice Story thus remarks: "The power of remission of fines, penalties and forfeitures, is also included in it; and may, in the last resort, be exercised by the Executive, although it is in many cases, by our laws confined to the Treasury Department. No law can abridge the constitutional powers of the Executive Department, or interrupt its right to interfere by pardon in such cases. Instances of the exercise of this power by the President, in remitting fines and penalties, in cases not within the scope of the laws, giving authority to the Treasury Department, have repeatedly occurred; and their obligatory force has never been questioned." (Story, Com. on Constitution, vol. ii. § 1504.)

It has been decided by the Supreme Court, after elaborate argument, that the Secretary of the Treasury has authority, under the Remission Act of the 3d March, 1797, cap. 361, "to remit a forfeiture or penalty accruing under the revenue laws, at any time, before or after a final sentence of condemnation or judgment for the penalty, until the money is actually paid over to the Collector for distribution; and such permission extends to the shares of the forfeiture or penalty to which the office of the customs is entitled, as well as to the interest of the United States." In giving his opinion in this case, Mr. Justice Johnson, of South Carolina, made use of language much in point. "Mercy and justice," he said, "could only have been administered by halves, if collectors could have hurried causes to judgment, and then clung to the one-half of the forfeiture, in contempt of the cries of distress, or the mandates of the Secretary." (*United States* v. *Morris*, 10 Wheaton, 303.)

A case has occurred in Kentucky, to which reference has been already made, in which it is confidently and broadly assumed that the pardoning power (under the Constitution) extends even to the penalties due to informers. The following passage occurs in the opinion of the Court: "The act of 1823 says that any prosecuting attorney, who shall prosecute any person to conviction under it, shall be entitled to twenty-five per cent. of the amount of such fine as shall be collected. The act gives the prosecuting attorney one-fourth of the money when collected, but vests him with no interest in the fine or sentence, separate and distinct from that of the Commonwealth, that would screen his share from the effect of any legal operation which should, before collection, abrogate the whole or a part of it. It would require language of the strongest and most explicit character to authorize a presumption that the Legislature intended to confer any such right. We could never presume an intention to control the Governor's constitutional power to remit fines and forfeitures. *If he can, in this way, be restrained in the exercise of his power to remit, for the fourth of a fine, so can he be from the half or the whole. This part of his prerogative cannot be curtailed. With the exception of the case of treason, his power to remit fines and forfeitures, grant reprieves and pardons, is unlimtied, illimitable and uncontrollable. It has no bounds but his own discretion.* It is no doubt politic and proper for the Legislature to incite prosecuting attorneys and informers, by giving them a portion of fines when collected; but in so doing, the citizen cannot be debarred of his right of appeal to Executive clemency." (*Routt* v. *Flemster*, 7 J. J. Marshall, 132.)

According to these authorities, it seems reasonable to infer that, under the Constitution of the United States, the pardoning power, which is clearly applicable to the offence of "transporting" slaves of the District, might remit the penalties in question. These penalties, though allotted to the owners and the county, when finally collected, are neither more nor less than the punishment, under sentence of a criminal court for an offence of which the parties stand convicted upon indictment. They can be collected and acquitted only by the United States. No process for this purpose is at the command of the slave owner. He had no control whatever over the prosecution at any stage, nor did it proceed at his suggestion or information. The very statute under which these public proceedings were instituted, in the name of the United States, secured to the slave owner his private action on the case for damages — thus separating the public from the private interests. These, it seems the duty of the President to keep separate, except on the final collection and distribution of the penalties. Public policy and the ends of justice require that the punishment for a criminal offence should, in every case, be exclusively subject to the supreme pardoning power, without dependence upon the will of any private person. An obvious case will illustrate this. Suppose, in the case of Drayton and Sayres, it should be ascertained beyond doubt that the conviction was procured by perjury. If, by virtue of the judgment, the slave owners have an interest in the imprisonment of these men, which cannot be touched, then the prisoners, unable to meet these heavy liabilities, must continue in perpetual imprisonment, or owe their release to the accident of private good-will. The President, notwithstanding his beneficent power to pardon, under the Constitution, will be powerless to remedy this evil. But such a state of things would be monstrous; and any interpretation of the Constitution is monstrous which thus ties his hands. Mercy and justice would be rendered *not merely by halves:* but, owing to the inability of prisoners, from poverty, to pay the other half of the fine, they would be entirely arrested.

The power of pardon, which is attached by the Constitution to offences generally, should not be curtailed. It is a generous prerogative, and should be exercised generously. *Boni judicis est ampliare jurisdictionem.* This is an old maxim of the law. But if it be the duty of a good judge to extend his jurisdiction, how much more true is it the duty of a good President to extend the field of his clemency. At least, no small doubt should deter him from the exercise of his prerogative.

The conclusion from this review is as follows:

1. By the English common law, the costs and one-half of the fines may be remitted. It is not certain

that by this law, as adopted in the United States, the other half of the fines may not also be remitted.

2. Under the statutes of Maryland, now the law of the District, the Governor, and, of course, the President, may remit "the whole or any part of any fine," without exception.

3. Under the Constitution of the United States, and according to its true spirit, the pardoning power of the President is co-extensive with the power to punish, except in the solitary case of impeachment.

Several courses are open to the President in the present case.

I. By a *general pardon* he may discharge Drayton and Sayres *from prison, and remit all the fines and costs for which they are detained.* Such a pardon would effectually operate unquestionably upon the imprisonment and upon the costs, and also upon the half of the fines due to the county. It would be for the courts, on a proper application, and in the exercise of their just powers, to restrain it, if the pardon did not operate upon the other moiety.

Among the opinions of the Attorney General, is a case which illustrates this point. In 1824, one Joshua Wingold prayed for a credit in the settlement of his accounts, for his proportion of a fine incurred by one P. Varney. It appeared that suit was instituted by the petitioner as Collector of the District of Bath, Maine, on which judgment was obtained in May, 1809; the defendant was arrested and committed to jail, under execution on that judgment, and the fine afterwards remitted by the President. The petitioner contended that the President had no constitutional or legal power to remit his proportion of the fine, the right to which had been vested by the institution of the suit. On this Mr. Wirt remarks, that it is unnecessary to express an opinion upon the correctness of this position, "because, if it be correct, the act of remission by the President being wholly inoperative as to that portion of the fine claimed by the collector, his legal right to recover it remained in full force, notwithstanding the remission; and it is his own fault if he has not enforced his right at law." (Opinions of Attorney General, vol. i. p. 479.)

A general pardon cannot conclude the question, so as to divest any existing rights. It can do no wrong. Why should the President hesitate to exercise it?

II. By a *limited pardon* the President may discharge Drayton and Sayres simply and exclusively *from their imprisonment, without touching their pecuniary liability;* but leaving them still exposed to proceedings for all fines and costs, to be satisfied out of any property they may hereafter acquire.

If the imprisonment had been a specific part of the sentence, — as if they had been sentenced to one year's imprisonment and a fine of one hundred dollars, — beyond all question they might be discharged, by pardon, from this imprisonment. But where the imprisonment, as in the present case, is not a specific part of the sentence, but simply an alternative in the nature of a remedy, to secure the payment of the fine, the power of the President cannot be less than in the former case.

So far as all private parties are concerned, the imprisonment is a mere matter of *remedy*, which can be discharged without divesting the beneficiaries of any rights; and, since imprisonment for debt has been abolished, it is reasonable, under the circumstances, that this peculiar remedy should be discharged.

III. By another form of *limited pardon*, the President may discharge Drayton and Sayres *from their imprisonment, also from all fines and costs in which the United States have an interest*, without touching the rights of other parties.

This would set them at liberty, but would leave them exposed to private proceedings at the investigation of the owners of the "transported slaves," if any should be so disposed.

IV. By still another form of pardon, reference may be made to the Maryland statute of 1782, under which the Governor is authorized "to remit the whole or any part of any fine," without any exception therefrom; and this power, now vested in the President, may be made the express ground for the remission of all fines and costs due from Drayton and Sayres. By this form of pardon, the case may be limited, as a precedent hereafter, to a very narrow circle of cases. It would not in any way affect cases arising under the general laws of the Union.

In either of these alternatives, the great object of this application would be gained — the discharge of these men from prison.

CHARLES SUMNER.

14 May, 1852.

# TRIBUTE TO MR. RANTOUL.

SPEECH IN THE SENATE OF THE UNITED STATES, ON THE DEATH OF HON. ROBERT RANTOUL, JR., 9TH AUGUST, 1852.

---

A message was received from the House of Representatives, by Mr. Hayes, its Chief Clerk, communicating to the Senate information of the death of the Hon. ROBERT RANTOUL, JR., a member of the House of Representatives from the State of Massachusetts, and the proceedings of the House thereon.

The resolutions of the House of Representatives were read.

MR. SUMNER said: — Mr. President, by formal message of the House of Representatives, we now learn that one of our associates in the public councils has died. Only a few brief days — I had almost said hours — have passed since he was in his accustomed seat. Now he is gone from us forever. He was my colleague and friend; and yet, so sudden has been this change, that no tidings of his illness even had reached me, before I learned that he was already beyond the reach of mortal aid or consolation, and that the shadows of the grave had already descended upon him. He died here in Washington, late on Saturday evening, 7th August; and his earthly remains, accompanied by the bereaved companion of his life, with a Committee of the other House, are now far on the way to Massachusetts, there to mingle dust to dust with his native soil.

The occasion does not permit me to speak at length of the character or services of Mr. Rantoul. A few words will suffice; nor will the language of eulogy be required.

He was born 13th August, 1805, at Beverly, in the county of Essex, the home of Nathan Dane, final author of the immortal Ordinance by which freedom was made a perpetual heir-loom in the broad region of the Northwest. Here, under happy auspices of family and neighborhood, he commenced life. Here his excellent father, honored for his public services, venerable also with years and flowing silver locks, yet lives to mourn his last surviving son. The sad fortune of Burke is renewed. He who should have been as posterity, is now to this father in the place of ancestor.

Mr. Rantoul was early a member of the Legislature of Massachusetts, and there won his first fame. For many years he occupied a place on the Board of Education in that State. He was also, for a time, Collector of the Port of Boston, and afterwards Attorney of the United States for Massachusetts. During a brief period he held a seat in this body. Finally, in 1851, by the choice of his native District, remarkable for its intelligence and public spirit, he became a Representative in the other branch of the National Legislature. In all these spheres he performed most acceptable service. And the future promised opportunities of a higher character, to which his abilities, industry, and fidelity would have amply responded. Massachusetts has many arrows in her well-stocked quiver; but few could she so ill spare at this moment as the servant we now mourn.

By original fitness, study, knowledge and various

experience, he was formed for public service. But he was no stranger to other pursuits. Early devoted to the profession of the law, he followed it with assiduity and success. In the antiquities of our jurisprudence, few were more learned. His arguments at the bar were thorough; nor was his intellectual promptness in all emergencies of a trial easily surpassed. Literature, neglected by many under the pressure of professional life, was always cultivated by him. His taste for books was enduring. He was a constant student. Amidst his manifold labors, professional and public, he cherished the honorable aspiration of adding to the historical productions of his country. A work on the history of France, wherein the annals and character of this great nation should be portrayed by an American pen, had occupied much of his thoughts. I know not if any part was ever matured for publication.

The practice of the law, while it sharpens the intellect, is too apt to cramp the faculties within the narrow limits of form, and to restrain the genial currents of the soul. It had no such influence on him. He was a Reformer. In the warfare with Evil, he was enlisted early and openly as a soldier for life. As such, he did not hesitate to encounter opposition, to bear obloquy, and to brave enmity. His conscience, pure as goodness, sustained him in every trial — even that sharpest of all, the desertion of friends. And yet, while earnest in his cause, his zeal was tempered beyond that of the common reformer. He knew well the difference between the *ideal* and the *actual*, and sought, by practical means, in harmony with the existing public sentiment, to promote the interests which he had at heart. He saw clearly that reform could not prevail at once, in an hour, or in a day, but that it would be the slow and certain result of constant labor, testimony, and faith. Determined and tranquil in his own convictions, he had the grace to respect the convictions of others. Recognizing in the social and political system the essential elements of stability and progress, he discerned at once the office of the conservative and the reformer. But he saw also that a blind conservatism was not less destructive than a blind reform. By the mingled caution, moderation, and earnestness of his labors, he seemed often to blend two characters in one and to be at the same time a *Reforming Conservative* and a *Conservative Reformer*.

I might speak of his devotion to public improvements of all kinds, particularly to the system of railroads. But here he was on the popular side. There were other causes, where his struggle was keener and more meritorious. At a moment when his services were much needed he was the faithful supporter of common schools, the peculiar glory of New England. By word and example he sustained the cause of temperance. Some of his most devoted labors, commencing in the Legislature of Massachusetts, were for the abolition of capital punishment. Perhaps no person since that consummate jurist, Edward Livingston, has done so much by reports, articles, letters and speeches to commend this reform to the country. With its final triumph, in the progress of civilization, his name will be indissolubly connected. There is another cause that commanded his early sympathies and some of his latest best endeavors, to which, had life been spared, he would have given the splendid maturity of his powers. Posterity cannot forget this; but I am forbidden by the occasion to name it here. Sir, in the long line of portraits on the walls of the ducal palace of Venice, commemorating its Doges, a single panel, where a portrait should have been, is shrouded by a dark curtain. But this darkened blank, in that place, attracts the beholder more than any picture. Let such a curtain fall to-day upon this theme.

In becoming harmony with these noble causes was the purity of his private life. Here he was blameless. In manners he was modest, simple, and retiring. In conversation he was disposed to listen rather than to speak, though all were well pleased when he broke silence, and in apt language declared his glowing thoughts. But in the public assembly, before the people, or in the legislative hall, he was bold and triumphant. As a debater he rarely met his peer. Fluent, earnest, rapid, sharp, incisive, his words came forth like a flashing cimeter. Few could stand against him. He always understood his subject; and then, clear, logical, and determined, seeing his point before him, pressed forward with unrelenting power. His speeches on formal occasions were enriched by study, and contain passages of beauty. But he was most truly at home in dealing with practical questions arising from the actual exigencies of life.

Few had studied public affairs more minutely or intelligently. As a constant and effective member of the Democratic party, he had become conspicuous by championship of its doctrines on the currency and free trade. These he often discussed; and from the amplitude of his knowledge, and his overflowing familiarity with facts, statistics and the principles of political economy, poured upon them a luminous flood.

But there was no topic within the wide range of our national concerns which did not occupy his thoughts. The resources and needs of the West were all known to him; and Western interests were near his heart. As the pioneer, resting from his daily labors, learns the death of RANTOUL, he will feel a personal grief. The fishermen on the distant Eastern coast, many of whom are dwellers in his District, will sympathize with the pioneer. As these hardy children of the sea, returning in their small craft from late adventures, hear the sad tidings, they, too, will feel that they have lost a friend. And well they may. During his last fitful hours of life, while reason still struggled against disease, he was anxious for their welfare. The speech which, in their behalf, he had hoped soon to make on the floor of Congress, was then chasing through his mind. Finally, in broken utterances, he gave to them some of his latest earthly thoughts.

The death of such a man, so suddenly, in mid-career, is well calculated to arrest attention, and to furnish admonition. From the love of family, the attachment of friends and the regard of fellow-citizens, he has been removed. Leaving behind the cares of life, the concerns of State, and the wretched strifes of party, he has ascended to those mansions where there is no strife, or concern, or care. At last he stands face to face in His presence whose service is perfect freedom. He has gone before. You and I, sir, and all of us, must follow soon. God grant that we may go with equal consciousness of duty done.

I beg leave to offer the following resolutions:

*Resolved, unanimously,* That the Senate mourns the death of HON. ROBERT RANTOUL, JR., late a member of the House of Representatives, from Massachusetts, and tenders to his relatives a sincere sympathy in this afflicting bereavement.

*Resolved*, As a mark of respect to the memory of the deceased, that the Senate do now adjourn.

The resolutions were adopted, and the Senate adjourned.

# FREEDOM NATIONAL; SLAVERY SECTIONAL.

## SPEECH IN THE SENATE OF THE UNITED STATES, 26TH AUGUST 1852, ON HIS MOTION TO REPEAL THE FUGITIVE SLAVE BILL.

---

IN THE SENATE, *Wednesday*, *26th May*, 1852, on the presentation of a Memorial against the Fugitive Slave Bill, the following passage occurred, which is properly introductory to the principal speech at a later day.

MR. SUMNER. I hold in my hand, and desire to present, a memorial from the representatives of the Society of Friends in New England, formally adopted at a public meeting, and authenticated by their clerk, in which they ask for the repeal of the Fugitive Slave Bill. After setting forth their sentiments on the general subject of slavery, the memorialists proceed as follows:

"We, therefore, respectfully, but earnestly and sincerely, entreat you to repeal the law of the last Congress respecting fugitive slaves; first and principally, because of its injustice towards a long sorely-oppressed and deeply-injured people; and, secondly, in order that we, together with other conscientious sufferers, may be exempted from the penalties which it imposes on all who, in faithfulness to their Divine Master, and in discharge of their obligations to their distressed fellow-men, feel bound to regulate their conduct, even under the heaviest penalties which man can inflict for so doing, by the Divine injunction, 'All things whatsoever ye would that men should do to you, do ye even so to them;' and by the other commandment, 'Thou shalt love the Lord thy God with all thy heart, and thy neighbor as thyself.'"

Mr. President, this memorial is commended by the character of the religious association from which it proceeds — men who mingle rarely in public affairs, but with austere virtue seek to carry the Christian rule into life.

The PRESIDENT. [Mr. King, of Alabama.] The Chair will have to interpose. The Senator is not privileged to enter into a discussion of the subject now. The contents of the memorial, simply, are to be stated, and then it becomes a question whether it is to be received, if any objection is made to its reception. Silence gives consent. After it is received, he can make a motion with regard to its reference, and then make any remarks he thinks proper.

Mr. SUMNER. I have but few words to add, and then I propose to move the reference of the memorial to the Committee on the Judiciary.

The PRESIDENT. The memorial has first to be received before any motion as to its reference can be entertained. The Senator presenting a memorial states distinctly its objects and contents; then it is sent to the Chair, if a reference of it is desired. But it is not in order to enter into a discussion of the merits of the memorial until it has been received.

Mr. SUMNER. I do not propose to enter into any such discussion. I have already read one part of the memorial, and it was my design merely to refer to the character of the memorialists — a usage which I have observed on this floor constantly — to state the course I should pursue, and then conclude with a motion for a reference.

The PRESIDENT. The Chair will hear the Senator,

if such is the pleasure of the Senate, if he does not go into an elaborate discussion.

Mr. SUMNER. I have no such purpose.

Mr. DAWSON. Let him be heard.

Several SENATORS. Certainly.

Mr. SUMNER. I observed that this memorial was commended by the character of the religious association from which it proceeds. It is commended, also, by its earnest and persuasive tone, and by the prayer which it presents. Offering it now, sir, I desire simply to say, that I shall deem it my duty, on some proper occasion hereafter, to express myself at length on the matter to which it relates. Thus far, during this session, I have foreborne. With the exception of an able speech from my colleague [Mr. Davis], the discussion of this all-absorbing question has been mainly left with Senators from another quarter of the country, by whose mutual differences it has been complicated, and between whom I have not cared to interfere. But there is a time for all things. Justice, also, requires that both sides should be heard; and I trust not to expect too much, when, at some fit moment, I bespeak the clear and candid attention of the Senate, while I undertake to set forth, frankly and fully, and with entire respect for this body, convictions, deeply cherished in my own State, though disregarded here — to which I am bound by every sentiment of the heart, by every fibre of my being, by all my devotion to country, by my love of God and man. But, upon these I do not now enter. Suffice it, for the present, to say, that when I shall undertake that service, I believe I shall utter nothing which, in any just sense, can be called *sectional*, unless the Constitution is *sectional*, and unless the sentiments of the fathers were *sectional*. It is my happiness to believe, and my hope to be able to show, that, according to the true spirit of the Constitution, and according to the sentiments of the fathers, FREEDOM, and not *slavery*, is NATIONAL; while SLAVERY, and not *freedom*, is SECTIONAL. In duty to the petitioners, and with the hope of promoting their prayer, I move the reference of their petition to the Committee on the Judiciary.

A brief debate ensued, in which Messrs. Mangum, of North Carolina, Badger, of North Carolina, Hale, of New Hampshire, Clemens, of Alabama, Dawson, of Georgia, Adams, of Mississippi, Butler, of South Carolina, and Chase, of Ohio, took part; and, on motion of Mr. Badger, the memorial was laid on the table.

ON THURSDAY, 27*th July*, the subject was again presented by Mr. Sumner to the Senate.

Mr. SUMNER. Mr. President, I have a Resolution which I desire to offer; and, as it is not in order to debate it to-day, I give notice that I shall expect to call it up to-morrow, at an early moment in the morning hour, when I shall throw myself upon the indulgence of the Senate to be heard upon it.

The Resolution was then read, as follows:

*Resolved*, That the Committee on the Judiciary be requested to consider the expediency of reporting a bill for immediate repeal of the Act of Congress, approved September 18, 1850, usually known as the Fugitive Slave Act.

In pursuance of this notice, on the next day, 28th July, during the morning hour, an attempt was made by Mr. Sumner to call it up.

Mr. SUMNER. Mr. President, I now ask permission of the Senate to take up the Resolution which I offered yesterday. For that purpose, I move that the prior orders be postponed, and upon this motion I desire to say a word. In asking the Senate to take up this Resolution for consideration, I say nothing now of its merits, nor of the arguments by which it may be maintained; nor do I at this stage anticipate any objections to it on these grounds. All this will properly belong to the discussion of the Resolution itself — the main question — when it is actually before the Senate. The single question now is, not the Resolution, but whether I shall be heard upon it.

As a Senator, under the responsibilities of my position, I have deemed it my duty to offer this Resolution. I may seem to have postponed this duty to an inconvenient period of the session, but had I attempted it at an earlier day, I might have exposed myself to a charge of a different character. It might then have been said that, a new-comer and inexperienced in this scene, without deliberation, — hastily, — rashly, — recklessly, I pushed this question before the country. This is not the case now. I have taken time, and, in the exercise of my most careful discretion, at last ask the attention of the Senate. I shrink from any appeal founded on a trivial personal consideration; but should I be blamed for delay latterly, I may add, that though in my seat daily, my bodily health for some time past, down to this very week, has not been equal to the service I have undertaken. I am not sure that it is now, but I desire to try.

And now again I say, the question is simply whether I shall be heard. In allowing me this privilege — this right, I might say — you do not commit yourselves in any way to the principle of the Resolution; but you merely follow the ordinary usage of the Senate, and yield to a brother Senator the opportunity which he craves, in the practical discharge of his duty, to express convictions dear to his heart, and dear to large numbers of his constituents. For the sake of these constituents, for my own sake, I now desire to be heard. Make such disposition of my Resolution afterward as to you shall seem best; visit upon me any degree of criticism, censure, or displeasure, but do not deprive me of a hearing. "Strike, but hear."

A debate ensued, in which Messrs. Mason, of Virginia, Brooke, of Mississippi, Charlton, of Georgia, Shields, of Illinois, Gwin, of California, Douglas, of Illinois, Butler, of South Carolina, and Borland, of Arkansas, took part. Objections to taking up the Resolution were pressed on the ground of "want of time," the "lateness of the session," and "danger to the Union."

The question being then taken upon the motion by Mr. Sumner to take up his Resolution, it was rejected — Yeas 10, Nays 32 — as follows:

YEAS. — Messrs. Clarke, Davis, Dodge, of Wisconsin, Foote, Hamlin, Seward, Shields, Sumner, Upham, and Wade — 10.

NAYS. — Messrs. Borland, Brodhead, Brooke, Cass, Charlton, Clemens, Desaussure, Dodge, of Iowa, Douglas, Downs, Felch, Fish, Geyer, Gwin, Hunter, King, Mallory, Mangum, Mason, Meriwether, Miller, Morton, Norris, Pearce, Pratt, Rusk, Sebastian, Smith, Soulé, Spruance, Toucey, and Weller — 32.

Mr. Sumner was thus deprived of an opportunity to present his views on this important subject, and it was openly asserted that he should not present them on the floor of the Senate during the pending session. He was thus driven to watch for an opportunity, when, according to the rules of the Senate, he might be heard without impediment. On one of the last days of the session it came.

THURSDAY, 26*th August*, 1852. — The Civil and Diplomatic Appropriation Bill being under consideration, the following amendment was moved by Mr. Hunter, of Virginia, on the recommendation of the Committee on Finance.

"That where the ministerial officers of the United States have or shall incur extraordinary expenses in executing the laws thereof, the payment of which is not specifically provided for, the President of the United States is authorized to allow the payment thereof, under the special taxation of the District or Circuit Court of the District in which the said services have been or shall be rendered, to be paid from the appropriation for defraying the expenses of the Judiciary."

Mr. SUMNER seized the opportunity for which he had been watching, and at once moved the following amendment to the amendment:

"*Provided*, That no such allowance shall be authorized for any expenses incurred in executing the Act of September 18, 1850, for the surrender of fugitives from service or labor; which said Act is hereby repealed."

On this he took the floor, and spoke as follows:

MR. PRESIDENT: Here is a provision for extraordinary expenses incurred in executing the laws of the United States. Extraordinary expenses! Sir, beneath these specious words lurks the very subject on which, by a solemn vote of this body, I was refused a hearing. Here it is; no longer open to the charge of being an "abstraction," but actually presented for practical legislation; not introduced by me, but by the Senator from Virginia [Mr. Hunter], on the recommendation of one of the important Committees of the Senate; not brought forward weeks ago, when there was ample time for discussion, but only at this moment, without any reference to the late period of the session. The amendment which I now offer, proposes to remove one chief occasion of these extraordinary expenses. Beyond all controversy or cavil, it is strictly in order. And now, at last, among these final crowded days of our duties here, but at this earliest opportunity, I am to be heard; not as a favor, but as a right. The graceful usages of this body may be abandoned, but the established privileges of debate cannot be abridged. Parliamentary courtesy may be forgotten, but parliamentary law must prevail. The subject is broadly before the Senate. By the blessing of God, it shall be discussed.

Sir, a severe lawgiver of early Greece vainly sought to secure permanence for his imperfect institutions, by providing that the citizen who, at any time, attempted their alteration or repeal, should appear in the public assembly with a halter about his neck, ready to be drawn if his proposition failed to be adopted. A tyrannical spirit among us, in unconscious imitation of this antique and discarded barbarism, seeks to surround an offensive institution with a similar safeguard. In the existing distemper of the public mind and at this present juncture, no man can enter upon the service which I now undertake, without a personal responsibility, such as can be sustained only by that sense of duty which, under God, is always our best support. That personal responsibility I accept. Before the Senate and the country let me be held accountable for this act, and for every word which I utter.

With me, sir, there is no alternative. Painfully convinced of the unutterable wrongs and woes of slavery; profoundly believing that, according to the true spirit of the Constitution and the sentiments of the fathers, it can find no place under our *National* Government — that it is in every respect *sectional*, and in no respect *national* — that it is always and everywhere the creature and dependent of the *States*, and never anywhere the creature or dependent of the *Nation*, and that the *Nation* can never, by legislative or other act, impart to it any support, under the Constitution of the United States; with these convictions, I could not allow this session to reach its close, without making or seizing an opportunity to declare myself openly against the usurpation, injustice, and cruelty, of the late enactment by Congress for the recovery of fugitive slaves. Full well I know, sir, the difficulties of this discussion, arising from prejudices of opinion and from adverse conclusions, strong and sincere as my own. Full well I know that I am in a small minority, with few here to whom I may look for sympathy or support. Full well I know that I must utter things unwelcome to many in this body, which I cannot do without pain. Full well I know that the institution of slavery in our country, which I now proceed to consider, is as sensitive as it is powerful — possessing a power to shake the whole land with a sensitiveness that shrinks and trembles at the touch. But, while these things may properly prompt me to caution and reserve, they cannot change my duty, or my determination to perform it. For this I willingly forget myself, and all personal consequences. The favor and good-will of my fellow-citizens, of my brethren of the Senate, sir, — grateful to me as it justly is — I am ready, if required, to sacrifice. All that I am or may be, I freely offer to this cause.

And here allow me, for one moment, to refer to myself and my position. Sir, I have never been a politician. The slave of principles, I call no party master. By sentiment, education, and conviction, a friend of Human Rights, in their utmost expansion, I have ever most sincerely embraced the Democratic Idea; not, indeed, as represented or professed by any party, but according to its real significance, as transfigured in the Declaration of Independence, and in the injunctions of Christianity. In this idea I saw no narrow advantages merely for individuals or classes, but the sovereignty of the people and the greatest happiness of all secured by equal laws. Amidst the vicissitudes of public affairs, I trust always to hold fast to this idea, and to any political party which truly embraces it.

Party does not constrain me; nor is my independence lessened by any relations to the office which gives me a title to be heard on this floor. And here, sir, I may speak proudly. By no effort, by no desire of my own, I find myself a Senator of the United States. Never before have I held public office of any kind. With the ample opportunities of private life I was content. No tombstone for me could bear a fairer inscription than this: "Here lies one who, without the honors or emoluments of public station, did something for his fellow-man." From such simple aspirations I was taken away by the free choice of my native Commonwealth, and placed in this responsible post of duty, without personal obligation of any kind, beyond what was implied in my life and published words. The earnest friends, by whose confidence I was first designated, asked nothing from me, and, throughout the long conflict which ended in my election, rejoiced in the position which I most carefully guarded. To all my language was uniform, that I did not desire to be brought forward; that I would do nothing to promote the result; that I had no pledges or promises to offer; that the office should seek me, and not I the office; and that it should find me in all respects an independent man, bound to no party and to no human being, but only, according to my best judgment, to act for the good of all. Again, sir, I speak with pride, both for myself and others, when I add that these avowals found a sympathizing response. In this spirit I have come here, and in this spirit I shall speak to-day.

Rejoicing in my independence, and claiming nothing from party ties, I throw myself upon the candor and magnanimity of the Senate. I now ask your attention; but I trust not to abuse it. I may speak strongly; for I shall speak openly and from the strength of my convictions. I may speak warmly; for I shall speak from the heart. But in no event can I forget the amenities which belong to debate, and which especially become this body. Slavery I must condemn with my whole soul; but here I need only borrow the language of slaveholders themselves; nor would it accord with my habits or my sense of justice to exhibit them as the impersonation of the institution — Jefferson calls it the "enormity" — which they cherish. Of them I do not speak; but without fear and without favor, as without impeachment of any person, I assail this wrong. Again, sir, I may err; but it will be with the Fathers. I plant myself on the ancient ways of the Republic, with its grandest names, its surest landmarks, and all its original altar-fires about me.

And now, on the very threshold, I encounter the objection that there is a final settlement, in principle and substance, of the question of Slavery, and that all discussion of it is closed. Both the old political parties of the country, by formal resolutions, in their recent conventions at Baltimore, have united in this declaration. On a subject which for years has agitated the public mind; which yet palpitates in every heart and burns on every tongue; which, in its immeasurable importance, dwarfs all other subjects; which, by its constant and gigantic presence, throws a shadow across these Halls; which at this very time calls for appropriations to meet extraordinary expenses it has caused, they have imposed the rule of silence. According to them, sir, we may speak of everything except that alone, which is most present in all our minds.

To this combined effort I might fitly reply, that, with flagrant inconsistency, it challenges the very discussion which it pretends to forbid. Such a declaration, on the eve of an election, is, of course, submitted to the consideration and ratification of the people. Debate, inquiry, discussion, are the necessary consequence. Silence becomes impossible. Slavery, which you profess to banish from the public attention, openly by your invitation enters every political meeting and every political convention. Nay, at this moment it stalks into this Senate, crying, like the daughters of the horseleech, "Give, give!"

But no unanimity of politicians can uphold the

baseless assumption, that a law, or any conglomerate of laws, under the name of Compromise, or howsoever called, is final. Nothing can be plainer than this; that, by no parliamentary device or knot, can any Legislature tie the hands of a succeeding Legislature, so as to prevent the full exercise of its constitutional powers. Each Legislature, under a just sense of its responsibility, must judge for itself; and, if it think proper, it may revise or amend, or absolutely undo the work of its predecessors. The laws of the Medes and Persians are proverbially said to have been unalterable; but they stand forth in history as a single example of such irrational defiance of the true principles of all law.

To make a law final, so as not to be reached by Congress, is, by mere legislation, to fasten a new provision on the Constitution. Nay, more; it gives to the law a character which the very Constitution does not possess. The wise fathers did not treat the country as a Chinese foot, never to grow after infancy; but, anticipating Progress, they declared expressly that their great Act is not final. According to the Constitution itself, there is not one of its existing provisions — not even that with regard to fugitives from labor — which may not at all times be reached by amendment, and thus be drawn into debate. This is rational and just. Sir, nothing from man's hands, nor law, nor constitution, can be final. Truth alone is final.

Inconsistent and absurd, this effort is tyrannical also. The responsibility for the recent Slave Act and for Slavery everywhere within the jurisdiction of Congress necessarily involves the right to discuss them.

To separate these is impossible. Like the twenty-fifth rule of the House of Representatives against petitions on Slavery — now repealed and dishonored — the Compromise, as explained and urged, is a curtailment of the actual powers of legislation, and a perpetual denial of the indisputable principle that the right to deliberate is co-extensive with the responsibility for an act. To sustain Slavery, it is now proposed to trample on *free speech.* In any country this would be grievous; but here, where the Constitution expressly provides against abridging freedom of speech, it is a special outrage. In vain do we condemn the despotisms of Europe, while we borrow the rigors with which they repress Liberty, and guard their own uncertain power. For myself, in no factious spirit, but solemnly and in loyalty to the Constitution, as a Senator of the United States, representing a free Commonwealth, I protest against this wrong. On Slavery, as on every other subject, I claim the right to be heard. That right I cannot, I will not abandon. "Give me the liberty to know, to utter and to argue freely, above all liberties;" these are the glowing words which flashed from the soul of John Milton, in his struggles with English tyranny. With equal fervor they should be echoed now by every American, not already a slave.

But, sir, this effort is impotent as tyrannical. The convictions of the heart cannot be repressed. The utterances of conscience must be heard. They break forth with irrepressible might. As well attempt to check the tides of Ocean, the currents of the Mississippi, or the rushing waters of Niagara. The discussion of Slavery will proceed, wherever two or three are gathered together — by the fireside, on the highway, at the public meeting, in the church. The movement against Slavery is from the Everlasting Arm. Even now it is gathering its forces, soon to be confessed everywhere. It may not yet be felt in the high places of office and power; but all who can put their ears humbly to the ground, will hear and comprehend its incessant and advancing tread.

The relations of the Government of the United States — I speak of the National Government — to Slavery, though plain and obvious, are constantly misunderstood. A popular belief at this moment makes Slavery a national institution, and, of course, renders its support a national duty. The extravagance of this error can hardly be surpassed. An institution, which our fathers most carefully omitted to name in the Constitution, which, according to the debates in the Convention, they refused to cover with any "sanction," and which, at the original organization of the Government, was merely *sectional*, existing nowhere on the *national* territory, is now, above all other things, blazoned as national. Its supporters plume themselves as national. The old political parties, while upholding it, claim to be national. A National Whig is simply a Slavery Whig, and a National Democrat is simply a Slavery Democrat, in contradistinction to all who regard Slavery as a sectional institution, within the exclusive control of the States, and with which the nation has nothing to do.

As Slavery assumes to be national, so, by an equally strange perversion, Freedom is degraded to be sectional, and all who uphold it, under the national Constitution, share this same epithet. The honest efforts to secure its blessings, everywhere within the jurisdiction of Congress, are scouted as sectional; and this cause, which the founders of our National Government had so much at heart, is called *sectionalism.* These terms, now belonging to the commonplaces of political speech, are adopted and misapplied by most persons without reflection. But herein is the power of Slavery. According to a curious tradition of the French language, Louis XIV., the grand monarch, by an accidental error of speech, among supple courtiers, changed the gender of a noun; but Slavery has done more. It has changed word for word. It has taught men to say *national* instead of *sectional*, and *sectional* instead of *national.*

Slavery national! Sir, this is all a mistake and absurdity, fit to take a place in some new collection of Vulgar Errors, by some other Sir Thomas Browne, with the ancient but exploded stories, that the toad has a stone in its head, and that ostriches digest iron. According to the true spirit of the Constitution, and the sentiments of the Fathers, *Slavery* and not Freedom is *sectional*, while *Freedom* and not Slavery is *national.* On this unanswerable proposition I take my stand, and here commences my argument.

The subject presents itself under *two* principal heads; FIRST, *the true relations of the National Government to Slavery*, wherein it will appear that there is no national fountain out of which Slavery can be derived, and no national power, under the Constitution, by which it can be supported. Enlightened by this general survey, we shall be prepared to consider, SECONDLY, *the true nature of the provision for the rendition of fugitives from service*, and herein especially the unconstitutional and offensive legislation of Congress in pursuance thereof.

I. And now for the TRUE RELATIONS OF THE NATIONAL GOVERNMENT TO SLAVERY. These will be readily apparent, if we do not neglect well-established principles.

If Slavery be national, if there be any power in the National Government to uphold this institution — as in the recent Slave Act — it must be by virtue of the Constitution. Nor can it be by mere inference, implication, or conjecture. According to the uniform admission of courts and jurists in Europe, again and again promulgated in our country, Slavery can be derived only from clear and special recognition. "The state of Slavery," said Lord Mansfield, pronouncing judgment in the great case of Somersett, "is of such a nature, that it is incapable of being introduced on any reasons moral or political, *but only by positive law*. It is so odious, that *nothing can be suffered to support it* but POSITIVE LAW." * And a slaveholding tribunal, — the Supreme Court of Mississippi, — adopting the same principle, has said:

> "Slavery is condemned by reason, and the laws of nature. It exists and can exist *only* through municipal regulations." — (*Harry* v. *Decker*, Walker, R. 42.)

And another slaveholding tribunal, — the Supreme Court of Kentucky, — has said:

> "We view this as a right existing by *positive law* of a municipal character, without foundation in the law of nature or the unwritten and common law." — (*Rankin* v. *Lydia*, 2 Marshall, 470.)

* Howell's State Trials, vol. 20, p. 82.

Of course every power to uphold Slavery must have an origin as distinct as that of Slavery itself. Every presumption must be as strong against such a power as against Slavery. A power so peculiar and offensive — so hostile to reason — so repugnant to the law of nature and the inborn Rights of Man; which despoils its victims of the fruits of their labor; which substitutes concubinage for marriage; which abrogates the relation of parent and child; which, by a denial of education, abases the intellect, prevents a true knowledge of God, and murders the very soul; which, amidst a plausible physical comfort, degrades man, created in the Divine image, to the level of a beast; — such a power, so eminent, so transcendent, so tyrannical, so unjust, can find no place in any system of Government, unless by virtue of *positive sanction.* It can spring from no doubtful phrases. It must be declared by unambiguous words, incapable of a double sense.

Slavery, I now repeat, is not mentioned in the Constitution. The name Slave does not pollute this Charter of our Liberties. No "positive" language gives to Congress any *power* to make a Slave or to hunt a Slave. To find even any seeming sanction for either, we must travel, with doubtful footsteps, beyond its express letter, into the region of interpretation. But here are rules which cannot be disobeyed. With electric might for Freedom, they send a pervasive influence through every provision, clause, and word of the Constitution. Each and all make Slavery impossible as a national institution. They efface from the Constitution every fountain out of which it can be derived.

*First* and foremost, is the *Preamble.* This discloses the prevailing objects and principles of the Constitution. This is the vestibule through which all must pass, who would enter the sacred temple. Here are the inscriptions by which they are earliest impressed. Here they first catch the genius of the place. Here the proclamation of Liberty is soonest heard. "We the People of the United States," says the Preamble, "in order to form a more perfect Union, *establish justice,* insure domestic tranquillity, provide for the common defence, *promote the general welfare, and secure the blessings of Liberty* to ourselves and our posterity, do ordain and establish this Constitution for the United States of America." Thus, according to undeniable words, the Constitution was ordained, not to establish, secure, or sanction Slavery — not to promote the special interests of slaveholders — not to make Slavery national, in any way, form, or manner; but to "establish justice," "promote the general welfare," and "secure the blessings of Liberty." Here, surely, Liberty is national.

*Secondly.* Next in importance to the Preamble are the explicit *contemporaneous declarations* in the Convention which framed the Constitution, and elsewhere, expressed in different forms of language, but all tending to the same conclusion. By the Preamble, the Constitution speaks for Freedom. By these declarations, the Fathers speak as the Constitution speaks. Early in the Convention, Gouverneur Morris, of Pennsylvania, broke forth in the language of an Abolitionist: "*He never would concur in upholding domestic slavery.* It was a nefarious institution. It was the curse of Heaven on the State where it prevailed."

Oliver Ellsworth, of Connecticut, said: "The morality or wisdom of Slavery are considerations belonging to the States themselves." According to him, Slavery was sectional.

At a later day, a discussion ensued on the clause touching the African slave trade, which reveals the definitive purposes of the Convention. From the report of Mr. Madison we learn what was said. Elbridge Gerry, of Massachusetts, "thought we had nothing to do with the conduct of the States as to Slavery, *but we ought to be careful not to give any sanction to it.*" According to these words, he regarded Slavery as sectional, and would not make it national. Roger Sherman, of Connecticut, "was opposed to any tax on slaves imported, as making the matter worse, *because it implied they were property.* He would not have Slavery national. After debate, the subject was committed to a Committee of eleven, who subsequently reported a substitute, authorizing "a tax on such migration or importation, at a rate *not exceeding the average of duties laid on imports.*" This language, classifying *persons* with merchandise, seemed to imply a recognition that they were *property.* Mr. Sherman at once declared himself "against this part, *as acknowledging men to be property*, by taxing them as such under the character of slaves." Mr. Gorham "thought Mr. Sherman should consider the duty *not as implying that slaves are property*, but as a discouragement to the importation of them." Mr. Madison in mild juridical phrase, "*thought it wrong to admit in the Constitution the idea that there could be property in man.*" After discussion it was finally agreed to make the clause read:

"But a tax or duty may be imposed on such importation, not exceeding ten dollars *for each person.*"

The difficulty seemed then to be removed, and the whole clause was adopted. This record demonstrates that the word "persons" was employed in order to show that slaves, everywhere under the Constitution, were always to be regarded as *persons*, and not as *property*, and thus to exclude from the Constitution all idea that there can be property in man. Remember well, that Mr. Sherman was opposed to the clause in its original form, "as acknowledging men to be *property;*" that Mr. Madison was also opposed to it, because he "thought it *wrong* to admit in the Constitution the idea that there could be property in man;" and that, after these objections, the clause was so amended as to exclude the idea. But Slavery cannot be national, unless this idea is distinctly and unequivocally admitted into the Constitution.

But the evidence still accumulates. At a still later day in the proceedings of the Convention, as if to set the seal upon the solemn determination to have no sanction of Slavery in the Constitution, the word "servitude" which appeared in the clause on the apportionment of representation was struck out, and the word "service" inserted. This was done on the motion of Mr. Randolph, of Virginia, and the reason assigned for this substitution, according to Mr. Madison, in his authentic report of the debate, was that "the former was thought to express the condition of slaves, and the latter *the obligations of free persons.*" With such care was Slavery excluded from the Constitution.

Nor is this all. In the Massachusetts Convention,

to which the Constitution, when completed, was submitted for ratification, a veteran of the Revolution, General Heath, openly declared that, according to his view, Slavery was sectional, and not national. His language was pointed. "I apprehend," he says, "that it is not in our power *to do anything for or against those who are in Slavery in the Southern States.* No gentleman within these walls detests every idea of Slavery more than I do; it is generally detested by people of this Commonwealth; and I ardently hope the time will soon come, when our brethren in the Southern States will view it as we do, and put a stop to it; but to this we have no right to compel them. Two questions naturally arise: *If we ratify the Constitution, shall we do anything by our act to hold the blacks in slavery — or shall we become partakers in other men's sins? I think neither of them.*"

Afterwards, in the first Congress under the Constitution, on a motion which was much debated, to introduce into the Impost Bill a duty on the importation of Slaves, the same Roger Sherman, who in the National Convention had opposed the idea of property in man, authoritatively exposed the true relations of the Constitution to Slavery. His language was, that "The Constitution does not consider these persons as property; it speaks of them as persons."

Thus distinctly and constantly, from the very lips of the framers of the Constitution, we learn the falsehood of the recent assumptions in favor of Slavery and in derogation of Freedom.

*Thirdly.* According to a familiar rule of interpretation, all laws concerning the same matter, ***in pari materia***, are to be construed together. By the same reason, *the grand political acts of the Nation are to be construed together*, giving and receiving light from each other. Earlier than the Constitution was the Declaration of Independence, embodying, in immortal words, those primal truths to which our country pledged itself with its baptismal vows as a Nation. "We hold these truths to be self-evident," says the Nation, "that all men are created equal; that they are endowed by their Creator with certain unalienable rights; that among them are life, *liberty*, and the pursuit of happiness; that to secure these rights governments are instituted among men, deriving their just powers from the consent of the governed." But this does not stand alone. There is another national act of similar import. On the successful close of the Revolution, the Continental Congress, in an address to the people, repeated the same lofty truth. "Let it be remembered," said the Nation again, "that it has ever been the pride and the boast of America, *that the rights for which she has contended were the rights of human nature*. By the blessing of the Author of *these rights*, they have prevailed over all opposition, and FORM THE BASIS of thirteen independent States." Such were the acts of the Nation in its united capacity. Whatever may be the privileges of States in their individual capacities, within their several local jurisdictions, no power can be attributed to the Nation, in the absence of positive, unequivocal grant, inconsistent with these two national declarations. Here, sir, is the national heart, the national soul, the national will, the national voice, which must inspire our interpretation of the Constitution, and enter into and diffuse itself through all the national legislation. Thus again is Freedom national.

*Fourthly.* Beyond these is a principle of the common law, clear, and indisputable, a supreme rule of interpretation from which in this case there can be no appeal. In any question under the Constitution *every word is to be construed in favor of liberty.* This rule, which commends itself to the natural reason, is sustained by time-honored maxims of our early jurisprudence. Blackstone aptly expresses it, when he says, that "The law is always ready to catch at anything in favor of liberty." * The rule is repeated in various forms. *Favores ampliandi sunt; odia restringenda.* Favors are to be amplified; hateful things to be restrained. *Lex Angliæ est lex misericordiæ.* The law of England is a law of mercy. *Angliæ jura in omni casu libertati dant favorem.* The laws of England in every case show favor to liberty. And this sentiment breaks forth in natural, though intense, force, in the maxim: *Impius et crudelis judicandus est qui libertati non favet.* He is to be adjudged impious and cruel who does not favor liberty. Reading the Constitution in the admonition of these rules, again I say Freedom is national.

*Fifthly.* From a learned judge of the *Supreme Court of the United States,* in an opinion of the court, we derive the same lesson. In considering the question, whether a State can prohibit the importation of slaves as merchandise, and whether Congress, in the exercise of its power to regulate commerce among the States, can interfere with the slave-trade between the States, a

* 2 Black. Com. 94.

principle has been enunciated, which, while protecting the trade from any intervention of Congress declares openly that the Constitution acts upon no man as property. Mr. Justice McLean says: "If slaves are considered in some of the States as merchandise, that cannot divest them of the leading and controlling quality of persons by which they are designated in the Constitution. The character of property is given them by the local law. This law is respected, and all rights under it are protected by the Federal authorities; *but the Constitution acts upon slaves as* PERSONS *and not as property*. . . . "The power over Slavery belongs to the States respectively. It is local in its character, and in its effects." * Here again Slavery is sectional, while Freedom is national.

Sir, such, briefly, are the rules of interpretation which, as applied to the Constitution, fill it with the breath of Freedom,

"Driving far off each thing of sin and guilt."

To the *history and prevailing sentiments* of the times we may turn for further assurance. In the Spirit of Freedom the Constitution was formed. In this spirit our Fathers always spoke and acted. In this spirit the National Government was first organized under Washington. And here I recall a scene, in itself a touchstone of the period, and an example for us, upon which we may look with pure national pride, while we learn anew the relations of the National Government to Slavery.

The Revolution had been accomplished. The feeble

* *Groves* v. *Slaughter*, 15 Peters, R. 507.

Government of the Confederation had passed away. The Constitution, slowly matured in a National Convention, discussed before the people, defended by masterly pens, had been already adopted. The thirteen States stood forth a nation, wherein was unity without consolidation, and diversity without discord. The hopes of all were anxiously hanging upon the new order of things and the mighty procession of events. With signal unanimity Washington was chosen President. Leaving his home at Mount Vernon, he repaired to New York, — where the first Congress had already commenced its session, — to assume his place as elected Chief of the Republic. On the thirtieth of April, 1789, the organization of the Government was completed by his inaguration. Entering the Senate Chamber, where the two Houses were assembled, he was informed that they awaited his readiness to receive the oath of office. Without delay, attended by the Senators and Representatives, with friends and men of mark gathered about him, he moved to the balcony in front of the edifice. A countless multitude, thronging the open street, and eagerly watching this great espousal,

> "With reverence look on his majestic face,
> Proud to be less, but of his god-like race." *

The oath was administered by the Chancellor of New York. At this time, and in this presence, beneath the uncovered heavens, Washington first took this vow upon his lips: "I do solemnly swear that I will faithfully execute the office of President of the United

* Dryden.

States, and will to the best of my ability, preserve, protect and defend the Constitution of the United States."

Over the President, on this high occasion, floated the national flag, with its stripes of red, and its stars on a field of blue. As his patriot eyes rested upon the glowing ensign, what currents must have rushed swiftly through his soul! In the early days of the Revolution, in those darkest hours about Boston, after the battle of Bunker Hill, and before the Declaration of Independence, the thirteen stripes had been first unfurled by him, as the emblem of Union among the Colonies for the sake of Freedom. By him, at that time, they had been named the Union Flag. Trial, struggle and war, were now ended, and the Union, which they first heralded, was unalterably established. To every beholder, these memories must have been full of pride and consolation. But looking back upon the scene, there is one circumstance which, more than all its other associations, fills the soul; more even than the suggestions of Union, which I prize so much. AT THIS MOMENT, WHEN WASHINGTON TOOK HIS FIRST OATH TO SUPPORT THE CONSTITUTION OF THE UNITED STATES, THE NATIONAL ENSIGN, NOWHERE WITHIN THE NATIONAL TERRITORY, COVERED A SINGLE SLAVE. Then, indeed, was Slavery sectional, and Freedom national.

On the sea, an execrable piracy, the trade in slaves, was still, to the national scandal, tolerated under the national flag. In the States, as a sectional institution, beneath the shelter of local laws, Slavery unhappily found a home. But in the only territories at this time belonging to the nation, the broad region of the

North-west, it had already, by the Ordinance of Freedom, been made impossible, even before the adoption of the Constitution. The District of Columbia, with its fatal incumbrance, had not yet been acquired.

The Government thus organized was Anti-Slavery in character. Washington was a slave-holder; but it would be unjust to his memory not to say that he was an Abolitionist also. His opinions do not admit of question. Only a short time before the formation of the National Constitution, he had declared, by letter, "That it was among his first wishes to see some plan adopted, by which Slavery may be abolished by law;" and again, in another letter, "That, in support of any legislative measure for the abolition of slavery, his suffrage should not be wanting;" and still further, in conversation with a distinguished European Abolitionist, a travelling propagandist of Freedom, Brissot de Warville, recently welcomed to Mount Vernon, he had openly announced, that to promote this object in Virginia, "He desired the formation of a SOCIETY, and that he would second it." By this authentic testimony, he takes his place with the early patrons of Abolition Societies.

By the side of Washington, as standing beneath the national flag he swore to support the Constitution, were illustrious men, whose lives and recorded words now rise in judgment. There was John Adams, the Vice-President — great vindicator and final negotiator of our national independence — whose soul, flaming with freedom, broke forth in the early declaration, that "Consenting to Slavery is a sacrilegious breach of trust," and whose immitigable hostility to this wrong has been made immortal in his descendants. There also was a companion in arms, and attached friend of incomparable genius, the yet youthful Hamilton, who, as a member of the Abolition Society of New York, had only recently united in a solemn petition for those who, "though *free by the laws of God*, are held in Slavery *by the laws of the State*." There, too, was a noble spirit, the ornament of his country, the exemplar of truth and virtue, who, like the sun, ever held an unerring course, John Jay. Filling the important post of Minister of Foreign Affairs under the Confederation, he found time to organize the Abolition Society of New York, and to act as its President, until, by the nomination of Washington, he became Chief Justice of the United States. In his sight, Slavery was an "iniquity," "a sin of crimson dye," against which ministers of the gospel should testify, and which the Government should seek in every way to abolish. "Were I in the Legislature," he wrote, "I would present a bill for this purpose with great care, and I would never cease moving it till it became a law, or I ceased to be a member. Till America comes into this measure, her prayers to heaven will be impious."

But they were not alone. The convictions and earnest aspirations of the country were with them. At the North these were broad and general. At the South they found fervid utterance from slaveholders. By early and precocious efforts for "total emancipation," the author of the Declaration of Independence placed himself foremost among the Abolitionists of the land. In language now familiar to all, and which can never die, he perpetually denounced Slavery. He exposed its pernicious influences upon master as well as slave; declared that the love of justice and the love of country pleaded equally for the slave, and that the "abolition of domestic slavery was the greatest object of desire." He believed that the "sacred side was gaining daily recruits," and confidently looked to the young for the accomplishment of this good work. In fitful sympathy with Jefferson, was another honored son of Virginia, the Orator of Liberty, Patrick Henry, who, while confessing that he was a master of slaves, said: "I will not, I cannot justify it. However culpable my conduct, I will so far pay my devoir to virtue, as to own the excellence and rectitude of her precepts, and lament my want of conformity to them." At this very period, in the Legislature of Maryland, on a bill for the relief of oppressed slaves, a young man, afterwards by his consummate learning and forensic powers, the acknowledged head of the American bar, William Pinkney, in a speech of earnest, truthful eloquence — better far for his memory than his transcendent professional fame — branded Slavery as "iniquitous and most dishonorable;" "founded in a disgraceful traffic;" "as shameful in its continuance as in its origin;" and he openly declared, that, "By the eternal principles of natural justice, no master in the State has a right to hold his slave in bondage a single hour."

Thus at this time spoke the NATION. The CHURCH also joined its voice. And here, amidst the diversities of religious faith, it is instructive to observe the general accord. The Quakers first bore their testimony. At the adoption of the Constitution, their whole body, under the early teaching of George Fox, and by the crowning exertions of Benezet and Woolman, had become an organized band of Abolitionists, penetrated by the conviction that it was unlawful to hold a fellow-man in bondage. The Methodists, numerous, earnest and faithful, never ceased by their preachers to proclaim the same truth. Their rules in 1788 denounced, in formal language, "the buying or selling of bodies and souls of men, women, and children, with an intention to enslave them." The words of their great apostle, John Wesley, were constantly repeated. On the eve of the National Convention the burning tract was circulated, in which he exposes American slavery as the "vilest" of the world—"such Slavery as is not found among the Turks at Algiers;" and, after declaring "Liberty the birthright of every human creature, of which no human law can deprive him," he pleads, "If, therefore, you have any regard to justice, (to say nothing of mercy or the revealed law of God,) render unto all their due. Give liberty to whom liberty is due, that is, to every child of man, to every partaker of human nature." At the same time, the Presbyterians, a powerful religious body, inspired by the principles of John Calvin, in more moderate language, but by a public act, recorded their judgment, recommending "to all the people under their care to use the most prudent measures consistent with the interest and the state of civil society, *to procure eventually the final abolition of Slavery in America.*" The Congregationalists of New-England, also of the faith of John Calvin, and with the hatred of Slavery belonging to the great non-conformist, Richard Baxter, were sternly united against this wrong. As early as 1776, Samuel Hopkins, their eminent leader and divine, published his tract, showing it to be the Duty and Interest of the American States to emancipate all their African slaves, and declaring that "Slavery is in every instance wrong, unrighteous and oppressive — a very great and crying sin — there being nothing of the kind equal to it on the face of the earth." And, in 1791, shortly after the adoption of the Constitution, the second Jonathan Edwards, a twice-honored name, in an elaborate discourse often published, called upon his country, "in the present blaze of light" on the injustice of slavery, to prepare the way for "its total abolition." This he gladly thought at hand. "If we judge of the future by the past," said the celebrated preacher, "within fifty years from this time, it will be as shameful for a man to hold a negro slave, as to be guilty of common robbery, or theft."

Thus, at this time, the Church, in harmony with the Nation, by its leading denominations, Quakers, Methodists, Presbyterians and Congregationalists, thundered against Slavery. The COLLEGES were in unison with the Church. Harvard University spoke by the voice of Massachusetts, which had already abolished Slavery. Dartmouth College, by one of its learned Professors, claimed for the slaves "equal privileges with the whites." Yale College, by its President, the eminent divine, Ezra Stiles, became the head of the Abolition Society of Connecticut. And the University of William and Mary, in Virginia, testified its sympathy with this cause at this very time, by conferring upon Granville Sharpe, the acknowledged chief of British Abolitionists, the honorary degree of Doctor of Laws.

The LITERATURE of the land, such as then existed, agreed with the Nation, the Church and the College.

Franklin, in the last literary labor of his life; Jefferson, in his Notes on Virginia; Barlow, in his measured verse; Rush, in a work which inspired the praise of Clarkson; the ingenious author of the Algerine Captive — the earliest American novel, and though now but little known, one of the earliest American books republished in London — were all moved by the contemplation of Slavery. "If our fellow-citizens of the Southern States are deaf to the pleadings of nature," the latter exclaims in his work, "I will conjure them, for the sake of consistency, to cease to deprive their fellow-creatures of freedom, which their writers, their orators, representatives and senators, and even their Constitution of Government, have declared to be the inalienable birthright of man." A female writer and poet, earliest in our country among the graceful throng, Sarah Wentworth Morton, at the very period of the National Convention admired by the polite society in which she lived, poured forth her sympathies also. The generous labors of John Jay in behalf of the crushed African inspired her muse; and, in another poem, commemorating a slave, who fell while vindicating his freedom, she rendered a truthful homage to his inalienable rights, in words which I now quote as part of the testimony of the times:

"Does not the voice of reason cry,
'Claim the first right that Nature gave;
From the red scourge of bondage fly,
Nor deign to live a burdened slave?'"

Such, sir, at the adoption of the Constitution and at the first organization of the National Government, was the out-spoken, unequivocal heart of the country.

9*

Slavery was abhorred. Like the slave trade, it was regarded as transitory; and, by many, it was supposed that they would both disappear together. As the oracles grew mute at the coming of Christ, and a voice was heard, crying to mariners at sea, "Great Pan is dead," so at this time Slavery became dumb, and its death seemed to be near. Voices of Freedom filled the air. The patriot, the Christian, the scholar, the writer, the poet, vied in loyalty to this cause. All were Abolitionists.

Glance now at the earliest Congress under the Constitution. From various quarters came memorials to this body against Slavery. Among these was one from the Abolition Society of Virginia, wherein Slavery is pronounced "not only an odious degradation, but an outrageous violation of one of the most essential rights of human nature, and utterly repugnant to the precepts of the Gospel." Still another, of a more important character, proceeded from the Abolition Society of Pennsylvania, and was signed by Benjamin Franklin, as President. This venerable man, whose active life had been devoted to the welfare of mankind at home and abroad — who, both as philosopher and statesman, had arrested the admiration of the world — who had ravished the lightning from the skies and the sceptre from the tyrant — who, as a member of the Continental Congress, had set his name to the Declaration of Independence, and, as a member of the National Convention, had again set his name to the Constitution — in whom more, perhaps, than in any other person, was embodied the true spirit of American institutions, at once practical and humane — than whom no one could be more familiar with the purposes and aspirations of the founders — this veteran, eighty-four years of age, within a few months of his death, now appeared by petition at the bar of that Congress, whose powers he had helped to define and establish. This was the last political act of his long life. Listen to the prayer of Franklin:

"Your memoralists, particularly engaged in attending to the distresses arising from Slavery, believe it to be their indispensable duty to present this subject to your notice. They have observed with real satisfaction that many important and salutary powers are vested in you for promoting the welfare and securing the blessings of liberty to the people of the United States; and as they conceive that these blessings ought rightfully to be administered, *without distinction of color* to all descriptions of people, *so they indulge themselves in the pleasing expectation, that nothing which can be done for the relief of the unhappy objects of their care, will be either omitted or delayed.*" "Under these impressions, they earnestly entreat your serious attention to the subject of Slavery; *that you would be pleased to countenance the restoration of liberty to those unhappy men, who alone, in this land of Freedom, are degraded into perpetual bondage*, and who, amidst the general joy of surrounding freemen, are groaning in servile subjection; that you will promote mercy and justice towards this distressed race, and *that you will step to the very verge of the power vested in you for* ***DISCOURAGING*** *every species of traffic in the persons of our fellow-men.*"

Important words! in themselves a key-note of the times. From his grave Franklin seems still to call upon Congress *to step to the very verge of the powers vested in it to* DISCOURAGE SLAVERY; and, in making this prayer, he proclaims the true national policy of the Fathers. Not encouragement but discouragement of Slavery was their rule.

Sir, enough has been said to show the sentiment which, like a vital air, surrounded the National Government as it stepped into being. In the face of this history, and in the absence of any positive sanction, it is absurd to suppose that Slavery, which under the Confederation was merely sectional, was now constituted a national institution. Our fathers did not say with the apostate angel, "Evil be thou my good!" In a different spirit they cried out to Slavery, "Get thee behind me, Satan!"

But there is yet another link in the argument. In the discussions which took place in the local conventions on the adoption of the Constitution, a sensitive desire was manifested to surround all persons under the Constitution with additional safeguards. Fears were expressed, from the supposed indefiniteness of some of the powers conceded to the National Government, and also from the absence of a Bill of Rights. Massachusetts, on ratifying the Constitution, proposed a series of amendments, at the head of which was this, characterized by Samuel Adams, in the Convention, as "A summary of a Bill of Rights:"

> "That it be explicitly declared, that all powers not expressly delegated by the aforesaid Constitution are reserved to the several States, to be by them exercised."

Virginia, South Carolina, and North Carolina, with minorities in Pennsylvania and Maryland, united in this proposition. In pursuance of these recommendations, the first Congress presented for adoption the following article, which, being ratified by a proper number of States, became part of the Constitution, as the 10th amendment:

> "The powers not delegated to the United States by the Constitution, nor prohibited by it to the States, are reserved to the States respectively, or to the people."

Stronger words could not be employed to limit the power under the Constitution, and to protect the people from all assumptions of the National Government, *particularly in derogation of Freedom.* Its guardian character commended it to the sagacious mind of Jefferson, who said: "I consider the foundation corner-stone of the Constitution of the United States to be laid upon the tenth article of the amendments." And Samuel Adams, ever watchful for Freedom, said: "It removes a doubt which many have entertained respecting the matter, gives assurance that, if any law made by the Federal Government shall be extended beyond the power granted by the Constitution, and inconsistent with the Constitution of this State, it will be an error, and adjudged by the courts of law to be void."

Beyond all question, the National Government, ordained by the Constitution, is not general or universal; but special and particular. It is a Government of limited powers. It has no power which is not delegated. Especially is this clear with regard to an institution like Slavery. The Constitution contains no power to make a King or to support kingly rule. With similar reason it may be said, that it contains no power to make a slave, or to support a system of Slavery. The absence of all such power is hardly more clear in one case than in the other. But if there be no such power, all national legislation upholding Slavery must be unconstitutional and void. The stream cannot be higher than the fountain-head. Nay more, *nothing can come out of nothing;* the stream cannot exist, if there be no springs from which it is fed.

At the risk of repetition, but for the sake of clearness, review now this argument, and gather it together. Considering that Slavery is of such an offensive character that it can find sanction only in "positive law," and that it has no such "positive" sanction in the Constitution; that the Constitution, according to its Preamble, was ordained "to establish justice" and "secure the blessings of liberty;" that, in the Convention which framed it, and also elsewhere at the time, it was declared not to sanction Slavery; that, according to the Declaration of Independence and the Address of the Continental Congress, the Nation was dedicated to "liberty" and the "rights of human nature;" that, according to the principles of the common law, the Constitution must be interpreted openly, actively, and perpetually, for Freedom; that, according to the decision of the Supreme Court, it acts upon slaves, *not as property*, but as PERSONS; that, at the first organization of the National Government under Washington, Slavery had no national favor, existed nowhere on the national territory, beneath the national flag, but was openly condemned by the Nation, the Church, the Colleges and Literature of the time; and, finally, that according to an Amendment of the Constitution, the National Government can only exercise powers delegated to it, among which there is none to support Slavery; considering these things, sir, it is impossible to avoid the single conclusion that Slavery is in no respect a national institution, and that the Constitution nowhere upholds property in man.

But there is one other special provision of the Constitution, which I have reserved to this stage, not so much from its superior importance, but because it may fitly stand by itself. This alone, if practically applied, would carry Freedom to all within its influence. It is an amendment proposed by the first Congress, as follows:

> "No *person* shall be deprived of life, *liberty* or property, *without due process of law.*"

Under this ægis the liberty of every person within the national jurisdiction is unequivocally placed. I say every person. Of this there can be no question. The word "person" in the Constitution embraces every human being within its sphere, whether Caucasian, Indian, or African, from the President to the slave. Show me a person, no matter what his condition, or race, or color, within the national jurisdiction, and I confidently claim for him this protection. The natural meaning of the clause is clear, but a single fact of its history places it in the broad light of noon. As originally recommended by North Carolina and Virginia, it was restrained to the *freeman.* Its language was, "No *freeman* ought to be deprived of his life, *liberty* or property, but by the law of the land." In rejecting this limitation, the authors of the amendment revealed their purpose, that no person, under the National Government, of whatever character, shall be deprived of liberty without due process of law; that is, without due presentment, indictment or other judicial proceedings. Here by this Amendment is an express guaranty of Personal Liberty, and an express prohibition against its invasion anywhere, at least within the national jurisdiction.

Sir, apply these principles, and Slavery will again be as when Washington took his first oath as President. The Union Flag of the Republic will become once more the flag of Freedom, and at all points within the national jurisdiction will refuse to cover a slave. Beneath its beneficent folds, wherever it is carried, on land or sea, Slavery will disappear, like darkness under the arrows of the ascending sun — like the Spirit of Evil before the Angel of the Lord.

In all national territories Slavery will be impossible.

On the high seas, under the national flag, Slavery will be impossible.

In the District of Columbia Slavery will instantly cease.

Inspired by these principles, Congress can give no sanction to Slavery by the admission of new Slave States.

Nowhere under the Constitution, can the Nation, by legislation or otherwise, support Slavery, hunt slaves, or hold property in man.

Such, sir, are my sincere convictions. According to the Constitution, as I understand it, in the light of the Past and of its true principles, there is no other conclusion which is rational or tenable; which does not defy the authoritative rules of interpretation; which does not falsify indisputable facts of history; which does not affront the public opinion in which it had its birth; and which does not dishonor the memory of the Fathers. And yet these convictions are now placed under formal ban by politicians of the hour. The generous sentiments which filled the early patriots, and which impressed upon the Government they founded, as upon the coin they circulated, the image and superscription of LIBERTY, have lost their power. The slave masters, few in number, amounting to not more than three hundred and fifty thousand, according to the recent census, have succeeded in dictating the policy of the National Government, and have written SLAVERY on its front. And now an arrogant and unrelenting ostracism is applied, not only to all who express themselves against Slavery, but to every man who is unwilling to be the menial of Slavery. A novel test for office is introduced, which would have excluded all the Fathers of the Republic — even Washington, Jefferson and Franklin! Yes, sir. Startling it may be, but indisputable. Could these revered demigods of history once again descend upon earth and mingle in our affairs, not one of them could receive a nomination from the National Convention of either of the two old political parties! Out of the convictions of their hearts and the utterances of their lips against Slavery they would be condemned.

This single fact reveals the extent to which the National Government has departed from its true course and its great examples. For myself, I know no better aim under the Constitution, than to bring the Government back to the precise position on this question which it occupied on the auspicious morning of its first organization by Washington;

> ——— nunc retrorsum
> Vela dare, atque iterare cursus
> Relictos; *

that the sentiments of the Fathers may again prevail with our rulers, and that the National Flag may nowhere shelter Slavery.

To such as count this aspiration unreasonable, let

* Horace, Carmina, Lib. I. 34.

me commend a renowned and life-giving precedent of English history. As early as the days of Queen Elizabeth, a courtier had boasted that the air of England was too pure for a slave to breathe, and the common law was said to forbid Slavery. And yet in the face of this vaunt, kindred to that of our Fathers, and so truly honorable, slaves were introduced from the West Indies. The custom of slavery gradually prevailed. Its positive legality was affirmed, in professional opinions, by two eminent lawyers, Talbot and Yorke, each afterwards Lord Chancellor. It was also affirmed on the bench by the latter as Lord Hardwicke. England was already a Slave State. The following advertisement, copied from a London newspaper, the *Public Advertiser*, of Nov. 22d, 1769, shows that the journals there were disfigured as some of ours, even in the District of Columbia:

"To be sold, a black girl, the property of J. B., eleven years of age, who is extremely handy, works at her needle tolerably, and speaks English perfectly well ; is of an excellent temper and willing disposition. Enquire of her Owner at the Angel Inn, behind St. Clement's Church, in the Strand."

At last, only three years after this advertisement, in 1772, the single question of the legality of Slavery was presented to Lord Mansfield, on a writ of *Habeas Corpus*. A poor negro, named Somersett, brought to England as a slave, became ill, and with an inhumanity disgraceful even to Slavery, was turned adrift upon the world. Through the charity of an estimable man, the eminent Abolitionist, Granville Sharpe, he was restored to health, when his unfeeling and avaricious master again claimed him as a bondman. The claim was repelled. After an elaborate and protracted discussion in Westminster Hall, marked by rare learning and ability, Lord Mansfield, with discreditable reluctance, sullying his great judicial name, but in trembling obedience to the genius of the British Constitution, pronounced a decree which made the early boast a practical verity, and rendered Slavery forever impossible in England. More than fifteen thousand persons, at that time held as slaves in English air — four times as many as are now found in this national metropolis — stepped forth in the happiness and dignity of freemen.

With this guiding example I cannot despair. The time will yet come when the boast of our Fathers will be made a practical verity also, and Court or Congress, in the spirit of this British judgment, will proudly declare that nowhere under the Constitution can man hold property in man. For the Republic such a decree will be the way of peace and safety. As Slavery is banished from the national jurisdiction, it will cease to vex our national politics. It may linger in the States as a local institution; but it will no longer engender national animosities, when it no longer demands national support.

II. From this general review of the relations of the National Government to Slavery, I pass to the consideration of the TRUE NATURE OF THE PROVISION FOR THE SURRENDER OF FUGITIVES FROM SERVICE, embracing an examination of this provision in the Constitution, and especially of the recent act of Congress in pursuance thereof. And here, as I begin this discussion, let me bespeak anew your candor. Not in prejudice, but in the light of history and of reason, let us consider this subject. The way will then be easy and the conclusion certain.

Much error arises from the exaggerated importance now attached to this provision, and from the assumptions with regard to its origin and primitive character It is often asserted that it was suggested by some special difficulty, which had become practically and extensively felt, anterior to the Constitution. But this is one of the myths or fables with which the supporters of Slavery have surrounded their false god. In the Articles of Confederation, while provision is made for the surrender of fugitive criminals, nothing is said of fugitive slaves or servants; and there is no evidence in any quarter, until after the National Convention, of any hardship or solicitude on this account. No previous voice was heard to express desire for any provision on the subject. The story to the contrary is a modern fiction.

I put aside as equally fabulous the common saying that this provision was one of the original compromises of the Constitution, and an essential condition of Union. Though sanctioned by eminent judicial opinions, it will be found that this statement has been hastily made, without any support in the records of the Convention, the only authentic evidence of the compromises; nor will it be easy to find any authority for it in any contemporary document, speech, published letter or pamphlet of any kind. It is true that there were compromises at the formation of the Constitution, which were the subject of anxious debate; but this was not of them.

There was a compromise between the small and

large States, by which equality was secured to all the States in the Senate. There was another compromise finally carried, under threats from the South, *on the motion of a New England member*, by which the Slave States were allowed Representatives according to the whole number of free persons, and "three-fifths of all other persons," thus securing political power on account of their slaves, in consideration that direct taxes should be apportioned in the same way. Direct taxes have been imposed at only four brief intervals. The political power has been constant, and, at this moment, sends twenty-one members to the other House.

There was a third compromise, which cannot be mentioned without shame. It was that hateful bargain by which Congress was restrained until 1808 from the prohibition of the foreign slave trade, thus securing, down to that period, toleration for crime. This was pertinaciously pressed by the South, even to the extent of an absolute restraint on Congress. John Rutledge said: "If the Convention thinks North Carolina, South Carolina and Georgia, will ever agree to this plan [the Federal Constitution] unless their right to import slaves be untouched, the expectation is vain. The people of those States will never be such fools as to give up so important an interest." Charles Pinckney said: "South Carolina can never receive the plan [of the Constitution] if it prohibits the slave trade." Charles Cotesworth Pinckney "thought himself bound to declare candidly that he did not think South Carolina would stop her importation of slaves in any short time." The effrontery of the slave-masters was matched by the sordidness of the Eastern members, who yielded again. Luther Martin, the eminent member of the Convention, in his contemporary address to the Legislature of Maryland, has described the compromise. "I found," he says, "that the Eastern members, notwithstanding their aversion to slavery, were very willing to indulge the Southern States, at least with a temporary liberty to prosecute the slave trade, *provided the Southern States would in their turn gratify them, by laying no restriction on navigation acts.*" The bargain was struck, and at this price the Southern States gained the detestable indulgence. At a subsequent day, Congress branded the slave trade as piracy, and thus, by solemn legislative act, adjudged this compromise to be felonious and wicked.

Such are the three chief original compromises of the Constitution and essential conditions of Union. The case of fugitives from service is not of these. During the Convention, it was not in any way associated with these. Nor is there any evidence, from the records of this body, that the provision on this subject was regarded with any peculiar interest. As its absence from the Articles of Confederation had not been the occasion of solicitude or desire, anterior to the National Convention, so it did not enter into any of the original plans of the Constitution. It was introduced tardily, at a late period of the Convention, and with very little and most casual discussion adopted. A few facts will show how utterly unfounded are the recent assumptions.

The National Convention was convoked to meet at Philadelphia on the second Monday in May, 1787. Several members appeared at this time; but a majority of the States not being represented, those present adjourned from day to day until the 25th, when the

Convention was organized by the choice of George Washington, as President. On the 28th, a few brief rules and orders were adopted. On the next day they commenced their great work.

On the same day, Edmund Randolph, of slaveholding Virginia, laid before the Convention a series of sixteen resolutions, containing his plan for the establishment of a New National Government. Here was no allusion to fugitive slaves.

On the same day, Charles Pinckney, of slaveholding South Carolina, laid before the Convention what is called " A draft of a Federal Government, to be agreed upon between the free and independent States of America," an elaborate paper, marked by considerable minuteness of detail. Here are provisions, borrowed from the Articles of Confederation, securing to citizens of each State equal privileges in the several States; giving faith to the public records of the States; and ordaining the surrender of fugitives from justice. But this draft, though from the flaming guardian of the slave interest, contained no allusion to fugitive slaves.

In the course of the Convention other plans were brought forward; on the 15th June a series of eleven propositions by Mr. Patterson, of New Jersey, " so as to render the Federal Constitution adequate to the exigencies of Government, and the preservation of the Union;" on the 18th June, eleven propositions by Mr. Hamilton of New York, " containing his ideas of a suitable plan of Government for the United States;" and on the 19th June, Mr. Randolph's resolutions, originally offered on the 29th May, " as altered, amended, and agreed to in Committee of the Whole House." On the 26th, twenty-three resolutions, already adopted on different days in the Convention, were referred to a "Committee of Detail," to be reduced to the form of a Constitution. On the 6th August this Committee reported the finished draft of a Constitution. And yet in all these resolutions, plans and drafts, *seven* in number, proceeding from eminent members and from able Committees, no allusion was made to fugitive slaves. For three months the Convention was in session, and not a word uttered on this subject.

At last, on the 28th August, as the Convention was drawing to a close, on the consideration of the article providing for the privileges of citizens in different States, we meet the first reference to this matter, in words worthy of note: "Gen. [Charles Cotesworth] Pinckney was not satisfied with it. He SEEMED *to wish some provision* should be included in favor of property in slaves." *But he made no proposition.* Unwilling to shock the Convention, and uncertain in his own mind, he only *seemed* to wish such a provision. In this vague expression of a vague desire, this idea first appeared. In this modest, hesitating phrase is the germ of the audacious, unhesitating Slave Act. Here is the little vapor, which has since swollen, as in the Arabian tale, to the power and dimensions of a giant. The next article under discussion provided for the surrender of fugitives from justice. Mr. Butler and Mr. Charles Pinckney, both from South Carolina, now moved openly to require "fugitive slaves and servants to be delivered up like criminals." Here was no disguise. With Hamlet it was now said in spirit:

"*Seems*, madam, nay, it is; I know not *seems*."

But the very boldness of the effort drew attention and opposition. Mr. Wilson, of Pennsylvania, at once objected: "This would oblige the Executive of the State to do it at the public expense." Mr. Sherman, of Connecticut, "saw no more propriety in the public seizing and surrendering a slave or servant, than a horse." Under the pressure of these objections, *the offensive proposition was quietly withdrawn* — never more to be renewed. The article for the surrender of criminals was then adopted. On the next day, 29th August, profiting by the suggestions already made, Mr. Butler moved a proposition — substantially like that now found in the Constitution — not for the surrender of "fugitive slaves," as originally proposed, but simply of "persons held to *service*," which, without debate or opposition of any kind, was unanimously adopted.

Here palpably was no labor of compromise — no adjustment of conflicting interests; nor even any expression of solicitude. The clause finally adopted was vague and faint as the original suggestion. In its natural import it is not applicable to slaves. If supposed by some to be so applicable, it is clear that it was supposed by others to be inapplicable to them. It is now insisted that the term "persons held *to service*" is an equivalent or synonym for "slaves." This interpretation is rebuked by an incident, to which reference has been already made, but which will bear repetition. On the 6th September — a little more than one brief week after the clause had been adopted, and when, if it was deemed to be of any significance, it could not have been forgotten — the very word "service" came under debate, and received a fixed meaning. It was unanimously adopted as a substitute for "servitude" in another part of the Constitution, for the reason that it "expressed the *obligation of free per-*

*sons*," while the other expressed "the condition of Slaves." * In the face of this authentic evidence of the sentiments of the Convention, reported by Mr. Madison, it is difficult to see how the term "persons held to *service*," can be deemed to express anything beyond "the obligations of *free persons*." Thus in the light of calm inquiry, does this exaggerated clause lose its importance.

The provision, which showed itself thus tardily, and was so slightly regarded in the National Convention, was neglected in much of the contemporaneous discussions before the people. In the Conventions of South Carolina, North Carolina and Virginia, it was commended as securing important rights, though on this point there was a difference of opinion. In the Virginia Convention, an eminent character, Mr. George Mason, with others, expressly declared that there was "no security of property coming within this section." In the other Conventions it was disregarded. Massachusetts, while exhibiting peculiar sensitiveness at any responsibility for Slavery, seemed to view it with unconcern. One of her leading statesmen, Gen. Heath, in the debates of the State Convention, strenuously asserted that, in ratifying the Constitution, the people of Massachusetts "would do nothing to hold the blacks in Slavery." The Federalist, (No. 42,) in its classification of the powers of Congress, describes and groups a large number as those "which provide for the harmony and proper intercourse among the States," and therein speaks of the power over public records, standing next in the Constitution to the provision on fugi-

* Madison's Papers, Vol. III. 1569.

tives from service; but it fails to recognize the latter among the means of promoting that "harmony and proper intercourse;" nor does it anywhere allude to the provision.

The indifference which had thus far attended this subject, still continued. The earliest Act of Congress, passed in 1793, drew little attention. It was not originally suggested by any difficulty or anxiety, touching fugitives from service, nor is there any record of the times, in debate or otherwise, showing that any special importance was attached to its provisions in this regard. The attention of Congress had been directed to fugitives from justice, and, with little deliberation, it undertook, in the same bill, to provide for both classes of cases. In this accidental manner was legislation on this subject first attempted.

There is no evidence that fugitives were often seized under this Act. From a competent inquirer we learn that twenty-six years elapsed before a single slave was surrendered under it in any Free State. It is certain that, in a case at Boston, towards the close of the last century, illustrated by Josiah Quincy as counsel, the crowd about the magistrate, at the examination, quietly and spontaneously opened a way for the fugitive, and thus the Act failed to be executed. It is also certain that, in Vermont, at the beginning of the century, a Judge of the Supreme Court of the State, on application for the surrender of an alleged slave, accompanied by documentary evidence, gloriously refused compliance *unless the master could show a Bill of Sale from the Almighty.* But even these cases passed without public comment.

In 1801, the subject was introduced in the House

of Representatives, by an effort for another Act, which, on consideration, was rejected. At a later day, in 1817–18, though still disregarded by the country, it seemed to excite a short-lived interest in Congress. A bill to provide more effectually "for reclaiming servants and slaves, escaping from one State into another," was introduced into the House of Representatives by Mr. Pindall, of Virginia, was considered for several days in Committee of the Whole, amended and passed by this body. In the Senate, after much attention and warm debate, it was also passed with amendments. But on its return to the House for the adoption of the amendments, it was dropped. This effort, which, in the discussions of this subject, has thus far been unnoticed, is chiefly remarkable as the earliest recorded evidence of the unwarrantable assertion, now so common, that this provision was originally of vital importance to the peace and harmony of the country.

At last, in 1850, we have another Act, passed by both Houses of Congress, and approved by the President, familiarly known as the Fugitive Slave Bill. As I read this statute, I am filled with painful emotions. The masterly subtlety with which it is drawn, might challenge admiration, if exerted for a benevolent purpose; but in an age of sensibility and refinement, a machine of torture, however skilful and apt, cannot be regarded without horror. Sir, in the name of the Constitution which it violates; of my country which it dishonors; of Humanity which it degrades; of Christianity which it offends; I arraign this enactment, and now hold it up to the judgment of the Senate and the world. Again, I shrink from no responsibility. I may seem to stand alone; but all the patriots and martyrs of history, all the Fathers of the Republic, are with me. Sir, there is no attribute of God which does not unite against this Act.

But I am to regard it now chiefly as an infringement of the Constitution. And here its outrages, flagrant as manifold, assume the deepest dye and broadest character only when we consider that by its language it is not restrained to any special race or class, to the African or to the person with African blood; but that any inhabitant of the United States, of whatever complexion or condition, may be its victim. Without discrimination of color even, and in violation of every presumption of freedom, the Act surrenders all, who may be claimed as "owing service or labor" to the same tyrannical proceedings. If there be any, whose sympathies are not moved for the slave, who do not cherish the rights of the humble African, struggling for divine Freedom, as warmly as the rights of the white man, let him consider well that the rights of all are equally assailed. "Nephew," said Algernon Sidney in prison, on the night before his execution, "I value not my own life a chip; but what concerns me is, that *the law* which takes away my life may hang every one of you, whenever it is thought convenient."

Though thus comprehensive in its provisions and applicable to all, there is no safeguard of Human Freedom which the monster Act does not set at naught.

It commits this great question — than which none is more sacred in the law — not to a solemn trial; but to summary proceedings.

It commits this question — not to one of the high tribunals of the land — but to the unaided judgment of a single petty magistrate.

It commits this question to a magistrate, appointed not by the President with the consent of the Senate but by the Court; holding his office, not during good behavior, but merely during the will of the Court; and receiving, not a regular salary, but fees according to each individual case.

It authorizes judgment on *ex parte* evidence, by affidavits, without the sanction of cross-examination.

It denies the writ of Habeas Corpus, ever known as the Palladium of the citizen.

Contrary to the declared purposes of the framers of the Constitution, it sends the fugitive back "at the public expense."

Adding meanness to the violation of the Constitution, it bribes the Commissioner by a double stipend to pronounce against Freedom. If he dooms a man to Slavery, the reward is ten dollars; but, saving him to Freedom, his dole is five dollars.

The Constitution expressly secures the "free exercise of religion;" but this Act visits with unrelenting penalties the faithful men and women, who may render to the fugitive that countenance, succor and shelter, which in their conscience "religion" seems to require.

As it is for the public weal that there should be an end of suits, so by the consent of civilized nations, these must be instituted within fixed limitations of time; but this Act, exalting Slavery above even this practical principle of universal justice, ordains proceedings against Freedom without any reference to the lapse of time.

Glancing only at these points, and not stopping for argument, vindication, or illustration, I come at once upon the two chief radical objections to this Act, identical in principle with those brought by our fathers against the British Stamp Act; *first*, that it is an usurpation by Congress of powers not granted by the Constitution, and an infraction of rights secured to the States; and, *secondly*, that it takes away Trial by Jury in a question of Personal Liberty and a suit at common law. Either of these objections, if sustained, strikes at the very root of the Act. That it is obnoxious to both, seems beyond doubt.

But here, at this stage, I encounter the difficulty, that these objections have been already foreclosed by the legislation of Congress and by the decisions of the Supreme Court; that as early as 1793, Congress assumed power over this subject by an Act, which failed to secure Trial by Jury, and that the validity of this Act, under the Constitution, has been affirmed by the Supreme Court. On examination this difficulty will disappear.

The Act of 1793 proceeded from a Congress that had already recognized the United States Bank, chartered by a previous Congress, which, though sanctioned by the Supreme Court, has been since in high quarters pronounced unconstitutional. If it erred as to the Bank, it may have erred also as to fugitives from service. But the very Act contains a capital error on this very subject, so declared by the Supreme Court, in pretending to vest a portion of the judicial power of the Nation in State officers. This error takes from the Act all authority as an interpretation of the Constitution. I dismiss it.

The decisions of the Supreme Court are entitled to great consideration, and will not be mentioned by me except with respect. Among the memories of my youth are happy days in which I sat at the feet of this tribunal, while MARSHALL presided, with STORY by his side. The pressure now proceeds from the case of *Prigg* v. *Pennsylvania*, (16 Peters, 539,) wherein the power of Congress over this matter is asserted. Without going into any minute criticism of this judgment, or considering the extent to which it is extra-judicial, and therefore of no binding force, all which has been already done at the bar in one State, and by an able court in another; but conceding to it a certain degree of weight as a rule to the judiciary on this particular point, still it does not touch the grave question arising from the denial of Trial by Jury. This judgment was pronounced by Mr. Justice Story. From the interesting biography of this great jurist, recently published by his son, we learn that the question of Trial by Jury was not considered as before the Court; so that, in the estimation of the judge himself, it was still an open question. Here are the words:

"One prevailing opinion, which has created great prejudice against this judgment, is, that it denies the right of a person claimed as a fugitive from service or labor to a trial by jury. This mistake arises from supposing the case to involve the general question as to the constitutionality of the Act of 1793. But in fact no such question was in the case; and the argument that the Act of 1793 was unconstitutional, because it did not provide for a trial by jury according to the requisitions of the sixth article in the amendments to the Constitution, having been suggested to my father on his return from Washington, he replied that this question was not argued by counsel nor considered by the Court, and that he should still consider it an open one."

But whatever may be the influence of this judgment as a rule to the judiciary, it cannot arrest our duty as legislators. And here I adopt with entire assent the language of President Jackson, in his memorable Veto, in 1832, of the Bank of the United States. To his course was opposed the authority of the Supreme Court, and this is his reply:

"If the opinion of the Supreme Court covers the whole ground of this Act, it ought not to control the coördinate authorities of this Government. The Congress, the Executive and the Court, must each for itself be guided by its own opinion of the Constitution. *Each public officer, who takes an oath to support the Constitution, swears that he will support it as he understands it, and not as it is understood by others.* It is as much the duty of the House of Representatives, of the Senate, and of the President, to decide upon the constitutionality of any bill or resolution, which may be presented to them for passage or approval, as it is of the Supreme Judges when it may be brought before them for judicial decision. The authority of the Supreme Court must not, therefore, be permitted to control the Congress or the Executive, when acting in their legislative capacities, but to have only such influence as the force of their reasoning may deserve."

With these authoritative words of Andrew Jackson I dismiss this topic. The early legislation of Congress, and the decisions of the Supreme Court cannot stand in our way. I advance to the argument.

(1.) *Now, first, of the power of Congress over this subject.*

The Constitution contains *powers* granted to Congress, *compacts* between the States, and *prohibitions* addressed to the Nation and to the States. A compact or prohibition may be accompanied by a power; but not necessarily, for it is essentially distinct in its nature. And here the single question arises, Whether the Constitution, by grant, general or special, confers upon Congress any *power* to legislate on the subject of fugitives from service.

The whole legislative power of Congress is derived from two sources; first, from the general grant of power, attached to the long catalogue of powers "to make all laws which shall be necessary and proper for the carrying into execution the foregoing powers and all other powers vested by this Constitution in the Government of the United States, or in any department or officer thereof;" and secondly, from special grants in other parts of the Constitution. As the provision in question does not appear in the catalogue of powers, and does not purport to vest any power in the Government of the United States, or in any department or officer thereof, no power to legislate on this subject can be derived from the general grant. Nor can any such power be derived from any special grant in any other part of the Constitution; for none such exists. The conclusion must be, that no power is delegated to Congress over the surrender of fugitives from service.

In all contemporary discussions and comments, the Constitution was constantly justified and recommended, on the ground that the powers not given to the Government were withheld from it. If under its original provisions any doubt could have existed on this head, it was removed, so far as language could remove it, by the Tenth Amendment, which, as we have already seen, expressly declares, that "The powers *not delegated* to the United States by the Constitution, nor prohibited by it to the States, are reserved to the States respectively or to the people." Here on the simple text of the Constitution I might leave this question. But its importance justifies a more extended examination in a two-fold light; *first*, in the history of the Convention, revealing the unmistakeable intention of its members; and *secondly*, in the true principles of our Political System, by which the powers of the Nation and of the States are respectively guarded.

Look first at the *history of the Convention*. The articles of the old Confederation, adopted by the Continental Congress, 15th November, 1777, though containing no reference to fugitives from service, had provisions substantially like those in our present Constitution, touching the privileges of citizens in the several States, the surrender of fugitives from justice, and the credit due to the public records of States. But, since the Confederation had no powers not "expressly delegated," and as no power was delegated to legislate on these matters, they were nothing more than articles of treaty or compact. Afterwards, at the National Convention, these three provisions found a place in the first reported draft of a Constitution, and they were arranged in the very order which they occupied in the Articles of Confederation. *The clause relating to public records stood last.* Mark this fact.

When this clause, being in form merely a *compact*, came up for consideration in the Convention, various efforts were made to graft upon it a *power*. This was on the very day of the adoption of the clause relating to fugitives from service. Charles Pinckney moved to commit it with a proposition for a *power* to establish uniform laws on the subject of bankruptcy and foreign bills of exchange. Mr. Madison was in favor of a *power* for the execution of judgments in other States. Gouverneur Morris on the same day moved to commit a further proposition for a *power* "to determine the proof and effect of such acts, records and proceedings." Amidst all these efforts to associate a power with this compact, it is clear that nobody supposed that any such already existed. This narrative places the views of the Convention beyond question.

The compact regarding public records, together with these various propositions, was referred to a Committee, on which were Mr. Randolph and Mr. Wilson, with John Rutledge, of South Carolina, as chairman. After several days, they reported the compact, with a *power* in Congress to prescribe by general laws the manner in which such records shall be proved. A discussion ensued, in which Mr. Randolph complained that the "definition of the powers of the Government was so loose as to give it opportunities of usurping all the State powers. *He was for not going further than the report, which enables the Legislature to provide for the effect of judgments.*" The clause of compact with the power attached was then adopted, and is now a part of the Constitution. In presence of this solicitude for the preservation of "State powers," even while considering a proposition for an express power, and also of the distinct statement of Mr. Randolph, that he "was not for going further than the report,' it is evident that the idea could not then have occurred, that a power was coupled with the naked clause of compact on fugitives from service.

At a later day, the various clauses and articles severally adopted from time to time in Convention, were referred to a committee of revision and arrangement, that they might be reduced to form as a connected whole. *Here another change was made.* The clause relating to public records, with the power attached, was taken from its original place at the bottom of the clauses of compact, and promoted to stand first in the article, as a distinct section, while the other clauses of compact concerning citizens, fugitives from justice, and fugitives from service, each and all without any power attached, by a natural association compose but a single section, thus:

"ARTICLE IV.

"SECTION 1. Full faith and credit shall be given in each State to the public acts, records and judicial proceedings of every other State. *And the Congress may by general laws prescribe the manner in which such acts, records, and proceedings shall be proved, and the effect thereof.*

"SECTION 2. The citizens of each State shall be entitled to all privileges and immunities of citizens in the several States.

"A person charged in any State with treason, felony, or other crime, who shall flee from justice, and be found in another State, shall, on demand of the Executive authority of the State from which he fled, be delivered up, to be removed to the State having jurisdiction of the crime.

"No person held to service or labor in one State, under the laws thereof, escaping into another, shall, in consequence of any law or regulation therein, be discharged from such service or labor, but shall be delivered up on claim of the party to whom such service or labor may be due.

"SECTION 3. New States *may be admitted by the Congress* into this Union; but no new State shall be formed or erected within the jurisdiction of any other State, nor any State be formed by the junction of two or more States, or parts of States, without the consent of the Legislatures of the States concerned, *as well as of the Congress.*

"*The Congress shall have power* to dispose of and make all needful rules and regulations respecting the territory or other property belonging to the United States; and nothing in this

Constitution shall be so construed as to prejudice any claims of the United States, or of any particular State.

"SECTION 4. The *United States shall guarantee* to every State in this Union a republican form of Government, and *shall protect* each of them against invasion, and on application of the Legislature, or of the Executive, (when the Legislature cannot be convened,) against domestic violence."

Here is the whole article. It will be observed that the third section immediately following the triad section of compacts, contains two specific powers, one with regard to new States, and the other with regard to the Public Treasury. These are naturally grouped together, while the fourth section of this same article, which is distinct in its character, is placed by itself. In the absence of all specific information, reason alone can determine why this arrangement was made. But the conclusion is obvious, that, in the view of the Committee and of the Convention, each of these sections differs from the others. The first contains a compact with a grant of power. The second contains provisions, all of which are simple compacts, and two of which were confessedly simple compacts in the old Articles of Confederation, from which, unchanged in letter or spirit, they were borrowed. The third is a two-fold grant of power to Congress, without any compact. The fourth is neither power nor compact merely, nor both united, but a solemn injunction upon the National Government to perform an important duty.

The framers of the Constitution were wise and careful men, who had a reason for what they did, and who understood the language which they employed. They did not, after discussion, incorporate into their work any superfluous provision; nor did they without design adopt the peculiar arrangement in which it appears. In adding to the record compact the express grant of power, they testified not only their desire for such power in Congress; but their conviction, that, without an express grant, it would not exist. But if an express grant was necessary in this case, it was equally necessary in all the other cases. *Expressum facit cessare tacitum.* Especially, in view of its odious character, was it necessary in the case of fugitives from service. In abstaining from any such grant, and then, in grouping the bare compact with other similar compacts, separate from every grant of power, they have most significantly testified their purpose. They not only decline all addition of any such power to the compact, but, to render misapprehension impossible, to make assurance doubly sure, to exclude any contrary conclusion, they punctiliously arrange the clauses, on the principle of *noscitur a sociis*, so as to distinguish all the grants of power, but especially to make the new grant of power, in the case of public records, stand forth in the front by itself, severed from the mere naked compacts with which it was originally associated.

Thus the proceedings of the Convention show that the founders understood the necessity of *powers* in certain cases, and, on consideration, most jealously granted them. A closing example will strengthen the argument. Congress is expressly empowered "*to establish an uniform rule of* Naturalization, and *uniform laws* on the subject of Bankruptcies, *throughout the United States.*" Without this provision these two subjects would have been within the control of the States, and the Nation would have had no power *to establish an uniform rule* thereupon. Now, instead of the existing compact on fugitives from service, it would have been easy, had any such desire prevailed, to add this case to the clause on Naturalization and Bankruptcies, and to empower Congress TO ESTABLISH AN UNIFORM RULE FOR THE SURRENDER OF FUGITIVES FROM SERVICE THROUGHOUT THE UNITED STATES. Then, of course, whenever Congress undertook to exercise the power, all State control of the subject would have been superseded. The National Government would have been constituted, like Nimrod, the mighty Hunter, with power to gather the huntsmen, to halloo the pack, and to direct the chase of men, ranging at will, without regard to boundaries or jurisdictions, throughout all the States. But no person in the Convention, not one of the reckless partisans of slavery, was so audacious as to make this proposition. Had it been distinctly made, it would have been distinctly denied.

The fact that the provision on this subject was adopted unanimously, while showing the little importance attached to it *in the shape it finally assumed*, testifies also that it could not have been regarded *as a source of National power over Slavery*. It will be remembered, that, among the members of the Convention, were Gouverneur Morris, who had said, that he "*never* would concur in upholding domestic slavery;" Elbridge Gerry, who thought "we ought to be careful NOT *to give any sanction to it;*" Roger Sherman, who was OPPOSED to any clause "acknowledging men to be property;" James Madison, who "thought it WRONG to admit in the Constitution the idea that there could be property in man;" and Benjamin Franklin, who likened American slaveholders to Algerine corsairs.

In the face of these unequivocal statements, it is absurd to suppose that they consented *unanimously* to any provision by which the National Government, the work of their hands, dedicated to Freedom, could be made the most offensive instrument of Slavery.

Thus much for the evidence from the history of the Convention. But the *true principles of our Political System* are in harmony with this conclusion of history; and here let me say a word of State Rights.

It was the purpose of our fathers to create a National Government, and to endow it with adequate powers. They had known the perils of imbecility, discord and confusion, during the uncertain days of the Confederation, and desired a Government which should be a true bond of Union and an efficient organ of the national interests at home and abroad. But while fashioning this agency, they fully recognized the Governments of the States. To the nation were delegated high powers, essential to the national interests, but specific in character and limited in number. To the States and to the people were reserved the powers, general in character and unlimited in number, not delegated to the Nation or prohibited to the States.

The integrity of our Political System depends upon harmony in the operations of the Nation and of the States. While the Nation within its wide orbit is supreme, the States move with equal supremacy in their own. But from the necessity of the case, the supremacy of each in its proper place excludes the other. The Nation cannot exercise rights reserved to the States; nor can the States interfere with the powers of the Nation. Any such action on either side is a usurpa-

12

tion. These principles were distinctly declared by Mr. Jefferson, in 1798, in words often adopted since; and which must find acceptance from all parties:

"That the several States composing the United States of America are not united upon the principle of unlimited submission to the General Government; but that by compact, under the style and title of the Constitution of the United States and of the amendments thereto, they constituted a General Government for special purposes, *delegated to that Government certain definite powers*, reserving each State to itself, the residuary mass of right to their own self-government, and that *wheresoever the General Government assumes undelegated powers, its acts are unauthorized, void, and of no force.*'

But I have already amply shown to-day that Slavery is in no respect national — that it is not within the sphere of national activity — that it has no "positive" support in the Constitution, and that any interpretation thereof consistent with this principle would be abhorrent to the sentiments of its founders. Slavery is a local institution, peculiar to the States and under the guardianship of State Rights. It is impossible, without violence, at once to the spirit and to the letter of the Constitution, to attribute to Congress any power to legislate, either for its abolition in the States or its support anywhere. *Non-Intervention* is the rule prescribed to the Nation. Regarding the question only in its more general aspects, and putting aside, for the moment, the perfect evidence from the records of the Convention, it is palpable that there is no *national fountain* out of which the existing Slave Act can be derived.

But this Act is not only an unwarrantable assumption of power by the Nation; it is also an infraction of rights reserved to the States. Everywhere within their borders the States are the peculiar guardians of *personal liberty*. By Jury and Habeas Corpus to save the citizen harmless against all assault is among their duties and rights. To his State the citizen when oppressed may appeal, nor should he find that appeal denied. But this Act despoils him of his rights, and despoils his State of all power to protect him. It subjects him to the wretched chances of false oaths, forged papers and facile commissioners, and takes from him every safeguard. Now, if the slaveholder has a right to be secure *at home* in the enjoyment of *Slavery*, so also has the freeman of the North — and every person there is presumed to be a freeman — an equal right to be secure *at home* in the enjoyment of *Freedom*. The same principle of State Rights by which Slavery is protected in the Slave States throws an impenetrable shield over Freedom in the Free States. And here, let me say, is the only security for Slavery in the Slave States as for Freedom in the Free States. In the present fatal overthrow of State Rights you teach a lesson which may return to plague the teacher. Compelling the National Government to stretch its Briarean arms into the Free States, for the sake of Slavery, you show openly how it may stretch these same hundred giant arms into the Slave States for the sake of Freedom. This lesson was not taught by our fathers.

And here I end this branch of the question. The true principles of our Political System, the history of the National Convention, the natural interpretation of the Convention, all teach that this Act is a usurpation by Congress of powers that do not belong to it, and an infraction of rights secured to the States. It is a sword, whose handle is at the National Capital, and whose point is everywhere in the States. A weapon so terrible to Personal Liberty the Nation has no power to grasp.

(2.) *And now of the denial of Trial by Jury.* Admitting, for the moment, that Congress is entrusted with power over this subject, which truth disowns, still the Act is again radically unconstitutional from its denial of Trial by Jury in a question of Personal Liberty and a suit at common law. Since on the one side there is a claim of property, and on the other of liberty, both property and liberty are involved in the issue. To this claim on either side is attached Trial by Jury.

To me, sir, regarding this matter in the light of the common law and in the blaze of free institutions, it has always seemed impossible to arrive at any other conclusion. If the language of the Constitution were open to doubt, which it is not, still all the presumptions of law, all the leanings for Freedom, all the suggestions of justice, plead angel-tongued for this right. Nobody doubts that Congress, if it legislates on this matter, *may* allow a Trial by Jury. But if it *may*, so overwhelming is the claim of justice, it MUST. Beyond this, however, the question is determined by the precise letter of the Constitution.

Several expressions in the provision for the surrender of fugitives from service, show the essential character of the proceedings. In the first place, the person must be, not merely *charged*, as in the case of fugitives from justice, but actually *held to service* in the State from which he escaped. In the second place, he must be "delivered up on claim of the party to whom such labor is *due*." These two facts, that he was *held* to service, and that his service was *due* to his claimant, are directly placed in issue, and must be proved. Two necessary incidents of the delivery may also be observed. First, it must be made in the State where the fugitive is found; and, secondly, it restores to the claimant his complete control over the person of the fugitive. From these circumstances it is evident that the proceedings cannot be regarded, in any just sense, as preliminary, or ancillary to some future formal trial, but as complete in themselves, final and conclusive.

And these proceedings determine on the one side the question of property, and on the other the sacred question of Personal Liberty in its most transcendent form; not merely Liberty for a day or a year, but for life, and the Liberty of generations that shall come after, so long as Slavery endures. To these questions, the Constitution, by two specific provisions, attaches the Trial by Jury. One of these is the familiar clause, already adduced: "No *person* shall be deprived of life, *liberty* or property, *without due process of law;*" that is, without due proceedings at law, with Trial by Jury. Not stopping to dwell on this, I press at once to the other provision, which is still more express: "In suits at common law, where the value in controversy shall exceed twenty dollars, the right of Trial by Jury shall be preserved." This clause, which was not in the original Constitution, when first adopted, was suggested by the very spirit of Freedom. At the close of the National Convention, Elbridge Gerry refused to sign the Constitution, because, among other things, it established a "tribunal *without juries*, a Star Chamber as to civil cases." Many united in his opposition, and on the recommendation of the First Congress this additional safeguard was adopted as an amendment.

Now, regarding the question as one of property, or of Personal Liberty, in either alternative the Trial by Jury is secured. For this position authority is ample. In the debate on the Fugitive Slave Bill of 1817–18, a Senator from South Carolina, Mr. Smith, anxious for the asserted right of property, objected, on this very floor, to a reference of the question, under the writ of Habeas Corpus, to a judge without a jury. Speaking solely for property, these were his words:

> "This would give the Judge the sole power of deciding *the right of property the master claims in his slaves, instead of trying that right by a jury, as prescribed by the Constitution.* He would be judge of matters of law and matters of fact; clothed with all the powers of a court. Such a principle is unknown in your system of jurisprudence. *Your Constitution has forbid it.* It preserves the right of Trial by Jury in all cases where the value in controversy exceeds twenty dollars." — (Debates in *National Intelligencer*, June 15, 1818.)

But this provision has been repeatedly discussed by the Supreme Court, so that its meaning is not open to doubt. Three conditions are necessary. *First*, the proceedings must be "a suit;" *secondly*, "at common law;" and *thirdly*, "where the value in controversy exceeds twenty dollars." In every such case "the right of Trial by Jury *shall* be preserved." The decisions of the Supreme Court expressly touch each of these points.

*First*. In the case of *Cohens* v. *Virginia*, (6 Wheaton, 407,) the Court say: "What is *a suit?* We understand it to be the prosecution of some *claim*, demand or request." Of course, then, the "claim" for a fugitive must be "a suit."

*Secondly.* In the case of *Parsons* v. *Bedford*, (3 Peters, 456,) while considering this very clause, the Court say: "By *common law* is meant not merely suits which the common law recognized among its old and settled proceedings, but suits in which *legal rights* were to be ascertained and determined. In a just sense, the Amendment may well be construed to embrace all suits, which are not of Equity or Admiralty jurisdiction, *whatever may be the peculiar form which they may assume to settle legal rights.*" Now, since the claim for a fugitive is not a suit in Equity or Admiralty, but a suit to settle what are called legal rights, it must, of course, be "a suit at common law."

*Thirdly.* In the case of *Lee* v. *Lee*, (8 Peters, 44,) on a question whether "the value in controversy" was "one thousand dollars and upwards," it was objected that the appellants, who were petitioners for Freedom, were not of the value of one thousand dollars. But the Court said: "The matter in dispute is the Freedom of the petitioners. *This is not susceptible of pecuniary valuation.* No doubt is entertained of the jurisdiction of the Court." Of course, then, since liberty is above price, the claim to any fugitive always and necessarily presumes that "the value in controversy exceeds twenty dollars."

By these successive steps, sustained by decisions of the highest tribunal, it appears, as in a diagram, that the right of Trial by Jury is secured to the fugitive from service.

This conclusion needs no further authority; but it may receive curious illustration from the ancient records of the common law, so familiar and dear to the framers of the Constitution. It is said by Mr. Burke, in his magnificent speech on Conciliation with America, that "nearly as many of Blackstone's Commentaries were sold in America as in England," carrying thither the knowledge of those vital principles of Freedom, which were the boast of the British Constitution. Imbued by these, the earliest Continental Congress, in 1774, declared, "That the respective Colonies are entitled to the common law of England, and especially to the great and inestimable privilege of being tried by their peers of the vicinage according to the course of that law." Thus, amidst the troubles which heralded the Revolution, the common law was claimed by our fathers as a birthright.

Now, although the common law may not be approached as a source of jurisdiction under the National Constitution — and on this point I do not dwell — *it is clear that it may be employed to determine the meaning of technical terms in the Constitution borrowed from this law.* This, indeed, is expressly sanctioned by Mr. Madison, in his celebrated report of 1799, while restraining the extent to which the common law may be employed. Thus by this law we learn the nature of *Trial by Jury*, which, though secured, is not described by the Constitution; also of *Bills of Attainder*, the *Writ of Habeas Corpus*, and *Impeachment*, all technical terms of the Constitution borrowed from the common law. By this law, and its associate Chancery, we learn what are *cases in law and equity* to which the judicial power of the United States is extended. These instances I adduce merely by way of example. Of course also in the same way we learn what in reality are *suits at common law.*

Now, on principle and authority, *a claim for the delivery of a fugitive slave is a suit at common law*, and is embraced naturally and necessarily in this class of judicial proceedings. This proposition can be placed beyond question. And here, especially, let me ask the attention of all learned in the law. On this point, as on every other other in this argument, I challenge inquiry and answer.

History painfully records, that during the early days of the common law, and down even to a late period, a system of slavery existed in England, known under the name of *villanage.* The slave was generally called a *villain*, though in the original Latin forms of judicial proceedings, he was termed *nativus*, implying slavery by birth. The incidents of this condition have been minutely described, and also the mutual remedies of master and slave, all of which were regulated by the common law. Slaves sometimes then, as now, *escaped* from their masters. The claim for them after such *escape* was prosecuted by a "suit at common law," to which, as to every suit at common law, the Trial by Jury was necessarily attached. Blackstone, in his Commentaries, (Vol. II. p. 93,) in words which must have been known to all the lawyers of the Convention, said of *villains:* "They could not leave their lord without his permission, but *if they ran away*, or were purloined from him, *might be* CLAIMED *and recovered by* ACTION, *like beasts or other cattle.*" This very word "action" of itself implies "a suit at common law," with Trial by Jury.

From other sources we learn precisely what the *action* was. That great expounder of the ancient law, Mr. Hargrave, says, "That Year Books and Books of Entries are full of the forms used in pleading a title to villains." Though no longer of practical value in England, they remain as monuments of jurisprudence, and as mementoes of a barbarous institution. He thus describes the remedy of the master at common law:

"The lord's remedy for a *fugitive villain* was, either by seizure or by suing out a writ of *Nativo Habendo*, or Neifty, as it is sometimes called. If the lord seized, the villain's most effectual mode of recovering liberty was by the writ of *Homine Replegiando*, which had great advantage over the writ of Habeas Corpus. In the *Habeas Corpus* the return cannot be contested by pleading against the truth of it, and consequently on a *Habeas Corpus the question of liberty cannot go to a jury for trial.* But in the *Homine Replegiando* it was otherwise. The plaintiff, on the defendant's pleading villanage, had the same opportunity of contesting it, as when impleaded by the lord in a *Nativo Habendo*. If the lord sued out a *Nativo Habendo*, and the villanage was denied, in which case the sheriff could not seize the villain, *the lord was then to enter his plaint in the county court*, and as the sheriff was not allowed to try the question of villanage in his court, the lord could not have any benefit from the writ, without removing the cause by the writ of *Pone* into the King's Bench or Common Pleas." — (20 Howell's State Trials, 38, *note*.)

The authority of Mr. Hargrave is sufficient. But I desire to place this matter beyond all cavil. From the Digest of Lord Chief Baron Comyns, which, at the adoption of the Constitution, was one of the classics of our jurisprudence, I derive another description of the remedy of the master:

"If the lord claims an inheritance in his villain, *who flies from his lord against his will*, and lives in a place out of the manor, to which he is regardant, the lord shall have a *Nativo Habendo*. And upon such writ, directed to the sheriff, he may seize him who does not deny himself to be a villain. But if the defendant say that he is a Free Man, the sheriff cannot seize him, but the lord must remove the writ by *Pone* before the Justices *in Eire*, or in C. B., *where he must count upon it.*" — (Comyns' Digest — Villanage, C. 1.)

An early writer of peculiar authority, Fitzherbert, in his *Natura Brevium*, on the writs of the common law, thus describes these proceedings:

"The writ *de Nativo Habendo* lieth for the lord who claimeth inheritance in any villain, *when his villain is run from him*, and is remaining within any place out of the manor unto which he is regardant, or when he departeth from his lord against the lord's will; and the writ shall be directed to the sheriff. And the sheriff may seize the villain, and deliver him unto his lord, if the villain confess unto the sheriff that he is his villain; but if the villain say to the sheriff that he is frank, then it seemeth that the sheriff ought not to seize him; as it is in a replevin, if the defendant claim property, the sheriff cannot replevy the cattle, but the party ought to sue a writ *de Proprietate Probanda;* and so if the villain say that he is a free man, &c., then the sheriff ought not to seize him, but then the lord ought to sue a *Pone* to remove the plea before the justices of the Common Pleas, or before the justices in eyre. But if the villain purchase a writ *de Libertate Probanda* before the lord hath sued the *Pone* to remove the plea before the justices, then that writ of *Libertate Probanda* is a *Supersedeas* unto the lord, that he proceed not upon the writ *Nativo Habendo* till the eyre of the justices, and that the lord ought not to seize the villain in the meantime." — (Vol. I. p. 76.)

These authorities are not merely applicable to the general question of freedom; but they distinctly contemplate the case of *fugitive* slaves, and the "suits at common law" for their rendition. Blackstone speaks of villains who "ran away;" Hargrave of "fugitive villains;" Comyns of a villain "who flies from his lord against his will;" and Fitzherbert of the proceedings of the lord "when his villain is run from him." The forms, writs, counts, pleadings, and judgments, in these suits, are all preserved among the precedents of the common law. The writs are known as original writs which the party on either side, at the proper stage, could sue out of right without showing cause. The writ of *Libertate Probanda* for a fugitive slave was in this form:

"LIBERTATE PROBANDA.

"The king to the sheriff, &c. A. and B. her sister, have showed unto us, that whereas they are free women, and ready to prove their liberty, F. claiming then to be his niefs unjustly, vexes them; and therefore we command you, that if the aforesaid A. and B. shall make you secure touching the proving of their liberty, then put that plea before our justices at the first assizes, when they shall come into those parts, because proof of this kind belongeth not to you to take; and in the meantime cause the said A. and B. to have peace thereupon, and tell the aforesaid F. that he may be there, if he will, to prosecute his plea thereof against the aforesaid A. and B. And have there this writ. Witness, &c." — (*Fitzherbert*, Vol. I. p. 77.)

By these various proceedings, all ending in Trial by Jury, Personal Liberty was guarded, even in the early, unrefined, and barbarous days of the common law. Any person claimed as a fugitive slave might invoke this Trial as a sacred right. Whether the master proceeded by seizure, as he might, or by legal process, the Trial by Jury in a suit at common law, before one of the high courts of the realm, was equally secured. In the case of seizure, the fugitive, reserving the proceedings, might institute process against his master and appeal to a court and jury. In the case of process by the master, the watchful law secured to the fugitive the same protection. By no urgency of force, by no device of process, could any person claimed as a slave be defrauded of this Trial. Such was the common law. If its early boast, that there could be no slaves in England, fails to be true, this at least may be its pride, that, according to its indisputable principles, the Liberty of every man was placed under the guard of Trial by Jury.

These things may seem new to us; but they must have been known to the members of the Convention, particularly to those from South Carolina, through whose influence the provision on this subject was adopted. Charles Cotesworth Pinckney and Mr. Rutledge had studied law at the Temple, one of the English Inns of Court. It would be a discredit to them, and also to other learned lawyers, members of the Convention, to suppose that they were not conversant with the principles and precedents directly applicable to this subject, all of which are set down in works of acknowledged weight, and at that time of constant professional study. Only a short time before, in the case of *Somersett*, they had been most elaborately examined in Westminster Hall. In a forensic effort of unsurpassed learning and elevation, which of itself vindicates for its author his great juridical name, Mr. Hargrave had fully made them known to such as were little acquainted with the more ancient sources. But even if we could suppose them unknown to the lawyers of the Convention, they are none the less applicable in determining the true meaning of the Constitution.

The conclusion from this examination is explicit. Clearly and indisputably, in England, the country of the common law, a claim for a fugitive slave was "a suit at common law," recognized "among its old and settled proceedings." To question this, in the face of authentic principles and precedents, would be preposterous. As well might it be questioned, that a writ of replevin for a horse, or a writ of right for land, was "a suit at common law." It follows, then, that this *technical term* of the Constitution, read in the illumination of the common law, naturally and necessarily embraces proceedings for the recovery of fugitive slaves, *if any such be instituted or allowed under the Constitution.* And thus, by the letter of the Constitution, in harmony with the requirements of the common law, all such persons, when claimed by their masters, are entitled to a Trial by Jury.

Such, sir, is the argument, briefly uttered, against the constitutionality of the Slave Act. Much more I might say on this matter; much more on the two chief grounds of objection which I have occupied. But I am admonished to hasten on.

Opposing this Act as doubly unconstitutional from a want of power in Congress and from a denial of Trial by Jury, I find myself again encouraged by the example of our Revolutionary Fathers, in a case which is one of the landmarks of history. The parallel is important and complete In 1765, the British Parliament, by a notorious statute, attempted to draw money from the colonies through a stamp tax, while the determination of certain questions of forfeiture under the statute was delegated — not to the courts of common law — but to

Courts of Admiralty without a jury. The Stamp Act, now execrated by all lovers of liberty, had this extent and no more. Its passage was the signal for a general flame of opposition and indignation throughout the Colonies. It was denounced as contrary to the British Constitution on two principal grounds; *first*, as a usurpation by Parliament of powers not belonging to it, and an infraction of rights secured to the Colonies; and *secondly*, as a denial of Trial by Jury in certain cases of property.

The public feeling was variously expressed. At Boston, on the arrival of the stamps, the shops were closed, the bells of the churches tolled, and the flags of the ships hung at half-mast. At Portsmouth, in New Hampshire, the bells were tolled, and notice given to the friends of Liberty to hold themselves in readiness to attend her funeral. At New York a letter was received from Franklin, then in London, written on the day after the passage of the Act, in which he said: "The sun of liberty is set." The obnoxious Act, headed "Folly of England and Ruin of America," was contemptuously hawked through the streets. The merchants of New York, inspired then by Liberty, resolved to import no more goods from England until the repeal of the Act; and their example was followed shortly afterwards by the merchants of Philadelphia and Boston. Bodies of patriots were organized everywhere under the name of "Sons of Liberty." The orators also spoke. James Otis with fiery tongue appealed to Magna Charta.

Of all the States, Virginia — whose shield bears the image of Liberty trampling upon chains — first declared herself by solemn resolutions, which the timid thought "treasonable;" but which soon found a response. New York followed. Massachusetts came next, speaking by the pen of the inflexible Samuel Adams. In an Address from the Legislature to the Governor, the true grounds of opposition to the Stamp Act, coincident with the two radical objections to the Slave Act, are clearly set forth:

"You are pleased to say that the Stamp Act is an act of Parliament, and as such ought to be observed. This House, sir, has too great reverence for the Supreme Legislature of the nation *to question its just authority*. It by no means appertains to us to presume to adjust the boundaries of the *power* of Parliament; *but boundaries there undoubtedly are.* We hope we may, without offence, put your Excellency in mind of that most grievous sentence of excommunication solemnly denounced by the Church in the name of the sacred Trinity, in the presence of King Henry the Third and the estates of the realm, *against all those who should make statutes* OR OBSERVE THEM, BEING MADE, *contrary to the liberties of Magna Charta.* The Charter of this province invests the General Assembly with the *power* of making laws for its internal government and taxation; and this Charter has never been forfeited. The Parliament has a right to make all laws within the limits of their own constitution." . . . "The people complain that the Act vests a single judge of Admiralty with the power to try and determine their property in controversies arising from internal concerns, *without a jury*, contrary to the very expression of Magna Charta, that no freeman shall be amerced, but by the oath of good and lawful men of the vicinage." . . . "We deeply regret that the Parliament has seen fit to pass such an act as the Stamp Act; we flatter ourselves that the hardships of it will shortly appear to them in such a light, as shall induce them in their wisdom to repeal it; *in the meantime, we must beg your Excellency will excuse us from doing anything to assist in the execution of it.*"

Thus in those days spoke Massachusetts! The parallel still proceeds. The unconstitutional Stamp Act was welcomed in the Colonies by the Tories of that day precisely as the unconstitutional Slave Act has been welcomed by large and imperious numbers among us. Hutchinson, at that time Lieutenant Governor and Judge in Massachusetts, wrote to Ministers in England: "The Stamp Act is received with as much decency as could be expected. It leaves no room for evasion, and will execute itself." Like the judges of our day, in charges to grand juries, he resolutely vindicated the Act, and admonished "the jurors and the people" to obey. Like Governors of our day, Bernard, in his speech to the Legislature of Massachusetts, demanded unreasoning submission. "I shall not," says this British Governor, "enter into any disquisition of the policy of this Act. I have only to say it is an Act of the Parliament of Great Britain; and I trust that the supremacy of that Parliament over all the members of their wide and diffused empire never was and never will be denied within these walls." Like marshals of our day, the officers of the Customs made "application for a military force to assist them in the execution of their duty." The military were against the people. A British major of artillery at New York exclaimed, in tones not unlike those now sometimes heard: "I will cram the stamps down their throats with the end of my sword." The elaborate answer of Massachusetts — a paper of historic grandeur — drawn by Samuel Adams, was pronounced "the ravings of a parcel of wild enthusiasts."

Thus in those days spoke the partisans of the Stamp Act. But their weakness soon became manifest. In the face of an awakened community, where discussion has free scope, no men, though surrounded by office and wealth, can long sustain injustice. Earth, water, nature, they may subdue; but Truth they cannot subdue. Subtle and mighty, against all efforts and devices, it fills every region of light with its majestic presence. The Stamp Act was discussed and understood. Its violation of constitutional rights was exposed. By resolutions of Legislatures and of town meetings, by speeches and writings, by public assemblies and processions, the country was rallied in peaceful phalanx *against the execution of the Act.* To this great object, within the bounds of law and the constitution, were bent all the patriot energies of the land.

And here Boston took the lead. Her records at this time are full of proud memorials. In formal instructions to her representatives, adopted unanimously, "having been read several times," in Town Meeting at Faneuil Hall, the following rule of conduct was prescribed:

"We, therefore, think it our indispensable duty, in Justice to ourselves and Posterity, as it is our undoubted Privilege, in the most open and unreserved, but decent and respectful Terms, to declare our greatest Dissatisfaction with this Law. *And we think it incumbent upon you by no Means to join in any public Measures for countenancing and assisting in the execution of the same.* But to use your best endeavors in the general Assembly to have the inherent inalienable Rights of the People of this Province asserted, and vindicated, and left upon the public record, that Posterity may never have reason to charge the present Times with the Guilt of tamely giving them away."

Virginia responded to Boston. Many of her justices of the peace surrendered their commissions "rather than aid in the enforcement of the law, or be instrumental in the overthrow of their country's liberties."

As the opposition deepened, its natural tendency was

to outbreak and violence. But this was carefully restrained. On one occasion in Boston it showed itself in the lawlessness of a mob. But the town, at a public meeting in Faneuil Hall, called without delay on the motion of the opponents of the Stamp Act, with James Otis as chairman, condemned the outrage. Eager in hostility to the execution of the Act, Boston cherished municipal order, and constantly discountenanced all tumult, violence and illegal proceedings. Her equal devotion to these two objects drew the praises and congratulations of other towns. In reply, March 27th, 1766, to an Address from the inhabitants of Plymouth, her own consciousness of duty done is thus expressed:

"If the inhabitants of Boston have taken *the legal and warrantable measures to prevent that misfortune, of all others the most to be dreaded, the execution of the Stamp Act*, and as a necessary means of preventing it, have made any spirited applications for opening the custom-houses and courts of justice; if *at the same time they have borne their testimony against outrageous tumults and illegal proceedings*, and given any example of the Love of Peace and good order, next to the consciousness of having done their duty is the satisfaction of meeting with the approbation of any of their fellow-countrymen."

Learn now from the Diary of John Adams the results of this system:

"The year 1765 has been the most remarkable year of my life. That enormous engine, fabricated by the British Parliament, for battering down all the rights and liberties of America — I mean the Stamp Act — has raised and spread through the whole continent a spirit that will be recorded to our honor with all future generations. In every Colony, from Georgia to New Hampshire inclusively, the stamp distributors and inspectors have been compelled by the unconquerable rage of the people to renounce their offices. Such and so universal has been the resentment of the people, that every man who has dared to speak in favor of the stamps, or to soften the detestation in which they are held, how great soever his abilities and virtues had been esteemed before, or whatever his fortune, connections and influence had been, has been seen to sink into universal contempt and ignominy."

The Stamp Act became a dead letter. At the meeting of Parliament numerous petitions were presented, calling for its instant repeal. Franklin, at that time in England, while giving his famous testimony before the House of Commons, was asked whether he thought the people of America would submit to this Act if modified. His brief emphatic response was: "No, never, unless compelled by force of arms." Chatham yet weak with disease, but mighty in eloquence, exclaimed in ever-memorable words: "We are told America is obstinate — America is almost in open rebellion. *Sir, I rejoice that America has resisted.* Three millions of people, so dead to all the feelings of liberty as voluntarily to submit to be slaves, would have been fit instruments to make slaves of all the rest. The Americans have been wronged; they have been driven to madness. I will beg leave to tell the House in a few words that is really my opinion. *It is that the Stamp Act be repealed, absolutely, totally and immediately.*" It was repealed. Within less than a year from its original passage, denounced and discredited, it was driven from the Statute Book. In the charnel-house of history, with the unclean things of the Past, it now rots. Thither the Slave Act is destined to follow.

Sir, regarding the Stamp Act candidly and cautiously, free from the animosities of the time, it is impossible not to see that, though gravely unconstitutional, it was at most an infringement of *civil* liberty only; not of *personal* liberty. There was an unjust tax of a few pence, with the chances of amercements by a single judge without a jury; but, by no provision of this Act was the *personal* liberty of any man assailed. Under it no freeman could be seized as a slave. Such an Act, though justly obnoxious to every lover of Constitutional Liberty, cannot be viewed with the feelings of repugnance, enkindled by a statute which assails the personal liberty of every man, and under which any freeman may be seized as a slave. Sir, in placing the Stamp Act by the side of the Slave Act, I do injustice to that emanation of British tyranny. Both, indeed, infringe important rights; one of property; the other the vital right of all, which is to other rights as the soul to the body — *the right of a man to himself.* Both are condemned; but their relative condemnation must be measured by their relative characters. As Freedom is more than property; as Man is above the dollar that he earns; as Heaven, to which we all aspire, is higher than the earth, where every accumulation of wealth must ever remain; so are the rights assailed by an American Congress higher than those once assailed by the British Parliament. And just in this degree must history condemn the Slave Act more than the Stamp Act.

Sir, I might here stop. It is enough in this place, and on this occasion, to show the unconstitutionality of this enactment. Your duty commences at once. All legislation hostile to the fundamental law of the land should be repealed without delay. But the argument is not yet exhausted. Even if this Act could claim any validity or apology under the Constitution, which it cannot, *it lacks that essential support in the Public Conscience of the States, where it is to be enforced, which is the life of all law, and without which any law must become a dead letter.*

The Senator from South Carolina (Mr. Butler) was right, when, at the beginning of the session, he pointedly said that a law which could be enforced only by the bayonet, was no law. Sir, it is idle to suppose that an Act of Congress becomes effective, merely by compliance with the forms of legislation. Something more is necessary. The Act must be in harmony with the prevailing public sentiment of the community upon which it bears. Of course, I do not suggest that the cordial support of every man or of every small locality is necessary; but I do mean that the public feelings, the public convictions, the public conscience, must not be touched, wounded, lacerated, by every endeavor to enforce it. With all these, it must be so far in harmony, that, like other laws, by which property, liberty and life are guarded, it may be administered by the ordinary process of courts, without jeoparding the public peace or shocking good men. If this be true as a general rule — if the public support and sympathy be essential to the life of all law, — this is especially the case in an enactment which concerns the important and sensitive rights of Personal Liberty. In conformity with this principle, the Legislature of Massachusetts, by formal resolution, in 1850, with singular unanimity, declared:

"We hold it to be the duty of Congress to pass such laws only in regard thereto as will be maintained by the sentiments of the Free States, where such laws are to be enforced."

The duty of consulting these sentiments was recognized by Washington. While President of the United States, at the close of his Administration, he sought to recover a slave who had fled to New Hampshire. His autograph letter to Mr. Whipple, the Collector at Portsmouth, dated at Philadelphia, 28th November, 1796, which I now hold in my hand, and which has never before seen the light, after describing the fugitive, and particularly expressing the desire of "her mistress," Mrs. Washington, for her return, employs the following decisive language:

"I do not mean, however, by this request, that such violent measures should be used AS WOULD EXCITE A MOB OR RIOT, WHICH MIGHT BE THE CASE IF SHE HAS ADHERENTS, OR EVEN UNEASY SENSATIONS IN THE MINDS OF WELL-DISPOSED CITIZENS. Rather than either of these should happen, I would forego her services altogether; and the example, also, which is of infinite more importance.

"GEORGE WASHINGTON."

Mr. Whipple, in his reply, dated at Portsmouth, December 22, 1796, an autograph copy of which I have, recognizes the rule of Washington:

"I will now, sir, agreeably to your desire, send her to Alexandria, *if it be practicable without the consequences which you except — that of exciting a riot or a mob, or creating uneasy sensations in the minds of well-disposed persons.* The first cannot be calculated beforehand; it will be governed by the popular opinion of the moment, or the circumstances that may arise in the transaction. The latter may be sought into and judged of by conversing with such persons without discovering the occasion. So far as I have had opportunity, I perceive that different sentiments are entertained on this subject."

The fugitive never was returned; but lived in freedom to a good old age, down to a very recent period, a monument of the just forbearance of him whom we aptly call the Father of his Country. It is true that he sought her return. This we must regret, and find its apology. He was at the time a slaveholder. Though often with various degrees of force expressing himself against slavery, and promising his suffrage for its abolition, he did not see this wrong as he saw it at the close of life, in the illumination of another sphere. From this act of Washington, still swayed by the policy of the world, I appeal to Washington writing his will. From Washington on earth I appeal to Washington in Heaven. Seek not by his name to justify any such effort. His death is above his life. His last testament cancels his authority as a slaveholder. However he may have appeared before man, he came into the presence of God only as the liberator of his slaves. Grateful for this example, I am grateful also that, while a slaveholder, and seeking the return of a fugitive, he has left in permanent record a rule of conduct which, if adopted by his country, will make Slave-Hunting impossible. The chances of a riot, or mob, or "even uneasy sensations among well-disposed persons," are to prevent any such pursuit.

Sir, the existing Slave Act cannot be enforced without violating the precept of Washington. Not merely "uneasy sensations of well-disposed persons," but rage, tumult, commotion, mob, riot, violence, death, gush from its fatal overflowing fountains;

> Hoc fonte derivata clades
> In patriam populumque fluxit.*

Not a case occurs without endangering the public

* Horace, Carmina, Lib. III. 6.

peace. Workmen are brutally dragged from employments to which they are wedded by years of successful labor; husbands are ravished from wives, and parents from children. Everywhere there is disturbance; at Detroit, Buffalo, Harrisburg, Syracuse, Philadelphia, New York, Boston. At Buffalo the fugitive was cruelly knocked by a log of wood against a red-hot stove, and his mock trial commenced while the blood still oozed from his wounded head. At Syracuse he was rescued by a sudden mob; so also at Boston. At Harrisburg the fugitive was shot; at Christiana the Slave-Hunter was shot. At New York unprecedented excitement, always with uncertain consequences, has attended every case. Again at Boston a fugitive, according to the received report, was first basely seized under pretext that he was a criminal; arrested only after a deadly struggle; guarded by officers who acted in violation of the laws of the State; tried in a Court-House surrounded by chains contrary to the common law; finally surrendered to Slavery by trampling on the criminal process of the State, under an escort in violation again of the laws of the State, while the pulpits trembled and the whole people, not merely "uneasy," but swelling with ill-suppressed indignation, for the sake of order and tranquillity, without violence witnessed the shameful catastrophe.

With every attempt to administer the Slave Act, it constantly becomes more revolting, particularly in its influence on the agents it enlists. Pitch cannot be touched without defilement, and all who lend themselves to this work seem at once and unconsciously to lose the better part of man. The spirit of the law passes into them, as the devils entered the swine.

Upstart commissioners, the mere mushrooms of courts, vie and revie with each other. Now by indecent speed, now by harshness of manner, now by a denial of evidence, now by crippling the defence, and now by open glaring wrong, they make the odious Act yet more odious. Clemency, grace, and justice, die in its presence. All this is observed by the world. Not a case occurs which does not harrow the souls of good men, and bring tears of sympathy to the eyes, also those other noble tears which "patriots shed o'er dying laws."

Sir, I shall speak frankly. If there be an exception to this feeling, it will be found chiefly with a peculiar class. It is a sorry fact that the "mercantile interest," in its unpardonable selfishness, twice in English history, frowned upon the endeavors to suppress the atrocity of Algerine Slavery; that it sought to baffle Wilberforce's great effort for the abolition of the African slave trade; and that, by a sordid compromise, at the formation of our Constitution, it exempted the same detested Heaven-defying traffic from American judgment. And now representatives of this "interest," forgetful that commerce is the child of Freedom, join in hunting the Slave. But the great heart of the people recoils from this enactment. It palpitates for the fugitive, and rejoices in his escape. Sir, I am telling you facts. The literature of the age is all on his side. The songs, more potent than laws, are for him. The poets, with voices of melody, are for Freedom. Who could sing for Slavery? They who make the permanent opinion of the country, who mould our youth, whose words, dropped into the soul, are the germs of character, supplicate for the Slave. And

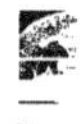

now, sir, behold a new and heavenly ally. A woman, inspired by Christian genius, enters the lists, like another Joan of Arc, and with marvellous power, sweeps the chords of the popular heart. Now melting to tears, and now inspiring to rage, her work everywhere touches the conscience, and makes the Slave-Hunter more hateful. In a brief period, nearly 100,000 copies of *Uncle Tom's Cabin* have been already circulated.* But this extraordinary and sudden success — surpassing all other instances in the records of literature — cannot be regarded merely as the triumph of genius. Higher far than this, it is the testimony of the people, by an unprecedented act, against the Fugitive Slave Bill.

These things I dwell upon as the incentives and tokens of an existing public sentiment, which renders this Act practically inoperative, except as a tremendous engine of terror. Sir, the sentiment is just. Even in the lands of slavery, the slave-trader is loathed as an ignoble character, from whom the countenance is turned away; and can the Slave-Hunter be more regarded while pursuing his prey in a land of Freedom? In early Europe, in barbarous days, while Slavery prevailed, a Hunting Master, *nach jagender Herr*, as the Germans called him, was held in aversion. Nor was this all. The fugitive was welcomed in the cities, and protected against pursuit. Sometimes vengeance awaited the Hunter. Down to this day, at Revel, now a Russian city, a sword is proudly preserved with which a Hunting Baron was beheaded, who, in viola-

* This was the number at the time of the delivery of this speech. But the circulation has gone on indefinitely.

tion of the municipal rights of this place, seized a fugitive slave. Hostile to this Act as our public sentiment may be, it exhibits no trophy like this. The State laws of Massachusetts have been violated in the seizure of a fugitive slave; but no sword, like that of Revel, now hangs at Boston.

I have said, sir, that this sentiment is just. And is it not? Every escape from slavery necessarily and instinctively awakens the regard of all who love Freedom. The endeavor, though unsuccessful, reveals courage, manhood, character. No story is read with more interest than that of our own Lafayette, when, aided by a gallant South Carolinian, in defiance of the despotic ordinances of Austria, kindred to our Slave Act, he strove to escape from the bondage of Olmutz. Literature pauses with exultation over the struggles of Cervantes, the great Spaniard, while a slave in Algiers, to regain the liberty for which he says, in his immortal work, "we ought to risk life itself, Slavery being the greatest evil that can fall to the lot of man." Science, in all her manifold triumphs, throbs with pride and delight, that Arago, the astronomer and philosopher — devoted republican also — was redeemed from barbarous Slavery to become one of her greatest sons. Religion rejoices serenely, with joy unspeakable, in the final escape of Vincent de Paul. Exposed in the public squares of Tunis to the inspection of the traffickers in human flesh, this illustrious Frenchman was subjected to every vileness of treatment compelled, like a horse, to open his mouth, to show his teeth, to trot, to run, to exhibit his strength in lifting burthens, and then, like a horse, legally sold in market overt. Passing from master to master, after a protracted servitude, he achieved his freedom, and regaining France, commenced that resplendent career of charity by which he is placed among the great names of Christendom. Princes and orators have lavished panegyrics upon this fugitive slave; and the Catholic Church, in homage to his extraordinary virtues, has introduced him into the company of saints.

Less by genius or eminent services, than by sufferings, are the fugitive slaves of our country now commended. For them every sentiment of humanity is aroused:

> ——— "Who could refrain
> That had a heart to love, and in that heart
> Courage to make his love known?"

Rude and ignorant they may be; but in their very efforts for Freedom, they claim kindred with all that is noble in the Past. They are among the heroes of our age. Romance has no stories of more thrilling interest than theirs. Classical antiquity has preserved no examples of adventurous trial more worthy of renown. Among them are men whose names will be treasured in the annals of their race. By their eloquent voice they have already done much to make their wrongs known, and to secure the respect of the world. History will soon lend them her avenging pen. Proscribed by you during life, they will proscribe you through all time. Sir, already judgment is beginning. A righteous public sentiment palsies your enactment.

And now, sir, let us review the field over which we have passed. We have seen that any compromise, finally closing the discussion of Slavery under the Constitution, is tyrannical, absurd and impotent; that as Slavery can exist only by virtue of positive law, and as it has no such positive support in the Constitution, it cannot exist within the National jurisdiction; that the Constitution nowhere recognizes property in man, and that, according to its true interpretation, Freedom and not Slavery is national, while Slavery and not Freedom is sectional; that, in this spirit, the National Government was first organized under Washington, himself an Abolitionist, surrounded by Abolitionists, while the whole country, by its Church, its Colleges, its Literature, and all its best voices, was united against Slavery, and the national flag at that time nowhere within the National Territory covered a single slave; still further, that the National Government is a Government of delegated powers, and as among these there is no power to support Slavery, this institution cannot be national, nor can Congress in any way legislate in its behalf; and, finally, that the establishment of this principle is the true way of peace and safety for the Republic. Considering next the provision for the surrender of fugitives from service, we have seen that it was not one of the original compromises of the Constitution; that it was introduced tardily and with hesitation, and adopted with little discussion, and then and for a long period after was regarded with comparative indifference; that the recent Slave Act, though many times unconstitutional, is especially so on two grounds—*first*, as a usurpation by Congress of powers not granted by the Constitution, and an infraction of rights secured to the States; and *secondly*, as a denial of Trial by Jury, in a question of Personal Liberty and a suit at common law; that its glaring unconstitu-

tionality finds a prototype in the British Stamp Act, which our fathers refused to obey as unconstitutional on two parallel grounds —*first*, because it was a usurpation by Parliament of powers not belonging to it under the British Constitution, and an infraction of rights belonging to the Colonies; and *secondly*, because it was a denial of Trial by Jury in certain cases of property; that as Liberty is far above property, so is the outrage perpetrated by the American Congress far above that perpetrated by the British Parliament; and, finally, that the Slave Act has not that support in the public sentiment of the States where it is to be executed, which is the life of all law, and which prudence and the precept of Washington require.

Sir, thus far I have arrayed the objections to this Act, and the false interpretations out of which it has sprung. But I am asked what I offer as a substitute for the legislation which I denounce. Freely I will answer. It is to be found in a correct appreciation of the provision of the Constitution, under which this discussion occurs. Look at it in the double light of reason and of Freedom, and we cannot mistake the exact extent of its requirements. Here is the provision:

> "No person held to service or labor in one State, under the laws thereof, escaping into another, shall, in consequence of any law or regulation therein, be discharged from such service or labor, but shall be delivered up on claim of the party to whom such service or labor may be due."

From the very language employed, it is obvious that this is merely a *compact* between the States, with a *prohibition* on the States, *conferring no power on the nation.* In its natural signification it is a compact. According to the examples of other countries, and the principles of jurisprudence, it is a compact. All arrangements for the extradition of fugitives have been customarily compacts. Except under the express obligations of treaty, no nation is bound to surrender fugitives. Especially has this been the case with fugitives for Freedom. In mediæval Europe, cities refused to recognize this obligation in favor of persons even under the same National Government. In 1531, while the Netherlands and Spain were united under Charles V., the Supreme Council of Mechlin rejected an application from Spain for the surrender of a fugitive slave. By express compact alone could this be secured. But the provision of the Constitution was borrowed from the Ordinance of the Northwestern Territory, which is expressly declared to be a compact; and this Ordinance, finally drawn by Nathan Dane, was again borrowed in its distinctive features from the early institutions of Massachusetts, among which, as far back as 1643, was a compact of like nature with other New England States. Thus this provision is a compact in language, in nature, in its whole history; as we have already seen it is a compact, according to the intentions of our Fathers and the genius of our institutions.

As a compact, its execution depends absolutely upon the States, without any intervention of the Nation. *Each State, in the exercise of its own judgment, will determine for itself the precise extent of the obligations assumed.* As a compact in derogation of Freedom, it must be construed strictly in every respect — leaning always in favor of Freedom, and shunning any meaning, not clearly necessary, which takes away important personal rights; mindful that the parties to whom it is applicable are regarded as "persons," of course with all the rights of "persons" under the Constitution; especially mindful of the vigorous maxim of the common law, that "he is cruel and impious who does not always favor Freedom;" and also, completely adopting in letter and in spirit, as becomes a just people, the rule of the great Commentator, that "the law is always ready to catch at anything in favor of Liberty." With this key the true interpretation is natural and easy.

Briefly, the States are prohibited from any "law or regulation" by which any "person" escaped from "service or labor" may be discharged therefrom, and on establishment of the claim to such "service or labor," he is to be "delivered up." But the mode by which the claim is to be tried and determined is not specified. All this is obviously within the control of each State. It may be done by virtue of express legislation, in which event any Legislature, justly careful of Personal Liberty, would surround the fugitive with every shield of the law and Constitution. But here a fact, pregnant with Freedom, must be studiously observed. The name Slave — that litany of wrong and woe — does not appear in the clause. Here is no unambiguous phrase, incapable of a double sense; no "positive" language, applicable only to slaves, and excluding all other classes; no word of that absolute certainty in every particular, which forbids any interpretation except that of Slavery, and makes it impossible "to catch at anything in favor of Liberty." Nothing of this kind is here. But passing from this; "cruelly and impiously" renouncing for the moment all leanings for Freedom; refusing "to catch at anything in favor of Liberty;" abandoning the cherished idea of the Fathers, that "It was *wrong* to admit in the Constitution the idea of property in man;" and, in the face of these commanding principles, assuming two things, first, that, in the evasive language of this clause, the Convention, whatever may have been the aim of individual members, really intended fugitive slaves, which is sometimes questioned, and, secondly, that, if they so intended, the language employed can be judicially regarded as justly applicable to fugitive slaves, which is often and earnestly denied; then the whole proceeding, without any express legislation, may be left to the ancient and authentic forms of the common law, familiar to the framers of the Constitution and ample for the occasion. If the fugitive be seized without process, he will be entitled at once to his writ *de Homine Replegiando*, while the master, resorting to process, may find his remedy in the writ *de Nativo Habendo* — each writ requiring Trial by Jury. If, from ignorance or lack of employment, these processes have slumbered in our country, still they belong to the great arsenal of the common law, and continue, like other ancient writs, *tanquam gladium in vagina*, ready to be employed at the first necessity. They belong to the safeguards of the citizen. But in any event and in either alternative the proceedings would be by "suit at common law," with Trial by Jury; and it would be the solemn duty of the court, according to all the forms and proper delays of the common law, to try the case on the evidence; strictly to apply all the protecting rules of evidence, and especially to require stringent proof, by competent witnesses under cross-examination, that the person claimed was *held* to service; that his service was *due* to the claimant; that he had *escaped* from the State where such service was due; and also proof of the *laws* of the State under which he was held. *Still further, to the Courts of each State must belong the determination of the question, to what classes of persons, according to just rules of interpretation, the phrase "persons held to service or labor" is strictly applicable.*

Such is this much-debated provision. The Slave States, at the formation of the Constitution, did not propose, as in the cases of Naturalization and Bankruptcy, to empower the National Government *to establish an uniform rule* for the rendition of fugitives from service, *throughout the United States;* they did not ask the National Government to charge itself in any way with this service; they did not venture to offend the country, and particularly the Northern States, by any such assertion of a hateful right. They were content, under the sanctions of compact, to leave it to the public sentiment of the States. There, I insist, it shall remain.

Mr. President, I have occupied much time; but the great subject still stretches before us. One other point yet remains, which I should not leave untouched, and which justly belongs to the close. The Slave Act violates the Constitution and shocks the Public Conscience. With modesty and yet with firmness let me add, sir, it offends against the Divine Law. No such enactment can be entitled to support. As the throne of God is above every earthly throne, so are his laws and statutes above all the laws and statutes of man. To question these, is to question God himself. But to assume that human laws are beyond question, is to claim for their fallible authors infallibility. To assume that they are always in conformity with the laws of God, is presumptuously and impiously to exalt man to an equality with God. Clearly human laws are not always in such conformity; nor can they ever be beyond question from each individual. Where the conflict is open, as if Congress should command the perpetration of murder, the office of conscience as final arbiter is undisputed. But in every conflict the same Queenly office is hers. By no earthly power can she be dethroned. Each person, after anxious examination, without haste, without passion, solemnly for himself must decide this great controversy. Any other rule attributes infallibility to human laws, places them beyond question, and degrades all men to an unthinking passive obedience.

According to St. Augustine, an unjust law does not appear to be a law; *lex esse non videtur quæ justa non fuerit;* and the great fathers of the Church, while adopting these words, declare openly that unjust laws are not binding. Sometimes they are called "abuses," and not laws; sometimes "violences," and not laws. And here again the conscience of each person is the final arbiter. But this lofty principle is not confined to the Church. A master of philosophy in early Europe, a name of intellectual renown, the eloquent Abelard, in Latin verses addressed to his son, has clearly expressed the universal injunction:

"Jussa potestatis terrenæ discutienda
Cœlestis tibi mox perficienda scias.

Siquis divinis jubeat contraria jussis
Te contra Dominum pactio nulla trahat."

The mandates of an earthly power are to be discussed; those of Heaven must at once be performed; nor can any agreement constrain us against God. Such is the rule of morals. Such, also, by the lips of judges and sages, has been the proud declaration of the English law, whence our own is derived. In this conviction patriots have fearlessly braved unjust commands, and martyrs have died.

And now, sir, the rule is commended to us. [The good citizen, as he thinks of the shivering fugitive, — guilty of no crime, — pursued, — hunted down like a beast, while praying for Christian help and deliverance, and as he reads the requirements of this Act, is filled with horror. Here is a despotic mandate, "to aid and assist in the prompt and efficient execution of this law." Again let me speak frankly. Not rashly would I set myself against any provision of law. This grave responsibility I would not lightly assume. But here the path of duty is clear. By the Supreme Law, which commands me to do no injustice; by the comprehensive Christian Law of Brotherhood; *by the Constitution, which I have sworn to support;* I AM BOUND TO DISOBEY THIS ACT. Never, in any capacity, can I render voluntary aid in its execution. Pains and penalties I will endure; but this great wrong I will not do. "I cannot obey; but I can suffer," was the exclamation of the author of Pilgrim's Progress, when imprisoned for disobedience to an earthly statute. Better suffer injustice than do it. Better be the victim than the instrument of wrong. Better be even the poor slave, returned to bondage, than the unhappy Commissioner.

There is, sir, an incident of history, which suggests a parallel, and affords a lesson of fidelity. Under the triumphant exertions of that Apostolic Jesuit, St. Francis Xavier, large numbers of the Japanese, amounting to as many as two hundred thousand — among them princes, generals, and the flower of the nobility — were converted to Christianity. Afterwards, amidst the frenzy of civil war, religious persecution arose, and the penalty of death was denounced against all who refused to trample upon the effigy of the Redeemer. This was the Pagan law of a Pagan land. But the delighted historian records that scarcely one from the multitude of converts was guilty of this apostacy. The law of man was set at naught. Imprisonment, torture, death, were preferred. Thus did this people refuse to trample on the painted image. Sir, multitudes among us will not be less steadfast in refusing to trample on the living image of their Redeemer.

Finally, sir, for the sake of peace and tranquillity, cease to shock the Public Conscience; for the sake of the Constitution, cease to exercise a power which is nowhere granted, and which violates inviolable rights expressly secured. Leave this question where it was left by our fathers, at the formation of our National Government, in the absolute control of the States, the appointed guardians of Personal Liberty. Repeal this enactment. Let its terrors no longer rage through the land. Mindful of the lowly whom it pursues; mindful of the good men perplexed by its requirements; in the name of charity, in the name of the

Constitution, repeal this enactment, totally and without delay. Be inspired by the *example of Washington.* Be admonished by those words of Oriental piety — "Beware of the groans of the wounded souls. Oppress not to the utmost a single heart; for a solitary sigh has power to overset a whole world."

# TRIBUTE TO MR. DOWNING.

SPEECH IN THE SENATE OF THE UNITED STATES, 26TH AUGUST, 1852, IN FAVOR OF AN ALLOWANCE TO THE WIDOW OF THE LATE ANDREW J. DOWNING.

---

The Civil and Diplomatic Appropriation Bill being under consideration, Mr. Pearce, of Maryland, under instructions from the Committee on Finance, moved the following amendment :

"For the payment of the arrears of salary due to the late Rural Architect, A. J. Downing, from the first of May, 1852, to the date of his death, and a further allowance to his widow, equal to the salary for one year, $2,500 ; *Provided*, that the said sum shall be in full of all claim for the services of the said deceased, and for all models, specifications and drawings designed for the benefit of the United States, which are not in its possession."

In the course of the debate which ensued, Mr. Sumner spoke as follows :

MR. SUMNER. — Mr. President: The laborer is worthy of his hire ; and I believe at this moment there is no question of charity to the widow of the late Mr. Downing. The simple proposition is to make compensation for services rendered to the United States by this eminent artist as superintendent of the public grounds in Washington. And, since the plans he has left behind and the impulses he has given to improvements here by his incomparable genius will continue to benefit us, though he has been removed, it is thought reasonable to continue his salary to the close of the unexpired year from which it commenced. These plans alone have been valued at five thousand dollars, and we are to have the advantage of them. In pursuance of these, his successor will be able to proceed in arranging the public grounds, and in embellishing the national capital, without any further expenditure to procure others instead. Thus, as I said at the outset, it is not a question of charity, but of compensation; and on this ground I submit that the estate of the departed artist deserves the small pittance which it is proposed to supply. For myself, I should be much happier to vote for a larger appropriation, believing that, over and above the services actually rendered in the discharge of his duties, these plans are amply worth it, and that we shall all feel better by such a recognition of our debt.

Few men in the public service have vindicated a title to regard above Mr. Downing. At the age of thirty-seven he has passed away, " dead ere his prime" — like Lycidas, also, " stretched on a watery bier " — leaving behind a reputation above that of any other citizen in the beautiful department of art to which he was devoted. His labors and his example cannot be forgotten. I know of no man among us, in any sphere of life, so young as he was at his death, who has been able to perform services of such true, simple and lasting beneficence. By his wide and active superintendence of rural improvements, by his labors of the pen, and by the various exercise of his genius, he has contributed essentially to the sum of human happiness. And now, sir, by practical services here in Washington, rendered at the call of his country, he has earned, it seems to me, this small appropriation — not as a charity to his desolate widow, but as a compensation for labor done. I hope the amendment will be agreed to.

# THE PARTY OF FREEDOM; ITS NECESSITY AND PRACTICABILITY.

SPEECH AT THE STATE CONVENTION OF THE FREE SOIL PARTY OF MASSACHUSETTS, HELD AT LOWELL, 16TH SEPTEMBER, 1852.

---

The President [Hon. STEPHEN C. PHILLIPS] remarked that there was one gentleman present whom the Convention would all delight to hear; he alluded to our distinguished Senator in Congress, Hon. Charles Sumner.

The name of Mr. Sumner was received with "three times three" rousing cheers, and the waving of hats, canes, handkerchiefs, &c., which demonstrations of regard were renewed as he made his appearance on the platform. The enthusiasm having in a degree subsided, he stepped forward and said: *

MR. PRESIDENT AND FELLOW-CITIZENS OF MASSACHUSETTS: — I should be dull indeed — dull as a weed — were I insensible to this generous, overflowing, heart-speaking welcome. After an absence of many months, I have now come home, to breathe anew this invigorating Northern air (applause), to tread again the free soil of our native Massachusetts (cheers), and to enjoy the sympathy of friends and fellow-citizens. (Renewed applause.) But, while glad in your greetings, thus bounteously lavished, I cannot accept them for myself. I do not deserve them. They belong to

* This report is copied from the newspapers of the time.

the cause (applause) which we all have at heart, and which binds us together. (Cheers.)

Fellow-citizens, I have not come here to-day to make a speech. The occasion requires no such effort. Weary with other labors, and desiring rest, I have little now to say, and that little must not be about myself. If, at Washington, during a long session of Congress — my own first experience of public life — I have been able to do anything which meets your acceptance, I am happy. (Cheers.) I have done nothing but my duty. ("Hear! hear!") Passing from this, and taking advantage of the kind attention with which you honor me, let me add one word in vindication of our position as a *third party*.

At this moment we are on the eve of two important elections; one of national officers and the other of State officers. A President and Vice President of the United States, and members of Congress are to be chosen; also, Governor and Lieutenant Governor of the Commonwealth, and members of the Legislature. And at these elections we are to cast our votes so as most to promote the cause of Freedom under the National Constitution. (Cheers.) This is our peculiar object, though associated with it are other aims, kindred in their humane and liberal character.

Against Freedom both the old parties are now banded. Opposed to each other in the contest for power, they concur in opposing every effort for the establishment of Freedom under the National Constitution. (Applause.) Divided as parties, *they are one* as supporters of slavery. On this question we can have no sympathy with either; but must necessarily be against both. ("Hear! hear!") They sustain slavery

in the District of Columbia; we are against it. They sustain the coastwise slave trade under the National Flag; we abhor it. (Cheers.) They sustain the policy of silence on Slavery in the territories; we urge the voice of positive prohibition. They sustain that paragon of legislative monsters — unconstitutional, unchristian and infamous, — the Fugitive Slave Bill (sensation); we insist on its repeal. (Great applause.) They concede to the Slave Power new life and protection; we cannot be content except with its total destruction. (Enthusiasm.) Such, fellow-citizens, is the difference between us.

And now, if here in Massachusetts, there be any persons, who, on grounds of policy or conscience, feel impelled to support slavery, let them go and sink in the embrace of the old parties. (Applause.) There they belong. But, on the other hand, all who are sincerely opposed to slavery — who desire to act against it — who seek to bear their testimony for Freedom, — who long to carry into public affairs those principles of morality and Christian duty which are the rule of private life, — let them come out from both the old parties, and join us. (Cheers.) In our third party, with the declared friends of Freedom, they will find a place in harmony with their aspirations. (Enthusiasm.)

But there is one apology, which is common to the supporters of both the old parties, and which is often in their mouths when pressed for their inconsistent persistence in adhering to these parties. It is dogmatically asserted that there can be but two parties; that a third party is impossible, particularly in our country, and that, therefore, all persons, however opposed to Slavery, must be content in one of the old parties. This assumption, which is without any foundation in reason, has been so often put forth, that it has acquired a certain currency; and many, who reason hastily, or who implicitly follow others, have adopted it as the all-sufficient excuse for their conduct. Confessing their own opposition to slavery, they yet yield to the domination of party, and become dumb. All this is wrong morally, and, therefore, must be wrong practically.

Party, in its true estate, is the natural expression and agency of different forms of opinion on important public questions; and itself assumes different forms precisely according to the prevalence of different opinions. Thus in the early Italian republics there were for a while the factions of the Guelphs and Ghibellins, supporters of the Pope and the Emperor; also of the Whites and the Blacks, taking their names from the color of their respective badges, and in England, the two factions of the white and red roses, in which was involved the succession to the crown. But in all these cases the party came into being, died out, or changed with the prevailing sentiment. If there be in a community only two chief antagonist opinions, then there will be but two parties, embodying these opinions. But as other opinions practically prevail and seek vent, so must parties change or multiply. This is so strongly the conclusion of reason and philosophy, that it could not be doubted, even if there were no examples of such change and multiplication. But we need only turn to the recent history of France and England, the two countries where opinion has had the freest scope to find such examples.

Thus, for instance, in France — and I dwell on this point because I have observed myself, in conversation, that it is of practical importance — under Louis Phillippe, anterior to the late Republic, there was the party of Legitimists, supporters of the old branch of Bourbons; the party of Orleanists, supporters of the existing throne; these two corresponding at the time in relative rank and power to our Whigs and Democrats. But besides these, there was a third party, *the small band of republicans, represented in the legislature by a few persons only*, but strong in principles and purposes, which in February, 1848, prevailed over both the others. (Applause.) On the establishment of the Republic the multiplicity of parties continued until, with the freedom of opinion and the freedom of the press, all were equally overthrown by Louis Napoleon, and their place supplied by the enforced unity of despotism.

In England, the most important measure of recent reform, the abolition of the laws imposing a protective duty on corn, was carried only by a third party. Neither of the two old parties could be brought to adopt this measure and press it to a consummation. A powerful public opinion, thus thwarted in the regular channel, found an outlet in another party, which was neither Whig nor Tory, but which was formed from both these parties, and wherein Sir Robert Peel, the great Conservative leader, took his place, side by side, in honorable coalition, with Mr. Cobden, the great Liberal leader. ("Hear! hear!") In this way the Corn Laws were finally overthrown. The multiplicity of parties in England, engendered by this contest, still continues. At the general election for the new Parliament which has just taken place, the strict lines of ancient parties seemed to be effaced, and many were returned, not as Whigs and Tories, but as Protectionists and anti-Protectionists.

Thus, by example in our own day we may confirm the principle of political philosophy, that parties must naturally adapt themselves in character and number to the prevailing public opinion.

Now at the present time in our country, there exists a deep controlling conscientious feeling against Slavery. (Cheers.) You and I, sir, and all of us confess it. While recognizing the Constitution we desire to do everything in our power to relieve ourselves of responsibility for this terrible wrong. ("Yes! yes!") We would vindicate the Constitution and the National Government which it has established, from all participation in this outrage. (Cheers.) Both the old political parties, forgetful of the sentiments of the Fathers and of the spirit of the Constitution, not only refuse to be in any degree the agents or representatives of our convictions, but expressly discourage and denounce them. Thus baffled in their efforts for utterance, these convictions naturally seek expression in a new agency, the party of Freedom. (Cheers.) Such is the party, which, representing the great doctrines of Human Rights, as enunciated in our Declaration of Independence, and inspired truly by the Democratic sentiment, is now assembled here under the name of the Free Democracy. (Cheers.)

The rising public opinion against Slavery cannot now flow in the old political channels. It is strangled, clogged, and dammed back. But if not *through* the old parties, then *over* the old parties, (tremendous cheering,) this irresistible current *shall* find its way. (Enthusiasm.) It cannot be permanently stopped. If the old parties will not become its organ, they must become its victim. (Cheers.) The party of Freedom will certainly prevail. (Sensation.) It may be by entering into, and possessing one of the old parties, filling it with our own strong life; or it may be by drawing from both to itself the good and true who are unwilling to continue members of any political combination when it ceases to represent their convictions. But, in one way or the other, its ultimate triumph is sure. (Great applause.) Of this let no man doubt. (Repeated cheers.)

At this moment we are in a minority. At the last popular election in Massachusetts, there were twenty-eight thousand Free Soilers, forty-three thousand Democrats, and sixty-four thousand Whigs. But this is no reason for discouragement. According to recent estimates, the population of the whole world amounts to about eight hundred millions. Of these only two hundred and sixty millions are Christians, while the remaining five hundred and forty millions are mainly Mahometans, Brahmins and Idolaters. Because the Christians are in this minority, that is no reason for renouncing Christianity and for surrendering to the false religions (cheers); nor do we doubt that Christianity will yet prevail over the whole earth, as the waters cover the sea. ("Hear! hear!") The friends of Freedom in Massachusetts are likewise in a minority; but they will not, therefore, renounce Freedom (cheers); nor surrender to the political Mahometans and idolaters of Baltimore ("never! never!"); nor can they doubt that their cause, like Christianity, will yet prevail. (Enthusiastic cheers.)

Our cause commends itself. But it is also commended by our candidates. (Cheers.) In all that makes the eminent civilian or the accomplished statesman fit for the responsibilities of government, they will proudly compare with any of their competitors (applause), while they are dear to our hearts as able, well-tried, loyal supporters of those vital principles of Freedom which we seek to establish under the Constitution of the United States. (Applause.) In the Senate, Mr. Hale (cheers) is admitted to be foremost in aptitude and readiness of debate, whether in the general legislation of the country, or in the constant and valiant championship of our cause. (Applause.) His genial and sun-like nature irradiates the antagonism of political controversy (cheers), while his active and practical mind, richly stored with various experience, never fails to render good service. (Great cheering.)

Of Mr. Julian, our candidate for the Vice-Presidency ("Hear! hear!"), let me say simply that, in ability and devotion to our principles, he is a worthy compeer of Mr. Hale. To vote for such men will itself be a pleasure. But it will be doubly so when we reflect that in this way we bear our testimony to a noble cause, with which the happiness, welfare and fame of our country are indissolubly connected. (Repeated and enthusiastic cheers.)

With such a cause and such candidates, let no man be disheartened. The tempest may blow, but ours is a life-boat, which cannot be harmed by wind or wave.

The genius of Liberty sits at the helm. I hear her voice of cheer saying, "Whoso sails with me comes to shore."

Mr. Sumner resumed his seat amid the heartiest and long protracted applause.

## CIVIL SUPERINTENDENTS OF ARMORIES.

SPEECH IN THE SENATE OF THE UNITED STATES, 23D FEBUARY, 1853, ON THE PROPOSITION TO CHANGE THE SUPERINTENDENTS OF ARMORIES.

---

The Army Appropriation Bill being under discussion, Mr. Davis, of Massachusetts, moved the following amendment:

"The Act of Congress, approved August 23, 1842, shall be so modified, that the President may, if in his opinion the public interest demands it, place over any of the armories a Superintendent who does not belong to the Army."

In the course of the debate Mr. Sumner spoke as follows:

MR. SUMNER. — Mr. President, I do not desire to speak upon the general subject of the manufacture of arms under the authority of the United States, which has been opened in debate by honorable Senators. What I have to say will be on the precise question before the Senate, and nothing else. That question, as I understand it, is on the amendment proposed by my colleague [Mr. Davis], according to which the act of 1842 is to be so far modified that the President, in his discretion, may place over the armories persons not of the army — leaving it, therefore to his judgment to determine whether the superintendent shall be a military man or a civilian. This is all.

The Senate has been exhorted not to act precipitately; but the character of this proposition excludes all idea of precipitation. We do not determine absolutely that the system shall be changed, but simply that it may be changed in the discretion of the President. This discretion, which naturally will be exercised only after ample inquiry, stands in the way of all precipitation; and this is my answer to the Senator from Illinois [Mr. Shields].

Again: it is urged that under a military head, the armories are better administered than they would be under a civil head, and that the arms are better and cheaper made; and here my friend from South Carolina, who sits before me [Mr. Butler], dwelt with his accustomed glow upon the success with which this manufacture has been conducted at the national armories, and the extent to which it has been recognized in Europe. But, sir, on the precise question now before you, the merits of the armories are not involved. We do not undertake to judge the military superintendents or their works. The determination of this question is referred to the President; and this is my answer to the Senator from South Carolina.

The objections to this amendment of my colleague, then, seem to disappear. But there are two distinct arguments in its favor, which, at the present moment, do not seem to me susceptible of any answer.

In the first place, there are complaints against the existing system which ought to be heard. A memorial from five hundred legal voters of Springfield, now on your table, bears testimony to them. Letters addressed to myself and others, from persons whose opinions I am bound to regard, set them forth sometimes in very strong language. The administration of the arsenal at Springfield is commended by many, but there are others who judge it differently. As now conducted, it is represented by some to be the seat of oppressive conduct, and the occasion of heart-burnings and strife, often running into the local politics. In the eyes of some, this arsenal is now little better than a sore on that beautiful town. Now, on these complaints and allegations I express no opinion. I do not affirm their truth or their untruth. What I know of the Superintendent, makes it difficult for me to believe that any thing unjust, oppressive, or hard, could proceed from him. But the whole case justifies inquiry at least, and such will be secured by the proposition now before the Senate. This is the smallest thing we can do.

But this proposition is enforced by another consideration which seems to me entitled to peculiar weight. I have nothing to say now on the general question of reducing the army or modifying the existing military system. But I do submit confidently that the genius of our institutions favors civil life rather than military life; and that, in harmony with this, it is our duty, whenever the public interests will permit, to limit and restrain the sphere of military influences. This is not a military monarchy, where the soldier is supreme, but a republic, where the soldier yields to the civilian. But the law, as it now stands, gives to the soldier an absolute preference in a service which is not military, and which from its nature, seems to belong to civil life. Now the manufacture of arms is a mechanical pursuit, and for myself, I can see no reason why it should not be placed in charge of one bred to the business. Among the intelligent mechanics of Massachusetts, there are many fully fit to be at the head of the arsenal at Springfield; but all these, by the existing law, are austerely excluded from any such trust. The idea which has fallen from so many Senators, that the superintendent of an armory ought to be a military man — that a military man only is competent — or even that a military man is more competent than a civilian, seems to me as illogical as the jocular fallacy of Dr. Johnson, that "He who drives fat oxen must himself be fat."

# AGAINST SECRECY IN THE PROCEEDINGS OF THE SENATE.

SPEECH IN THE SENATE OF THE UNITED STATES, 6TH APRIL, 1853, ON THE PROPOSITION TO LIMIT THE SECRET SESSIONS OF THE SENATE.

---

The following resolution was submitted by Mr. Chase, of Ohio : —

"*Resolved*, That the sessions and all proceedings of the Senate shall be public and open, except when matters communicated in confidence by the President, shall be received and considered, and in such other cases as the Senate by resolution from time to time shall specially order, and so much of the 38th, 39th and 40th rules as may be inconsistent with this resolution is hereby rescinded."

In the debate which ensued, Mr. Sumner spoke as follows :

MR. SUMNER. — Party allusions and party considerations have been brought to bear upon this question. I wish to regard it for a moment in the light of the Constitution and in the spirit of our institutions. In the Constitution there is no injunction of secrecy on any of the proceedings of the Senate; nor is there any requirement of publicity. To the Senate is left absolutely the determination of its rules of proceedings. In thus abstaining from all regulation of this matter the framers of the Constitution have obviously regarded it as in all respects within the discretion of the Senate, to be exercised from time to time as it thinks best.

The Senate exercises three important functions: *first*, the legislative or parliamentary power, wherein it acts concurrently with the House of Representatives, as well as the President; *secondly*, the power "to advise and consent" to treaties with foreign countries in concurrence with the President; and, *thirdly*, the power "to advise and consent" to nominations by the President to offices under the Constitution. I say nothing of another, rarely called into exercise, the sole power to try impeachments.

At the first organization of the Government the proceedings of the Senate, whether in legislation or on treaties or on nominations, were with closed doors. In this respect the legislative business and executive business were conducted alike. This continued down to the second session of the Third Congress, in 1794, when, in pursuance of a formal resolution, the galleries were allowed to be opened so long as the Senate were engaged in their legislative capacity, unless in such cases as might, in the opinion of the Senate, require secrecy; and this rule has continued ever since. Here was an exercise of the discretion of the Senate, in obvious harmony with public sentiment and the spirit of our institutions.

The change now proposed goes still further. It opens the doors on all occasions, whether legislative or executive, except when specially ordered otherwise. The Senator from South Carolina [Mr. Butler] says that the Senate is a confidential body, and should be ready to receive confidential communications from the President. But this will still be the case if we adopt the resolution now under consideration. The limitation proposed seems adequate to all exigencies, while the general rule will be publicity. The Executive sessions with closed doors, shrouded from the public gaze and public criticism, constitute an exceptional part of our system, too much in harmony with the proceedings of other Governments less liberal in character. The genius of our institutions requires publicity. The ancient Roman, who bade his architect so to construct his house that his guests and all that he did could be seen by the world, is a fit model for the American people.

# THE POWERS OF A STATE OVER THE MILITIA.

SPEECHES ON THE MILITIA GENERALLY AND A COLORED MILITIA, IN THE CONVENTION TO REVISE AND AMEND THE CONSTITUTION OF MASSACHUSETTS * 21ST AND 22D JUNE, 1853.

---

The propositions of amendment on the general subject of the Militia being under consideration in Committee of the Whole, Mr. Sumner spoke as follows:

I SHOULD like to call the attention of the Committee to the precise question on which we are to vote. This does not, as it seems to me, properly open the discussion to which we have been listening. I do not understand that it involves the topics introduced by my friend opposite [Mr. Wilson], — the present condition of Europe, the prospects of the liberal cause in that quarter of the globe, or the extent to which that cause may be affected by a contemporaneous movement for peace. Nor do I understand that the important considerations introduced by the gentleman on my right [Mr. Whitney, of Boylston], on the extent to which Government may be entrusted with the power

* The members of this Convention were not required to have their domicil in the places which they represented. Mr. Sumner sat as the member for Marshfield, for which place he was chosen while absent from the State.

of the sword, can materially influence our decision. I put these things aside at this time.

The question is on the final passage of the fifteen resolutions reported by the Committee on the Militia; and here let me catch and adopt one word from my friend opposite [Mr. Wilson]. He regretted, if I understood him, that this whole subject was not compressed into one or two resolutions. Am I right?

Mr. WILSON. The gentleman is correct.

Mr. SUMNER. I agree with him. I regret that it was not compressed into one or two resolutions. I object to these resolutions for several reasons. In the first place, there are too many. In the second place, at least two of them seem to be an assumption of power belonging to Congress, and, therefore, at least, of doubtful constitutionality; and in the third place, because twelve of them undertake to control matters which it were better to leave to the Legislature.

On the formation of the Constitution of Massachusetts, in 1780, it was natural that our fathers should introduce into it details with regard to the militia and its organization. The Constitution of the United States had not then been made. But since the establishment of this Constitution, the whole condition of the militia is changed. Among the powers expressly given to Congress, is the power "to provide for organizing, arming and disciplining the militia, and for governing such part of them as may be employed in the service of the United States, *reserving* to the States respectively the appointment of the officers and the authority of training the militia, according to the discipline prescribed by Congress." And Congress have proceeded to exercise this power by the organization of a national militia. I submit that whatever might have been the original inducements to introduce multiform provisions on this subject into the Constitution of Massachusetts, none such exist at this day; and it is impolitic, at least, to introduce them.

But I fear that they are more than impolitic. I will not argue here the question of constitutional law; but I submit to the better judgment of my professional brethren — and I am happy to see some of them lingering at this late hour — that any attempt on the part of the State to interfere, in any way, by addition or subtraction, with the organization of the national militia, is an experiment which we should not introduce into the permanent text of our organic law. If the decisions of the Supreme Court of the United States on the powers of Congress are to prevail, then, it seems to me, any such assumption, in a case where the original power of Congress is clear, will be unconstitutional and void. In the famous case of *Prigg* v. *Pennsylvania*, after an elaborate discussion at the bar, all State legislation on the subject of fugitive slaves was declared to be unconstitutional and void, while Congress was recognized as the sole depository of power on this subject. According to my recollection, it was expressly held, that the legislation by Congress excluded all State legislation on the same subject, whether to control, qualify or *superadd to* the remedy enacted by Congress. I commend gentlemen, who are now so swift to introduce these provisions into our Constitution, to the study of this precedent. It is comparatively recent; and the principle of interpretation which it establishes is applicable to State laws on the militia, even though entirely inapplicable to State

laws on fugitive slaves; for the simple reason that in the former case the original power of Congress is clear, while in the latter it is denied.

But the States are not without power over the militia. In the very grant to Congress is a reservation to them as follows: "reserving to the States respectively the appointment of the officers and the authority of training the militia, according to the discipline prescribed by Congress." And here is precisely what the States can do. They may appoint the officers and train the militia.

Now, sir, the first two resolutions before us transcend the powers of the State. They touch the enrolment and organization of the militia, and on this account are an assumption of power, forbidden by the principle to which I have referred. The other thirteen resolutions, with the exception of the seventh, are in the nature of a military code, concerning the choice of officers, all of which should be left to the action of the Legislature.

In conformity with these views, Mr. Chairman, and in the hope of presenting a proposition on which the Convention may unite, I propose to strike out all after the preamble and insert two resolutions, as follows:

*Art.* 1. The Governor shall be the Commander-in-Chief of the Army and Navy of the State, and the Militia thereof, excepting when these forces shall be actually in the service of the United States; and shall have power to call out the same to aid in the execution of the laws, to suppress insurrection, and to repel invasion.

*Art.* 2. The appointment of officers and the training of the Militia shall be regulated in such manner as may hereafter be deemed expedient by the Legislature, and all persons, who from scruples of conscience, shall be averse to bearing arms shall be excused on such conditions as shall hereafter be prescribed by law.

The first of these resolutions is identical with the seventh resolution of the Committee. The second provides for the exercise, by the Legislature, of the powers expressly reserved to the States, over the appointment of officers and the training of the militia; and taking advantage of the Act of Congress, which allows the States to determine who shall be exempted from military duty, it plants in the text of the Constitution a clause by which this immunity is secured to all persons, who, from scruples of conscience, shall be averse to bearing arms. I believe we cannot go far beyond these without doing too much, while these seem to me to be enough. I send the resolutions to the Chair, and leave the Convention to dispose of them as they think proper.

On the next day, 22d June, the following resolution was brought forward by Mr. Wilson:

*Resolved,* That no distinction shall ever be made in the organization of the volunteer militia of the Commonwealth on account of color or race.

On this proposition Mr. Sumner spoke as follows:

I have a suggestion to make to my friend opposite [Mr. Wilson], in regard to the form of his proposition, which, if he will accept it, will, as it seems to me, absolutely remove his proposition from the criticism of my most eloquent friend before me [Mr. Choate], and from the criticism of other gentlemen who have addressed the Convention. I suggest to him to strike out the word "militia," and substitute therefor the words, "military companies," so that his proposition will read "that in the organization of the volunteer military companies of the Commonwealth there shall be no distinction of color or race."

Mr. Wilson. I accept the suggestion, and will amend my proposition accordingly.

Mr. Sumner. Now that proposition, as amended, I submit, is absolutely consistent with the Constitution of the United States, and, I believe, in conformity with the public sentiment of Massachusetts.

A brief inquiry will show that it is consistent with the Constitution of the United States, and in no respect interferes with the organization of the National Militia. That Constitution provides for organizing, arming and disciplining a militia, and gives Congress full power over the subject — in which particular, be it observed, it is clearly distinguishable from that of fugitive slaves, over whom no such power is given. To be more explicit, I will read the clause. It is found in the long list of enumerated powers of Congress, and is as follows: — "Congress shall have power to provide for organizing, arming and disciplining the militia, and of governing such part of them as may be employed in the service of the United States, reserving to the States respectively the appointment of the officers, and the authority of training the militia, according to the discipline prescribed by Congress." And then at the close of the section it is further declared "that Congress shall make *all laws which shall be necessary and proper* for carrying into execution the foregoing powers."

In pursuance of this power, Congress have proceeded by various laws, "to provide for organizing, arming and disciplining the militia, and for governing such part of them as may be engaged in the service of the United States." The earliest of these laws, which is still in force, is entitled, "An act more effectually to provide for the national defence, by *establishing an uniform* militia throughout the United States." [Act of May 8th, 1792, ch. 33.] This has been followed by several acts in addition thereto. Congress, then, have undertaken to exercise the power of "organizing" the militia under the Constitution.

And here the question arises, to what extent, if any, this power, when already exercised by Congress, is exclusive in its character. Among the powers delegated to Congress, there may be some which are not for the time being exercised. For instance, there is the power "to fix the standard of weights and measures." Practically this has never been exercised by Congress; but it has been left to each State within its own jurisdiction. On the other hand, there is a power belonging to the same group, "to establish uniform laws on the subject of bankruptcies throughout the United States," which, when exercised by Congress, has been held so far exclusive, as to avoid at once all the bankrupt and insolvent laws of the several States.

Sir, I might go over all the powers of Congress, and find constant illustration of the subject. For instance, there is the power "to establish an uniform rule of naturalization," on which Chief Justice Marshall once remarked: — "That the power of naturalization is *exclusively* in Congress, does not seem to be, and certainly ought not to be controverted." There is the power "to regulate commerce with foreign nations and among the several States," which was early declared by the Supreme Court, to be exclusive, so as to prevent the exercise of any part of it by the States. There is the power over patents and copyrights, which has also been regarded as exclusive. So, also, is the power "to define and punish piracies and felonies, committed on the high seas, and offences against the law of nations." So, also, is still another power, viz: "to establish post-offices and post-roads. All of these powers, as in the case of the power over the National Militia, have been exercised by Congress, and even if not absolutely exclusive in their original character, have become so by the exercise.

Now, sir, upon what ground do gentleman make any discrimination in the case of the power over the National Militia? I know of no ground which seems to be tenable. It is natural that the States should desire to exercise this power, since it was so important to them before the Union; but I do not see how any discrimination can be maintained at the present time. Whatever may have been the original importance of the militia to each State, yet when the Constitution of the United States was formed, and Congress exercised the power delegated to it over this subject, the militia of the several States was absorbed into one uniform body, organized, armed and disciplined as the National Militia. To the States respectively was left, according to the express language of the Constitution, "the appointment of the officers and the authority of training the militia, according to the discipline prescribed by Congress." To this we may add the implied power of "governing" them when in the service of the State. This is all. The distinct specification of certain powers, as reserved to the States, seems to exclude them from the exercise of all others, which are not specified or

clearly implied. In other words, they are excluded from all power over the "organizing, arming, and disciplining the militia," at least after Congress have undertaken to enact laws for this purpose.

The history of the adoption of the several parts of this clause in the Federal Convention reflects light upon its true meaning. The first part, in regard to organizing, arming and disciplining the militia, was passed by a vote of nine States against two; the next, referring the appointment of officers to the States, after an ineffectual attempt to amend it by confining the appointment to officers under the rank of general officers, was passed without a division; and the last, reserving to the States the authority to train the militia, according to the discipline prescribed by Congress, was passed by a vote of seven States against four. It seems, then, that there was a strong opposition in the Convention, even to the express reservation to the States of "the authority of training the militia." But this power is not reserved unqualifiedly. The States are to train the militia "according to the *discipline prescribed* by Congress;" not according to any discipline determined by the States, or by the States concurrently with the General Government; but absolutely *according to the discipline prescribed by Congress*; nor more, nor less; thus distinctly recognizing the exclusive character of the legislation of Congress on this subject.

This interpretation derives confirmation from the manner in which the militia of England was constituted or organized at the time of the adoption of the Federal Constitution. To the crown was given the "*sole right* to govern and command them," though they were "officered" by the Lord Lieutenant of the county, the Deputy Lieutenant, and other principal landholders of the county. The commentaries of Sir William Blackstone, from which this description is drawn, were familiar to the members of the Convention; and it is reasonable to suppose that in the distribution of powers between the General Government and the States, on this subject, the peculiar arrangement which prevailed in the mother country was not disregarded.

If it should be said that the adoption of this conclusion would affect the character of many laws enacted by States, and thus far recognized as ancillary to the National Militia, it may be replied, that the possibility of these consequences cannot justly influence our conclusions on a question which must be determined by acknowledged principles of constitutional law. In obedience to these same principles, the Supreme Court, in the case of *Prigg* v. *Pennsylvania*, after asserting a power over fugitive slaves, which I cannot admit, has proceeded to annul a large number of statutes in different States. Mr. Justice Wayne in this case said: "That the legislation by Congress upon the provision, as the supreme law of the land, *excludes all State legislation upon the same subject;* and that no State can pass any law or regulation, or interpose such as may have been a law or regulation when the Constitution of the United States has ratified *to superadd to*, control, qualify, or impede a remedy enacted by Congress for the delivery of fugitive slaves to the parties to whom their service or labor is due." Without the sanction of any express words in the Constitution, and chiefly, if not solely, impressed by the importance of consulting "unity of purpose or uniformity of operation" in the legislation with regard to fugitive slaves, the Court has assumed a power over this subject, and then, as a natural incident to this assumption, it has excluded the States from all sovereignty in the premises.

Now, if this rule be applicable to the pretended power over fugitive slaves, it is more applicable to the power over the militia which nobody questions. Besides, I know of no power which so absolutely requires what has been regarded as an important criterion, "unity of purpose or uniformity of operation," as that over the militia. No uniform military organization can spring from opposite or inharmonious systems, and all systems proceeding from different sources are liable to be opposite or inharmonious.

Now, sir, let us apply this reasoning to the matter in hand, that we may arrive at a just conclusion. In Massachusetts, there exists, and has for a long time existed, an anomalous system, familiarly and loosely described as the Volunteer Militia, not composed absolutely of those enrolled under the laws of the United States, but a smaller, more select and peculiar body. Now it cannot be doubted that the State, by virtue of its *police powers* within its own borders, has power to constitute or organize a body of *volunteers*, to aid in enforcing its laws. But it does not follow that it has power to constitute or organize a body of volunteers, who shall be regarded as a part of the National Militia. And, sir, I make bold to say that the volunteer militia — I prefer to call it the volunteer military companies — cannot be regarded as a part of the National Militia. It is no part of that *uniform militia* which it was the object of the early Act of Congress to organize. It may appear to be a part of this system — it may affect to be, but I submit, it is a mistake to suppose that it is so in any just constitutional sense.

As a local system, disconnected from the national militia, and not in any way constrained by its organization, it is within our jurisdiction. We are free to declare the principles which shall govern it. We may declare that, whatever may be the existing law of the United States with regard to its enrolled militia — and with this I propose no interference, because it would be futile — I say, Massachusetts may proudly declare that in her own volunteer military companies, marshalled under her own local laws, there shall be no distinction of color or race.

## THE REPRESENTATIVE SYSTEM AND ITS PROPER BASIS.

SPEECH ON THE PROPOSITION TO AMEND THE BASIS OF THE HOUSE OF REPRESENTATIVES OF MASSACHUSETTS, IN THE CONVENTION TO REVISE AND AMEND THE CONSTITUTION OF THAT STATE, 7TH JULY, 1853.

Mr. President, if the question under consideration were less important in its bearings, or less embarrassed by conflicting opinions, I should hesitate to break the silence which I have been inclined to preserve in this Convention. In taking the seat to which, while absent from the Commonwealth, in another sphere of duty, I have been unexpectedly chosen, I felt that it would be becoming in me — and that my associates here would recognize the propriety of my course — considering the little opportunities I had of late enjoyed to make myself acquainted with the sentiments of the people on proposed changes, especially in comparison with friends to whom this movement is mainly due — on these accounts, and, also, on other accounts, I felt that it would be becoming in me to interfere as little as possible with these debates. To others, I have willingly left the part which I might have taken.

And now, when I think that since our labors began, weeks, even months, have passed, and that the term has been already reached, when, according to the just expectations and earnest desires of many, they should be closed, I feel that acts rather than words — that votes rather than speeches — at least such as I might hope to make — are needed here, to the end that the Convention, seasonably, and effectively completing its beneficent work, may itself be hailed as a Great Act in the history of the Commonwealth.

But the magnitude of this question justifies debate: and allow me to add that the State, our common mother, may feel proud of the ability, the eloquence, and the good temper with which it has thus far been conducted. Gentlemen have addressed the Convention in a manner which would grace any assembly, which it has been my fortune to know, at home or abroad. Sir, the character of these proceedings gives us new assurance for the future. The alarmist, who starts at every suggestion of change, and the croaker, who augurs constant evil from the irresistible tendency of events, must confess, that there are men here, to whose intelligence and patriotism, under God, the interests of our beloved Commonwealth may be entrusted. Yes, sir, Massachusetts is safe. Whatever may be the result even of the present important question — whichsoever scheme of representation may be adopted — Massachusetts will continue to prosper as in times past.

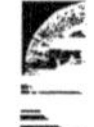

In the course of human history, two States, small in territory, have won enviable renown by their genius and devotion to Freedom, so that their very names awaken echoes; I refer to Athens and Scotland. But Athens — even at Salamis, repelling the Persian host, or afterwards, in the golden days of Pericles — and Scotland, throughout her long struggles with England down to the very act of Union at the beginning of the last century — were inferior, each of them, in population and in wealth, to Massachusetts at this moment. It belongs to us, according to our capacities, to see that this comparison does not end here. Others may believe that our duty will be best accomplished by standing still. I believe that it can be completely done only by a constant incessant advance in all things — in knowledge, in science, in art, and lastly in government itself, destined to be the bright consummation, on earth, of all knowledge, all science, and all art.

And now, sir, in framing anew our Constitution, we encounter a difficulty which at its original formation in 1780, perplexed our fathers — which perplexed the Convention of 1820 — which with its perplexities has haunted successive Legislatures and the whole people down to this day — and which now perplexes us. This difficulty occurs in determining the Representative System, and it arises mainly from the corporate claims of towns. From an early period, the towns in the State, both great and small, with slight exceptions, have sent one or more representatives to the Legislature. In primitive days, when the towns were few and the whole population was scanty, this arrangement was convenient at least, if not equitable. But now, with the increased number of towns, and the unequal distribution of a large population, it has become inconvenient, if not inequitable. The existing system does not work well, and we are summoned to reform it.

And here, sir, let me congratulate the Convention that, on this most important question, transcending every other, all of us, without distinction of party, are in favor of reform. We are all Reformers. The existing system finds no advocate on this floor. Nobody here will do it reverence. If the call of the Convention were not already amply vindicated — if there were doubt anywhere of its expediency, the remarkable concurrence of all sides in condemning the existing representative system shows that we have not come together without cause.

The orders of the day have been filled with the various plans offered to meet the exigency. Most of these aimed to preserve the corporate representation of towns; some of them, at least one from the venerable gentleman from Taunton [Mr. Morton], and another from the venerable gentleman from Boston [Mr. Hale], adopted an opposite system, hitherto untried among us, and proposed to divide the State into districts. And the question has been between these hostile propositions; and that is the question which I propose to consider, in the light of history and abstract principle, and, also, with reference to present exigencies. I shall speak *first* of the origin and nature of the Representative System and its proper conditions under American institutions. And *secondly*, I shall endeavor to indicate the principles which may conduct us to a practical conclusion on the present occasion. In entering upon this service, at this late stage of the debate, I feel like a tardy gleaner in a well-traversed field; but I shall proceed.

I. And I begin with the origin and nature of the Representative System. This is an invention of modern times. In antiquity there were republics and democracies; but there was no Representative System.

Rulers were chosen by the people, as in many Commonwealths; senators were designated by the king or by the censors, as in Rome; ambassadors or legates were sent to a Federal Council, as to the Assembly of the Amphictyons; but, in no ancient State, was any body of men ever constituted by the people to represent them in the administration of their internal affairs. In Athens, the people met in public assembly, and directly acted for themselves in all questions, foreign or domestic. This was possible there, as the State was small, and the Assembly at no time exceeded five thousand citizens, — a large town-meeting, or mass-meeting, we might call it, — not inaptly termed the "fierce democracie" of Athens.

But where the territory was extensive, and the population scattered and numerous, there could be no Assembly of the whole body of citizens. To meet this precise difficulty, the Representative System was devised. By a machinery, so obvious that we are astonished it was not employed in the ancient Commonwealths, the people, though scattered and numerous, are gathered, by their chosen representatives, into a small and deliberative assembly, where, without tumult or rashness, they may consider and determine all questions which concern them. In every representative body, properly constituted, the people are practically present.

Nothing is invented and perfected at the same time; and this system has been no exception to the rule. In England, where it reached its earliest vigor, it has been, and still is, anomalous in its character. The existing divisions of the country, composed of boroughs, cities, and counties, were summoned by the king's writ to send representatives, with little regard to equality of any kind, whether of population, of taxation, or of territory. Their existence as corporate units was the prevailing title. The irregular operation of the system, increasing with the lapse of time, provoked a cry for Parliamentary Reform, which, after a struggle of more than fifty years, ending in a debate which occupied the House of Commons more than fifty days, was finally carried; but, though many abuses and inequalities were removed, yet, the anomalous representation by counties, cities and boroughs, was still continued. And this, sir, is the English system.

Pass now, sir, to the American system. I say American system, for to our country belongs the honor of first giving to the world the idea of a system, which, discarding corporate representation, founded itself absolutely on equality. Let us acknowledge with gratitude, that from England have come five great and ever memorable institutions, by which Liberty is secured — I mean the Trial by Jury, — the writ of *Habeas Corpus*, — the Representative System, — the Rules and Orders of Debate; and, lastly, that benign principle which pronounces *that its air is too pure for a slave to breathe* — perhaps the five most important political establishments of modern times. This glory cannot be taken from the mother country. But America has added to the Representative System another principle, without which it is incomplete, and which, in the course of events, is destined, I cannot doubt, to find acceptance wherever the Representative System is employed. I mean the principle of equality.

Here in Massachusetts, home of the ideas out of which sprung the Revolution, this principle had its earliest expression. And it is not a little curious that this very expression was suggested by the two evils of which we now complain — namely, a practical inequality of representation and a too numerous House. Let me furnish some details of its history.

In the earliest days of the Colony, while the number of freemen was small and gathered in one neighborhood, there was no occasion for any representative body. All could then meet as at ancient Athens, in public assembly; and in fact, they did so meet, and in this way discharged the duties of legislation. But as the freemen became scattered and numerous, it was found grievous to compel the personal attendance of the whole body, and, as a substitute therefor, the towns were directed, in 1634, to assemble in General Court, by deputies. Here was the establishment of the Representative System in Massachusetts, which has continued, without interruption, down to our day. The size of the House and the relative representation of towns have varied at different times; but the great principle of representation — by which a substitute is provided for the whole body of the people — has been constantly preserved. Still a feeling has long prevailed, that the system had not yet received its final form, while, in more than vision, has been discerned that principle of equality which is essential to its completeness.

Among the acts of the first General Court of the Revolution, was one passed in the summer of 1775, after the battle of Bunker Hill, "declaratory of the rights of the towns and districts to elect and depute a representative or representatives to serve for and represent them in the General Court." By this act, all pre-

vious acts taking from towns and districts the right of sending a representative to the General Court were repealed, and every town containing thirty qualified voters, was authorized to send a representative. The immediate consequence was the two evils to which I have already referred — namely, inequality of representation, and a too numerous House; but the whole number of representatives which aroused the complaints of that day, was two hundred and sixty.

These grievances were the occasion of a Convention of delegates from the towns of Essex County, at Ipswich, April 25th, 1776, where a memorial to the Legislature was adopted, which was afterwards presented and enforced at the bar of the House by John Lowell. In this remarkable document occurs the first development, if not the first proclamation of the principle of equality in representation. Here, sir, is the fountain and origin of an idea, full of strength, beauty and glory. Listen to the words of these Revolutionary fathers: —

"If the representation is equal, it is perfect; as far as it deviates from this equality, so far it is imperfect, and approaches to the state of slavery; and the want of a just weight in representation is an evil nearly akin to being totally destitute of it. An inequality of representation has been justly esteemed the cause, which has, in a great degree, sapped the foundation of the once admired, but now tottering fabric of the British empire; and we fear that if a different mode of representation from the present is not adopted in this colony, our Constitution will not continue to the late period of time which the glowing heart of every true American now anticipates. . . .

"We cannot realize that your honors, our wise political fathers, have adverted to the present inequality of representation in this colony, to the growth of the evil, or to the fatal consequences which will probably ensue from the continuance of it.

"Each town and district in the colony is, by some late regulations, permitted to send one representative to the General Court, if such town or district consists of thirty freeholders and other inhabitants qualified to elect; if of one hundred and twenty, to send two. No town is permitted to send more than two except the town of Boston, which may send four. There are some towns and districts in the colony, in which there are between thirty and forty freeholders and other inhabitants qualified to elect only; there are others beside Boston, in which there are more than five hundred. The first of these may send one representative, the latter can send only two. If these towns as to property are to each other in the same respective proportion, is it not clear to a mathematical demonstration that the same number of inhabitants of equal property in the one town, have but an *eighth* part of the weight in representation with the other; and with what colorable pretext we would decently inquire."

Under the pressure of this powerful state paper the obnoxious law was repealed; but the evil was not remedied. Then followed the unsuccessful effort to make a Constitution in 1777, which failed partly through dissatisfaction with its disposition of this very question. The county of Essex was again heard in another document, now known as the "Essex Result," and, among the most able and instructive in our history, from which I take the following important words: "The rights of representation should be so equally and impartially distributed, that the representatives should have the same views and interests with the people at large. They should think, feel, and act like them, and, in fine, should be an exact miniature of their constituents. They should be, if we may use the expression, the whole body politic, with all its property, rights and privileges, reduced to a similar scale, *every part being diminished in just proportion.* To pursue the metaphor, if, in adjusting the representation of freemen, *any ten are reduced into one, all the other tens should be alike reduced; or, if any hundred should be reduced to one, all the other hundreds should have just the same reduction.*" Mark well these words. Here is the Rule of Three, for the first time in history, applied to representation. This, Sir, is not the English system. I call it, with pride, the American system.

In another place the document proceeds as follows:

"The rights of representation should also be held sacred and inviolable, and for this purpose, representation should be fixed upon known and easy principles; and the Constitution should make provision that recourse should constantly be had to those principles within a very small period of years, to rectify the errors that will creep in through lapse of time or alteration of situations."

It then distinctly proposes a system of districts, in words which I quote:—

"In forming the first body of legislators, let regard be had only to the representation of persons, not of property This body we call the House of Representatives. Ascertain the number of representatives. It ought not to be so large as will induce an enormous expense to government, nor too unwieldy to deliberate with coolness and attention; nor so small as to be unacquainted with the situation and circumstances of the State. One hundred will be large enough, and, perhaps, it may be too large. We are persuaded that any number of men exceeding that, cannot do business with such expedition and propriety as a smaller number could. However, let that at present be considered as the number. Let us have the number of freemen in the several counties in the State; and let these representatives be apportioned among the respective counties, in proportion to their number of freemen.

"As we have the number of freemen in the county, and the number of county representatives, by dividing the greater by the less we have the number of freemen entitled to send one representative. Then add as many adjoining towns together as contain that number of freemen, or as near as may be, and let those towns form one district, and proceed in this manner through the country."

Mr. HALLETT, for Wilbraham (interrupting). Will the gentleman state who was the author of that Essex paper.

Mr. SUMNER. Theophilus Parsons is the reputed author of the document known as the "Essex Result."

Mr. HALLETT. Yes, Sir, it was Theophilus Parsons who was the author of that, and John Lowell of the other, and good old Tory doctrines they are.

Mr. SUMNER. If these be Tory doctrines, I must think well of Toryism.

Mr. BIRD, of Walpole. The gentleman for Marshfield speaks of the basis of representation in one House. I should like to know what was the basis proposed at that time for the other branch?

Mr. SUMNER. Property, I believe. But, Sir, I put these inquiries aside. I do not concern myself with the authorship of these doctrines, or with the character of other doctrines with which they were associated in the minds of their authors. All this is irrelevant and unimportant. I refer to them in the history of the question and hasten on.

Sir, notwithstanding these appeals, sustained by unsurpassed ability, the American system failed to be adopted in the Constitution of 1780. The anomalous English system was still continued; but, as if to cover the departure from principle, it was twice declared that the representation of the people should be "founded on the principle of equality." This declaration still continues as our guide, while the irregular operation of the existing system, with its inequalities and large numbers, is a beacon of warning.

Following closely upon these efforts in Massachusetts, this principle found an illustrious advocate in Thomas Jefferson. In his Notes on Virginia, written in 1780, he sharply exposes the inequalities of representation, and, a short time afterwards, when the victory at Yorktown had rescued Virginia from invasion and secured the independence of the United Colonies, he prepared a draught of a Constitution for his native State, which, disowning the English System and recognizing the very principle that had failed in Massachusetts, expressly provided that, "the number of delegates which each county may send shall be *in proportion to the number of its qualified electors;* and the whole number of delegates for the State shall be so *proportioned to the whole number of qualified electors in it*, that they shall never exceed three hundred, nor be fewer than one hundred; and if any county be reduced in its qualified electors below the number authorized to send one delegate, let it be annexed to some adjoining county." This proposition, which is substantially the Rule of Three, was not adopted in Virginia. This State, like Massachusetts, was not yet prepared for such a charter of electoral equality; but it still stands as a monument at once of its author and of the true system of representation.

The American System, though first showing itself in Massachusetts and in Virginia, found its earliest practical exemplification only a few years later in the Constitution of the United States. By the Articles of Confederation each State was entitled to send to Congress not less than two, nor more than seven representatives, and in the determination of questions, each State had one vote only. This plan was rejected by the framers of the new Constitution; and another, until then untried in the history of the world, was adopted. It was declared that "representatives and direct taxes shall be *apportioned* among the several States which may be included in this Union, *according to their respective numbers;*" not according to property; not according to territory; not according to any corporate rights; *but according to their respective numbers.* And this system has continued down to our day, and will continue immortal as the Union itself. Here is the Rule of Three actually incorporated into the Representative System of the United States.

An attempt has been made to render this system odious, or at least questionable, by charging upon it something of the excesses of the great French Revolution. Even if this rule had prevailed at that time in France, it would be bold to attribute to it any such consequences. But it is a mistake to suppose that it was then adopted in that country. The republican Constitution of 1791 was not founded upon numbers only; but upon numbers, territory and taxation combined; a mixed system, which excluded the true idea of personal equality. But at the peaceful — almost bloodless — revolution of 1848, under the lead of Lamartine, a National Assembly was convened on the simple basis of population, and one representative was allowed for every forty thousand inhabitants. Here again is the Rule of Three; but the idea originally came from our country.

Mr. HALLETT. Will the gentleman from Marshfield allow me to make one more inquiry?

Mr. SUMNER. Certainly.

Mr. HALLETT. Do I understand the gentleman to say that the Rule of Three was applied to representation in the United States?

Mr. SUMNER. I mean to say, that the representation in the lower House of Congress was apportioned according to numbers; and this is the Rule of Three. The gentleman has in mind, perhaps, the anomalous exception with reference to Slavery.

Mr. HALLETT. No, sir. I do not refer to that at all. The first apportionment of representation by Congress, was made by applying the divisor of thirty thousand, which was the ratio of representation, to the whole population of the United States. That bill was vetoed by General Washington, upon the ground that the Constitution required that representation should be apportioned among the States according to their respective numbers, and that it did not allow of a numerical representation of all the people of the United States. I ask the gentleman if that rule was the Rule of Three?

Mr. SUMNER. The learned gentleman is substantially right in his statement; but he will pardon me if I say, that it does not interfere with my proposition. The language of the Constitution is explicit: "representatives shall be *apportioned* among the several States *according to their respective numbers.*" This is the rule; I call it the Rule of Three. There are minor details in its operation, arising from Slavery, and from the division into States, on which I do not dwell, as they do not interfere with its paramount principle, and I am admonished to proceed.

A practical question here arises, whether this rule

should be applied to the whole body of population, including women, children, and unnaturalized foreigners, or whether it should be applied to those only who exercise the electoral franchise ; in other words, to voters. It is probable that the rule would generally produce nearly similar results, in both cases ; as the voters, except in a few places, would bear a uniform proportion to the whole population. But it will be easy to determine what the principle of the Representative System requires. Since the object of the system is to provide a practical substitute for the meetings of the people, it should be founded in just proportion on the numbers of those who, according to our Constitution, can take part in those meetings ; that is, upon the qualified voters. The representative body should be a minature or abridgment of the electoral body ; in other words, of those allowed to participate in public affairs. If this conclusion needs authority, it may be found in the words of Mr. Madison, in the Debates on the Federal Constitution. "It has been very properly observed," he says, "that representation was an expedient by which the meeting of the people themselves was rendered unnecessary, *and that representatives ought, therefore, to bear a proportion to the votes which their constituents, if convened, would respectively have.*" — [Madison's Debates, vol. ii. p. 1103.]

The Rule of Three, then, applied to voters, seems to me sound ; but whether applied to voters or population, it is the true rule of representation, and stands on adamantine principles. In my view, it commends itself so obviously, so instinctively, to the natural reason, that I do not feel disposed to dwell upon it. But since it has been called in question, I shall be excused for saying a few words in its behalf. Its advantages present themselves in several aspects.

*First.* And I put in the front its constant and equal operation throughout the Commonwealth. Under it, every man will have a representative each year; and every man will have the same representative power as every other man. In this respect, it carries out a darling idea of our institutions, which cannot be disowned without weakening their foundations. It gives to the great principle of human equality a new expansion and application. It makes all men, in the enjoyment of the electoral franchise, whatever be their diversities of intelligence, of education, or of wealth, or wheresoever they may be within the borders of the Commonwealth, in small town or in populous city, absolutely equal at the ballot-box.

I know that there are persons, sir, who do not hesitate to assail the whole doctrine of the equality of men, as enunciated in our Declaration of Independence, and in our Bill of Rights. In this work two eminent statesmen, of our own country, and of England, have led the way. But it seems to me, that if they had chosen to comprehend the meaning of the principle, much, if not all of their objection would have been removed. It is a palpable truth, that men are not born equal in physical strength or in mental capacities; in beauty of form or health of body. These mortal cloaks of flesh differ, as do these worldly garments. Diversity or inequality in these respects, is the law of creation. But as God is no respecter of persons, and as all are equal in his sight, whether rich or poor, whether dwellers in cities or in fields, so are all equal in natural rights; and it is a childish sophism — of which no gentleman in this Convention is guilty — to adduce in argument against them the physical or mental inequalities by which men are characterized. Now, I do not pretend to class the electoral franchise among those inherent, natural rights, which are common to the human family, without distinction of age, sex or residence; but I do say, that from the equality of men, which we so proudly proclaim, we may derive a just rule for its exercise. For myself, I accept this principle, and just so far and just so soon as possible, I would be guided by it in the system of Representation. But there are other reasons still.

*Secondly.* The rule of Three, as applied to representation, is commended by its simplicity. It supersedes all the painful calculations to which we have been driven, the long agony of mathematics as it was called by my friend over the way [Mr. Giles], and is as easy in its application as it seems to me to be just.

*Thirdly.* This rule is founded in nature, and not in art; on natural bodies, and not on artificial bodies; on men, and not on corporations; on souls, and not on petty geographical lines. On this account it may be called a natural rule, and when once established, will become fixed and permanent, beyond all change or desire of change.

And, *fourthly*, this rule removes, to every possible extent, those opportunities of political partiality and calculation in the adjustment of the representation, which are naturally incident to any departure from precise rule. It was beautifully said of law by the greatest intellect of Antiquity, that it is *mind without passion*, and this very definition I would extend to a rule which, with little intervention from human will, is graduated by numbers, passionless as law itself in the conception of Aristotle. The object of free institutions is, to withdraw all concerns of State, so far as practicable, from human discretion, and place them under the shield of human principles, to the end, according to the words of our Constitution, that there may be a government of laws, and not of men. But, just in proportion as we depart from precise rule, it becomes a government of men, and not of laws.

Such considerations as these, thus briefly expressed, seem to vindicate this rule of representation. But let me not forget the arguments adduced against it. These have assumed two distinct forms; one is founded on the character of our towns and the importance of preserving their influence; the other is founded on the alleged necessity of counteracting the centralization of power in the cities. Now, of these in their order.

And, first, of the importance of preserving our towns. Sir, I yield to no man in appreciation of the good done by these free municipalities. The able member for Erving [Mr. Griswold], who began this debate, the eloquent member for Berlin [Mr. Boutwell], and my excellent friend of many years, the accomplished member for Manchester [Mr. Dana], in the masterly speeches which they have addressed to the Convention, have attributed no good influence to the towns which I do not recognize also. With them I agree, cordially, that the towns in Massachusetts, like the municipalities of Switzerland, have been schools and nurseries of freedom; and that in these small bodies, men were early disciplined in those primal duties of citizenship, which, on a grander scale, have been made the founda-

tion of our whole political fabric. But, I cannot go so far as to attribute this remarkable influence to the assumed fact, that each town by itself was entitled to a representative in the legislative body. At the time of the Revolution, this was the prerogative of most towns, though not of all; but it cannot be regarded as the distinctive, essential, life-giving attribute. At most it was only an incident.

Sir, the true glory of the towns then was, that they were organized on the principles of self-government, at a time when these principles were not generally recognized; that each town by itself was a little republic, where the whole body of freemen were voters, with powers of local legislation, taxation and administration, and, especially, with the power to choose their own head and all subordinate magistrates. Sir, the boroughs of England have possessed the power to send a member — often two members — to Parliament; but this has not saved them from corruption; nor has any person attributed to them, though in the enjoyment of this franchise, the influence which has proceeded from our municipalities. And the reason is obvious. They were organized under charters from the crown, by which the local government was vested — not in the whole body of freeman — but in small councils, or select classes, originally nominated by the crown, and ever afterwards renewing themselves. No such abuse prevailed in our municipalities; and this political health at home, sir, and not the incident of exclusive representation in a distant Legislature, has been the secret of their strength. This I would ever cherish.

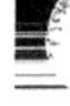

And this brings me, in the next place, to the objection founded on centralization of power in the cities. It is said that wealth, business, population and talent, in its multitudinous forms, all tend to the cities, and that the excessive influence of this concentrated mass, quickened by an active press, by facilities of concert, and by social appliances ought to be counterbalanced by an allotment to the towns of a representative weight beyond their proportion of numbers. Now, sir, while confessing and regretting the present predominance of the cities, I must be permitted to question the propriety of the proposed remedy. And here, as I differ in some respects from friends on both sides, I make an appeal for a candid judgment of what I shall candidly say.

I would not be unjust to cities. But no student of history can fail to perceive that they have performed different parts at different stages of the world. In antiquity, they were the acknowledged centres of power, often of tyranny. But in the middle ages, they became the home of freedom, and the bridle to feudalism. For this service they should be gratefully remembered. And now there is another change. The armed feudalism is overthrown; but it is impossible not to see that it has yielded to a commercial feudalism, whose seat is in the cities, and which, in its way, is hardly less selfish and exacting than the feudalism of the iron hand. My friend, the member for Manchester [Mr. Dana], was clearly right when he said, that the Boston of to-day is not the Boston of our fathers. But let me be understood. I make no impeachment of individuals; but simply indicate those combined influences proceeding from the potent Spirit of Trade — alas! how unlike that Spirit of the Lord, where is liberty! — which are not inconsistent with

the most exalted individual worth. I think, while confessing the abounding charities of the rich men, whose eulogy we have heard more than once in this debate, it must be admitted that those pure principles which are the breath of the republic, now find their truest atmosphere in calm retreats, away from the strife of gain, and the hot pavements of crowded streets. Sir, it is not only when we look upon the fields, hills and valleys, clad in verdure, and shining with silver lake or rivulet, that we may be ready to exclaim: —

> "God made the country, and man made the town."

But, sir, while maintaining these opinions, I cannot admit the argument, that the centralized power of the cities may be counteracted by degrading them in the scale of representation. This cannot be purposely done without departing from fundamental principles, and without overthrowing the presiding doctrine of personal equality. Cities are but congregations of men; and men exert influence in various ways; by the accident of position; by the accident of intelligence; by the accident of property; by the accident of birth; and lastly, by the vote. It is the vote only which is not an accident; and it should be the boast of Massachusetts, that all men, whatever may be their accidents, are equal in their votes. [Here the hammer of the President fell, as the hour expired; but by unanimous consent, Mr. Sumner proceeded.] The idea of property as a check upon numbers, which, on a former occasion, found such favor in this hall, is now rejected in the adjustment of our Representative System. And, sir, I venture to predict that the proposition, newly broached in this Commonwealth, to restrain the cities by a curtailment of their just representative power, will hereafter be as little regarded.

II. Mr. President, such is what I have to say on the history and principles of the Representative System, particularly in the light of American institutions, and this brings me to the *practical question* at this moment. I cannot doubt that the District System, as it is generally called, whereby the representative power will be distributed in just proportion, according to the Rule of Three, among the voters of the Commonwealth, is the true system, destined at no distant day to prevail. And, gladly, would I see this Convention hasten the day by presenting it to the people for adoption in the organic law. To this end I have striven by my votes. But, sir, I am not blind to what has passed. The votes already taken show that the Convention is not prepared for this change, and I am assured by gentlemen more familiar with public sentiment than I can pretend to be, that the people are not yet prepared for it.

And thus, sir, we are brought to the position occupied successively by the Conventions of 1780 and 1820, each of which, though containing warm partisans of the District System, shrank from its adoption; as in Virginia, the early recommendation of Jefferson, and his vehement support at a later day, have been powerless to produce this important amendment. John Lowell, who appeared at the bar of the Massachusetts Legislature in 1776, to vindicate the principle of equality in representation, and Theophilus Parsons, the author of the powerful tract which proposed to found the

Representative System on the Rule of Three, were both members of the first Convention; and, I know not if the District System has since had any abler defenders. To these I might add the great name of John Adams, who had early pleaded for equality of representation, and had declared in words adopted by the Essex Convention, that the Representative Assembly should be an exact portrait in miniature of the people at large. — (*Works*, Vol. iv., pp. 186, 195, 205.) In the Convention of 1820, the District System was cherished and openly extolled by a distinguished jurist, at that time a Justice of the Supreme Court of the United States,— Joseph Story, — whose present fame gives additional importance to his opinions. And yet, the desire of these men failed. The corporate representation of towns was preserved, and the District System pronounced impracticable. In the address put forth by the Convention of 1780, and signed by its President, James Bowdoin, these words may be found: —

"You will observe that we have resolved that representatives ought to be founded on the principle of equality; but it cannot be understood thereby, that each town in the Commonwealth shall have weight and importance in a just proportion to its numbers and property. An exact representation would be unpracticable, even in a system of government arising from the state of nature, and much more so in a state already divided into nearly three hundred corporations."

The Convention seem to have recognized the theoretic fitness of an "exact representation;" but did not regard it as feasible in a State already divided into nearly three hundred corporations. In the Convention of 1820, Joseph Story, who has been already quoted by my eloquent friend [Mr. Choate], used language which, though not so strong as that of the early address, yet has the same result : —

"In the Select Committee, I was in favor of a plan of representation in the House founded on population, as the most just and equal in its operation. I still retain that opinion. There were serious objections against this system, and it was believed by others that the towns could not be brought to consent to yield up the corporate privileges of representation which had been enjoyed so long, and were so intimately connected with their pride and their interests. I felt constrained, therefore, with great reluctance to yield up a favorite plan. I have lived long enough to know, that in any question of government, something is to be yielded up on all sides. Conciliation and compromise lie at the origin of every free government; and the question never was, and never can be, what is absolutely best, but what is relatively wise, just and expedient. I have not hesitated, therefore, to support the plan of the Select Committee as one that, on the whole, was the best that, under existing circumstances, could be obtained."

Sir, I am not insensible to these considerations, nor to the authority of these examples. A division of the State into districts would be a change, in conformity with abstract principles, which would interfere with the existing opinions, habitudes and prejudices of the towns, all of which must be respected. A change so important in its character, cannot be advantageously made, unless supported by the permanent feelings and convictions of the people. Institutions are formed *from within*, and not *from without*. They spring from custom and popular faith, silently operating with internal power, and not from the imposed will of a lawgiver. And our present duty here, at least on this question, may be, in some measure, satisfied, if we aid this growth.

Two great schools of jurisprudence, for a while,

divided the learned mind of Germany; one known as the Historic, the other as the Didactic. The question between them was similar to that now before the Convention. The first regarded all laws and institutions as the growth of custom under the constant influences of history; the other insisted upon giving to them, by positive legislation, a form in conformity with abstract reason. It is clear that both were, in a measure, right. No law-giver or statesman can disregard either history or abstract reason. He must contemplate both. He will faithfully study the Past, and will recognize its treasures and traditions; but, with equal fidelity, he will set his face towards the Future, where all institutions shall, at last, be in harmony with truth.

I have been encouraged to believe in the practicability of the District System, by its conformity with reason, and by seeing how naturally it went into operation under the Constitution of the United States. But there is a difference between that case and the present. A new Government was then founded, with new powers, applicable to a broad expanse of country; but the Constitution of Massachusetts was little more than a continuation of pre-existing usages and institutions, with all dependence upon royalty removed. This distinction may help us now. If the country were absolutely new, with no embarrassments from existing corporate rights — claims I would rather call them — it might easily be arranged, according to the most approved theory, as Philadelphia was originally laid out by its great founder, on the model of the German city which he had seen in his youth. But to bring our existing system into symmetry and to lay it out anew, would seem to be a task — at least I am reluctantly led to this conclusion by what I have heard here — not unlike that of rebuilding Boston, and of shaping its compact mass of crooked streets into the regular rectangular forms of the city of Penn. And yet this is not impossible. With each day, by demolishing ancient houses and widening ancient ways, changes are made, which tend to this result.

Sir, we must recognize the existing condition of things, remedy all practical grievances, so far as possible, and set our faces towards the true system. We must act in the Present; but be mindful also of the Future. There are proper occasions for compromise, as most certainly there are rights which are beyond compromise. But the Representative System is an expedient or device, for ascertaining the popular will, and though well satisfied that this can be best founded on numbers, I would not venture to say, in the present light of political science, that the right of each man to an equal representation, according to the Rule of Three and without regard to existing institutions or controlling usages, is of that inherent and lofty character — like the God-given right to life or liberty — which admits of no compromise.

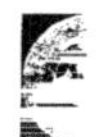

Several grievances exist, which will be removed by the proposed amendments. There is one which I had hoped would disappear, but which is the necessary incident of corporate representation; I mean the unwieldy size of the House.

It is generally said, that a small body is more open to bribery and corruption than a large body; but, on the other hand, I have heard it asserted, that the larger is more exposed than the smaller. I put this consider-

ation aside. My objection to a large House is, that it is inconvenient for the dispatch of public business. There is a famous saying of Cardinal de Retz, that every assembly, of more than one hundred, is a mob; and Lord Chesterfield applied this same term to the British House of Commons. This body, at present, nominally has six hundred and fifty-five members. It is called, by Lord Brougham, "preposterously large," but a quorum for business is forty only; and it is only on rare occasions of political importance, that its benches are completely occupied. The House of Lords, nominally, has four hundred and forty-seven members; but a quorum in this body consists of three only; and much of its business is transacted in a very thin attendance.

The experience of Congress, and also of other States, points to a reduction of our present number. Indeed, for many years, this was a general desire through the State. In the earliest colonial days, every town was allowed three deputies; but in five years the number, on reaching thirty-three, was reduced to two for each. At a later day, in 1694, a great contest in the House was decided by a vote of twenty-six against twenty-four. In the agitating period between 1762 and 1773, covering the controversies which heralded the Revolution, the House contained about one hundred and ten. Only on one occasion, the magnitude of the interest is said by Governor Hutchinson to have drawn together one hundred and thirty. At the last session of the Provincial Legislature, in May, 1774, when the revolutionary conflict was at hand, the complete returns of the journals show one hundred and forty; and in 1776, there was a House of two hundred and sixty.

But this "enormous and very unwieldy size," as it was then called, was assigned as a reason for a new Constitution. I regret that we cannot profit by this experience. A House of two hundred and fifty, or, since we are accustomed to large congregations, of three hundred at most, would be an improvement on the present system.

But, there are two proposed improvements which I hail with satisfaction; one relates to the small towns, and the other to the cities. The small towns will have a more constant representation, and this of itself is an approach to the true principle of representation, which should be constant as well as equal. The cities will be divided into districts, and this I regard of two-fold importance — first, as the beginning of a true system; and secondly, as reducing the power, which the cities, by the large number of their representatives, chosen by the general ticket, now exercise.

A respected gentleman, now in my eye, has reminded me that in boyhood, his attention was arrested in this House by what was called the Boston seat, reserved exclusively for the Boston members, who sat together, on cushions, while other members were left to such accommodations as they could find on bare benches. This discrimination ceased long ago. But it seems to me that this reserved and cushioned seat is typical of another discrimination, which Boston, in common with the cities, still enjoys. Sir, in voting for forty-four representatives, the elector in Boston exercises a representative power transcending far that of electors in the country; and the majority which rules Boston and determines the whole delegation, exercises a representative power transcending far that of any

similar number in the Commonwealth. This is apparent on the bare statement, as forty-four sticks are stronger in one compact bundle, than when apart or in small parcels. Thus, while other counties are divided, the delegation from Boston is united. In all political contests, it is like the well-knit Macedonian phalanx, or the iron front of the Roman legion, in comparison with the disconnected, individual warriors, against whom they were matched. But this abuse is to be removed; and here is the beginning — I had almost said the inauguration — of a true electoral equality in our Commonwealth.

And now, in conclusion, while thanking gentlemen for the kind attention with which they have honored me, let me express briefly the result to which I have come. I have openly declared my convictions with regard to the District System, and in accordance with these, have recorded my votes in this Convention. These votes, which reveal my inmost desires on this matter, I would not change. But the question is not now between the District System, which I covet so much for Massachusetts, and the proposed amendments; but between these amendments and the existing system. On this issue I decide without hesitation. I shall vote, sir, for the propositions of amendment now before the Convention, should they come to a question on their final passage; not because they are all that I desire; not because they seem to satisfy the requirements of principles which I cannot deny; not because they constitute a permanent adjustment of this difficult question; but because, they are the best which I can now obtain; because they reform grievances of the existing system; and, because,

they begin a change, which can end only in the establishment of a Representative System, founded in reality, as in name, on equality. Their adoption will be a triumph of conciliation and harmony, and will furnish new testimony to the well-tempered spirit of our institutions,

> "Where jarring interests, reconciled, create
> The according music of a well mixed State."

# BILLS OF RIGHTS; THEIR HISTORY AND POLICY.

SPEECH ON THE REPORT FROM THE COMMITTEE ON THE BILL OF RIGHTS, IN THE CONVENTION TO REVISE AND AMEND THE CONSTITUTION OF MASSACHUSETTS, 25TH JULY, 1853.

---

As Chairman of the Committee on the Bill of Rights, Mr. Sumner submitted a Report, on which, in Committee of the Whole, he spoke as follows:

MR. CHAIRMAN: As chairman of the Committee on the Preamble and Bill of Rights, it belongs to me to introduce and explain their Report. It will be perceived that it is brief and proposes no important changes. But in justice to the distinguished gentlemen with whom I had the honor of being associated on that Committee, I deem it my duty to suggest that the extent of their labors should not be judged by this result. It appears from the proceedings of the Convention of 1820, that the Committee on the Bill of Rights at that time sat longer than any other Committee. I believe that the same Committee in the present Convention might claim the same pre-eminence. Their records show twenty different sessions.

At these sessions, the Preamble and the Bill of Rights, in its thirty different propositions, were passed in review and considered, clause by clause; the various orders of the Convention, amounting to twelve in number; the petitions addressed to the Convention and referred to the Committee; and also informal propositions from members of the Convention and others, were considered; some of them repeatedly and at length. On many questions there was a decided difference of opinion and on a few the Committee was nearly equally divided. But after the best consideration we could bestow upon them in our protracted series of meetings, it was found that the few simple propositions, now on your table, were all upon which a majority of the Committee could be brought to unite. As such I was directed to present them to the Convention. And here, sir, admonished by the lapse of time and the desire to close these proceedings, I might be content with this simple statement.

But, notwithstanding the urgency of our business, I cannot allow the opportunity to pass — indeed I should not do my duty — without attempting for a brief moment to show the origin and character of this part of our Constitution. In this way we may learn its weight and authority and appreciate the difficulty and delicacy of any change in its substance or even its form. I will try not to abuse your patience.

The Preamble and Bill of Rights, like the rest of our Constitution, were from the pen of John Adams; among whose published works the whole document, in its original draught, may be found. At the time when he rendered this important service to his native Commonwealth and to the principles of free institutions everywhere, he was forty-five years of age. But he was not unprepared. The natural maturity of his powers had been enriched by the well-ripened fruit of assiduous study and of an active life, both of which concurred in him. The examples of Greece and Rome and the writings of Sidney and Locke were especially familiar to his mind. The common law he had made his own, and mastered well its whole arsenal of Freedom. For a long time the vigorous and unfailing partisan of the liberal cause in Boston, throughout its many conflicts; then in Congress, whither he was transferred, the irresistible champion of Independence; and then the republican representative of the united but still struggling Colonies at the Court of France; in the brief interval between his two foreign missions, only seven days after landing from his long ocean voyage, he was chosen a delegate to the Constitutional Convention, and at once brought all his varied experience, rare political culture and eminent powers to the task of adjusting the frame-work of government for Massachusetts. As his work, it all claims our regard; and no part bears the imprint of his mind so much as the Preamble and Bill of Rights; nor is any other part authenticated as coming so exclusively from him.

At the time of its first adoption, the Massachusetts Bill of Rights was more ample in its provisions, and more complete in form, than any similar Declaration in English or Colonial history. Glancing at its predecessors, we shall learn something of its sources. First came, long back in the thirteenth century, Magna Charta, with its generous safeguards of Freedom, wrung from King John by the Barons at Runnymede. From time to time these liberties were confirmed, and, after an interval of centuries, they were again ratified, at the beginning of the unhappy reign of Charles I. by a

Parliamentary Declaration, to which the monarch assented, known as the Petition of Right, which, in its very title, reveals the humility with which the rights of the people were then maintained. And, finally, in a different tone and language, at the revolution of 1688, when James II. was driven from his dominions, a "Declaration of the true, ancient and indubitable rights and liberties of the people of the kingdom," familiarly known as the Bill of Rights, was delivered by the Convention Parliament to the new sovereigns, William and Mary, and embodied in the Act of Settlement, by virtue of which they sat on the throne. These, sir, are the English examples.

Their influence was not restrained to England. It crossed the ocean. From the beginning the colonists were tenacious of the rights and liberties of Englishmen, and, at various times and in various forms, declared them. Connecticut, as early as 1639; Virginia in 1624 and 1676; Pennsylvania in 1682; New York in 1691; — and I might mention others still — put forth Declarations, brief and meagre, but kindred to those of the mother country. In the colony of New Plymouth, the essential principles of Magna Charta were proclaimed in 1636, under the name of the General Fundamentals; and in 1672, the inhabitants of Massachusetts Bay announced in words, worthy of careful study, that "the free fruition of such Liberties, Immunities, Privileges, as Humanity, Civility, and Christianity call for, as due to every man in his place and proportion, without impeachment and infringement, hath ever been and ever will be, the tranquillity and stability of churches and Commonwealth, and the denial or deprival thereof, the disturbance, if not the ruin, of both."

In the animated discussions, which immediately preceded the revolution, the rights and liberties of Englishmen were constantly asserted as the birth-right of the colonists. This was often done by formal resolutions or declarations, couched at first in moderate phrase. At the outrage of the Stamp Act, a Congress of delegates from nine States, held at New York in October, 1765, put forth a series of resolution entitled, "*Declaration of our humble opinion* respecting the most essential rights and liberties of the colonists." The humility of this language may recall the English Petition of Right under Charles I. This was followed in 1774 by the Declaration of the Continental Congress, which, in another tone and with admirable force, arrays in ten different propositions, the rights which "by the immutable laws of nature, the principles of English liberty and the several charters of compacts" belong to "the inhabitants of the English colonies in North America,"

"Time's noblest offspring is the last;"

and the whole colonial series was aptly closed by the Declaration of Independence, which declared not merely the rights of Englishmen, but the rights of men.

But only a few brief weeks before the Declaration of Independence, Virginia, taking the lead of her sister colonies, had established a Constitution to which was prefixed an elaborate Bill of Rights. This remarkable document, which has been the grand precedent for the whole country, marks an epoch in political history.

In all English Declarations of Rights and even in those of the Colonies, unless we except the early declaration of the inhabitants of Massachusetts Bay, stress had been laid upon the liberties and privileges of Englishmen. The rights claimed even by the Continental Congress of 1774, in their masculine Declaration, were the rights of "free and natural-born subjects within the realm of England." But the Virginia Bill of Rights, standing at the front of its first Constitution, discarded all narrow title from mere English precedent, planted itself on the eternal law of God, above every human ordinance, and openly proclaimed that "all men are equally free and independent;" a declaration, which is repeated, though in other language, by the Massachusetts Bill of Rights.

The policy of Bills of Rights has been sometimes called in question. It has been said that they were originally privileges or concessions extorted from the King, and, though expedient in a monarchy, are of little value in a Republic. As late as 1821, in the Convention for revising the Constitution of New York, doubts of their utility were openly expressed by Mr. Van Buren. But they are now above question. Each new State, ending with California, follows the example of Virginia and Massachusetts, and places its Bill of Rights in the front of its Constitution. Nor can I doubt that much good is done by this frank assertion of fundamental principles. The public mind is instructed; people learn to know their rights; liberal institutions are confirmed; and the Constitution is made stable in the hearts of the community. The provisions in the Bill of Rights are lessons of political wisdom and anchors of liberty. They are also the

constant index and scourge of injustice and wrong. In Massachusetts, Slavery itself disappeared before the declaration that "all men are born free and equal," interpreted by a liberty-loving Court.

In the Convention of 1780, the Bill of Rights formed a prominent subject of interest. The necessity of such a safeguard had been pressed upon the people, and its absence from the Constitution of 1777, was unquestionably a reason for the rejection of that ill-fated effort. Indeed this Constitution was openly opposed because it had no Bill of Rights. In the array of objections to it, at the period, was the following, which I take from an important contemporaneous publication. "That a Bill of Rights, clearly ascertaining and defining the rights of conscience and that security of person and property, which every member of the State hath a right to expect from the supreme power thereof, ought to be settled and established previous to the ratification of any Constitution for the State." Accordingly, at the earliest moment after the organization of the Convention, a motion was made "that there be a Declaration of Rights prepared previous to the framing of the Constitution of Government;" and this motion, after "a general and extensive debate," prevailed by a nearly unanimous vote. The whole number present, as returned by the monitors, was two hundred and fifty-one, of whom two hundred and fifty were in the affirmative. By this triumphant vote did the early fathers of Massachusetts manifest their watchfulness for the rights of the people; and there is good reason to believe also, that among the motives which stimulated it, was a determination in this way to abolish Slavery. The Convention then resolved "to proceed

to the framing a new Constitution of Government." A grand Committee of thirty was chosen to perform these two important duties; and this Committee, after extended discussion, entrusted to John Adams alone the preparation of a Declaration of Rights, and to a Sub-Committee, consisting of James Bowdoin, Samuel Adams and John Adams, the duty of preparing the Form of a Constitution, which Sub-Committee again delegated the task to John Adams; so that to the pen of this illustrious citizen, we are indebted primarily both for the Declaration of Rights and the Form of the Constitution.

It is not difficult to trace most, if not all, of the ideas and provisions of our Preamble and Declaration of Rights, to their primitive sources. The Preamble, wherein the body politic is founded on the fiction of the social compact, was doubtless inspired by the writings of Sidney and Locke, and by the English discussions at the period of the Revolution of 1688, when this questionable theory did good service in response to the assumptions of Filmer, and as a shield against arbitrary power. Of the different provisions in the Bill of Rights, some are in the very words of Magna Charta; others are derived from the ancient common law, the Petition of Right and the Bill of Rights of 1688, while no less than sixteen may be found substantially in the Virginia Bill of Rights; but these again are in great part derived from the earlier fountains.

And now, sir, you have before you for revision and amendment this early work of our Fathers. I do not stop to consider its peculiar merits. With satisfaction I might point to special safeguards by which our rights have been protected against usurpations, whether executive, legislative or judicial. With pride I might dwell on those words which banished Slavery from our soil, and rendered the Declaration of Independence here with us a living letter. But the hour does not require or admit any such service. You have a practical duty which I seek to promote; and I now take leave of the whole subject, with the simple remark, that a document proceeding from such a pen — drawn from such sources — with such an origin in all respects — speaking so early for Human Rights — and now for more than threescore years and ten a household word to the people of Massachusetts — should be touched by the Convention only with extreme care.

# FINGER-POINT FROM PLYMOUTH ROCK.

SPEECH AT THE PLYMOUTH FESTIVAL IN COMMEMORATION OF THE EMBARKATION OF THE PILGRIMS, 1ST AUGUST, 1853.

---

The President, in giving the next toast, said they had already been delighted with the words of a distinguished member of the Senate of the United States. They were favored with the presence of another; and he would give as a sentiment: —

"*The Senate of the United States,* — The concentrated light of the stars of the Union."

Mr. Sumner responded as follows: —

MR. PRESIDENT. — You bid me speak for the Senate of the United States. But I cannot forget that there is another voice here, of classical eloquence, which might more fitly render this service. As one of the humblest members of that body, and associated with the public councils for a brief period only, I should prefer that my distinguished colleague [Mr. Everett], whose fame is linked with a long political life, should speak for it. And there is yet another here [Mr. Hale], who, though not at this moment a member of the Senate, has, throughout an active and brilliant career, marked by a rare combination of ability, eloquence, and good humor, so identified himself with it in the public mind, that he might well speak for it always, and when he speaks all are pleased to listen. But, sir, you have ordered it otherwise.

From the tears and trials at Delft Haven, from the deck of the "Mayflower," from the landing at Plymouth Rock, to the Senate of the United States, is a mighty contrast, covering whole spaces of history, hardly less than from the wolf that suckled Romulus and Remus to that Roman Senate which, on curule chairs, swayed Italy and the world. From these obscure beginnings of poverty and weakness, which you now piously commemorate, and on which all our minds naturally rest to-day, you bid us leap to that marble Capitol, where thirty-one powerful republics, bound in indissoluble union, a Plural Unit, are gathered together in legislative body, constituting a part of One Government, which, stretching from ocean to ocean, and counting millions of people beneath its majestic rule, surpasses far in wealth and might any Government of the Old World when the little band of Pilgrims left it, and now promises to be a clasp between Europe and Asia, bringing the most distant places near together, so that there shall be no more Orient or Occident. It were interesting to dwell on the stages of this grand procession; but it is enough on this occasion merely to glance at them and pass on.

Sir, it is the Pilgrims that we commemorate to-day; not the Senate. For this moment, at least, let us tread under foot all pride of empire, — all exultation in our manifold triumphs of industry, of science, of literature, — with all the crowding anticipations of the vast untold Future, — that we may reverently bow before the forefathers. The day is theirs. In the contemplation of their virtue we shall derive a lesson, which, like truth, may judge us sternly; but, if we can really follow it, like truth, it shall make us free. For myself, I accept the admonitions of the day. It may teach us all never, by word or act, although we may be few in numbers or alone, to swerve from those primal principles of duty, which, from the landing at Plymouth Rock, have been the life of Massachusetts. Let me briefly unfold the lesson; though to the discerning soul it unfolds itself.

Few persons in history have suffered more from contemporary misrepresentation, abuse, and persecution, than the English Puritans. At first a small body, they were regarded with indifference and contempt. But by degrees they grew in numbers, and drew into their company men of education, intelligence, and even of rank. Reformers in all ages have had little of blessing from the world which they sought to serve; but the Puritans were not disheartened. Still they persevered. The obnoxious laws of conformity they vowed to withstand till, in the fervid language of the time, "they be sent back to the darkness from whence they came." Through them the spirit of modern Freedom made itself potently felt in its great warface with Authority, in Church, in Literature and in the State; in other words, for religious, intellectual and political emancipation. The Puritans primarily aimed at religious Freedom; for this they contended in Parliament, under Elizabeth and James; for this they suffered; but so connected are all these great and glorious interests, that the struggles for one have always helped the others. Such service did they do, that Hume, whose cold nature sympathized little

with their burning souls, is obliged to confess that to the Puritans alone "the English owe the whole freedom of their constitution."

As among all reformers, so among them there were differences of degree. Some continued within the pale of the National Church, and there pressed their ineffectual attempts in behalf of the good cause. Some at length, driven by conscientious convictions, and unwilling to be partakers longer in its enormities, stung also by the cruel excesses of magisterial power, openly disclaimed the National Establishment and became a separate sect, first under the name of Brownists, from the person who had led in this new organization, and then under the better name of *Separatists.* I like this word, sir. It has a meaning. After long struggles in Parliament and out of it, in Church and State, continued through successive reigns, the Puritans finally triumphed, and the despised sect of Separatists, swollen in numbers, and now under the denomination of Independents, with Oliver Cromwell at their head and John Milton as his Secretary, ruled England. Thus is prefigured the final triumph of all, however few in numbers, who sincerely devote themselves to Truth.

The Pilgrims of Plymouth were among the earliest of the Separatists. As such, they knew by bitter experience all the sharpness of persecution. Against them the men in power raged like the heathen. Against them the whole fury of the law was directed. Some were imprisoned; all were impoverished, while their name became a by-word of reproach. For safety and freedom the little band first sought shelter in Holland, where they continued in indigence and obscurity for more than ten years, when they were inspired to seek a home in this unknown Western world. Such, in brief, is their history. I could not say more of it without intruding upon your time; I could not say less without injustice to them.

Rarely have austere principles been expressed with more gentleness than from their lips. By a covenant with the Lord, they had vowed to walk in all His ways, according to their best endeavors, *whatsoever it should cost them*, — and also to receive whatsoever truth should be made known from the written word of God. Repentance and prayers, patience and tears, were their weapons. "It is not with us," said they, "as with other men, whom small things can discourage or small discontentments cause to wish themselves at home again." And then, again, on another occasion, their souls were lifted to utterance like this: "When we are in our graves it will be all one, whether we have lived in plenty or penury, whether we have died in a bed of down or on locks of straw." Self-sacrifice is never in vain, and they foresaw, with the clearness of prophecy, that out of their trials should come a transcendent Future. "As one small candle," said an early Pilgrim Governor, "may light a thousand, so the light kindled here may in some sort shine even to the whole nation."

And yet these men, with such sublime endurance and such lofty faith, are among those who are sometimes called "Puritan knaves" and "knaves-Puritans," and who were branded by King James as the "very pests in the Church and Commonwealth." The small company of our forefathers became the jest and gibe of fashion and power. The phrase "men of one idea" had not been invented then; but, in equivalent language, they were styled "the pinched fanatics of Leyden." A contemporary poet and favorite of Charles the First, Thomas Carew, lent his genius to their defamation. A masque, from his elegant and careful pen, was performed by the monarch and his courtiers, wherein the whole plantation of New England was turned to royal sport. The jeer broke forth in the exclamation, that it had "purged more virulent humors from the politic bodies than guaiacum and all the West Indian drugs from the natural bodies of the kingdom." *

And these outcasts, despised in their own day by the proud and great, are the men whom we have met in this goodly number to celebrate; not for any victory of war; not for any triumph of discovery, science, learning, or eloquence; not for worldly success of any kind. How poor are all these things by the side of that divine virtue which made them, amidst the reproach, the obloquy and the hardness of the world, hold fast to Freedom and Truth! Sir, if the honors of this day are not a mockery; if they do not expend themselves in mere selfish gratulation; if they are a sincere homage to the character of the Pilgrims — and I cannot suppose otherwise, — then is it well for us to be here. Standing on Plymouth Rock, at their great anniversary, we cannot fail to be elevated by their example. We see clearly what it has done for the world, and what it has done for their fame. No pusillanimous soul here to-day will declare their self-sacrifice, their deviation from received

* This masque, entitled *Cælum Britannicum*, was performed at Whitehall, 18th February, 1673.

opinions, their unquenchable thirst for liberty, an error or illusion. From gushing multitudinous hearts we now thank these lowly men that they dared to be true and brave. Conformity or compromise might, perhaps, have purchased for them a profitable peace, but not peace of mind; it might have secured place and power, but not repose; it might have opened a present shelter, but not a home in history and in men's hearts till time shall be no more. All will confess the true grandeur of their example, while, in vindication of a cherished principle, they stood alone, against the madness of men, against the law of the land, against their king. Better be the despised Pilgrim, a fugitive for freedom, than the halting politician, forgetful of principle, "with a Senate at his heels."

Such, sir, is the voice from Plymouth Rock, as it salutes my ears. Others may not hear it. But to me it comes in tones which I cannot mistake. I catch its words of noble cheer: —

"New occasions teach new duties; Time makes ancient good uncouth;
They must upward still and onward who would keep abreast of Truth:
Lo, before us gleam her camp-fires! we ourselves must Pilgrims be,
Launch our Mayflower, and steer boldly through the desperate winter sea."

# THE LANDMARK OF FREEDOM; FREEDOM NATIONAL.

SPEECH IN THE SENATE OF THE UNITED STATES, AGAINST THE REPEAL OF THE MISSOURI PROHIBITION OF SLAVERY NORTH OF 36° 30′ IN THE NEBRASKA AND KANSAS BILL, 21ST FEBRUARY, 1854.

---

On the 14th December, 1853, Mr. Dodge of Iowa, asked and obtained leave to introduce a Bill to organize the Territory of Nebraska, which was read a first and second time, by unanimous consent, and referred to the Committee on Territories. This was a simple Territorial Bill, in the common form, containing no allusion to Slavery, and not in any way undertaking to touch the existing Prohibition of Slavery in this Territory.

On the 4th January, 1854, Mr. Douglas, of Illinois, as Chairman of the Committee on Territories, reported this Bill back to the Senate, with various amendments, accompanied by a Special Report. By this Bill only a single Territory was constituted under the name of Nebraska; the existing Prohibition of Slavery was not directly overthrown, but it was declared that the States formed out of this Territory, should be admitted into the Union "with or without Slavery," as they should desire.

On the 16th January, Mr. Dixon, of Kentucky, in order to accomplish directly what the Bill did only indirectly, gave notice of an amendment, to the effect that the existing Prohibition of Slavery "shall not be so construed as to apply to the Territory contemplated by this Act, or to any other Territory of the United States; but that the citizens of the several States or Territories shall be at liberty to take and hold their Slaves within any of the Territories of the United States, or of the States to be formed therefrom."

On the next day, 17th January, Mr. Sumner, in order to keep alive the existing prohibition, gave notice of the following amendment: —

"*Provided*, That nothing herein contained shall be construed to abrogate or in any way contravene the Act of March 6, 1820, entitled 'An Act to authorize the people of Missouri Territory to form a constitution and State government, and for the admission of such State into the Union on an equal footing with the original States, and to prohibit Slavery in certain Territories;' wherein it is expressly enacted that 'in all that territory ceded by France to the United States, under the name of Louisiana, which lies north of thirty-six degrees and thirty minutes north latitude, not included within the limits of the State contemplated by this act, Slavery and involuntary servitude, otherwise than in the punishment of crimes, whereof the party shall have been duly convicted, shall be, and is hereby, forever prohibited.'"

It is worthy of remark that at this stage the proposition of Mr. Dixon, and also that of Mr. Sumner, were equally condemned by the *Washington Union*, the official organ of the Administration. It had not then been determined to sustain the repeal.

On the 23d January, Mr. Douglas, from the Committee on Territories, submitted a new Bill as a substitute for that already reported. Here was a sudden change, by which the Territory was divided into two, Nebraska and Kansas, and the prohibition of Slavery was directly overthrown. According to his language at the time, there was "incorporated into it one or two other amendments, which make the provisions of the Bill upon other and more delicate questions, more clear and specific, so as to avoid all conflict of opinion." It was formally enunciated in the Bill, that the prohibition of Slavery "was superseded by the principles of the legislation of 1850, commonly called the Compromise Measures, and is hereby declared inoperative." This, of course, superseded the proposed amendment of Mr. Dixon, who subsequently declared his entire assent to the Bill in its new form. It also presented the issue directly raised in Mr. Sumner's proposed amendment.

On the next day, 24th January, when the amended Bill had just been laid upon the tables of Senators, and without allowing the necessary time even for its perusal, Mr. Douglas pressed its consideration upon the Senate. After some debate it was postponed until the 30th January, and made the special order from day to day until disposed of.

Meanwhile an appeal to the country was put forth by certain Senators and Representatives in Congress, calling themselves Independent Democrats. It was entitled, "Shall Slavery be permitted in Nebraska?" and proceeded in strong language to expose the violation of plighted faith and the wickedness about to be perpetrated. This document was extensively circulated, and did much to arouse the public.

On the 30th January, the Senate proceeded to the consideration of the Bill, when Mr. Douglas took the floor, and devoted himself to a denunciation of the appeal put forth by the Independent Democrats, characterizing its authors as "Abolition confederates," and particularly arraigning Mr. Chase of Ohio, and Mr. Sumner, the two Senators who had signed it. When he sat down, Mr. Chase replied at once in admirable remarks to the personal matters introduced, and was followed in a few words by Mr. Sumner; and this was the opening of the great debate which occupied for months the attention of the country.

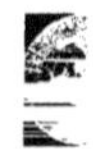

Mr. Sumner. — Mr. President, before the Senate adjourns I crave a single moment. As one of the signers of the address referred to by the Senator from Illinois [Mr. Douglas], I accept now openly, before the Senate and the country, my full responsibility for it, and deprecate no criticism from any quarter. That document was put forth in the discharge of a high public duty; on the precipitate introduction into this body of a measure which, as it seems to me, is not only subversive of an ancient landmark, but hostile to the peace, the harmony, and the best interests of the country. But, sir, in doing this, I judged the act, and not its author. I saw only the enormous proposition, and nothing of the Senator.

The language used is strong, but it is not stronger than the exigency required. Here is a measure which reverses the time-honored policy of our fathers in the restriction of Slavery; which sets aside the Missouri Compromise — a solemn compact, by which all the territory ceded by France under the name of Louisiana, was "forever" consecrated to freedom — and which violates, also, the alleged compromises of 1850; and all this is to open an immense territory to Slavery. Such a measure cannot be regarded without emotions too strong for speech; nor can it be justly described in common language. It is a soulless, eyeless monster — horrid, unshapely, vast; and this monster is now let loose upon the country.

Allow me one other word of explanation. It is true I desired that the consideration of this measure should not be pressed at once with indecent haste, as was proposed, even before the Senate could read the Bill in which it was embodied. I had not forgotten that the Missouri Bill, as appears from the Journals of Congress, when first introduced in December, 1819, was allowed to rest upon the table nearly two months before the discussion commenced. The proposition to undo the only part of that work which is now in any degree within the reach of Congress should be approached with even greater caution and reserve. The people have a right to be heard on this monstrous scheme; and there is no apology for that driving, galloping speed, which shall anticipate their voice, and, in its consequences, must despoil them of this right.

The debate was continued from day to day. On the 7th February, Mr. Douglas proposed still another change in his Bill. There seemed to be a perpetual difficulty in adjusting the language by which the existing prohibition of Slavery should be overthrown. He now moved to strike out the words referring to this prohibition, and to insert the following: —

"Which being inconsistent with the principles of non-intervention by Congress with Slavery in the States and Territories, as recognized by the legislation of 1850, commonly called the Compromise Measures, is hereby declared inoperative and void, it being the true intent and meaning of this Act not to legislate Slavery into any Territory or State, nor to exclude it therefrom; but to leave the people thereof perfectly free to form and regulate their domestic institutions in their own way, subject only to the Constitution of the United States."

On the 15th February this amendment was adopted by a vote of thirty-five yeas to ten nays. The debate was then continued upon the pending substitute reported by the Committee for the original Bill.

On the 21st February, Mr. Sumner took the floor and spoke as follows: —

Mr. President: I approach this discussion with awe. The mighty question, with its untold issues, oppresses me. Like a portentous cloud, surchanged with irresistible storm and ruin, it seems to fill the whole heavens, making me painfully conscious how unequal I am to the occasion — how unequal, also, is all that I can say, to all that I feel.

In delivering my sentiments here to-day, I shall speak frankly — according to my convictions, without concealment or reserve. But if anything fell from the Senator from Illinois [Mr. Douglas], in opening this discussion, which might seem to challenge a personal contest, I desire to say that I shall not enter upon it.

Let not a word or a tone pass my lips, to direct attention, for a moment, from the transcendent theme, — by the side of which Senators and Presidents are but dwarfs. I would not forget those amenities which belong to this place, and are so well calculated to temper the antagonism of debate; nor can I cease to remember and to feel, that, amidst all diversities of opinion, we are the representatives of thirty-one sister republics, knit together by indissoluble tie, and constituting that Plural Unit, which we all embrace by the endearing name of country.

The question presented for your consideration is not surpassed in grandeur by any which has occurred in our national history since the Declaration of Independence. In every aspect it assumes gigantic proportions, whether we simply consider the extent of territory it concerns, or the public faith and national policy which it assails, or that higher question — that *Question of Questions*, as far above others as Liberty is above the common things of life — which it opens anew for judgment.

It concerns an immense region, larger than the original thirteen States, vying in extent with all the existing free States — stretching over prairie, field and forest — interlaced by silver streams, skirted by protecting mountains, and constituting the heart of the North American continent — only a little smaller, let me add, than three great European countries combined — Italy, Spain and France — each of which, in succession, has dominated over the globe. This territory has already been likened, on this floor, to the Garden of God. The similitude is found, not merely in its present pure and virgin character, but in its actual geographical situation, occupying central spaces on this hemisphere, which, in their general relations, may well compare with that early Asiatic home. We are told that,

> Southward through Eden went a river large ;

so here a stream flows southward which is larger than the Euphrates. And here, too, amidst all the smiling products of nature, lavished by the hand of God, is the lofty tree of Liberty, planted by our fathers, which, without exaggeration, or even imagination, may be likened to

> ——————— the tree of life,
> High eminent, blooming ambrosial fruit
> Of vegetable gold.

It is with regard to this territory, that you are now called to exercise the grandest function of the lawgiver, by establishing those rules of polity which will determine its future character. As the twig is bent the tree inclines; and the influences impressed upon the early days of an empire, like those upon a child, are of inconceivable importance to its future weal or woe. The Bill now before us, proposes to organize and equip two new territorial establishments, with Governors, Secretaries, Legislative Councils, Legislators, Judges, Marshals, and the whole machinery of civil society. Such a measure, at any time, would deserve the most careful attention. But, at the present moment, it justly excites a peculiar interest, from the effort made — on pretences unsustained by facts — in violation of solemn covenant, and in disregard of the early principles of our fathers — to open this immense region to Slavery.

According to existing law, this territory is now guarded against Slavery by a positive prohibition, embodied in the Act of Congress, approved 6th March, 1820, preparatory to the admission of Missouri into the Union, as a sister State, and in the following explicit words:

"SEC. 8. *Be it further enacted,* That in all that territory *ceded by France to the United States, under the name of Louisiana,* which lies north 36° 30′ of north latitude, not included within the limits of the State contemplated by this Act, SLAVERY AND INVOLUNTARY SERVITUDE, otherwise than as the punishment of crimes, SHALL BE, AND IS HEREBY, FOREVER PROHIBITED."

It is now proposed to set aside this prohibition; but there seems to be a singular indecision as to the way in which the deed shall be done. From the time of its first introduction, in the report of the Committee on Territories, the proposition has assumed different shapes; and it promises to assume as many as Proteus; now, one thing in form, and now, another; now, like a river, and then, like flame; but, in every form and shape, identical in substance; with but one end and aim — its be-all and end-all — the overthrow of the Prohibition of Slavery. At first, it proposed simply to declare, that the States formed out of this territory should be admitted into the Union, "with or without Slavery," and did not directly assume to touch this prohibition. For some reason this was not satisfactory, and then it was precipitately proposed to declare, that the prohibition in the Missouri Act "was superseded by the principles of the legislation of 1850, commonly called the Compromise Measures, and is hereby declared inoperative." But this would not

do; and it is now proposed to enact, that the prohibition, "being inconsistent with the principles of non-intervention, by Congress, with Slavery in the States and Territories, as recognized by the legislation of 1850, commonly called the Compromise Measures, is hereby declared inoperative and void."

All this is to be done on pretences founded upon the Slavery enactments of 1850, thus seeking, with mingled audacity and cunning, "by indirection to find direction out." Now, sir, I am not here to speak in behalf of those measures, or to lean in any way upon their support. Relating to different subject-matters, contained in different acts, which prevailed successively, at different times, and by different votes — some persons voting for one measure, and some voting for another, and very few voting for all — they cannot be regarded as a *unit*, embodying conditions of compact, or compromise, if you please, adopted equally by all, and therefore obligatory on all. But since this broken series of measures has been adduced as an apology for the proposition now before us, I desire to say, that, such as they are, they cannot, by any effort of interpretation, by any distorting wand of power, by any perverse alchemy, be transmuted into a repeal of that original Prohibition of Slavery.

On this head there are several points to which I would merely call attention, and then pass on. *First:* The Slavery enactments of 1850 did not pretend, in terms, to touch, much less to change, the condition of the Louisiana Territory, which was already fixed by Congressional enactment. The two transactions related to different subject-matters. *Secondly:* The enactments do not directly touch the subject of Slavery, during the Territorial existence of Utah and New Mexico; but they provide prospectively, that, when admitted as States, they shall be received "with or without Slavery." Here certainly can be no overthrow of an Act of Congress which directly concerns a Territory *during its Territorial existence. Thirdly:* During all the discussion of these measures in Congress, and afterwards before the people, and through the public press, at the North and the South alike, no person was heard to intimate that the Prohibition of Slavery in the Missouri Act was in any way disturbed. And, *fourthly*, The acts themselves contain a formal provision, that "nothing herein contained shall be construed to impair or qualify anything" in a certain article of the resolutions annexing Texas, wherein it is expressly declared, that in territory north of the Missouri Compromise line, "Slavery, or involuntary servitude, except for crime, shall be prohibited."

But I do not dwell on these things. These pretences have been already amply refuted by able Senators who have preceded me. It is clear, beyond contradiction, that the Prohibition of Slavery in this Territory has not been superseded or in any way contravened by the Slavery Acts of 1850. The proposition before you is, therefore, original in its character, without sanction from any former legislation, and it must, accordingly, be judged by its merits, as an original proposition.

Here, sir, let it be remembered, that the friends of Freedom are not open to any charge of aggression. They are now standing on the defensive, guarding the early intrenchments thrown up by our fathers. No proposition to abolish Slavery anywhere is now before you; but, on the contrary, a proposition to abolish Freedom. The term Abolitionist, which is so often applied in reproach, justly belongs, on this occasion, to him who would overthrow this well-established landmark. He is, indeed, no Abolitionist of Slavery; let him be called, sir, an Abolitionist of Freedom. For myself, whether with many or few, my place is taken. Even if alone, my feeble arm should not be wanting as a bar against this outrage.

On two distinct grounds, "both strong against the deed," I arraign it: *First*, in the name of Public Faith, as an infraction of solemn obligations, assumed beyond recall by the South, on the admission of Missouri into the Union as a Slave State. *Secondly*, I arraign it, in the name of Freedom, as an unjustifiable departure from the original Anti-slavery policy of our fathers. These two heads I propose to consider in their order, glancing under the latter at the objections to the Prohibition of Slavery in the Territories.

And here, sir, before I approach the argument, indulge me with a few preliminary words on the character of this proposition. Slavery is the forcible subjection of one human being, in person, labor and property, to the will of another. In this simple statement is involved its whole injustice. There is no offence against religion, against morals, against humanity, which may not, in the license of this enormity, stalk "unwhipt of justice." For the husband and wife there is no marriage; for the mother there is no assurance that her infant child will not be ravished from her breast; for all who bear the name of Slave, there is nothing that they can call their own. Without a father, without a mother, almost without a God, the slave has nothing but a master. It would be contrary to that Rule of Right, which is ordained by God, if such a system, though mitigated often by a patriarchal kindness, and by a plausible physical comfort, could be otherwise than pernicious in its influences. It is confessed that the master suffers not less than the slave. And this is not all. The whole social fabric is disorganized; labor loses its dignity; industry sickens; education finds no schools, and all the land of Slavery is impoverished. And now, sir, when the conscience of mankind is at last aroused to these things; when, throughout the civilized world, a slave-dealer is a by-word and a reproach, we, as a nation, are about to open a new market to the traffickers in flesh, that haunt the shambles of the South. Such an act, at this time, is removed from all reach of that palliation often vouchsafed to Slavery. This wrong, we are speciously told, by those who seek to defend it, is not our original sin. It was entailed upon us, so we are instructed, by our ancestors; and the responsibility is often, with exultation, thrown upon the mother country. Now, without stopping to inquire into the value of this apology, which is never adduced in behalf of other abuses, and which availed nothing against that kingly power imposed by the mother country, which our fathers overthrew, it is sufficient for the present purpose to know, that it is now proposed to make Slavery our own original act. Here is a fresh case of actual transgression, which we cannot cast upon the shoulders of any progenitors, nor upon any mother country, distant in time or place. The Congress of the United States, the people of the

United States, at this day, in this vaunted period of light, will be responsible for it, so that it shall be said hereafter, so long as the dismal history of Slavery is read, that, in the year of Christ, 1854, a new and deliberate act was passed, by which a vast Territory was opened to its inroads.

Alone in the company of nations does our country assume this hateful championship. In despotic Russia, the serfdom which constitutes the "peculiar institution" of that great empire, is never allowed to travel with the imperial flag, according to the American pretension, into provinces newly acquired by the common blood and treasure, but is carefully restricted by positive prohibition, in harmony with the general conscience, within its ancient confines; and this prohibition — the Wilmot proviso of Russia — is rigorously enforced on every side, in all the provinces, as in Besarabia on the south, and Poland on the west, so that, in fact, no Russian nobleman has been able to move into these important territories with his slaves. Thus Russia speaks for Freedom, and disowns the slave-holding dogma of our country. Far away in the East, at the "gateways of the day," in effeminate India, Slavery has been condemned. In Constantinople, the queenly seat of the most powerful Mohammedan empire, where barbarism still mingles with civilization, the Ottoman Sultan has fastened upon it the stigma of disapprobation. The Barbary States of Africa, occupying the same parallels of latitude with the Slave States of our Union, and resembling them in the nature of their boundaries, their productions, their climate, and the "peculiar institution," which sought shelter in both, have been changed into Abolitionists.

Algiers, seated on the line of 36° 30′, has been dedicated to Freedom. Morocco, by its untutored ruler, has expressed its desire, stamped in the formal terms of a treaty, that the very name of Slavery may perish from the minds of men; and only recently, from the Bey of Tunis, has proceeded that noble act, by which, "in honor of God, and to distinguish man from the brute creation" — I quote his own words — he decreed its total abolition throughout his dominions. Let Christian America be willing to be taught by these examples. God forbid that our republic — "heir of all the ages, foremost in the files of time" — should adopt anew the barbarism which they have renounced.

As the effort now making is extraordinary in character, so no assumption seems too extraordinary to be wielded in its support. The primal truth of the Equality of men, proclaimed in our Declaration of Independence, has been assailed, and this Great Charter of our country discredited. Sir, you and I will soon pass away, but that charter will continue to stand above impeachment or question. The Declaration of Independence was a Declaration of Rights, and the language employed, though general in its character, must obviously be restrained within the design and sphere of a Declaration of Rights, involving no such absurdity as was attributed to it yesterday by the Senator from Indiana [Mr. Pettit]. Sir, it is a palpable fact that men are not born equal in physical strength or in mental capacities, in beauty of form or health of body. These mortal cloaks of flesh differ, as do these worldly garments. Diversity or inequality, in these respects, is the law of creation. But as God is no respecter of persons, and as all are equal in His

sight, whether Dives or Lazarus, master or slave, so are all equal in natural inborn rights; and pardon me if I say, it is a vain sophism to adduce in argument against this vital axiom of Liberty, the physical or mental inequalities by which men are characterized, or the unhappy degradation to which, in violation of a common brotherhood, they are doomed. To deny the Declaration of Independence is to rush on the bosses of the shield of the Almighty, — which, in all respects, the supporters of this measure seem to do.

To the delusive suggestion of the Senator from North Carolina [Mr. Badger], that, by the overthrow of this prohibition, the number of slaves will not be increased; that there will be simply a beneficent diffusion of Slavery, and not its extension, I reply at once, that this argument, if of any value — if not mere words and nothing else — would equally justify and require the overthrow of the Prohibition of Slavery in the Free States, and indeed, everywhere throughout the world. All the dikes which, in different countries, from time to time, with the march of civilization, have been painfully set up against the inroads of this evil, must be removed, and every land opened anew to its destructive flood. It is clear, beyond dispute, that by the overthrow of this prohibition, Slavery will be quickened, and slaves themselves will be multiplied, while new room and verge will be secured for the gloomy operations of slave law, under which free labor will droop, and a vast territory be smitten with sterility. Sir, a blade of grass would not grow where the horse of Attila had trod; nor can any true prosperity spring up in the foot-prints of the slave.

But it is argued, that slaves will not be carried into

Nebraska in large numbers, and that, therefore, the question is of small practical moment. My distinguished colleague [Mr. Everett], in his eloquent speech, hearkened to this apology, and allowed himself, while upholding the prohibition, to disparage its importance in a manner, from which I feel obliged kindly, but most strenuously, to dissent. Sir, the very census attests its vital consequence. There is Missouri, at this moment, with Illinois on the east and Nebraska on the west, all covering nearly the same spaces of latitude, and resembling each other in soil, climate and natural productions. Mark now the contrast! By the potent efficacy of the ordinance of the Northwestern Territory, Illinois is a free State, while Missouri has eighty-seven thousand four hundred and twenty-two slaves; and the simple question which challenges an answer is, whether Nebraska shall be preserved in the condition of Illinois, or surrendered to that of Missouri? Surely this cannot be treated lightly. But for myself, I am unwilling to measure the exigency of the prohibition by the number of persons, whether many or few, whom it may protect. Human rights, whether in a vast multitude or a solitary individual, are entitled to an equal and unhesitating support. In this spirit, the flag of our country only recently became the impenetrable panoply of a homeless wanderer, who claimed its protection in a distant sea; and in this spirit I am constrained to declare that there is no place accessible to human avarice, or human lust, or human force — whether in the lowest valley, or on the loftiest mountain top, whether on the broad flower-spangled prairies, or the snowy caps of the Rocky Mountains — where the prohibition of Slavery, like the commandments of the Decalogue, should not go.

I. And now, sir, in the name of that Public Faith, which is the very ligament of civil society, and which the great Roman orator tells us it is detestable to break even with an enemy, I arraign this scheme, and hold it up to the judgment of the country. There is an early Italian story of an experienced citizen, who, when told by his nephew that he had been studying, at the University of Bologna, the science of *right*, said in reply, "You have spent your time to little purpose. It would have been better had you learned the science of *might*, for that is worth two of the other;" and the bystanders of that day all agreed that the veteran spoke the truth. I begin, sir, by assuming that honorable Senators will not act in this spirit — that they will not substitute *might* for *right* — that they will not wantonly and flagitiously discard any obligation, pledge, or covenant, because they chance to possess the power; but that, as honest men, desirous to do right, they will confront this question.

Sir, the proposition before you involves not merely the repeal of an existing law, but the infraction of solemn obligations originally proposed and assumed by the South, after a protracted and embittered contest, as a covenant of peace — with regard to certain specified territory therein described, namely: "All that territory ceded by France to the United States, under the name of Louisiana;" according to which, in consideration of the admission into the Union of Missouri as a slave State, Slavery was forever prohibited in all the remaining part of this territory which lies north of 36° 30′. This arrangement, between different sections of the Union — the slave States of the first part and the free States of the second part — though usually known as the Missouri Compromise, was at the time styled a COMPACT. In its stipulations for Slavery, it was justly repugnant to the conscience of the North, and ought never to have been made; but on that side it has been performed. And now the unperformed outstanding obligations to Freedom, originally proposed and assumed by the South, are resisted.

Years have passed since these obligations were embodied in the legislation of Congress, and accepted by the country. Meanwhile, the statesmen by whom they were framed and vindicated have, one by one, dropped from this earthly sphere. Their living voices cannot now be heard, to plead for the conservation of that Public Faith to which they were pledged. But this extraordinary lapse of time, with the complete fruition by one party of all the benefits belonging to it, under the compact, gives to the transaction an added and most sacred strength. Prescription steps in and with new bonds, confirms the original work, to the end that while men are mortal, controversies shall not be immortal. Death, with inexorable scythe, has mowed down the authors of this compact; but, with conservative hour-glass, the dread destroyer has counted out a succession of years, which now defile before us, like so many sentinels, to guard the sacred landmark of Freedom.

A simple statement of facts, derived from the journals of Congress and contemporary records, will show the origin and nature of this compact, the influence by which it was established, and the obligations which it imposed.

As early as 1818, at the first session of the fifteenth Congress, a Bill was reported to the House of Representatives, authorizing the people of the Missouri Territory to form a Constitution and State Government, for the admission of such State into the Union; but, at that session, no final action was had thereon. At the next session, in February, 1819, the Bill was again brought forward, when an eminent Representative of New York, whose life has been spared till this last summer, Mr. James Tallmadge, moved a clause prohibiting any further introduction of slaves into the proposed State, and securing Freedom to the children born within the State after its admission into the Union, on attaining twenty-five years of age. This important proposition, which assumed a power not only to prohibit the ingress of Slavery into the State itself, *but also to abolish it there*, was passed in the affirmative, after a vehement debate of three days. On a division of the question, the first part, prohibiting the further introduction of slaves, was adopted by eighty-seven yeas to seventy-six nays; the second part, providing for the emancipation of children, was adopted by eighty-two yeas to seventy-eight nays. Other propositions to thwart the operation of these amendments were voted down, and on the 17th February the Bill was read a third time, and passed with these important restrictions.

In the Senate, after debate, the provision for the emancipation of children was struck out by thirty-one yeas to seven nays; the other provision, against the further introduction of Slavery, was struck out by twenty-two yeas to sixteen nays. Thus emasculated, the Bill was returned to the House, which, on 2d March, by a vote of seventy-eight nays to seventy-six yeas, refused its concurrence. The Senate adhered to their amendments, and the House, by seventy-eight yeas to sixty-six nays, adhered to their disagreement; and so at this session the Missouri Bill was lost; and here was a temporary triumph for Freedom.

Meanwhile, the same controversy was renewed on the Bill pending at the same time for the organization of the Territory of Arkansas, then known as the southern part of the Territory of Missouri. The restrictions already adopted in the Missouri Bill were moved by Mr. Taylor, of New York, subsequently Speaker; but after at least six close votes, on the yeas and nays, in one of which the House was equally divided, eighty-eight yeas to eighty-eight nays, they were lost. Another proposition by Mr. Taylor, simpler in form, that Slavery should not hereafter be introduced into this Territory, was lost by ninety nays to eighty-six yeas; and the Arkansas Bill on 25th February was read the third time and passed. In the Senate, Mr. Burrill, of Rhode Island, moved, as an amendment, the prohibition of the further introduction of Slavery into this Territory, which was lost by nineteen nays to fourteen yeas. And thus, without any provision for Freedom, Arkansas was organized as a Territory; and here was a triumph of Slavery.

At this same session, Alabama was admitted as a slave State, without any restriction or objection.

It was in the discussion on the Arkansas Bill, at this session, that we find the earliest suggestion of a Compromise. Defeated in his efforts to prohibit Slavery in this Territory, Mr. Taylor stated that "he thought it important that some line should be designated beyond which Slavery should not be permitted," and he moved its prohibition hereafter in all territories of the United States north of 36° 30′ north latitude, *without any exception of Missouri, which is north of this line.* This proposition, though withdrawn after debate, was at once welcomed by Mr. Livermore, of New Hampshire, "as made in the true spirit of compromise." It was opposed by Mr. Rhea, of Tennessee, on behalf of Slavery, who avowed himself against every restriction; and also by Mr. Ogle, of Pennsylvania, on behalf of Freedom, who was "against any Compromise by which Slavery, in any of the Territories, should be recognized or sanctioned by Congress." In this spirit it was opposed and supported by others, among whom was General Harrison, afterwards President of the United States, who "assented to the expediency of establishing some such line of discrimination;" but proposed a line due west from the mouth of the Des Moines, thus constituting the northern, and not the southern boundary of Missouri, the partition line between Freedom and Slavery.

But this idea of Compromise, though suggested by Mr. Taylor, was thus early adopted and vindicated in this very debate, by an eminent character, — Mr. Louis McLane, of Delaware, — who has since held high office in the country, and enjoyed no common measure of public confidence. Of all the leading actors in these early scenes, he and Mr. Mercer alone are yet spared. On this occasion he said:

"The fixing of a line on the west of the Mississippi, north of which Slavery shall not be tolerated, *had always been with him a favorite policy*, and he hoped the day was not distant when, upon principles of *fair compromise*, it might constitutionally be effected. The present attempt he regarded as premature."

After opposing the restriction on Missouri, he concluded by declaring:

"At the same time, I do not mean to abandon the policy to which I alluded in the commencement of my remarks. I think it but fair that both sections of the Union should be accommodated on this subject, with regard to which so much feeling has been manifested. The same great motives of policy which reconciled and harmonized the jarring and discordant elements of our system originally, and which enabled the framers of our happy Constitution to compromise the different interests which then prevailed on this and other subjects, if properly cherished by us, will enable us to achieve similar objects. If we meet upon principles of reciprocity, we cannot fail to do justice to all. *It has already been avowed, by gentlemen on this floor from the South and the West, that they will agree upon a line which shall divide the slaveholding from the non-slaveholding States. It is this proposition I am anxious to effect; but I wish to effect it by some* COMPACT *which shall be binding upon all parties, and all subsequent Legislatures;* which cannot be changed, and will not fluctuate with the diversity of feeling and of sentiment to which this empire, in its march, must be destined. There is a vast and immense tract of country west of the Mississippi yet to be settled, and intimately connected with the Northern section of the Union, *upon which this compromise can be effected.*"

The suggestions of Compromise were at this time vain; each party was determined. The North, by the prevailing voice of its representatives, claimed all for Freedom; the South, by its potential command of the Senate, claimed all for Slavery.

The report of this debate aroused the country. For the first time in our history, Freedom, after an animated struggle, hand to hand, had been kept in check by Slavery. The original policy of our fathers in the restriction of slavery was suspended, and this giant wrong threatened to stalk into all the broad national domain. Men at the North were humbled and amazed. The imperious demands of Slavery seemed incredible. Meanwhile, the whole subject was adjourned from Congress to the people. Through the press and at public meetings, an earnest voice was raised against the admission of Missouri into the Union without the restriction of Slavery. Judges left the bench and clergymen the pulpit, to swell the indignant protest which went up from good men, without distinction of party or of pursuit.

The movement was not confined to a few persons, nor to a few States. A public meeting at Trenton, in New Jersey, was followed by others in New York and Philadelphia, and finally at Worcester, Salem and Boston, where Committees were organized to rally the country. The citizens of Baltimore, in public meeting at the court-house with the Mayor in the chair, resolved that the future admission of slaves into the States hereafter formed west of the Mississippi, ought to be prohibited by Congress. Villages, towns and cities, by memorial, petition and prayer, called upon Congress to maintain the great principle of the prohibition of Slavery. The same principle was also commended by the resolutions of State Legislatures; and Pennsylvania, inspired by the teachings of Franklin and the convictions of the respectable denomination of Friends, unanimously asserted at once the right and the duty of Congress to prohibit Slavery west of the Mississippi, and solemnly appealed to her sister States, "to refuse to covenant with crime." New Jersey and Delaware followed, both also unanimously. Ohio asserted the same principle: so did also Indiana. The latter State, not content with providing for the future, severely censured one of its Senators, for his vote to organize Arkansas without the prohibition of Slavery. The resolutions of New York were reinforced by the recommendation of De Witt Clinton.

Amidst these excitements, Congress came together in December, 1819, taking possession of these Halls of the Capitol for the first time since their desolation by the British. On the day after the receipt of the President's Message, two several Committees of the House were constituted, one to consider the application of Maine, and the other of Missouri, to enter the Union as separate and independent States. With only the delay of a single day, the bill for the admission of Missouri was reported to the House without the restriction of Slavery; but, as if shrinking from the immediate discussion of the great question it involved, afterwards, on the motion of Mr. Mercer, of Virginia, its consideration was postponed for several weeks; all which, be it observed, is in open contrast with the manner in which the present discussion has been precipitated upon Congress. Meanwhile, the Maine Bill, when reported to the House, was promptly acted upon, and sent to the Senate.

In the interval between the report of the Missouri Bill and its consideration by the House, a Committee was constituted on motion of Mr. Taylor, of New York, to inquire into the expediency of prohibiting the introduction of Slavery into the Territories west of the Mississippi. This Committee, at the end of a fortnight, was discharged from further consideration of the subject, which, it was understood, would enter into the postponed debate on the Missouri Bill. This early effort to interdict Slavery in the Territories by a special law, is worthy of notice, on account of some of the expressions of opinion which it drew forth. In the course of his remarks, Mr. Taylor declared, that "he presumed there were no members — he knew of none — who doubted the constitutional power of Congress to impose such a restriction on the Territories."

A generous voice from Virginia recognized at once the right and duty of Congress. This was from Charles Fenton Mercer, who declared that "When the question proposed should come fairly before the House, he should support the proposition. He should record his vote against suffering the dark cloud of inhumanity, which now darkened his country, from rolling on beyond the peaceful shores of the Mississippi."

At length, on the 26th January, 1820, the House resolved itself into a Committee of the Whole on the Missouri Bill, and proceeded with its discussion, day by day, till the 28th February, when it was reported back with amendments. But meanwhile the same question was presented to the Senate, where a conclusion was reached earlier than in the House. A clause for the admission of Missouri was moved by way of tack to the Maine Bill. To this an amendment was moved by Mr. Roberts, of Pennsylvania, prohibiting the further introduction of Slavery into the State, which, after a fortnight's debate, was defeated by twenty-seven nays to sixteen yeas.

The debate in the Senate was of unusual interest and splendor. It was especially illustrated by an effort of transcendent power from that great lawyer and orator, William Pinkney. Recently returned from a succession of missions to foreign courts, and at this time the acknowledged chief of the American bar, particularly skilled in questions of constitutional law, his course as a Senator from Maryland was calculated to produce a profound impression. In a speech which for two days drew to this chamber an admiring throng, and at the time was fondly compared with the best examples of Greece and Rome, he first authoritatively proposed and developed the Missouri Compromise. His masterly effort was mainly directed against the restriction upon Missouri, but it began and ended with the idea of compromise. "Notwithstanding," he says, "occasional appearances of rather an unfavorable description, I have long since persuaded myself that the *Missouri question*, as it is called, might be laid to rest, with innocence and safety, by some *conciliatory Compromise* at least, by which, as is our duty, we might reconcile the extremes of conflicting views and feelings, without any sacrifice of constitutional principles." And he closed with the hope that the restriction on Missouri would not be pressed, but that the whole question "might be disposed of in a manner satisfactory to all, *by a positive prohibition of Slavery in the Territory to the north and west of Missouri.*"

This authoritative proposition of Compromise, from the most powerful advocate of the unconditional admission of Missouri, was made in the Senate on the 21st January. From various indications, it seems to have found prompt favor in that body. Finally, on the 17th February, the union of Maine and Missouri in one Bill prevailed there, by twenty-three yeas to twenty-one nays. On the next day, Mr. Thomas, of Illinois, who had always voted with the South against any restriction upon Missouri, introduced the famous clause prohibiting Slavery north of 36° 30′, which now constitutes the eighth section of the Missouri Act. An effort was made to include the Arkansas Territory within this prohibition; but the South united against this extension of the area of Freedom, and it was defeated by twenty-four nays to twenty yeas. The prohibition, as moved by Mr. Thomas, then prevailed, by thirty-four yeas to only ten nays. Among those in the affirmative were both the Senators from each of the Slave States, Louisiana, Tennessee, Kentucky, Delaware, Maryland and Alabama, and also one of the Senators from each of the Slave States, Mississippi and North Carolina, including in the honorable list the familiar names of William Pinkney, James Brown and William Rufus King.

This Bill, thus amended, is the first legislative embodiment of the Missouri Compact or Compromise, the essential conditions of which were, the admission of Missouri as a State without any restriction of Slavery; and the prohibition of Slavery in all the remaining territory of Louisiana north of 36° 30′. Janus-faced, with one front towards Freedom and another towards Slavery, this must not be confounded with the simpler proposition of Mr. Taylor, at the last session, to prohibit Slavery in all the territory north of 36° 30′, including Missouri. The Compromise now brought forward — following the early lead of Mr. McLane — both recognized and prohibited Slavery north of 36° 30′. Here, for the first time, these two opposite principles commingled in one legislative channel; and it is immediately subsequent to this junction that we discern the precise responsibility assumed by different parties. And now observe the indubitable and decisive fact. This Bill, thus composed, containing these two elements — this double measure — finally passed the Senate by a test vote of twenty-four yeas to twenty nays. The yeas embraced every Southern Senator, except Nathaniel Macon, of North Carolina, and William Smith, of South Carolina.

Mr. BUTLER, of S. C. (interrupting). Mr. Gaillard, of South Carolina, voted with Mr. Smith.

Mr. SUMNER. No, sir. The journal, which I now hold in my hand, shows that he voted for the Compromise. I repeat, that the yeas on this vital question embraced every Southern Senator, except Mr. Macon and Mr. Smith. The nays embraced every Northern Senator, except the two Senators from Illinois and one Senator from Rhode Island, and one from New Hampshire. And this, sir, is the record of the first stage in the adoption of the Missouri Compromise. First openly announced and vindicated on the floor of the Senate, by a distinguished Southern statesman, it was forced on the North by an almost unanimous Southern vote.

While things had thus culminated in the Senate, discussion was still proceeding in the other House on the original Missouri Bill. This was for a moment arrested by the reception from the Senate of the Maine Bill, embodying the Missouri Compromise. Upon this the debate was brief and the decision prompt. But here, even at this stage, as at every other, a Southern statesman intervenes. Mr. Smith, of Maryland, for many years an eminent Senator of that State, but at this time a representative, while opposing the restriction of Missouri, vindicated the prohibition of Slavery in the Territories, and thus practically accepted the Compromise:

"Mr. S. Smith said that he rose principally with a view to state his understanding of the proposed amendment, viz.: That it retained the boundaries of Missouri as delineated in the Bill; that it prohibited the admission of slaves west of the west line of Missouri, and north of the north line; that it did not interfere with the Territory of Arkansas, or the uninhabited land west thereof. *He thought the proposition not exceptionable*, but doubted the propriety of its forming a part of the Bill. He considered the power of Congress over the Territory as supreme, unlimited, before its admission; that Congress could impose on its Territories any restriction it thought proper; that if citizens go into the Territories thus restricted, they cannot carry with them slaves. They will be without slaves, and will be educated with prejudices and habits such as will exclude all desire, on their part, to admit Slavery when they shall become sufficiently numerous to be admitted as a State. And this is the advantage proposed by the amendment."

But the House was not disposed to abandon the substantial restriction of Slavery in Missouri, for what seemed its unsubstantial prohibition in an unsettled Territory. The Compromise was rejected, and the Bill left in its original condition. This was done by large votes. Even the prohibition of Slavery was thrown out by one hundred and fifty-nine yeas to eighteen nays, both the North and the South uniting against it; though, in this small but persistent minority, we find two Southern statesmen, Samuel Smith and Charles Fenton Mercer. The Senate, on receiving the Bill back from the House, insisted on their amendments. The House in turn insisted on their disagreement. According to parliamentary usage, a Committee of

Conference between the two Houses was appointed. Mr. Thomas, of Illinois, Mr. Pinkney, of Maryland, and Mr. James Barbour, of Virginia, composed this important Committee on the part of the Senate; and Mr. Holmes, of Maine, Mr. Taylor, of New York, Mr. Lowndes, of South Carolina, Mr. Parker, of Massachusetts, and Mr. Kinsey, of New Jersey, on the part of the House.

Meanwhile, the House had voted on the original Missouri Bill. An amendment, peremptorily interdicting all Slavery in the new State, was adopted by ninety-four yeas to eighty-six nays; and thus the Bill passed the House, and was sent to the Senate on the 1st March. Thus, after an exasperated and protracted discussion, the two Houses were at a dead-lock. The double-headed Missouri Compromise was the ultimatum of the Senate. The restriction of Slavery in Missouri, involving, of course, its prohibition in all the unorganized Territories, was the ultimatum of the House.

At this stage, on the 2d March, the Committee of Conference made their report, which was urged at once upon the House by Mr. Lowndes, the distinguished representative from South Carolina, and one of her most precious sons. And here sir, at the mention of this name, still so fragrant among us, let me for one moment stop this current of history, to express the tender admiration with which I am inspired. Mr. Lowndes died before my memory of political events; but he is still endeared by the self-abnegation of a single utterance — *that the Presidency is an office not to be sought or declined* — a sentiment, which, by its beauty, in one part at least, shames the vileness of aspiration in our day, and will ever live as an amaranthine flower. Such a man, on any occasion, would be a host; but he now threw his great soul into the work. He even objected to a motion to print the report, on the ground "that it would imply a determination in the House to delay a decision of the subject to-day, which he had hoped the House was fully prepared for." The question then came on striking out the restriction in the Missouri Bill. The report in the *National Intelligencer* says:

"Mr. Lowndes spoke briefly in support of the Compromise recommended by the Committee of Conference, and urged with great earnestness the propriety of a decision which would restore tranquillity to the country, which was demanded by every consideration of discretion, of moderation, of wisdom and of virtue.

"Mr. Mercer, of Virginia, followed on the same side with great earnestness, and had spoken about half an hour, when he was compelled, by indisposition, to resume his seat."

Such efforts, pressed with Southern ardor, were not unavailing. In conformity with the report of the Committee, the whole question was forthwith put at rest. Maine and Missouri were each admitted into the Union as independent States. The restriction of Slavery in Missouri was abandoned by a vote in the House of ninety yeas to eighty-seven nays; and the prohibition of Slavery in Territories north of 36° 30′, exclusive of Missouri, was substituted by a vote of one hundred and thirty-four yeas to forty-two nays. Among the distinguished Southern names in the affirmative, are Louis McLane, of Delaware; Samuel Smith, of Maryland; William Lowndes, of South Carolina; and Charles Fenton Mercer, of Virginia.

The title of the Missouri Bill was amended in conformity with this prohibition, by adding the words, "and to prohibit Slavery in certain Territories." *The bills then passed both Houses without a division;* and, on the morning of the 3d March, 1820, the *National Intelligencer* contained an exulting article, entitled "The Question Settled."

Another paper, published in Baltimore, immediately after the passage of the Compromise, vindicated it as a perpetual compact, which could not be disturbed. The language is so clear and strong that I will read it, although it has been already quoted by my able and most excellent friend from Ohio [Mr. Chase]:

> "*It is true the Compromise is supported only by the letter of the law, repealable by the authority which enacted it; but the circumstances of the case give this law a* MORAL FORCE *equal to that of a positive provision of the Constitution; and we do not hazard anything by saying that the Constitution exists in its observance.* Both parties have sacrificed much to conciliation. *We wish to see the* COMPACT *kept in good faith*, and we trust that a kind Providence will open the way to relieve us of an evil which every good citizen deprecates as the supreme curse of the country." — *Niles's Register.*

Sir, the distinguished leaders in this settlement were all from the South. As early as February, 1819, Louis McLane, of Delaware, had urged it upon Congress, in the form of "compact binding upon all subsequent Legislatures." It was in 1820 brought forward and upheld in the Senate by William Pinkney, of Maryland, and passed in that body by the vote of every Southern Senator except two, against the vote of every Northern Senator except four. In the House, it was welcomed at once by Samuel Smith, of Maryland, and Charles Fenton Mercer, of Virginia. The Committee of Conference, through which it finally prevailed, was filled, on the part of the Senate, with inflexible partisans of the South, such as might fitly represent the sentiments of its President, John Gaillard, a Senator from South Carolina; on the part of the House, it was nominated by Henry Clay, the Speaker, and Representative from Kentucky. This Committee, thus constituted, drawing its double life from the South, was unanimous in favor of the Compromise. A private letter from Mr. Pinkney, written at the time, and preserved by his distinguished biographer, shows that the report made by the Committee came from him:

"The bill for the admission of Missouri into the Union (*without* restriction as to Slavery) may be considered as past. That bill was sent back again this morning from the House, *with the restriction as to Slavery.* The Senate voted to amend it by striking out the restriction (twenty-seven to fifteen), and proposed, as another amendment, *what I have all along been the advocate of, a restriction upon the vacant territory to the north and west, as to Slavery.* To-night the House of Representatives have agreed to *both* of these amendments, in opposition to their former votes, and this affair is settled. To-morrow we shall (of course) recede from our amendments as to Maine (our object being effected), and both States will be admitted. *This happy result has been accomplished by the Conference, of which I was a member on the part of the Senate, and of which I proposed the report which has been made.*" — *Wheaton's Life of Pinkney.*

Thus again the Compromise takes its life from the South. Proposed in the Committee by Mr. Pinkney, it was urged on the House of Representatives, with great earnestness, by Mr. Lowndes, of South Carolina, and Mr. Mercer, of Virginia; and here again is the most persuasive voice of the South. When passed by Congress, it next came before the President, James

Monroe, of Virginia, for his approval, who did not sign it till after the unanimous opinion, in writing, of his Cabinet, composed of John Quincy Adams, William H. Crawford, Smith Thompson, John C. Calhoun, and William Wirt — a majority of whom were Southern men — that the prohibition of Slavery in the Territories was constitutional. Thus yet again the Compromise takes its life from the South.

As the Compromise took its life from the South, so the South, in the judgment of its own statesmen at the time, and according to unquestionable facts, was the conquering party. It gained forthwith its darling desire, the first and essential stage in the admission of Missouri as a Slave State, successfully consummated at the next session; and subsequently the admission of Arkansas, also as a Slave State. From the crushed and humbled North, it received more than the full consideration stipulated in its favor. On the side of the North the contract has been more than executed. And now the South refuses to perform the part which it originally proposed and assumed in this transaction. With the consideration in its pocket, it repudiates the bargain which it forced upon the country. This, sir, is a simple statement of the present question.

A subtle German has declared, that he could find heresies in the Lord's Prayer — and I believe it is only in this spirit that any flaw can be found in the existing obligations of this compact. As late as 1848, in the discussions of this body, the Senator from Virginia, who usually sits behind me [Mr. Mason], but who is not now in his seat, while condemning it in many aspects, says:

"Yet as it was agreed to as a Compromise by the *South* for

the sake of the Union, *I would be the last to disturb it.*" — *Cong. Globe, Appendix,* 1st *sess.* 30*th Cong., vol.* xix. p. 887.

Even this determined Senator recognized it as an obligation which he would not disturb. And, though disbelieving the original constitutionality of the arrangement, he was clearly right. I know, sir, that it is in form simply a legislative Act; but as the Act of Settlement in England, declaring the rights and liberties of the subject, and settling the succession of the Crown, has become a permanent part of the British Constitution, irrepealable by any common legislation, so this Act under all the circumstances attending its passage, also by long acquiescence and the complete performance of its conditions by one party, has become a part of our fundamental law, irrepealable by any common legislation. As well might Congress at this moment undertake to overhaul the original purchase of Louisiana, as unconstitutional, and now, on this account, thrust away that magnificent heritage, with all its cities, States and territories, teeming with civilization. The Missouri Compact, in its unperformed obligations to Freedom, stands at this day as impregnable as the Louisiana purchase.

I appeal to Senators about me, not to disturb it. I appeal to the Senators from Virginia, to keep inviolate the compact made in their behalf by James Barbour and Charles Fenton Mercer. I appeal to the Senators from South Carolina, to guard the work of John Gaillard and William Lowndes. I appeal to the Senators from Maryland, to uphold the Compromise which elicited the constant support of Samuel Smith, and was first triumphantly pressed by the unsurpassed eloquence of Pinkney. I appeal to the Senators from

Delaware, to maintain the landmark of Freedom in the Territory of Louisiana, early espoused by Louis McLane. I appeal to the Senators from Kentucky, not to repudiate the pledges of Henry Clay. I appeal to the Senators from Alabama, not to break the agreement sanctioned by the earliest votes in the Senate of their late most cherished fellow-citizen, William Rufus King. Sir, I have heard of an honor that felt a stain like a wound. If there be any such in this chamber — as surely there is — it will hesitate to take upon itself the stain of this transaction.

Sir, Congress may now set aside this obligation, repudiate this plighted faith, annul this compact; and some of you, forgetful of the *majesty of honest dealing*, in order to support Slavery, may consider it advantageous to use this power. To all such let me commend a familiar story: An eminent leader in antiquity, Themistocles, once announced to the Athenian Assembly, that he had a scheme to propose, highly beneficial to the State, but which could not be expounded to the many. Aristides, surnamed the Just, was appointed to receive the secret, and to report upon it. His brief and memorable judgment was, that, while nothing could be more advantageous to Athens, nothing could be more unjust; and the Athenian multitude, responding at once, rejected the proposition. It appears that it was proposed to burn the combined Greek fleet, which then rested in the security of peace in a neighboring sea, and thus confirm the naval supremacy of Athens. A similar proposition is now brought before the American Senate. You are asked to destroy a safeguard of Freedom, consecrated by solemn compact, under which the country is now reposing in the secu-

rity of peace, and thus confirm the supremacy of Slavery. To this institution and its partisans the proposition may seem to be advantageous; but nothing can be more unjust. Let the judgment of the Athenian multitude be yours.

This is what I have to say upon this head. I now pass to the second branch of the argument.

II. Mr. President, it is not only as an infraction of solemn compact, embodied in ancient law, that I arraign this bill. I arraign it also as a flagrant and extravagant departure from the original policy of our fathers, consecrated by their lives, opinions and acts.

And here, sir, bear with me in a brief recital of unquestionable facts. At the period of the Declaration of Independence, there was upwards of half a million colored persons in slavery throughout the United Colonies. These unhappy people were originally stolen from Africa, or were the children of those who had been stolen, and, though distributed throughout the whole country, were to be found in largest number in the Southern States. But the spirit of Freedom then prevailed in the land. The fathers of the Republic, leaders in the war of Independence, were struck with the inconsistency of an appeal for their own liberties, while holding in bondage their fellow-men, only "guilty of a skin not colored like their own." The same conviction animated the hearts of the people, whether at the North or South. In a town meeting, at Danbury, Connecticut, held on the 12th December, 1778, the following declaration was made:

"It is with singular pleasure we note the second article of the Association, in which it is agreed to import no more negro slaves, as we cannot but think it a palpable absurdity so loudly to complain of attempts to enslave *us* while we are actually enslaving *others*. — *Am. Archives, 4th Series*, vol. i. p. 1038.

The South responded in similar strains. At a meeting in Darien, Georgia, in 1775, the following important resolution was put forth:

"To show the world that we are not influenced by any contracted or interested motives, but by a general philanthropy for all mankind, of whatever climate, language, or complexion, *we hereby declare our disapprobation and abhorrence of the unnatural practice of Slavery in* (however the uncultivated state of the country or other specious arguments may plead for it) *a practice founded in injustice and cruelty, and highly dangerous to our liberties as well as lives, debasing part of our fellow-creatures below men and corrupting the virtue and morals of the rest*, and laying the basis of that liberty we contend for, and which we pray the Almighty to continue to the latest posterity, upon a very wrong foundation. We therefore resolve at all times to *use our utmost endeavors for the manumission* of our slaves in this Colony, upon the most safe and equitable footing for the masters and themselves." — *Am. Archives, 4th Series*, vol. i. p. 1135.

The soul of Virginia, during this period, found fervid utterance through Jefferson, who, by precocious and immortal words, has enrolled himself among the earliest Abolitionists of the country. In his address to the Virginia Convention of 1774, he openly avowed, while vindicating the rights of British America, that "the abolition of domestic Slavery is the greatest object of desire in these Colonies, *where it was unhappily introduced in their infant state.*" And then again, in the Declaration of Independence, he embodied sentiments, which, when practically applied, will give Freedom to every slave throughout the land. "We hold these truths to be self-evident," says our country, speaking by the voice of Jefferson, "that all men are created equal — that they are endowed with certain inalienable rights — that among these are life, *liberty*, and the pursuit of happiness." And again, in the Congress of the Confederation, he brought forward, as early as 1784, a resolution to exclude Slavery from all the territory "ceded or to be ceded" by the States of the Federal Government, including the whole territory now covered by Tennessee, Mississippi and Alabama. Lost at first by a single vote only, this measure was renewed in a more restricted form, at a subsequent day, by a son of Massachusetts, and in 1787 was finally confirmed in the Ordinance of the Northwestern Territory, by a unanimous vote of the States.

Thus early and distinctly do we discern the Anti-Slavery character of the founders of our Republic, and their determination to place the National Government, within the sphere of its jurisdiction, openly, actively and perpetually, on the side of Freedom.

The National Constitution was adopted in 1788. And here we discern the same spirit. The emphatic words of the Declaration of Independence, which our country took upon its lips as baptismal vows, when it claimed its place among the nations of the earth, were not forgotten. The preamble to the Constitution renews them, when it declares its object to be, among other things, "to establish justice, to promote the general welfare, and to secure the blessings of liberty to ourselves and posterity." Thus, according to undeniable words, the Constitution was ordained, not to establish, secure, or sanction Slavery — not to promote the special interest of slaveholders — not to make Slavery national in any way, form, or manner — not to foster this great wrong, but to "establish justice," "promote the general welfare," and "secure the blessings of Liberty." The discreditable words *Slave* and *Slavery* were not allowed to find a place in this instrument, while a clause was subsequently added by way of amendment, and, therefore, according to the rules of interpretation, particularly revealing the sentiments of the founders, which is calculated, like the Declaration of Independence, if practically applied, to carry Freedom everywhere within the sphere of its influence. It was specifically declared, that "no person shall be deprived of life, *liberty*, or property, without due process of law;" that is, without due presentment, indictment, or other judicial proceeding. Here is an express guard of personal Liberty, and an express interdict upon slavery anywhere within the national jurisdiction.

It is evident, from the debates on the National Constitution, that Slavery, like the Slave trade, was regarded as temporary; and it seems to have been supposed by many that they would both disappear together. Nor do any words employed in our day denounce it with an indignation more burning than those which glowed on the lips of the Fathers. Early in the Convention, Gouverneur Morris, of Pennsylvania, broke forth in the language of an Abolitionist: "He never would concur in upholding domestic Slavery. It was a nefarious institution. It was the curse of Heaven." In another mood, and with mild, juridical phrase, Mr. Madison "thought it wrong to admit in the Constitution the idea of property in man." And Washington, in letters written near this period —

which completely describe the aims of an Abolitionist — avowed "that it was among his first wishes to see some plan adopted by which Slavery may be abolished by law," and that to this end "his suffrage should not be wanting."

In this spirit was the National Constitution adopted. In this spirit the National Government was first organized under Washington. And here there is a fact of peculiar significance, to which I have already, on a former occasion, called attention, but which is well worthy of perpetual memory. At the time that this great chief took his first oath to support the Constitution of the United States, *the national ensign nowhere within the national territory covered a single slave.* On the sea, an execrable piracy, the trade in slaves, was still, to the national scandal, tolerated under the national flag. In the States, as a sectional institution, beneath the shelter of local laws, Slavery unhappily found a home. But in the only Territories at this time belonging to the nation, the broad region of the Northwest, it had already, by the Ordinance of Freedom, been made impossible, even before the adoption of the Constitution. The District of Columbia, with its Fatal Dowry, had not yet been acquired.

Entering upon his high duties, Washington, himself an Abolitionist, was surrounded by men, who, by their lives and declared opinions, were pledged to warfare with Slavery. There was John Adams, the Vice President — great vindicator and final negotiator of our National Independence — whose soul, flaming with Freedom, broke forth in the early declaration, that "consenting to Slavery is a sacrilegious breach of trust," and whose immitigable hostility to this wrong has been made immortal in his descendants. By his side, also, was a companion in arms and attached friend, the yet youthful and "incomparable" Hamilton — fit companion in early fame and genius with that darling of English history, Sir Philip Sidney, to whom the latter epithet has been reserved — who, as a member of the Abolition Society of New York, had only recently united in a solemn petition for those who, "though *free by the laws of God*, are held in Slavery *by the laws of the State*." There, too, was a noble spirit, of spotless virtue, and commanding influence, the ornament of human nature, who, like the sun, ever held an unerring course, John Jay. Filling the important post of Minister of Foreign Affairs under the Confederation, he found time to organize the Abolition Society of New York, and to act as its President, until by the nomination of Washington he became Chief Justice of the United States. In his sight, Slavery was an "iniquity" — "a sin of crimson dye," against which ministers of the gospel should testify, and which the Government should seek in every way to abolish. "Were I in the Legislature," he wrote, "I would present a bill for this purpose with great care, and I would never cease moving it till it became a law or I ceased to be a member. Till America comes into this measure, her prayers to Heaven will be impious." By such men was Washington surrounded, while from his own Virginia came the voice of Patrick Henry, amidst confessions that he was a master of slaves, crying, "I will not, I cannot justify it. However culpable my conduct, I will so far pay my devoir to virtue as to own the excellence and rectitude of her precepts, and lament my want of con-

formity to them." Such words as these, fitly coming from our leaders, belong to the true glories of the country:

> "While we such precedents can boast at home,
> Keep thy Fabricius and thy Cato, Rome!"

The earliest Congress under the Constitution adopted the Ordinance of Freedom for the Northwestern Territory, and thus ratified the prohibition of Slavery in all the existing Territories of the Union. In the list of those who sanctioned this act were men fresh from the labors of the Convention, and therefore familiar with its policy. But there is another voice which bears testimony in the same direction. Among the petitions presented to the first Congress, was one from the Abolition Society of Pennsylvania, signed by Benjamin Franklin, as President. This venerable votary of Freedom, who throughout a long life had splendidly served his country at home and abroad — who, as statesman and philosopher, had won the admiration of mankind — who had ravished the lightning from the skies and the sceptre from the tyrant — whose name, signed to the Declaration of Independence, gave added importance even to that great instrument, and then again signed to the Constitution of the United States, filled it with the charm of wisdom — in whom, more than in any other man, the true spirit of American Institutions, at once practical and humane, was embodied — who knew intimately the purposes and aspirations of the founders — this veteran statesman, then eighty-four years of age, appeared at the bar of that Congress, whose powers he had helped to define and establish, and, by the last political act of his long life, solemnly entreated "that it would be pleased to countenance the restoration of liberty to those unhappy men, who alone, in this land of Freedom, are degraded into perpetual bondage," and "that it would step to the very verge of the power vested in it for DISCOURAGING every species of traffic in the persons of our fellow-men." Only a short time after uttering this prayer, the patriot sage descended to the tomb; but he seems still to call upon Congress, in memorable words, *to step to the very verge of the powers vested in it to discourage Slavery;* and this prayer, now sounding from the tomb of Franklin, proclaims the true national policy of the Fathers. Not encouragement, but discouragement of slavery, not its *nationalization*, but its *denationalization*, was their rule.

The memorial of Franklin, with other memorials of a similar character, was referred to a Committee, and much debated in the House, which finally sanctioned the following resolution, and directed the same to be entered upon its journals, viz:

"That Congress have no authority to interfere in the emancipation of slaves, or in the treatment of them, within any of the States; *it remaining with the several States to provide any regulations therein which humanity may require.*"

This resolution, declaring the principle of non-intervention by Congress with Slavery in the States, was adopted by the same Congress which had solemnly affirmed the prohibition of Slavery in all the existing territory of the Union; and not only by the same Congress, but at the same session, so that one may be regarded as the complement of the other. And it is on these double acts, at the first organization of the Government, and the recorded sentiments of the founders, that I take my stand, and challenge all question.

At this time, there was strictly no dividing line in the country between Anti-Slavery and Pro-Slavery. The Anti-Slavery sentiment was thoroughly national, broad and general, pervading alike all parts of the Union, and uprising from the common heart of the entire people. The Pro-Slavery interest was strictly personal and pecuniary, and had its source simply in the self-interest of individual slaveholders. It contemplated Slavery only as a domestic institution — not as a political element — and merely stipulated for its security where it actually existed within the States.

Sir, the original policy of the country, begun under the Confederation, and recognized at the initiation of the new Government, is clear and unmistakable. Compendiously expressed, it was *non-intervention by Congress with Slavery in the States, and its prohibition in all the national domain.* In this way, the discordant feelings on this subject were reconciled. Slave-masters were left at home in their respective States, under the protection of local laws, to hug Slavery without any interference from Congress, while all opposed to it were exempted from any responsibility therefor in the national domain. This, sir, is the common ground on which our political fabric was reared; and I do not hesitate to say that it is the only ground on which it can stand in permanent peace.

It is beyond question, sir, that our Constitution was framed by the lovers of Human Rights; that it was animated by their divine spirit; that the institution of Slavery was regarded by them with aversion, so that, though covertly alluded to, it was not named in the instrument; that, according to the debates in the Convention, they refused to give it any "sanction," and looked forward to the certain day when it would be obliterated from the land. But the original policy of the Government did not long prevail. The generous sentiments which filled the early patriots, giving to them historic grandeur, gradually lost their power. The blessings of Freedom being already secured to themselves, the freemen of the land grew indifferent to the freedom of others. They ceased to think of the slaves. The slave-masters availed themselves of this indifference, and, though few in numbers, compared with the non-slaveholders, even in the slave States (according to the late census they are fewer than three hundred and fifty thousand), they have, under the influence of an imagined self-interest, by the skilful tactics of party, and especially by an unhesitating, persevering union among themselves — swaying, by turns, both the great political parties — succeeded, through a long succession of years, in obtaining the control of the National Government, bending it to their purposes, compelling it to do their will, and imposing upon it a policy friendly to Slavery — offensive to Freedom only — and directly opposed to the sentiments of its founders. Our Republic has swollen in population and power; but it has shrunk in character. It is not now what it was in the beginning, a Republic merely permitting, while it regretted Slavery; tolerating it only where it could not be removed, and interdicting it where it did not exist — but a mighty Propagandist, openly favoring and vindicating it; visiting, also, with displeasure all who oppose it.

Sir, our country early reached heights which it could

not keep. Its fall was gentle but complete. At the session of Congress immediately following the ratification of the prohibition of Slavery in the national domain, a transfer of the territory now constituting Tennessee was accepted from North Carolina (2d April, 1790), loaded with the express condition "that no regulation made, or to be made, should tend to emancipate slaves;" a formal provision, which, while admitting the power of Congress over Slavery in the Territories, waived the prevailing policy of executing it. This was followed, in 1798, by the transfer from Georgia of the region between her present western limit and the Mississippi, under a similar condition. In both these cases, an apology may be found in the very terms of the transfers, and in the fact that the region constituted a part of two States where Slavery actually existed; though it will be confessed that even here there was a descent from that summit of Freedom on which the Nation had so proudly rested:

> "From morn
> To noon he fell; from noon to dewy eve—
> A summer's day, and with the setting sun
> Drop'd from the zenith, like a falling star."

But, without tracing this downward course through its successive stages, let me refer to facts, which too palpably reveal the abyss that has been reached. Early in our history, no man was disqualified for public office by reasons of his opinions on this subject; and this condition continued for a long period. As late as 1821, John W. Taylor, Representative from New York, who had pressed with so much energy, not merely the prohibition of Slavery in the Territories, but its restriction in the State of Missouri, was elected to the chair of Henry Clay, as Speaker of the other House. It is needless to add, that no determined supporter of the prohibition of Slavery in the Territories at this day could expect that eminent trust. An arrogant and unrelenting ostracism is now applied, not only to all who express themselves against Slavery, but to every man who will not be its menial. A novel test for office has been introduced, which would have excluded all the Fathers of the Republic — even Washington, Jefferson and Franklin. Yes, sir; startling it may be, but indisputable. Could these illustrious men descend from their realms above, and revisit the land which they once nobly dedicated to Freedom, they could not, with their well-known and recorded opinions against Slavery, receive a nomination for the Presidency from either of the old political parties. Nor could John Jay, our first Chief Justice, and great exemplar of Judicial virtue — who hated Slavery as he loved Justice — be admitted to resume those duties with which his name on earth is indissolubly associated; nor could either of the patriots, whose names are now our greatest pride, be confirmed by the Senate for any political function whatever. To such lowest deep has our Government descended.

These things prepare us to comprehend the true character of the change with regard to the Territories. In 1787, all the existing national domain was promptly and unanimously dedicated to Freedom, without opposition or criticism. The interdict of Slavery then covered every inch of soil belonging to the National Government. Louisiana, an immense region beyond the bounds of the original States, was subsequently acquired, and in 1820, after a vehement struggle, which shook the whole land, discomfited Freedom was compelled, by a dividing line, to a partition with Slavery. This arrangement, which, in its very terms, was exclusively applicable to a particular territory purchased from France, has been *accepted* as *final* down to the present session of Congress; but now sir, here in 1854, Freedom is suddenly summoned to surrender even her hard-won moiety. Here are the three stages: at the first, all is consecrated to Freedom; at the second, only half; while at the third, all is grasped by Slavery. Thus is the original policy of the Government absolutely reversed. Slavery, which, at the beginning, was a sectional institution, with no foothold anywhere on the National Territory, is now exalted as a National Institution, and all our broad domain is threatened by its blighting shadow.

Thus much for what I have to say, at this time, of the original policy, consecrated by the lives, opinions and acts of our Fathers. Summoning to my side the majestic forms of those civil heroes, whose firmness in council was only equalled by the firmness of Washington in war, I might leave the cause in their care. But certain reasons are adduced for the proposed departure from their great example, and, though these seem of little validity, yet I would not pass them in silence.

The Prohibition of Slavery in the Territories is assailed, as beyond the power of Congress, and an infringement of the local sovereignty. On this account it is, at this late day, pronounced unconstitutional. Now, without considering minutely the sources from which the power of Congress over the national domain is derived — whether from the express grant in the Constitution to make rules and regulations for the government of the Territory, or from the power, necessarily implied, to govern Territory acquired by conquest or purchase — it seems to me impossible to deny its existence, without invalidating a large portion of the legislation of the country, from the adoption of the Constitution down to the present day. This power was asserted before the Constitution. It was not denied or prohibited by the Constitution itself. It has been exercised from the first existence of the Government, and has been recognized by the three departments — the Executive, the Legislative and the Judicial. Precedents of every kind are thick in its support. Indeed, the very Bill now before us, assumes a control of the Territory clearly inconsistent with those principles of sovereignty, which are said to be violated by a Congressional prohibition of Slavery.

Here are provisions, determining the main features in the Government — the distribution of powers in the Executive, the Legislative and Judicial departments, and the manner in which they shall be respectively constituted; securing to the President, with the consent of the Senate, the appointment of the Governor, the Secretary and the Judges, and to the people only the election of the Legislature; and even ordaining the qualifications of voters, the salaries of the public officers, and the daily compensation of the members of the Legislature. Surely, if Congress may establish these provisions, without any interference with the rights of territorial sovereignty, it is absurd to say that it may not also prohibit Slavery.

But in the very Bill there is an express prohibition on the Territory, borrowed from the Ordinance of 1787, and repeated in every Act organizing a Territory, or even a new State, down to the present time, wherein it is expressly declared, that "no tax shall be imposed upon the property of the United States." Now, here is a clear and unquestionable restraint upon the sovereignty of Territories and States. The public lands of the United States, situated within an organized Territory or State, cannot be regarded as the *instruments* and *means* necessary and proper to execute the sovereign powers of the nation, like fortifications, arsenals and navy yards. They are strictly in the nature of *private property* of the nation, and as such, unless exempted by the foregoing prohibition, would clearly be within the field of local taxation, liable, like the lands of other proprietors, to all customary burdens and incidents. Mr. Justice Woodbury has declared, in a well-considered judgment, that "where the United States own lánd situated within the limits of particular States, and over which they have no cession of jurisdiction, for objects either special or general, little doubt exists that the rights and remedies in relation to it are usually the same as apply to other landholders within the States."—(*United States* v. *Ames*, 1 Woodbury & Minot, p. 76). I assume, then, that without this prohibition these lands would be liable to taxation. Does any one question this? Nobody. The conclusion then follows, that by this prohibition you propose to deprive the present Territory, as you have deprived other Territories — ay, and States — of an essential portion of its sovereignty.

And these, sir, are not vain words. The Supreme

Court of the United States have given great prominence to the sovereign right of taxation in the States. In the case of *Providence Bank* v. *Pittman*, 4 Peters, 514, they declare —

"That the taxing power is of vital importance; *that it is essential to the existence of Government;* that the relinquishment of such power is never to be assumed."

And again, in the case of *Dobbins* v. *Commissioners of Erie County*, 16 Peters, 447, they say —

"Taxation is a sacred right, *essential to the existence of Government — an incident of sovereignty.* The right of legislation is co-extensive with the incident to attach it upon all persons and property within the jurisdiction of the State."

Now, I call upon Senators to remark, that this sacred right, said to be essential to the very existence of Government, is abridged in the Bill before us.

For myself, I do not doubt the power of Congress to fasten this restriction upon the Territory, and afterwards upon the State, as has been always done; but I am at a loss to see on what grounds this restriction can be placed, which will not also support the Prohibition of Slavery. The former is an unquestionable infringement of sovereignty, as declared by our Supreme Court, far more than can be asserted of the latter.

I am unwilling to admit, sir, that the Prohibition of Slavery in the Territories is in any just sense an infringement of the local sovereignty. Slavery is an infraction of the immutable law of nature, and as such, cannot be considered a natural incident to any sovereignty, especially in a country which has solemnly declared, in its Declaration of Independence, the inalienable right of all men to life, *liberty* and the pursuit of happiness.] In an age of civilization and in a land of rights, Slavery may still be tolerated *in fact;* but its prohibition, within a municipal jurisdiction, by the Government thereof — as by one of the States of the Union — cannot be considered an infraction of natural rights; nor can its prohibition by Congress in the Territories be regarded as an infringement of the local sovereignty, founded, as it must be, on natural rights.

But another argument is pressed, most fallacious in its character. It is asserted that, inasmuch as the Territories were acquired by the common treasure, they are the common property of the whole Union; and, therefore, no citizen can be prevented from moving into them with his slaves, without an infringement of the equal rights and privileges which belong to him as a citizen of the United States. But, it is admitted that the people of this very Territory, when organized as a State, may exclude slaves, and in this way abridge an asserted right founded on the common property in the Territory. Now, if this can be done by the few thousand settlers who constitute the State Government, the whole argument founded on the acquisition of the Territories, by a common treasure, seems futile and evanescent.

But this argument proceeds on an assumption which cannot stand. It assumes that Slavery is a National Institution, and that property in slaves is recognized by the Constitution of the United States. Nothing can be more false. By the judgment of the Supreme Court of the United States, and also by the principles of the common law, Slavery is a local municipal institution, which derives its support exclusively from local municipal laws, and beyond the sphere of these laws it ceases to exist, except so far as it may be preserved by the clause for the rendition of fugitives from service. Madison thought it wrong to admit into the Constitution the idea that there can be property in man; and I rejoice to believe that no such idea can be found there. The Constitution regards slaves always as "persons," with the rights of "persons," never as property. When it is said, therefore, that every citizen may enter the national domain with his property, it does not follow, by any rule of logic or of law, that he may carry his slaves. On the contrary, he can only carry that property which is admitted to be such by the universal law of nature, written by God's own finger on the heart of man.

Again: The relation of master and slave is sometimes classed with the domestic relations. Now, while it is unquestionably among the powers of any State, within its own jurisdiction, to change the existing relation of husband and wife, and to establish polygamy, I presume no person would contend that a polygamous husband, resident in one of the States, would be entitled to enter the National Territory with his harem — his property, if you please — and there claim immunity. Clearly, when he passes the bounds of that local jurisdiction, which sanctions polygamy, the peculiar domestic relation would cease; and it is precisely the same with Slavery.

Sir, I dismiss these considerations. The Prohibition of Slavery in the Territory of Kansas and Nebraska stands on foundations of adamant, upheld by the early policy of the Fathers, by constant precedent, and time-honored compact. It is now in your power to overturn it; you may remove the sacred landmark, and open the whole vast domain to Slavery. To you is committed this high prerogative. Our fathers, on the eve of the Revolution, set forth in burning words, among their grievances, that George III. "in order to keep open a market where men should be bought and sold, had prostituted his negative for suppressing every legislative attempt to prohibit or restrain this execrable commerce." Sir, like the English monarch, you may now prostitute your power to this same purpose. But you cannot escape the judgment of the world, nor the doom of history.

It will be in vain, that, while doing this thing, you plead, in apology, the principle of *self-government*, which you profess to recognize in the Territories. Sir, this very principle, when truly administered, secures equal rights to all, without distinction of color or race, and makes Slavery impossible. By no rule of justice, and by no subtlety of political metaphysics, can the right to hold a fellow-man in bondage be regarded as essential to self-government. The inconsistency is too flagrant. It is apparent on the bare statement. It is like saying *two* and *two* make *three*. In the name of Liberty you open the door to Slavery. With professions of Equal Rights on the lips, you trample on the rights of Human Nature. With a kiss upon the brow of that fair Territory, you betray it to wretchedness and shame. Well did the patriot soul exclaim, in bitter words, wrung out by bitter experience: "Oh Liberty! what crimes are done in thy name!"

In vain, sir, you will plead, that this measure proceeds from the North, as has been suggested by the

Senator from Kentucky [Mr. Dixon]. Even if this were true, it would be no apology. But, precipitated as this Bill has been upon the Senate, at a moment of general calm, and in the absence of any controlling exigency, and then hurried to a vote in advance of the public voice, as if fearful of arrest, it cannot justly be called the offspring of any popular sentiment. In this respect it differs widely from the Missouri Prohibition, which, after solemn debate, extending through two sessions of Congress, and ample discussion before the people, was adopted. Certainly there is, as yet, no evidence that this attempt, though espoused by Northern politicians, proceeds from that Northern sentiment which throbs and glows, strong and fresh, in the schools, the churches and homes of the people. *Populi omnes* AD AQUILONEM *positi Libertatem quandam spirant.* And could the abomination which you seek to perpetrate be now submitted to the awakened millions whose souls have been truly ripened under Northern skies, it would be flouted at once with indignant and undying scorn.

But the race of men, "white slaves of the North," described and despised by a Southern statesman, is not yet extinct there, sir. It is one of the melancholy tokens of the power of Slavery, under our political system, and especially through the operations of the National Government, that it loosens and destroys the character of Northern men, exerting its subtle influence even at a distance — like the black magnetic mountain in the Arabian story, under whose irresistible attraction the iron bolts, which held together the strong timbers of a stately ship, securely floating on the distant wave, were drawn out, till the whole fell apart, and became a disjointed wreck. Alas! too often those principles, which give consistency, individuality and form, to the Northern character, which render it staunch, strong and seaworthy, which bind it together as with iron, are sucked out, one by one, like the bolts of the ill-fated vessel, and from the miserable, loosened fragments is formed that human anomaly — *a Northern man with Southern principles.* Sir — No such man can speak for the North.

[Here there was an interruption of prolonged applause in the galleries.]

The PRESIDENT (Mr. Stuart in the chair). The Chair will be obliged to direct the galleries to be cleared, if order is not preserved. No applause will be allowed.

SEVERAL VOICES. Let them be cleared now.

Mr. SUMNER. Mr. President, I advance now to considerations of a more general character, to which I ask your best attention. Sir, this Bill is proposed as a measure of peace. In this way you vainly think to withdraw the subject of Slavery from National Politics. This is a mistake. Peace depends on mutual confidence. It can never rest secure on broken faith and injustice. And, sir permit me to say, frankly, sincerely and earnestly, that the subject of Slavery can never be withdrawn from the National Politics, until we return once more to the original policy of our fathers, at the first organization of the Government, under Washington, when the National ensign nowhere on the National Territory covered a single slave.

Slavery, which our fathers branded as an "evil," a "curse," an "enormity," a "nefarious institution," is condemned at the North by the strongest convictions of the reason and the best sentiments of the heart. It is the only subject within the field of National Politics which excites any real interest. The old matters which have divided the minds of men have lost their importance. One by one they have disappeared, leaving the ground to be occupied by a question grander far. The Bank, Sub-Treasury, the Distribution of the Public Lands, are each and all obselete issues. Even the Tariff is not a question on which opposite political parties are united in taking opposite sides. And now, instead of these superseded questions, which were filled for the most part with the odor of the dollar, the country is directly summoned to consider face to face a cause, which is connected with all that is divine in religion, with all that is pure and noble in morals, with all that is truly practical and constitutional in politics. Unlike the other questions, it is not temporary or local in its character. It belongs to all times and to all countries. Though long kept in check, it now, by your introduction, confronts the people, demanding to be heard. To every man in the land it says, with clear, penetrating voice, "Are you for Freedom, or are you for Slavery?" And every man in the land must answer this question when he votes.

Pass this Bill, and it will be in vain that you say, the Slavery Question is settled. Sir, *nothing can be settled which is not right.* Nothing can be settled which is adverse to Freedom. God, nature and all the holy sentiments of the heart, repudiate any such false seeming settlement.

Now, sir, mark the clear line of our duty. And here let me speak for those with whom, in minority and defeat, I am proud to be associated, — the Independent Democrats, — who espouse that Democracy which is transfigured in the Declaration of Independence and the injunctions of Christianity. The testimony which we bear against Slavery, as against all other wrong, is in different ways, according to our position. The Slavery, which exists under other Governments — as in Russia or Turkey — or in other States of the Union, as in Virginia and Carolina, we can oppose only through the influence of literature, morals and religion, without in any way invoking the Political Power. Nor is it proposed to act otherwise. But Slavery, where we are parties to it — where we are responsible for it — everywhere within our jurisdiction — must be opposed, not only by all the influence of literature, morals and religion, but directly by every instrument of Political Power. In the States it is sustained by local laws, and although we may be compelled to share the shame, which its presence inflicts upon the fair fame of the country, yet it receives no direct sanction at our hands. We are not responsible for it. The wrong is not at our own particular doors. It is not within our jurisdiction. But Slavery everywhere under the Constitution of the United States — everywhere within the exclusive jurisdiction of the National Government — everywhere under the National Flag, is at our own particular doors, within the sphere of our own personal responsibility, and exists there in defiance of the original policy of our Fathers, and of the true principles of the Constitution.

It is a mistake to say, as is often charged, that we seek to interfere, through Congress, with Slavery in the States, or in any way to direct the legislation of

Congress upon subjects not within its jurisdiction. Our *political* aims, as well as our *political* duties, are co-extensive with our *political* responsibilities. And since we at the North are responsible for Slavery wherever it exists under the jurisdiction of Congress, it is unpardonable in us not to exert every power we possess to enlist Congress against it.

Such is our cause. To men of all parties and opinions, who wish well to the Republic, and would preserve its good name, it appeals. Alike to the Conservative and the Reformer, it appeals ; for it stands on the truest Conservatism and the truest Reform. In seeking the reform of existing evils, we seek also the conservation of the principles of our fathers. The cause is not sectional. Oh, no ! sir, it is not sectional ; for it simply aims to establish under the National Government those great principles of Justice and Humanity, which are broad and universal as man. As well might it be said that Jefferson, Franklin and Washington, were sectional. It is not aggressive ; for it does not seek in any way to interfere, through Congress, with Slavery in the States. It is not contrary to the Constitution ; for it recognizes this paramount law, and in the administration of the Government invokes the spirit of its founders. Sir, it is not hostile to the quiet of the country ; for it proposes the only course by which agitation can be allayed, and quiet be permanently established.

It is not uncommon to hear persons declare that they are against Slavery, and are willing to unite in any practical efforts to make this opposition felt. At the same time, they pharisaically visit with condemnation, with reproach or contempt, the earnest souls who for years have striven in this struggle. To such I would say — could I reach them now with my voice — if you are sincere in what you declare; if your words are not merely lip-service; if in your hearts you are entirely willing to join in any practical efforts against Slavery, then by your lives, by your conversation, by your influence, by your votes — disregarding "the ancient forms of party strife" — seek to carry the principles of Freedom into the National Government, wherever its jurisdiction is acknowledged and its power can be felt. Thus, without any interference with the States, which are beyond this jurisdiction, may you help to erase the blot of Slavery from our National brow.

Do this, and you will most truly promote the harmony which you so much desire. You will establish tranquillity throughout the country. Then at last, sir, the Slavery Question will be settled. Banished from its usurped foothold under the National Government, Slavery will no longer enter, with distracting force, into the National Politics — making and unmaking laws, making and unmaking Presidents. Confined to the States, where it was left by the Constitution, it will take its place as a local institution — if, alas! continue it must! — for which we are in no sense responsible, and against which we cannot exert any political power. We shall be relieved from our present painful and irritating connection with it. The existing antagonism between the North and the South will be softened; crimination and recrimination will cease; the wishes of the Fathers will be fulfilled, and this Great Evil will be left to the kindly influences of morals and religion, and the prevailing laws of social economy.

I am not blind to the adverse signs. But this I see clearly. Amidst all seeming discouragements, the great omens are with us. Art, literature, poetry, religion — everything which elevates man — all are on our side. The plough, the steam-engine, the railroad, the telegraph, the book, every human improvement, every generous word anywhere, every true pulsation of every heart which is not a mere muscle, and nothing else, gives new encouragement to the warfare with Slavery. The discussion will proceed. The devices of party can no longer stave it off. The subterfuges of the politician cannot escape it. The tricks of the office-seeker cannot dodge it. Wherever an election occurs, there this question will arise. Wherever men come together to speak of public affairs, there again will it be. No political Joshua now, with miraculous power, can stop the sun in his course through the heavens. It is even now rejoicing, like a strong man, to run its race, and will yet send its beams into the most distant plantations — ay, sir, and melt the chains of every slave.

But this movement — or agitation, as it is reproachfully called — is boldly pronounced injurious to the very object desired. Now, without entering into details which neither time nor the occasion justifies, let me say that this objection belongs to those commonplaces, which have been arrayed against every beneficent movement in the world's history — against even knowledge itself — against the abolition of the slave-trade. Perhaps it was not unnatural for the Senator from North Carolina [Mr. Badger] to press it, even as vehemently as he did; but it sounded less natural when it came, though in more moderate phrase, from my distinguished friend and colleague from Massachusetts [Mr. Everett]. The past furnishes a controlling example by which its true character may be determined. Do not forget, sir, that the efforts of William Wilberforce encountered this precise objection, and that the condition of the kidnapped slave was then vindicated, in language not unlike that of the Senator from North Carolina, by no less a person than the Duke of Clarence, of the royal family of Great Britain. In what was called his maiden speech, on 3d May, 1792, and preserved in the Parliamentary Debates, he said: "The negroes were not treated in the manner which had so much agitated the public mind. He had been an attentive observer of their state, and had no doubt that he could bring forward proofs to convince their lordships that their state was far from being miserable; on the contrary, that when the various ranks of society were considered, they were comparatively in a state of humble happiness." And only the next year this same royal prince, in debate in the House of Lords, asserted that the promoters of the abolition of the slave-trade were "either fanatics or hypocrites," and in one of these classes he ranked Wilberforce. Mark now the end. After years of weary effort, the slave-trade was finally abolished; and at last, in 1833, the early vindicator of this enormity, the maligner of a name hallowed among men, was brought to give his royal assent, as William IV., King of Great Britain, to the immortal Act of Parliament, greater far than any victory of war, by which slavery was abolished throughout the British dominions. Sir, time and the universal conscience have vindicated the labors of Wilberforce. The movement against American Slavery, auspicated by the august names of Washington, Franklin and Jefferson, can calmly await a similar judgment.

But it is suggested that, in this movement, there is danger to the Union. In this solicitude I cannot share. As a lover of concord and a jealous partisan of all things that make for peace, I am always glad to express my attachment to the Union; but I believe that this bond will be most truly preserved and most beneficently extended (for I shrink from no expansion where Freedom leads the way) by firmly upholding those principles of Liberty and Justice which were made its early corner-stones. The true danger to this Union proceeds, not from any abandonment of the "peculiar institution" of the South, but from the abandonment of the spirit in which the Union was formed; not from any warfare, within the limits of the Constitution, upon Slavery; but from warfare, like that waged by this very Bill, upon Freedom. The Union is most precious; but more precious far are that "general welfare," "domestic tranquillity," and those "blessings of Liberty," which it was established to secure; all which are now wantonly endangered. Not that I love the Union less, but Freedom more, do I now, in pleading this great cause, insist that Freedom, at all hazards, shall be preserved.

One word more, and I have done. The great master, Shakespeare, who, with all-seeing mortal eye, observed mankind, and with immortal pen depicted the manners as they rise, has presented a scene which may be read with advantage by all who would plunge the South into tempestuous quarrel with the North. I refer to the well-known dialogue between Brutus and Cassius. Reading this remarkable passage, it is difficult not to see in Brutus our own North, and in Cassius the South:

*Cas.* Urge me no more, I shall forget myself;
Have a mind upon your health, tempt me no further.
*Bru.* Hear me, for I will speak.
Must I give way and room to your rash choler?
*Cas.* O ye gods! ye gods! Must I endure all this?
*Bru.* All this? ay, more: Fret, till your proud heart break:
*Go, show your slaves how choleric you are,*
*And make your bondmen tremble.* Must I budge?
Must I observe you? Must I stand and crouch
Under your testy humor?
*Cas.* Do not presume too much upon my love,
I may do that I shall be sorry for.
*Bru.* *You have done that you should be sorry for.*
There is no terror, Cassius, in your threats;
For I am arm'd so strong in honesty,
That they pass by me, as the idle wind,
Which I respect not.
*Cas.* A friend should bear his friend's infirmities,
But Brutus makes mine greater than they are.
*Bru.* I do not, TILL YOU PRACTISE THEM ON ME.
*Cas.* You love me not.
*Bru.* I do not like your faults.

*Julius Cæsar, Act* iv. *Scene* 3.

And the colloquy proceeding, each finally comes to understand the other, appreciates his character and attitude, and the impetuous gallant Cassius exclaims, "Give me your hand;" to which Brutus replies, "And my heart too." Afterwards, with hand and heart united, on the field of Philippi they together upheld the liberties of Rome.

The North and the South, sir, as I fondly trust,

amidst all differences, will ever have a hand and heart for each other; and, believing in the sure prevalence of Almighty Truth, I confidently look forward to the good time, when both will unite, according to the sentiments of the Fathers and the true spirit of the Constitution, in declaring Freedom and not Slavery NATIONAL, to the end that the Flag of the Republic, wherever it floats, on sea or land, within the National jurisdiction, may not cover a single slave. Then will be achieved that Union contemplated at the beginning, against which the storms of faction and the assaults of foreign power shall beat in vain, as upon the Rock of Ages; and LIBERTY, seeking a firm foothold, WILL HAVE AT LAST WHEREON TO STAND AND MOVE THE WORLD.

## FINAL PROTEST FOR HIMSELF AND THE CLERGY OF NEW ENGLAND AGAINST SLAVERY IN NEBRASKA AND KANSAS.

SPEECH IN THE SENATE OF THE UNITED STATES ON THE NIGHT OF THE FINAL PASSAGE OF THE NEBRASKA AND KANSAS BILL, 25TH MAY, 1854.

---

The original debate in the Senate, on the Nebraska and Kansas Bill, in which Mr. Sumner took part, was closed by the passage of that Bill — after a protracted session throughout the night — on the morning of Saturday, 4th March, 1854, by a vote of thirty-seven yeas to fourteen nays. The Bill was then sent to the House of Representatives for action there. It was there taken up and referred to the Committee of the Whole; but, owing to the mass of prior business, it became impossible to reach it. Under these circumstances a fresh Bill, identical with that which had passed the Senate, was introduced and passed the House. This, of course, required the action of the Senate. On the 23d May, a message from the House announced its passage and asked the concurrence of the Senate. It was at once read a first time; but, on the objection of Mr. Sumner, its second reading was stopped on that day. On the next day, on motion of Mr. Douglas, all prior orders were postponed for the purpose of considering it. The debate upon it continued during that day and the next. Late in the night of the last day, after the Bill had been reported to the Senate, and the question had been put by the Chair, "Shall the Bill be engrossed and read a third time?" Mr. SUMNER took the floor and said:

Mr. President: It is now midnight. At this late hour of a session drawn out to an unaccustomed length,

I shall not fatigue the Senate by argument. There is a time for all things, and the time for this has passed. The determination of the majority is fixed; but it is not more fixed than mine. The Bill which they sustain, I oppose. On a former occasion I met it by argument, which, though often attacked in debate, still stands unanswered and unanswerable. At present, I am admonished that I must be content with a few words of earnest protest against the consummation of a great wrong. Duty to myself, and also to the honored Commonwealth, of which I find myself the sole representative in this immediate exigency, will not allow me to do less.

But I have a special duty, which I would not omit. Here on my desk are remonstrances against the passage of this Bill, some of which have been placed in my hands since the commencement of the debate to-day, and I desire that these voices, direct from the people, should be heard. With the permission of the Senate, I will offer them now.

The Presiding Officer (Mr. Stuart in the chair). The remonstrances can be received by unanimous consent.

Several Voices. Let them be received.

The Presiding Officer. The Chair hears no objection.

Mr. Sumner. Taking advantage of this permission, I now present the remonstrance of a large number of citizens of New York against the repeal of the Missouri Compromise.

I also present the memorial of the religious Society of Friends in Michigan, against the passage of the

Nebraska Bill, or any other Bill annulling the Missouri Compromise Act of 1820.

I also present the remonstrance of the clergy and laity of the Baptist denomination in Michigan and Indiana, against the wrong and bad faith contemplated in the Nebraska Bill.

But this is not all.

I hold in my hand, and now present to the Senate, one hundred and twenty-five separate remonstrances, from clergymen of every Protestant denomination in Maine, New Hampshire, Vermont, Massachusetts, Rhode Island, and Connecticut, constituting the six New England States. These remonstrances are identical in character with the larger one presented by my distinguished colleague [Mr. Everett] — whose term of service here ends in a few days, by voluntary resignation, and who is now detained at home by illness — and were originally intended as a part of it, but did not arrive in season to be annexed to that interesting and weighty document. They are independent in form, though supplementary in their nature — helping to swell the protest of the pulpits of New England.

With pleasure and pride I now do this service, and, at this last stage, interpose the sanctity of the pulpits of New England to arrest an alarming outrage; believing that the remonstrants, from their eminent character and influence, as representatives of the intelligence and conscience of the country, are peculiarly entitled to be heard; and, further, believing that their remonstrances, while respectful in form, embody just conclusions, both of opinion and fact. Like them, sir, I do not hesitate to protest here against the Bill yet pending before the Senate, as a great moral wrong;

as a breach of public faith; as a measure full of danger to the peace, and even existence of our Union. And, sir, believing in God as I profoundly do, I cannot doubt that the opening of an immense region to so great an enormity as Slavery is calculated to draw down upon our country His righteous judgments.

"In the name of Almighty God, and in His presence," these remonstrants protest against the Nebraska Bill. In this solemn language, which has been strangely pronounced blasphemous on this floor, there is obviously no assumption of ecclesiastical power, as has been perversely charged, but simply a devout observance of the scriptural injunction: "Whatsoever ye do, in word or deed, do all in the name of the Lord." Let me add, also, that these remonstrants, in this very language, have followed the example of the Senate, which, at our present session, has ratified at least one important treaty, beginning with these precise words: "In the name of Almighty God." Surely, if the Senate may thus assume to speak, the clergy may do likewise, without imputation of blasphemy or any just criticism, at least in this body.

But I am unwilling, particularly at this time, to be betrayed into anything that shall seem like a defence of the clergy. They need no such thing at my hands. There are men in this Senate, justly eminent for eloquence, learning and ability; but there is no man here competent, except in his own conceit, to sit in judgment on the clergy of New England. Honorable Senators, who have been so swift with criticism and sarcasm, might profit by their example. Perhaps the Senator from South Carolina [Mr. Butler], who is not insensible to scholarship, might learn from them something of its graces. Perhaps the Senator from Virginia [Mr. Mason], who finds no sanction under the Constitution for any remonstrance from clergymen, might learn from them something of the privileges of an American citizen. And perhaps the Senator from Illinois [Mr. Douglas], who precipitated this odious measure upon the country, might learn from them something of political wisdom. Sir, from the first settlement of these shores, from those early days of struggle and privation — through the trials of the Revolution — the clergy have been associated, not only with the piety and the learning, but with the liberties of the country. For a long time, New England was governed by their prayers more than by any acts of the Legislature; and at a later day, their voices aided even the Declaration of Independence. The clergy of our time may speak, then, not only from their own virtues, but from the echoes which yet live in the pulpits of their fathers.

For myself, I desire to thank them for their generous interposition. They have already done much good in moving the country. They will not be idle. In the days of the Revolution, John Adams, yearning for Independence, said: "Let the pulpits thunder against oppression!" And the pulpits thundered. The time has come for them to thunder again.

There are lessons taught by these remonstrances, which, at this moment, should not pass unheeded. The Senator from Ohio [Mr. Wade], on the other side of the Chamber, has openly declared that the Northern Whigs can never again combine with their Southern brethren in support of Slavery. This is a good augury. The clergy of New England, some of whom, forgetful of the traditions of other days, once made their pulpits vocal for the Fugitive Slave Bill, now, by the voices of learned divines, eminent bishops, accomplished professors and faithful pastors, uttered in solemn remonstrance, at last unite in putting a permanent brand upon this hateful wrong. Surely, from this time forward, they can never more render it any support. Thank God for this! Here is a sign full of promise for Freedom.

These remonstrances have especial significance, when it is urged, as has been often done in this debate, that the proposition still pending proceeds from the North. Yes, sir, proceeds from the North; for that is its excuse and apology. The ostrich is reputed to hide its head in the sand, and then vainly imagine its coward body beyond the reach of pursuers. In similar spirit, honorable Senators seem to shelter themselves behind scanty Northern votes, and then vainly imagine that they are protected from the judgment of the country. The pulpits of New England, representing to an unprecedented extent the popular voice there, now proclaim that six States protest, with all the fervor of religious conviction, against your outrage. To this extent, at least, I confidently declare it does not come from the North.

From these expressions, and other tokens which daily greet us, it is evident that at last the religious sentiment of the country is touched, and, under this sentiment, I rejoice to believe that the whole North will be quickened with the true life of Freedom. Sir Philip Sidney, speaking to Queen Elizabeth of the spirit which animated every man, woman and child in the Netherlands, against the Spanish power, exclaimed, "It is the spirit of the Lord, and is irresistible." A kindred spirit now animates the free States against the Slave Power, breathing everywhere its precious inspiration, and forbidding repose under the attempted usurpation. I repeat, it is the spirit of the Lord, and is irresistible. The threat of disunion, too often sounded in our ears, will be disregarded by an aroused and indignant people. Ah, sir, Senators vainly expect peace. Not in this way can peace come. In passing this Bill, as is now threatened, you scatter, from this dark midnight hour, no seeds of harmony and good-will, but broadcast through the land, dragon's teeth, which haply may not, spring up in direful crops of armed men, but yet, I am assured, sir, will they fructify in civil strife and feud.

From the depths of my soul, as a loyal citizen and as a Senator, I plead, remonstrate, protest, against the passage of this Bill. I struggle against it as against death; but, as in death itself, corruption puts on incorruption, and this mortal body puts on immortality, so from the sting of this hour I find assurances of that triumph by which Freedom will be restored to her immortal birthright in the Republic.

*Sir, the Bill which you are now about to pass, is at once the worst and the best Bill on which Congress ever acted.* Yes, sir, WORST and BEST at the same time.

It is the worst Bill, inasmuch as it is a present victory of Slavery. In a Christian land, and in an age of civilization, a time-honored statute of Freedom is struck down, opening the way to all the countless woes and wrongs of human bondage. Among the crimes of history, another is about to be recorded, which no tears can blot out, and which, in better days, will be read with universal shame. Do not start. The Tea Tax and Stamp Act, which aroused the patriot rage of our fathers, were virtues by the side of your transgression; nor would it be easy to imagine, at this day, any measure which more openly and perversely defied every sentiment of justice, humanity and Christianity. Am I not right, then, in calling it the worst Bill on which Congress ever acted?

But there is another side to which I gladly turn. Sir, it is the best Bill on which Congress ever acted; *for it annuls all past Compromises with Slavery, and makes all future Compromises impossible.* Thus it puts Freedom and Slavery face to face, and bids them grapple. Who can doubt the result? It opens wide the door of the Future, when, at last, there will really be a North, and the Slave Power will be broken; when this wretched Despotism will cease to dominate over our Government, no longer impressing itself upon everything at home and abroad; when the National Government shall be divorced in every way from Slavery, and, according to the true intention of our fathers, Freedom shall be established by Congress everywhere, at least beyond the local limits of the States.

Slavery will then be driven from its usurped foothold here in the District of Columbia, in the National Territories, and elsewhere beneath the National flag; the Fugitive Slave Bill, as vile as it is unconstitutional, will become a dead letter; and the domestic Slave-trade, so far as it can be reached, but especially on the high seas, will be blasted by Congressional Prohibition. Everywhere within the sphere of Congress, the great *Northern Hammer* will descend to smite the wrong;

and the irresistible cry will break forth, "No more Slave States!"

Thus, sir, now standing at the very grave of Freedom in Nebraska and Kansas, I lift myself to the vision of that happy resurrection, by which Freedom will be secured, not only in these Territories, but everywhere under the National Government. More clearly than ever before, I now penetrate that "All-Hail-Hereafter," when Slavery must disappear. Proudly I discern the flag of my country, as it ripples in every breeze, at last become in reality, as in name, the Flag of Freedom — undoubted, pure and irresistible. Am I not right, then, in calling this Bill the best on which Congress ever acted?

Sorrowfully I bend before the wrong you are about to commit. Joyfully I welcome all the promises of the future.

When Mr. Sumner took his seat, he was followed by Mr. Mason, of Virginia, who spoke as follows:

I understand that the petitions which the Senator [Mr. Sumner] who has just taken his seat offers, were to be admitted as they were offered by the unanimous consent of the Senate. Two of them, when offered, were sent to the President's table. The last he has reserved, and made the vehicle for communicating the sentiments of the pulpits of New England to the Senate, on the subject of this Bill. I object to its reception, and I object to it, because I understand that Senator to say that it is *verbatim* the petition that was presented by his honorable colleague who is not now with us, in which the clergy presented themselves in this Senate and to the country, as a third estate, speaking not as American citizens, but as clergymen, and in that character only. I object to its reception. I object to it, that I may not in any manner minister to the unchristian purposes of the clergy of New England, as the Senator has just announced them. I object to it, that I may be in no manner responsible for the prostitution of their office, (once called holy and sacred, with them no longer so,) in the face of the Senate and of the American people. I object to it, that the clergymen of my own honored State, and of the South, may, as holding a common office in the ministry of the gospel, be in no manner confounded with or contaminated by these clergymen of New England, if the Senator represents them correctly.

Sir, if the Senator has represented these clergymen correctly, I rejoice that there is to be a separation between the church North and the church South ; for, I say, if these men dare to lay aside the character of American citizens, and come here profaning their office, profaning the name of the Almighty, for the purpose of political alliances, they are unworthy of their associates in the church. Sir, it is the first time in the history of this country that a church of any denomination has asserted a right to be heard, as a church, upon the floors of legislation ; and if the Senator represents that body correctly, they have profaned their office, and I predict now a total separation between the church North and the church South, if I understand the sentiments of the church South. The church there, I know, is yet pure in its great and holy mission. When its ministers address themselves from the pulpit, they are heard with respect, under the sanctity of their office. You find none of them coming here to the doors of legislation to mingle in political strife. They truly hold themselves "unspotted from the world."

If the Senator who has just taken his seat has correctly expounded the clergymen of New England, I object to that petition. If he has correctly stated that it is *verbatim* copied from the petition presented by his colleague, I say it is a prostitution of their office to the embrace of political party ; and the Senate shall not, by my assent, be made the medium of so unholy an alliance. I do not mean to go further into this debate ; but I object to the reception of the petition.

The PRESIDING OFFICER said : The petitions cannot be received without unanimous consent.

Mr. SUMNER in reply. It may be, sir, at this moment, within the competency of the honorable Senator from Virginia to object to the reception of these remonstrances; but I am satisfied that, at another time, his calmer judgment will not approve this course, much less the ground on which now, as well as on a former occasion, he has undertaken to impeach the right of clergymen to appear, by petition or remonstrance, at the bar of Congress. Sir, in refusing to receive these remonstrances, or in neglecting them in any way, on reasons assigned in this Chamber, you treat them with an indignity which becomes more marked, because it is the constant habit of the Senate to welcome remonstrances from members of the Society of Friends, in their religious character, and from all other persons, by any designation which they may adopt. Booksellers remonstrate against the international copyright treaty; last makers against a proposed change in the patent laws; and only lately the tobacconists have remonstrated against certain regulations touching tobacco; and all these remonstrances have been received with respect, and referred to appropriate Committees in the Senate. But the clergy of New England, when protesting against a measure which they believe, with singular unanimity, full of peril and shame to our country, are told to stay at home. Almost the jeer has gone forth, "Go up, thou bald head!" If not well, it is at least natural, that the act you are about to commit should be attended by this congenial outrage.

# DEFENCE OF MASSACHUSETTS.

SPEECHES IN THE SENATE OF THE UNITED STATES, 26TH AND 28TH JUNE, ON THE BOSTON MEMORIAL FOR THE REPEAL OF THE FUGITIVE SLAVE BILL, AND IN REPLY TO MESSRS. JONES, OF TENNESSEE, BUTLER, OF SOUTH CAROLINA, AND MASON, OF VIRGINIA.

---

On the 22d June, Mr. Rockwell, of Massachusetts, presented the following Memorial, stating that it was signed by twenty-nine hundred persons, chiefly of Boston, and moved its reference to the Committee on the Judiciary:

"To the Honorable the Senate and House of Representatives in Congress assembled: The undersigned, *men of Massachusetts*, ask for the repeal of the Act of Congress of 1850, known as the FUGITIVE SLAVE BILL."

On 26th June, on the motion to refer the memorial, a debate ensued, in which Mr. Jones, of Tennessee, Mr. Rockwell, of Massachusetts, and then again Mr. Jones, took part. At this stage, Mr. SUMNER took the floor, and spoke as follows:

MR. PRESIDENT: I begin by answering the interrogatory propounded by the Senator from Tennessee [Mr. Jones]. He asks, "Can any one suppose that, if the Fugitive Slave Act be repealed, this Union can exist?" To which I reply at once, that if the Union be in any way dependent on an Act — I cannot call it a law — so revolting in every regard as that to which he refers, then it ought not to exist. To much else that has fallen from that Senator I do not desire to reply. He has discussed at length matters already handled again and again in the long drawn out debates of this session. Like the excited hero of Macedonia, he has renewed past conflicts,

> "And thrice he routed all his foes,
> And thrice he slew the slain."

Of what the Senator has said on the relations of Senators, North and South, of a particular party, it is not my province to speak. And yet I cannot turn from it without expressing, at least, a single aspiration, that men from the North, whether Whigs or Democrats, will neither be cajoled or driven by any temptation, or lash, from the support of those principles of freedom which are inseparable from the true honor and welfare of the country. At last, I trust, there will be a backbone in the North.

My colleague has already remarked, that this memorial proceeds from persons of whom many were open supporters of the alleged Compromises of 1850, including even the odious Fugitive Slave Bill. I have looked over the long list, and, so far as I can judge, find this to be true. And, in my opinion, the change shown by these men is typical of the change in the community of which they constitute a prominent part. Once the positive upholders of the Fugitive Slave Bill, they now demand its unconditional repeal.

There is another circumstance worthy of especial remark. This memorial proceeds mainly from persons connected with trade and commerce. Now, it is a fact too well known in the history of England, and of our own country, that these persons, while often justly distinguished by their individual charities and munificence, have been lukewarm in their opposition to Slavery. Twice in English history the "mercantile interest" frowned upon the endeavors to suppress the atrocity of Algerine Slavery; steadfastly in England it sought to baffle Wilberforce's great effort for the abolition of the African Slave-trade; and, at the formation of our own Constitution, it stipulated a sordid compromise, by which this same detested, Heaven-defying traffic, was saved for twenty years from American judgment. But now it is all changed — at least in Boston. The representatives of the "mercantile interest" place themselves in the front of the new movement against Slavery, and, by their explicit memorial, call for the abatement of a grievance which they have bitterly felt in Boston.

Mr. President, this memorial is interesting to me, first, as it asks a repeal of the Fugitive Slave Bill, and secondly, as it comes from Massachusetts. That repeal I shall be glad at any time, now and hereafter, as in times past, to sustain by vote and argument; and I trust never to fail in any just regard for the sentiments or interests of Massachusetts. With these few remarks, I would gladly close. But there has been an arraignment here to-day, both of myself and of the Commonwealth which I represent. To all that has been said of myself or the Commonwealth — so far as it is an impeachment of either — so far as it subjects either to any just censure, I plead openly, for myself and for Massachusetts, "not guilty." But pardon me, if I do not submit to be tried by the Senate, fresh from the injustice of the Nebraska Bill. In the language of the common law I put myself upon "God and the country," and claim the same trial for my honored Commonwealth.

So far as the arraignment touches me personally, I hardly care to speak. It is true that I have not hesitated, here and elsewhere, to express my open, sincere, and unequivocal condemnation of the Fugitive Slave Bill. I have denounced it as at once a violation of the law of God, and of the Constitution of the United States; and I here repeat this denunciation.

Its violation of the Constitution is manifold.

It commits the great question of human freedom — than which none is more sacred in the law — not to a solemn trial, but to summary proceedings.

It commits this question — not to one of the high tribunals of the land — but to the unaided judgment of a single petty magistrate.

It commits this question to a magistrate, appointed, not by the President with the consent of the Senate, but by the court; holding his office, not during good behavior, but merely during the will of the court; and receiving, not a regular salary, but fees according to each individual case.

It authorizes judgment on *ex parte* evidence, by affidavits, without the sanction of cross-examination.

It denies the writ of *habeas corpus*, ever known as the palladium of the citizen.

Contrary to the declared purposes of the framers of the Constitution, it sends the fugitive back "at the public expense."

Adding meanness to the violation of the Constitution, it bribes the Commissioner by a double fee to pronounce against Freedom. If he dooms a man to

Slavery, the reward is ten dollars; but, saving him to Freedom, his dole is five dollars.

But this is not all. On two other capital grounds do I oppose this Act as unconstitutional; first, as it is an assumption by Congress of powers not delegated by the Constitution, and in derogation of the rights of the States; and, secondly, as it takes away that essential birthright of the citizen, trial by jury, in a question of personal liberty and a suit at common law. Thus obnoxious, I have regarded it as an enactment totally devoid of all constitutional obligation, as it is clearly devoid of all moral, while it is disgraceful to the country and the age. And, sir, I have hoped and labored for the creation of such a Public Opinion, firm, enlightened and generous, as should render the Act practically inoperative, and should press, without ceasing, upon Congress for its repeal. For all that I have said on this head, I have no regrets or apologies; but rather joy and satisfaction. Glad I am in having said it; glad I am now in the opportunity of affirming it all anew. Thus much for myself.

In response for Massachusetts, there are other things. Something surely must be pardoned to her history. In Massachusetts stands Boston. In Boston stands Faneuil Hall, where, throughout the perils which preceded the Revolution, our patriot fathers assembled to vow themselves to Freedom. Here, in those days, spoke James Otis, full of the thought that "the people's safety is the law of God." Here, also, spoke Joseph Warren, inspired by the sentiment that "death with all its tortures is preferable to Slavery." And here, also, thundered John Adams, fervid with the conviction that "consenting to Slavery is a sacrilegious breach of trust." Not far from this venerable hall — between this temple of freedom and the very court-house, to which the Senator [Mr. Jones] has referred — is the street, where, in 1770, the first blood was spilt in conflict between British troops and American citizens, and among the victims was one of that African race which you so much despise. Almost within sight is Bunker Hill; further off, Lexington and Concord. Amidst these scenes, a Slave-Hunter from Virginia appears, and the disgusting rites begin by which a fellow-man is doomed to bondage. Sir, can you wonder that the people were moved?

> "Who can be wise, amazed, temperate and furious,
> Loyal and neutral, in a moment? *No man.*"

It is true that the Slave Act was with difficulty executed, and that one of its servants perished in the effort. On these grounds the Senator from Tennessee charges Boston with fanaticism. I express no opinion on the conduct of individuals; but I do say, that the fanaticism, which the Senator condemns, is not new in Boston. It is the same which opposed the execution of the Stamp Act, and finally secured its repeal. It is the same which opposed the Tea Tax. It is the fanaticism which finally triumphed on Bunker Hill. The Senator says that Boston is filled with traitors. That charge is not new. Boston, of old, was the home of Hancock and Adams. Her traitors now are those who are truly animated by the spirit of the American Revolution. In condemning them, in condemning Massachusetts, in condemning these remonstrants, you simply give a proper conclusion to the utterance on this floor, that the Declaration of Independence is "a self-evident lie."

Here I might leave the imputations on Massachusetts. But the case is stronger yet. I have referred to the Stamp Act. The parallel is of such aptness and importance, that, though on a former occasion I presented it to the Senate, I cannot forbear from pressing it again. As the precise character of this Act may not be familiar, allow me to remind the Senate, that it was an attempt to draw money from the Colonies through a stamp tax, while the determination of certain questions of forfeiture under the statute was delegated, not to the courts of common law, but to courts of admiralty, without trial by jury. This Act was denounced in the Colonies at once on its passage, as contrary to the British Constitution, on two principal grounds, identical in character with the two chief grounds on which the Slave Act is now declared to be unconstitutional; first, as an assumption by Parliament of powers not belonging to it, and an infraction of rights secured to the Colonies; and secondly, as a denial of trial by jury in certain cases of property. On these grounds the Stamp Act was held to be an outrage.

The Colonies were aroused against it. Virginia first declared herself by solemn resolutions, which the timid thought "treasonable;" — yes, sir, "treasonable," — even as that word is now applied to recent manifestations of opinion in Boston — even to the memorial of her twenty-nine hundred merchants. But these "treasonable" resolutions soon found a response. New York followed. Massachusetts came next. In an address from the Legislature to the Governor, the true ground of opposition to the Stamp Act, coincident with the two radical objections to the Slave Act, are clearly set forth, with the following pregnant conclusion:

"We deeply regret that the Parliament has seen fit to pass such an Act as the Stamp Act; we flatter ourselves that the hardships of it will shortly appear to them in such a light as shall induce them, in their wisdom, to repeal it; *in the mean time, we must beg your Excellency to excuse us from doing anything to assist in the execution of it.*"

The Stamp Act was welcomed in the Colonies by the Tories of that day, precisely as the unconstitutional Slave Act has been welcomed by imperious numbers among us. Hutchinson, at that time Lieutenant Governor and Judge in Massachusetts, wrote to Ministers in England:

"The Stamp Act is received with as much decency as could be expected. It leaves no room for evasion, and will execute itself."

Like the Judges of our day, in charges to Grand Juries, he resolutely vindicated the Act, and admonished "the jurors and the people" to obey. Like Governors in our day, Bernard, in his speech to the Legislature of Massachusetts, demanded unreasoning submission. "I shall not," says this British Governor, "enter into any disquisition of the policy of the Act. I have only to say it is an Act of the Parliament of Great Britain." Like Marshals of our day, the Officers of the Customs are recorded as having made "application for a military force to assist them in the execution of their duty." The elaborate answer of Massachusetts — the work of Samuel Adams, and one of the corner-stones of our history — was pronounced "the ravings of a parcel of wild enthusiasts," even as recent proceedings in Boston, resulting in the memorial before you, have been characterized on this floor. Was I not right in adducing this parallel?

The country was aroused against the execution of this Act. And here Boston took the lead. In formal instructions to her Representatives, adopted unanimously in town meeting at Fanueil Hall, the following rule of conduct was prescribed:

"We, therefore, think it our indispensable duty, in justice to ourselves and posterity, as it is our undoubted privilege, in the most open and unreserved, but decent and respectful terms, to declare our greatest dissatisfaction with this law. *And we think it incumbent upon you by no means to join in any public measures for countenancing and assisting in the execution of the same*, but to use your best endeavors in the General Assembly to have the inherent, inalienable rights of the people of this Province asserted, and vindicated, and left upon the public record, that posterity may never have reason to charge the present times with the guilt of tamely giving them away."

The opposition spread and deepened, and one of its natural tendencies was to outbreak and violence. On one occasion in Boston, it showed itself in the lawlessness of a mob, of a most formidable character, even as is now charged. Liberty, in her struggles, is too often driven to force. But the town, at a public meeting in Fanueil Hall, called without delay, on the motion of the opponents of the Stamp Act, with James Otis as Chairman, condemned the outrage. Eager in hostility to the execution of the Act, Boston cherished municipal order, and constantly discountenanced all tumult, violence and illegal proceedings. On these two grounds she then stood; and her position was widely recognized. In reply, March 27, 1766, to an address from the inhabitants of Plymouth, her own consciousness of duty done is thus expressed:

"If the inhabitants of Boston have taken *the legal and warrantable measures to prevent that misfortune, of all others the most to be dreaded, the execution of the Stamp Act,* and as a necessary means of preventing it, have made any spirited applications for opening the custom houses and courts of justice; if, *at the same time, they have borne their testimony against outrageous tumults and illegal proceedings,* and given any example of the love of peace and good order, next to the consciousness of having done their duty is the satisfaction of meeting with the approbation of any of their fellow-countrymen."

Thus was the Stamp Act annulled, even before its actual repeal, which was pressed with assiduity by petition and remonstrance, on the next meeting of Parliament. Among the potent influences was the entire concurrence of the merchants, and especially a remonstrance against the Stamp Act by the merchants of New York, like that now made against the Slave Act by the merchants of Boston. Some sought at first only for its modification. Even James Otis began with this moderate aim. The King himself showed a disposition to yield to this extent. But Franklin, who was then in England, when asked whether the Colonies would submit to the Act, if mitigated in certain particulars, replied: "No, never, unless compelled by force of arms." Then it was, that the great Commoner, William Pitt, in an ever-memorable speech, uttered words which fitly belong to this occasion. He said:

"Sir, I have been charged with giving birth to sedition in America. They have spoken their sentiments with freedom against this unhappy Act, and that freedom has become their crime. Sorry I am to hear the liberty of speech in this House imputed as a crime. But the imputation shall not discourage me. It is a liberty I mean to exercise. No gentleman ought to be afraid to exercise it. It is a liberty by which the gentleman who calumniates it might and ought to have profited. The gentleman tells us America is obstinate ; America is almost in open rebellion. I rejoice that America has resisted. Three millions of slaves, so dead to all the feelings of liberty as voluntarily to submit to be slaves, would have been fit instruments to make slaves of all the rest. I would not debate a particular point of law with the gentleman ; but I draw my ideas of Freedom from the vital powers of the British Constitution — not from the crude and fallacious notions too much relied upon, as if we were but in the morning of liberty. I can acknowledge no veneration for any procedure, law, or ordinance, that is repugnant to reason and the first elements of our Constitution. The Americans have been wronged. They have been driven to madness. Upon the whole, I will beg leave to tell the House what is really my opin ion. *It is, that the Stamp Act be repealed, absolutety, totally and immediately, and that the reason for the repeal be assigned because it was founded on an erroneous principle.*"

Thus spoke this great orator, at the time tutelary guardian of American liberty. He was not unheeded. Within less than a year from its original passage, the Stamp Act — assailed as unconstitutional on the precise grounds which I now occupy in assailing the Slave Act — was driven from the statute book.

But, sir, the Stamp Act was, at most, an infringement of *civil* liberty only, not of *personal* liberty. It touched questions of property only, but not the personal liberty of any man. Under it, no freeman could be seized as a slave. There was an unjust tax of a few pence, with the chances of amercement by a single judge without jury ; but, by this statute, no person could be deprived of that vital right of all, which is to other rights as the soul to the body — *the right of a man to himself.* As liberty is more than property, as man is above the beasts that perish, as heaven is higher than earth, so are the rights assailed by an American Congress above those once assailed by the British

Parliament; and just in this proportion must be our condemnation of the Slave Act by the side of the Stamp Act. And this will yet be declared by history.

I call upon you, then, to receive the memorial, and hearken to its prayer. All other memorials asking for changes in existing legislation are treated with respect, promptly referred, and acted upon. This should not be an exception. The memorial simply asks the repeal of an obnoxious statute, which is entirely within the competency of Congress. It proceeds from a large number of respectable citizens whose autograph signatures are attached. It is brief and respectful in form; and, in its very brevity, shows that spirit of freedom which should awaken a generous response. In refusing to receive it or refer it, according to the usage of the Senate, or in treating it with any indignity, you offer an affront, not only to these numerous petitioners, but also to the great right of petition, which is never more sacred than when exercised in behalf of Freedom against an obnoxious statute. Permit me to add, that by this course you provoke the very spirit which you would repress. There is a certain plant which is said to grow when trodden upon. It remains to be seen if the Boston petitioners have not something of this quality. But this I know, sir, that the Slave Act, like vice, is of so hideous a mien, that "to be hated it needs only to be seen;" and the occurrences of this day will make it visible and palpable to the people in new forms of injustice.

This speech was followed by an angry debate, of a highly personal character, in which Mr. Butler, of South Carolina, Mr. Mason, of Virginia, Mr. Pettit, of Indiana, Mr. Dixon, of Kentucky, Mr. Mallory, of Florida, and Mr. Clay, of Alabama, took part — all directed against Mr. Sumner. On the 28th June, an effort was made to close the debate, or at least to postpone it, when Mr. SUMNER remarked :

I am unwilling to stand in the way of the general wish of the Senate to go on with its business. I desire at all times to promote its business; but this question has been presented and debated. Several Senators have already expressed themselves on it. Other Senators within my knowledge expect to be heard. I too, sir, claim the privilege of being heard again in reply to remarks which have fallen from honorable Senators. I hope, therefore, the memorial will have no disposition that will preclude its complete discussion.

## SECOND SPEECH.

The Senate refused to postpone the discussion, and the assault on Mr. Sumner went on. At last he obtained the floor and spoke as follows :

MR. PRESIDENT : Since I had the honor of addressing the Senate two days ago, various Senators have spoken. Among these, several have alluded to me in terms clearly beyond the sanctions of parliamentary debate. Of this I make no complaint, though, for the honor of the Senate, at least, it were well that it were otherwise. If to them it seems fit, courteous, parliamentary,

—— "to unpack the heart with words,
And fall a cursing, like a very drab,
A scullion,"

I will not interfere with the enjoyment which they find in such exposure of themselves. They have certainly given us a taste of their characters. Two of them, the Senator from South Carolina [Mr. Butler], who sits immediately before me, and the Senator from Virginia [Mr. Mason], who sits immediately behind me, are not young. Their heads are amply crowned by time. They did not speak from any ebullition of youth, but from the confirmed temper of age. It is melancholy to believe that, in this debate, they showed themselves as they are. It were charitable to believe that they are in reality better than they showed themselves.

I think, sir, that I am not the only person on this floor, who, in lately listening to these two self-confident champions of the peculiar fanaticism of the South, was reminded of the striking words by Jefferson, picturing the influence of Slavery, where he says, "The whole commerce between master and slave is a perpetual exercise of the most boisterous passions, the most unremitting despotism on the one part, and degrading submission on the other. Our children see this, and learn to imitate it; for man is an imitative animal. The parent storms. The child looks on, catches the lineaments of wrath, puts on the same airs in the circle of smaller slaves, gives loose to his worst passions, and, thus nursed, educated and daily exercised in tyranny, cannot but be stamped by it with odious peculiarities. *The man must be a prodigy who can retain his manners and morals undepraved by such circumstances.*" Nobody who witnessed the Senator from South Carolina or the Senator from Virginia in this debate, will place either of them among the "prodigies" described by Jefferson. As they spoke, the Senate Chamber must have seemed to them, in the characteristic fantasy of the moment, a plantation well-stocked with slaves, over which the lash of the overseer had free swing. Sir, it gives me no pleasure to say these things. It is not according to my nature. Bear witness, that I do it only in just self-defence against the unprecedented assaults and provocations of this debate. And, in doing it, I desire to warn certain Senators, that if they expect, by any ardor of menace or by any tyrannical frown, to shake my fixed resolve, they expect a vain thing.

There was, perhaps, little that fell from these two champions, as the fit was on, which deserves reply. Certainly not the hard words they used so readily and congenially. The veteran Senator from Virginia [Mr. Mason] complained that I had characterized one of his "constituents" — a person who went all the way from Virginia to Boston in pursuit of a slave — as a Slave-hunter. Sir, I choose to call things by their right names. White I call white, and black I call black. And where a person degrades himself to the work of chasing a fellow-man, who, under the inspiration of Freedom and the guidance of the north star, has sought a freeman's home far away from the coffle and the chain — that person, whomsoever he may be, I call a Slave-hunter. If the Senator from Virginia, who professes nicety of speech, will give me any term which more precisely describes such an individual, I will use it. Until then, I must continue to use the language which seems to me so apt. But this very sensibility of the veteran Senator at a just term, which truly depicts an odious character, shows a shame in which I exult. It was said by one of the philosophers of antiquity, that a blush is the sign of virtue, and permit me to add, that, in this violent sensibility, I recognize a blush mantling the cheek of the honorable Senator, which even his plantation manners cannot conceal.

And the venerable Senator from South Carolina, too, [Mr. Butler] — he has betrayed his sensibility. Here let me say that this Senator knows well that I always listen with peculiar pleasure to his racy and exuberant speech, as it gurgles forth — sometimes tinctured by generous ideas — except when, forgetful of history, and in defiance of reason, he undertakes to defend what is obviously indefensible. This Senator was disturbed, when to his inquiry, personally, pointedly and vehemently addressed to me, whether I would join in returning a fellow-man to Slavery, I exclaimed, "Is thy servant a dog, that he should do this thing?" In fitful phrases, which seemed to come from the unconscious excitement so common with the Senator, he shot forth various cries about "dogs;" and, among other things, asked if there was any "dog" in the Constitution? The Senator did not seem to bear in mind, through the heady currents of that moment, that, by the false interpretation he has fastened upon the Constitution, he has helped to nurture there a whole kennel of Carolina bloodhounds, trained, with savage jaws and insatiable scent, for the hunt of flying bondmen. No, sir, I do not believe that there is any "kennel of bloodhounds," or even any "dog," in the Constitution of the United States.

But, Mr. President, since the brief response which I made to the inquiry of the Senator, and which leaped unconsciously to my lips, has drawn upon me various attacks, all marked by grossness of language and manner; since I have been charged with openly declaring my purpose to violate the Constitution, and to break the oath which I have taken at that desk, I shall be pardoned for showing simply how a few plain words will put all this down. The authentic report in the *Globe* shows what was actually said. The report in the *Sentinel* is substantially the same; and one of the New York papers, which has been put into my hands since I entered the Senate Chamber to-day, under its telegraphic head, states the incident with substantial accuracy, though it omits the personal individual appeal addressed to me by the Senator, and which is preserved in the *Globe*. Here is the New York report:

"Mr. BUTLER. I would like to ask the Senator, if Congress repealed the Fugitive Slave Law, would Massachusetts execute the constitutional requirements, and send back to the South the absconding slaves?

"Mr. SUMNER. Do you ask if I would send back a slave?

"Mr. BUTLER. Why, yes.

"Mr. SUMNER. 'Is thy servant a dog, that he should do this thing?' "

To any candid mind, either of these reports renders anything further superfluous. The answer is explicit and above impeachment. It indignantly spurns a service from which the soul recoils; but it denies no Constitutional obligation. But the Senators, who have been so swift in misrepresentation and in assault upon me as disloyal to the Constitution, deserve to be exposed, and it shall be done.

Now, sir, I begin by adopting as my guide the authoritative words of Andrew Jackson, in 1832, in his memorable veto of the Bank of the United States.

To his course, at that critical time, were opposed the authority of the Supreme Court *and his oath to support the Constitution.* Here is his triumphant reply:

"If the opinion of the Supreme Court covers the whole ground of this act, it ought not to control the co-ordinate authorities of this Government. The Congress, the Executive and the Court, must each for itself be guided by its own opinion of the Constitution. *Each public officer, who takes an oath to support the Constitution, swears that he will support it as he understands it, and not as it is understood by others.* It is as much the duty of the House of Representatives, of the Senate, and of the President, to decide upon the constitutionality of any bill or resolution, which may be presented to them for passage or approval, as it is of the Supreme Judges when it may be brought before them for judicial decision. The authority of the Supreme Court must not, therefore, be permitted to control the Congress or the Executive, when acting in their legislative capacities, but to have only such influence as the force of their reasoning may deserve."

Mark these words, and let them sink into your minds. "Each public officer, who takes an oath to support the Constitution, swears that he will support it as he understands it, and not as it is understood by others." Yes, sir, AS HE UNDERSTANDS IT, *and not as it is understood by others.* Does any Senator here dissent from this rule? Does the Senator from Virginia? Does the Senator from South Carolina? [Here Mr. Sumner paused, but there was no reply.] At all events, I accept the rule as just and reasonable; in harmony, too, let me assert, with that liberty which scorns the dogma of *passive obedience,* and asserts the inestimable right of private judgment, whether in religion or politics. In swearing to support the Constitution at your desk, Mr. President, I did not swear to support it as *you* understand it. Oh, no, sir. Or as the Senator from Virginia understands it. Oh, no, sir. Or as the Senator from South Carolina understands it, with a kennel of bloodhounds; or, at least, a "dog" in it, "pawing to get free its hinder parts," in pursuit of a slave. No such thing. Sir, I swore to support the Constitution *as I understand it;* nor more, nor less.

Now, I will not occupy your time, nor am I so disposed at this moment, nor does the occasion require it, by entering upon any minute criticism of the clause in the Constitution touching the surrender of "fugitives from service." A few words only are needful. Assuming, sir, in the face of commanding rules of interpretation, all leaning towards Freedom, that in the evasive language of this clause, paltering in a double sense, the words employed can be judicially regarded as justly applicable to fugitive slaves, which, as you ought to know, sir, is often most strenuously and conscientiously denied — thus sponging the whole clause out of existence, except as a provision for the return of persons actually bound by lawful contract, — but on which I now express no opinion; assuming, I say, this interpretation, so hostile to Freedom, and derogatory to the members of the Federal Convention, who solemnly declared that they would not yield any sanction to Slavery, or admit into the Constitution the idea of property in man; assuming, I repeat, an interpretation which every principle of the common law, claimed by our fathers as their birthright, must disown; admitting, for the moment only, and with shame, that the Constitution of the United States has any words, which, in any legal intendment, can constrain fugitive slaves, then I desire to say, that, as I understand the Constitution, this clause does not impose upon me, as a Senator or citizen, any obligation to take part, directly or indirectly, in the surrender of a fugitive slave.

Sir, as a Senator, I have taken at your desk the oath to support the Constitution, *as I understand it.* And understanding it as I do, I am bound by that oath, Mr. President, to oppose all enactments by Congress on the subject of fugitive slaves, as a flagrant violation of the Constitution; especially must I oppose the last act as a tyrannical usurpation, kindred in character to the Stamp Act, which our fathers indignantly refused to obey. Here my duties, under the oath which I have taken as a Senator, end. There is nothing beyond. They are all absorbed in the constant, inflexible, righteous obligation to oppose every exercise by Congress of any power over the subject. In no respect, by that oath can I be constrained to duties *in other capacities, or as a simple citizen*, especially when revolting to my conscience. Now, in this interpretation of the Constitution I may be wrong; others may differ from me; the Senator from Virginia may differ from me, and the Senator from South Carolina also; and they will, each and all, act according to their respective understandings. For myself, I shall act according to mine. On this explicit statement of my constitutional obligations, I stand, as upon a living rock, and, to the inquiry, in whatever form addressed to my personal responsibility, whether I would aid, directly or indirectly, in reducing or surrendering a fellow-man to bondage, I reply again, "Is thy servant a dog, that he should do this thing?"

And, sir, looking round upon this Senate, I might ask fearlessly, how many there are — even in this body — if, indeed, there be a single Senator, who would stoop to any such service? Until some one rises and openly confesses his willingness to become a Slave-hunter, I will not believe there can be one. [Here Mr. Sumner paused, but nobody rose.] And yet honorable and chivalrous Senators have rushed headlong to denounce me because I openly declared my repudiation of a service at which every manly bosom must revolt. "Sire, I have found in Bayonne brave soldiers and good citizens, *but not one executioner*," was the noble utterance of the Governor of that place to Charles IX. of France, in response to the royal edict for the massacre of St. Bartholomew; and such a spirit, I trust, will yet animate the people of this country, when pressed to the service of "dogs!"

To that other question, which has been proposed, whether Massachusetts, by State laws, will carry out the offensive clause in the Constitution, according to the understanding of the venerable Senator from South Carolina, I reply that Massachusetts, at all times, has been ready to do her duty under the Constitution, as she understands it; and, I doubt not, will ever continue of this mind. More than this I cannot say.

In quitting this topic, I cannot forbear to remark that the assault on me for my disclaimer of all constitutional obligation, resting upon me as a Senator or citizen, to aid in making a man a slave, or in surrendering him to Slavery, comes with an ill grace from the veteran Senator from Virginia, a State which, by its far-famed resolutions of 1798, assumed to determine its constitutional obligations, even to the extent of openly declaring two different Acts of Congress null and void; and it comes also with an ill grace from the venerable

Senator from South Carolina, a State which, in latter days, has arrayed itself openly against the Federal authorities, and which threatens nullification as often as babies cry.

Surely the Senator from South Carolina, with his silver-white locks, would have hesitated to lead this assault upon me, had he not, for the moment, been entirely oblivious of the history of the State which he represents. Not many years have passed since an incident occurred at Charleston, in South Carolina — not at Boston, in Massachusetts — which ought to be remembered. The postmaster of that place, acting under a controlling Public Opinion there, informed the head of his Department at Washington that he had determined to suppress all *Anti-slavery* publications, and requested instructions for the future. Thus, in violation of the laws of the land, the very mails were rifled, and South Carolina smiled approbation of the outrage. But this is not all. The Postmaster General, Mr. Kendall, after prudently alleging that, as he had not seen the papers in question, he could not give an opinion of their character, proceeded to say, that he had been *informed* that they were incendiary, inflammatory and insurrectionary, and then announced:

"By no act or direction of mine, official or private, could I be induced to aid knowingly in giving circulation to papers of this description, directly or indirectly. *We owe an obligation to the laws*, but a *higher* one to the communities in which we live: and if the former be perverted to destroy the latter, *it is patriotism to disregard them*. Entertaining these views, I cannot sanction, and will not condemn, the step you have taken."

Such was the approving response of the National Government to the Postmaster of Charleston, when, for the sake of Slavery, and without any constitutional scruple, he set himself against an acknowledged law of the land; and yet the venerable Senator from South Carolina now presumes to denounce me, when, for the sake of Freedom, and in the honest interpretation of my constitutional obligations, I decline an offensive service.

But there is another incident in the history of South Carolina, which as a loyal son of Massachusetts, I cannot forget, and which rises now in judgment against the venerable Senator. Massachusetts had commissioned a distinguished gentleman, of blameless life and eminent professional qualities, who served with honor in the other House [Hon. Samuel Hoar], to reside at Charleston for a brief period, in order to guard the rights of her free colored citizens, assailed on arrival there by an inhospitable statute, so gross in its provisions that an eminent character of South Carolina, a Judge of the Supreme Court of the United States, [Hon. William Johnson,] had characterized it as "trampling on the Constitution," and "a direct attack upon the sovereignty of the United States." Massachusetts had read in the Constitution a clause closely associated with that touching "fugitives from service," to the following effect: "The citizens of each State shall be entitled to all privileges and immunities of citizens in the several States," and supposed that this would yet be recognized by South Carolina. But she was mistaken. Her venerable representative, an unarmed old man, with hair as silver-white almost as that of the Senator before me, was beset in Charleston by a "respectable" mob, prevented from entering upon his duties, and driven from the State; while the Legisla-

ture stepped in to sanction this shameless, lawless act, by placing on the statute book an order for his expulsion. And yet, sir, the excitable Senator from South Carolina is fired by the fancied delinquencies of Massachusetts towards Slave-hunters, and also by my own refusal to render them any aid or comfort; he shoots questions in volleys, assumes to measure our duties by his understanding, and ejaculates a lecture at Massachusetts and myself. Sir, before that venerable Senator again ventures thus, let him return to his own State, seamed all over with the scars of nullification, and first lecture there. Ay, sir, let him look into his own heart, and lecture to himself.

But enough for the present on the extent of my constitutional obligations to become a Slave-hunter. There are, however, yet other things in the assault of the venerable Senator, which, for the sake of truth, in just defence of Massachusetts, and in honor of Freedom, shall not be left unanswered. Alluding to those days when Massachusetts was illustrated by Otis, Hancock, and "the brace of Adamses;" when Faneuil Hall sent forth echoes of liberty which resounded even to South Carolina, and the very stones in the streets of Boston rose in mutiny against tyranny, the Senator with the silver-white locks, in the very ecstasy of Slavery, broke forth in the ejaculation that Massachusetts was then "slaveholding;" and he presumed to hail these patriots as representatives of "hardy, slaveholding Massachusetts." Sir, I repel the imputation. It is true that Massachusetts was "hardy;" but she was not, *in any just sense*, "slaveholding." And had she been so, she could not have been "hardy." The two characteristics are inconsistent as weakness and strength, as sickness and health — I had almost said, as death and life.

The Senator opens a page, which I would willingly present. Sir, Slavery never flourished in Massachusetts; nor did it ever prevail there at any time, even in early Colonial days, to such a degree as to be a distinctive feature in her powerful civilization. Her few slaves were merely for a term of years, or for life. If, in point of fact, their issue was sometimes held in bondage, it was never by sanction of any statute or law of Colony or Commonwealth. Such has been the solemn judgment of her Supreme Court.* In all her annals, no person was ever born a slave on the soil of Massachusetts. This, of itself, is a response to the imputation of the Senator.

A benign and brilliant Act of her Legislature, as far back as 1646, shows her sensibility on this subject. A Boston ship had brought home two negroes, seized on the coast of Guinea. Thus spoke Massachusetts:

> "The General Court, conceiving themselves bound by the first opportunity to bear witness against the heinous and crying sin of man-stealing, also to prescribe such timely redress for what is past, *and such a law for the future as may sufficiently deter all those belonging to us, to have to do in such vile and most odious conduct, justly ahhorred of all good and just men*, do order that the negro interpreter, with others unlawfully taken, be, by the first opportunity, at the charge of the country, for the present, sent to his native country of Guinea, and a letter with him of the indignation of the Court thereabout and justice thereof."

The Colony that could issue this noble decree was

* *Lanesboro* v. *Westfield*, 16 Mass. 74.

inconsistent with itself, when it allowed its rocky face to be pressed by the footsteps of a single slave. But a righteous public opinion early and constantly set its face against Slavery. As early as 1701, a vote was entered upon the records of Boston to the following effect: "The Representatives are desired to promote the encouraging the bringing of white servants, and *to put a period to negroes being slaves.*" Perhaps, in all history, this is the earliest testimony from any official body against Negro Slavery, and I thank God that it came from Boston, my native town. In 1705, a heavy duty was imposed upon every negro imported into the province; in 1712, the importation of Indians as servants or slaves was strictly forbidden; but the general subject of Slavery attracted little attention till the beginning of the controversy, which ended in the Revolution, when the rights of the blacks were blended by all true patriots with those of the whites. Sparing all unnecessary details, suffice it to say, that, as early as 1769, one of the courts of Massachusetts, anticipating, by several years, the renowned judgment in Somersett's case, established within its jurisdiction the principle of emancipation and, under its touch of magic power, changed a slave into a freeman. Similar decisions followed in other places. In 1776, the whole number of blacks, both free and slave, sprinkled thinly over "hardy" Massachusetts, was five thousand two hundred and forty-nine, being to the whites as one is to sixty-five; while in "slaveholding" South Carolina the number of negro slaves, at that time, was not far from one hundred thousand, being nearly one slave for every freeman, thus rendering that Colony anything but "hardy." At last, in 1780, even before the triumph of Yorktown had led the way to that peace which set its seal upon our National Independence, Massachusetts, animated by the struggles of the Revolution, and filled by the sentiments of Freedom, placed in front of her Bill of Rights the emphatic words, that "all men are born free and equal," and by this declaration exterminated every vestige of Slavery within her borders. All hail, then, to Massachusetts, the just and generous Commonwealth in whose behalf I have the honor to speak.

Thus, sir, does the venerable Senator err when he presumes to vouch Massachusetts for Slavery, and to associate this odious institution with the names of her great patriots.

Mr. ROCKWELL. Will my honorable colleague allow me to send to the Chair, and have read in this connection with his present remarks, a passage from Graham's History of the United States?

Mr. SUMNER. I do not know the passage to which my colleague refers, but I welcome any interruption from him.

The Secretary read as follows:

"Among other subjects of dispute with the British Government and its officers, was one more creditable to Massachusetts than even her magnanimous concern for the liberty of her citizens and their fellow-colonists. Negro Slavery still subsisted in every one of the American Provinces, and the unhappy victims of this yoke were rapidly multiplied by the progressive extension of the slave-trade. Georgia, the youngest of all the States, contained already fourteen thousand negroes; and in the course of the present year alone, more than six thousand were imported into South Carolina. In New England, the number of Slaves was very insignificant, and their treatment so mild and humane as in some measure to veil from the public eye the iniquity of their bondage. But the recent discussions with regard to liberty and the rights of human nature, were calculated to awaken in generous minds a juster impression of Negro Slavery; and during the latter part of Governor Bernard's administration, a Bill prohibitory of all traffic in negroes was passed by the Massachusetts Assembly. Bernard, however, in conformity with his instructions from the Crown, refused to affirm this law; and thus opposed himself to the virtue as well as to the liberty of the people whom he governed.

"On three subsequent occasions, laws abolishing the slave-trade were passed by the same Assembly during Hutchinson's administration; but all were, in like manner, negatived by the Governor. And yet it was at this very period, when Britain permitted her merchants annually to make slaves of more than fifty thousand men, and refused to permit her Colonies to decline a participation in this injustice, that her orators, poets and statesmen, loudly celebrate the generosity of English virtue, in suffering no slaves to exist on English ground, and the transcendent equity of her judicial tribunals in liberating one negro who had been carried there. Though Massachusetts was thus prevented from abolishing the slave-trade, the relative discussions that took place were by no means unproductive of good. A great amelioration became visible in the condition of all the negroes in the Province; and most of the proprietors gave liberty to their slaves. This *just* action — for such, and such only, it deserves to be termed — has obtained hitherto scarcely any notice from mankind, while the subsequent and similar conduct of the Quakers in Pennsylvania has been celebrated with warmth and general encomium. So capricious is the distribution of fame, and so much advantage does the reputation of virtue derive from alliance with sectarian spirit and interest."

Mr. Sumner. I am obliged to my colleague. The extract is in substantial conformity with clear historic truth, which the Senator from South Carolina, in one of his oratorical effluxes, has impeached. But the venerable Senator errs yet more, if possible, when he attributes to "slaveholding" communities a leading part in those contributions of arms and treasure by which independence was secured. Here are his exact words, as I find them in the *Globe*, revised by himself:

> "Sir, when blood was shed upon the plains of Lexington and Concord, in an issue made by Boston, to whom was an appeal made, and from whom was it answered? The answer is found in the acts of slaveholding States — *animis opibusque parati.* Yes, sir, the independence of America, to maintain republican liberty, was won by the arms and treasure, by the patriotism and *good faith* of slaveholding communities."

Mark the language, sir, as emphasized by himself. Surely, the Senator with his silver-white locks, all fresh from the outrage of the Nebraska Bill, cannot stand here and proclaim "the *good faith* of slaveholding communities," except in irony. Yes, sir, in irony. And let me add, that when this Senator presumes to say that American Independence "was won by the arms and treasure of *slaveholding* communities," he speaks either in irony or in ignorance.

The question which the venerable Senator from South Carolina here opens, by his vaunt, I have no desire to discuss; but, since it is presented, I confront it at once. This is not the first time, during my brief service here, that this Senator has sought on this floor to provoke a comparison between slaveholding communities and the free States.

Mr. Butler (from his seat). You cannot quote a single instance in which I have done it. I have always said I thought it was in bad taste, and I have never attempted it.

Mr. Sumner. I beg the Senator's pardon. I always listen to him, and I know wherof I affirm. He has profusely dealt in it. I allude now only to a single ccasion. In his speech on the Nebraska Bill, running through two days, it was one of his commonplaces. In that he openly presented a contrast between the free States and "slaveholding communities," in certain essential features of civilization, and directed shafts at Massachusetts, which called to his feet my distinguished colleague at that time [Mr. Everett], and which more than once compelled me to take the floor. And now, sir, the venerable Senator not rising from his seat, and standing openly before the Senate, assumes to deny that he has dealt in such comparisons.

Mr. Butler. Will the Senator allow me?

Mr. Sumner. Certainly; I yield the floor to the Senator.

Mr. Butler. Whenever that speech is read — and I wish the Senator had read it before he commented on it with a good deal of rhetorical enthusiasm — it will be found that I was particular not to wound the feelings of the Northern people who were sympathizing with us in the great movement to remove odious distinctions. I was careful to say nothing that would provoke invidious comparisons; and when that speech is read, notwithstanding the vehement assertion of the honorable Senator, he will find that when I quoted the laws of Massachusetts, particularly one Act which I termed the *toties quoties* Act, by which every negro was whipped every time he came into Massachusetts, I quoted them with a view to show, not a contrast between South Carolina and Massachusetts, but to show that, in the whole of this country, from the beginning to this time — even in my own State, I made no exception — public opinion had undergone a change, and that it had undergone the same change in Massachusetts, for at one time they did not regard this institution of Slavery with the same odium that they do at this time. That was the purpose; and I challenge the Senator as an orator of fairness to look at it, and see if it is not so.

Mr. SUMNER. Has the Senator done?

Mr. BUTLER. I may not be done presently; but that is the purport of that speech.

Mr. SUMNER. Will the Senator refer to his own speech? He now admits that, under the guise of an argument, he did draw attention to what he evidently regarded an odious law of Massachusetts. And, sir, I did not forget that, in doing this, there was, at the time, an apology which ill-concealed the sting. But let that pass. The Senator is strangely oblivious of the statistical contrasts, which he borrowed from the speech of a member of the other House, and which, at his request, were read by a Senator before him on this floor. The Senator, too, is strangely oblivious of yet another imputation, which, at the very close of his speech, he shot as a Parthian arrow at Massachusetts. It is he, then, who is the offender; and no hardihood of denial can extricate him. For myself, sir, I understand the sensibilities of Senators from slaveholding communities, and would not wound them by a superfluous word. Of Slavery I speak strongly, as I must; but thus far, even at the expense of my argument, I have avoided the contrasts, founded on details of figures and facts, which are so obvious between the free States and "slaveholding communities;" especially have I shunned all allusion to South Carolina. But the venerable Senator, to whose discretion that State has intrusted its interests here, will not allow me to be still.

God forbid that I should do injustice to South Carolina. I know well the gallantry of many of her sons. I know the response which she made to the appeal of Boston for union against the Stamp Act — the Fugitive Slave Act of that day — by the pen of Christopher Gadsden. And I remember with sorrow that this patriot was obliged to confess, at the time, her "weakness in having such a number of slaves," though it is to his credit that he recognized Slavery as a "crime." * I have no pleasure in dwelling on the humiliations of South Carolina; I do not desire to expose her sores; I would not lay bare her nakedness. But the Senator, in his vaunt for "slaveholding communities," has made a claim for Slavery which is so inconsistent with history, and so derogatory to Freedom, that I cannot allow it to pass unanswered.

This, sir, is not the first time, even during my little experience here, that the same claim has been made on this floor; and this seems more astonishing, because the archives of the country furnish such ample and undoubted materials for its refutation. The question of the comparative contributions of men by different States and sections of the country in the war of the Revolution, was brought forward as early as 1790, in the first Congress under the Constitution, in the animated and protracted debate on the assumption of State debts by the Union. On this occasion Fisher Ames, a Representative from Massachusetts, memorable for his classic eloquence, moved a call upon the War

* Bancroft's History of United States, vol. v. p. 426.

Department for the number of men furnished by each State to the Revolutionary armies. This motion, though vehemently opposed, was carried by a small majority. Shortly afterwards, the answer to the call was received from the Department, at that time under the charge of General Knox. This answer, which is one of the documents of our history, places beyond cavil or criticism the exact contributions in arms of each State. Here it is — copied from the first volume of the *American Archives.*

*Statement of the number of troops and militia furnished by the several States, for the support of the Revolutionary war, from* 1775 *to* 1783, *inclusive.*

| | Number of continental troops. | Number of militia. | Total militia & continental troops. | Conjectural estimate of militia. |
|---|---|---|---|---|
| NORTHERN STATES. | | | | |
| New Hampshire | 12,496 | 2,093 | 14,598 | 7,300 |
| Massachusetts | 67,937 | 15,155 | 83,092 | 9,500 |
| Rhode Island | 5,908 | 4,284 | 10,192 | 1,500 |
| Connecticut | 32,039 | 7,792 | 39,831 | 3,000 |
| New York | 17,781 | 3,312 | 21,093 | 8,750 |
| Pennsylvania | 25,608 | 7,357 | 32,965 | 2,000 |
| New Jersey | 10,727 | 6,055 | 16,782 | 2,500 |
| Total | 172,496 | 46,048 | 218,553 | 30,950 |
| SOUTHERN STATES. | | | | |
| Delaware | 2,387 | 376 | 2,763 | 1,000 |
| Maryland | 13,912 | 5,464 | 19,376 | 4,000 |
| Virginia | 26,672 | 4,163 | 30,835 | 21,880 |
| North Carolina | 7,263 | 2,716 | 9,969 | 12,000 |
| South Carolina | 5,508 | —— | 5,508 | 28,000 |
| Georgia | 2,679 | —— | 2,679 | 9,930 |
| Total | 58,421 | 12,719 | 71,130 | 76,810 |

It should be understood that, at this time, there was but little difference in numbers between the population of the Southern States and that of the Northern States. By the census of 1790, the Southern had a population of 1,956,354; the Northern had a population of 1,968,455. But, notwithstanding this comparative equality of population in the two sections, the North furnished vastly more men than the South.

Of continental troops, the Southern States furnished 58,421; the Northern furnished 172,496; making about three men furnished to the continental army by the Northern States to one from the Southern.

Of militia, whose services are authenticated by the War Office, the Southern States furnished 12,719; the Northern furnished 46,048; making nearly four men furnished to the militia by the Northern States to one from the Southern.

Of militia, whose services were not authenticated by the War Office, but are set down in the return as conjectural only, we have 76,810 furnished by the Southern States and 30,950 furnished by the Northern; making, under this head, more than two men furnished by the Southern to one from the Northern. The chief services of the Southern States — for which the venerable Senator now claims so much — it will be observed with a smile, were *conjectural* only!

Looking, however, at the sum total of continental troops, authenticated militia and conjectural militia, we have 147,940 furnished by the Southern States, while 249,503 were furnished by the Northern; making 100,000 men furnished to the war by the Northern more than the Southern.

But the disparity swells when we directly compare South Carolina and Massachusetts. Of continental troops, and authenticated militia, and conjectural militia, South Carolina furnished 33,508, while Massachusetts furnished 92,592; making in the latter sum nearly three men for one furnished by South Carolina. Look, however, at the continental troops and the authenticated militia furnished by the two States, and here you will find only 5,508 furnished by South Carolina, while 83,092 were furnished by Massachusetts — *being sixteen times more than by South Carolina, and much more than by all the Southern States together.* Here are facts and figures of which the Senator ought not to be ignorant.

Did the occasion require, I might go further, and minutely portray the imbecility of the Southern States, and particularly of South Carolina, in the war of the Revolution, as compared with the Northern States. This is a sad chapter of history, upon which I unwillingly dwell. Faithful annals record that, as early as 1778, the six South Carolina regiments, composing, with the Georgia regiment, the regular force of the Southern Department, did not, in the whole, muster above eight hundred men; nor was it possible to fill up their ranks. During the succeeding year, the Governor of South Carolina, pressed by the British forces, offered to stipulate the neutrality of his State during the war, leaving it to be decided at the peace to whom it should belong — a premonitory symptom of the secession proposed in our own day! At last, after the fatal field of Camden, no organized American force was left in this region. The three Southern States — *animis opibusque parati,* according to the vaunt of the Senator — had not a single battalion in the field! During all this period the men of Massachusetts were serving their country, not at home, but away from their own borders; for, from the time of the Declaration of Independence, Massachusetts never saw the smoke of an enemy's camp.

At last, by the military genius and remarkable exertions of General Greene, a Northern man, who assumed the command of the Southern army, South Carolina was rescued from the British power. But the trials of this successful leader reveal, in a striking manner, the weakness of the "slaveholding" State which he saved. Some of these are graphically presented in his letters. Writing to Governor Reed, of Pennsylvania, under date of 3d May, 1781, he says: —

"Those whose true interest it was to have informed Congress and the people to the *northward* of the real state of things, have joined in the deception, and *magnified the strength and resources of this country infinitely above their ability.* Many of those, who adhere to our party, are so fond of pleasure, that they cannot think of making the necessary sacrifices to support the Revolution. *There are many good and virtuous people to the southward; but they cannot animate the inhabitants in general, as you can to the northward.*" — *Gordon's History of American Revolution*, vol. iv. p. 87.

Writing to Colonel Davies, under date of 23d May, 1781, he exposes the actual condition of the country: —

"The animosity between the Whigs and Tories of this State renders their situation truly deplorable. There is not a day passes but there are more or less who fall a sacrifice to this savage disposition. The Whigs seem determined to extirpate the Tories, and the Tories the Whigs. Some thousands have fallen in this way in this quarter, and the evil rages with more violence than ever. If a stop cannot be soon put to these massacres, the country will be depopulated in a few months more, as neither Whig nor Tory can live."

To Lafayette, General Greene, under date of 29th December, 1780, describes the weakness of his troops:

"It is now within a few days of the time you mentioned of being with me. Were you to arrive, you would find a few ragged, half-starved troops in the wilderness, destitute of everything necessary for either the comfort or convenience of soldiers." . . . "The country is almost laid waste, and the inhabitants plunder one another with little less than savage fury. We live from hand to mouth, and have nothing to subsist on but what we collect with armed parties. In this situation, I believe you will agree with me, there is nothing inviting this way, especially when I assure you our whole force fit for duty, that are properly clothed and properly equipped, does not amount to eight hundred men." — *Johnson's Life of Greene*, vol. i. p. 340.

Writing to Mr. Varnum, a member of Congress, he says: —

"There is a great spirit of enterprise prevailing among the militia of these Southern States, especially with the volunteers. But their mode of going to war is so destructive, that *it is the greatest folly in the world to trust the liberties of a people to such a precarious defence.*" — *Johnson's Life of Greene*, vol. i. p. 397.

Nothing can be more authentic or complete than this testimony. Here, also, is what is said by David Ramsay, an estimable citizen of South Carolina, in his History of the Revolution in that State, published in 1785, only a short time after the scenes which he describes: —

"While the American soldiers lay encamped (in the low country near Charleston), their tattered rags were so completely worn out, that seven hundred of them were as naked as they were born, excepting a small strip of cloth about their waists, and they were nearly as destitute of meat as of clothing." — vol. ii. p. 258.

The military weakness of this "slaveholding community" is too apparent. Learn now its occasion; and then join with me in amazement that a Senator from South Carolina should attribute our independence to anything "slaveholding." The records of the country, and various voices, all disown his brag for Slavery. The State of South Carolina, by authentic history, disowns it. Listen, if you please, to peculiar and decisive testimony, under date of 29th March, 1779, from the Secret Journal of the Continental Congress: —

"The Committee appointed to take into consideration the *circumstances of the Southern States*, and the ways and means for *their* safety and defence, report, that the State of South Carolina (as represented by the Delegates of the said State, and by Mr. Huger, who has come here at the request of the Governor of the said State, on purpose to explain the circumstances thereof) is UNABLE to make any effectual efforts with militia, by reason of the great proportion of citizens *necessary to remain at home, to prevent insurrection among the negroes*, and to prevent the desertion of them to the enemy. That the state of the country, and *the great number of these people among them*, expose the inhabitants to great *danger*, from the endeavors of the enemy to excite them to revolt or desert." — Vol. i. p. 105.

Here is South Carolina secretly disclosing her military weakness, and its ignoble occasion; thus repudiating, in advance, the vaunt of her Senator, who finds strength and gratulation in Slavery rather than in Freedom. It was during the war that she thus shrived herself, on bended knees, in the confessional of the Continental Congress. But the same ignominious confession was made, some time after the war, in open debate, on the floor of Congress, by Mr. Burke, a Representative from South Carolina: —

"There is not a gentleman on the floor who is a stranger to the feeble situation of our State, when we entered into the war to oppose the British power. *We were not only without money, without an army or military stores, but we were few in number, and likely to be entangled with our domestics, in case the enemy invaded us.*" — *Annals of Congress*, 1789, 1791, vol. ii. p. 1484.

Similar testimony to the weakness engendered by Slavery was also borne by Mr. Madison, in open debate in Congress : —

"Every addition they (Georgia and South Carolina) receive to their number of slaves, *tends to weaken them, and render them less capable of self-defence.*" — *Annals of Congress*, vol. i. p. 340.

The historian of South Carolina, Dr. Ramsay, a contemporary observer of the very scenes which he describes, also exposes this weakness : —

"The forces under the command of General Provost marched through the richest settlements of the State, where are the fewest white inhabitants in proportion to the number of slaves. *The hapless Africans, allured with the hope of Freedom, forsook their owners*, and repaired in great numbers to the royal army. They endeavored to recommend themselves to their new masters by discovering where their owners had concealed their property, and were assisting in carrying it off." — *History of South Carolina*, vol. i. p. 312.

And the same candid historian, describing the invasion of the next year, says : —

"The slaves a *second* time *flocked* to the British army." — Vol. i. p. 336.

And at a still later day, Mr. Justice Johnson, of the Supreme Court of the United States, and a citizen of

South Carolina, in his elaborate Life of General Greene, speaking of negro slaves, makes the same unhappy admission. He says: —

"But the number dispersed through these (Southern) States was very great; *so great, as to render it impossible for the citizens to muster freemen enough to withstand the pressure of the British arms*." — Vol. ii. p. 472.

Surely, sir, this is enough, and more. Thus, from authentic documents — including the very muster-rolls of the Revolution — we learn the small contributions of men and the military weakness of the Southern States, particularly of South Carolina, as compared with the Northern States; and from the very lips of South Carolina, on four different occasions, speaking by a Committee; by one of her representatives in Congress; by her historian; and by an eminent citizen, we have the confession not only of weakness, but that this weakness was caused by Slavery. And yet, in the face of this cumulative and unimpeachable testimony, we are called to listen, in the American Senate, to a high-flying boast, from a venerable Senator, that American Independence was achieved by the arms and treasure of "slaveholding communities;" an assumption, baseless as the fabric of a vision, in any way it may be interpreted; whether as meaning baldly that independence was achieved by those Southern States, which were the peculiar home of Slavery, or that it was achieved by any strength or influence which came from that noxious source. Sir, I speak here for a Commonwealth of just renown, but I speak also for a cause which is more than any Commonwealth, even that which I represent; and I cannot allow the Senator, with his silver-white locks, to discredit either. Not by Slavery, but in spite of it, was independence achieved. Not *because*, but *notwithstanding*, there were "slaveholding communities," did triumph descend upon our arms. It was the inspiration of Liberty Universal that conducted us through the Red Sea of the Revolution, as it had already given to the Declaration of Independence its mighty tone, resounding through the ages. "Let it be remembered," said the nation, speaking by the voice of the Continental Congress, at the close of the war, "that it has ever been the pride and boast of America, that the rights for which she has contended WERE THE RIGHTS OF HUMAN NATURE!" Yes, sir, in this behalf, and by this sign, we conquered.

Such, sir, is my answer on this head to the Senator from South Carolina. If the work which I undertook has been done thoroughly, he must not blame me. Whatever I undertake, I am apt to do thoroughly. But while thus repelling the insinuations against Massachusetts, and the assumptions for Slavery, I would not unnecessarily touch the sensibilities of that Senator, or of the State which he represents. I cannot forget that, amidst all diversities of opinion, we are bound together by the ties of a common country — that Massachusetts and South Carolina are sister States, and that the concord of sisters ought to prevail between them; but I am constrained to declare, that throughout this debate I have sought in vain any token of that just spirit which, within the sphere of its influence, is calculated to promote the concord of States or of individuals

And now, for the present, I part with the venerable Senator from South Carolina. In pursuing his inconsistencies, and exposing them to judgment, I had almost forgotten his associate leader in the wanton and personal assault to which I have been exposed — I mean the veteran Senator from Virginia [Mr. Mason], who is now directly in my eye. With imperious look, and in the style of Sir Forcible Feeble, that Senator has undertaken to call in question my statement that the Fugitive Slave Bill denied the writ of *Habeas Corpus ;* and, in doing this, he has assumed a superiority for himself which, permit me to tell him now in this presence, nothing in him can sanction. Sir, I claim little for myself; but I shrink in no respect from any comparison with that Senator, veteran, though he be. Sitting near him, as has been my fortune since I have been on this floor, I have come to know something of his conversation, something of his manners, something of his attainments, something of his abilities, something of his character — ay, sir, and something of *his* associations ; and, while I would not undertake to disparage him in any of these respects, yet I feel that I do not exalt myself unduly — that I do not claim too much for the position which I hold, or the name which I have established — when I openly declare that, as a Senator of Massachusetts, and as a man, I place myself at every point in unhesitating comparison with that honorable assailant. And to his peremptory assertion that the Fugitive Slave Bill does not deny the *Habeas Corpus*, I oppose my assertion, as peremptory as his own, that it does, and there I leave that question.

Mr. President, I welcome the sensibility which the

Senator from Virginia displays at the exposure of the Fugitive Slave Bill in its true character. He is the author of that enormity. From his brain came forth the soulless monster. He is, therefore, its natural guardian. The Senator is, I believe, a lawyer. And now, since at last he has shown a parental solicitude to shield his offspring, he must do more than vainly parry the objection, that it denies the great writ of *Habeas Corpus*. It is true, sir, if anything but Slavery were in question, such an objection, if merely plausible, would be fatal; but it is not to be supposed that the partisans of an institution founded on a denial of human rights, can appreciate the proper efficacy of that writ of Freedom. Sir, I challenge the Senator to defend his progeny; not by assertion, but by reason. Let him rally all the ability, learning and subtlety, which he can command, and undertake the impossible work.

Let him answer this objection. The Constitution, by an amendment which Samuel Adams hailed as a protection against the usurpations of the National Government, and which Jefferson asserted was our "foundation corner-stone," has solemnly declared that "the powers not delegated to the United States by the Constitution, nor prohibited by it to the States, are reserved to the States respectively, or to the people." Stronger words could not be employed to limit the powers under the Constitution, and to protect the people from all assumptions of the National Government, particularly in derogation of Freedom. By the Virginia resolutions of 1798, which the Senator is reputed to accept, this limitation of the powers of the National Government is recognized and enforced. The Senator himself is understood, on all questions not affecting the claims of Slavery, to espouse this rule in its utmost strictness. Let him now indicate, if he can, any article, clause, phrase, or word, in the Constitution, which gives to Congress any power to establish a "uniform law throughout the United States" on the subject of fugitive slaves. Let him now show, if he can, from the records of the Federal Convention, one jot of evidence inclining to any such power. Whatever may be its interpretation in other respects, the clause on which this Bill purports to be founded gives no such power. Sir, nothing can come out of nothing, and the Fugitive Slave Bill is, therefore, without any source or origin in the Constitution. It is an open and unmitigated usurpation.

And, sir, when the veteran Senator of Virginia has answered this objection: when he has been able to find in the Constitution a power which is not to be found, and to make us see what is not to be seen, then let him answer another objection. The Constitution has secured the inestimable right of Trial by Jury in "suits at common law," where the value in controversy exceeds twenty dollars. Of course, Freedom is not susceptible of pecuniary valuation, therefore there can be no question that the claim for a fugitive slave is within this condition. In determining what is meant by "suits at common law," recourse must be had to the common law itself, precisely as we resort to that law in order to determine what is meant by "Trial by Jury." Let the Senator, if he be a lawyer, now undertake to show that a claim for a fugitive slave is not, according to the early precedents and writs — well known to the framers of the Constitution, especially to Charles Cotesworth Pinckney and John Rutledge, of South Carolina, both of whom had studied law at the Temple — a *suit at common law*, to which, under the solemn guaranty of the Constitution, is attached the Trial by Jury, as an inseparable incident. Let the Senator undertake to show this, if he can.

And, sir, when the veteran Senator has found a power in the Constitution where none exists, and has set aside the right of Trial by Jury in a suit at common law, then let him answer yet another objection. By the judgment of the Supreme Court of the United States, a claim for a fugitive slave is declared to be *a case under the Constitution*, within the judicial power; and this judgment of the court is confirmed by common sense and common law. Let the Senator undertake to show, if he can, how such an exalted exercise of judicial power can be confided to a single petty magistrate, appointed, not by the President, with the advice and consent of the Senate, but by the Court; holding his office, not during good behavior, but merely during the will of the Court; and receiving, not a regular salary, but fees according to each individual case. Let the Senator answer this objection, if, in any way, by any twist of learning, logic, or law, he can.

Thus, sir, do I present the issue directly on this outrageous enactment. Let the author of the Fugitive Slave Bill meet it. He will find me ready to follow him in argument, though I trust never to be led, even by his example, into any departure from those courtesies of debate which are essential to the harmony of every legislative body.

Such, Mr. President, is my response to all that has been said — in this debate — so far as I deem it in any way worthy of attention. To the two associate chieftains in this personal assault, the veteran Senator from Virginia, and the Senator from South Carolina with the silver-white locks, I have replied completely. It is true that others have joined in the cry, which these associates first started; but I shall not be tempted further. Some there are who are best answered by silence; best answered by withholding the words which leap impulsively to the lips.

And now, turning my back upon these things, let me, as I close, dwell on a single aspect of this discussion which will render it memorable. On former occasions like this, the right of petition has been vehemently assailed, or practically denied. Only two years ago, memorials for the repeal of the Fugitive Slave Bill, presented by me, were laid on your table, Mr. President, without reference to any Committee. All is changed now. Senators have condemned the memorial, and sounded the cry of "treason," "treason," in our ears; but thus far, throughout this excited debate, no person has so completely outraged the spirit of our institutions, or forgotten himself, as to persevere in objecting to the reception of the memorial, and its proper reference. It is true, the remonstrants and their representatives here have been treated with indignity; but the great right of petition — the sword and buckler of the citizen — though thus discredited, has not been denied. Here, sir, is a triumph for Freedom.

# STRUGGLE FOR THE REPEAL OF THE FUGITIVE SLAVE BILL

IN THE SENATE OF THE UNITED STATES, 31ST JULY, 1854.

The efforts of the friends of Freedom in Congress have encountered opposition at every stage. The presentation of petitions by John Quincy Adams was thwarted in every way that vindictive rage could prompt. All propositions for the repeal of obnoxious laws sustaining Slavery have been stifled. To accomplish this result, parliamentary courtesy and parliamentary law have both been set at defiance. On a former occasion, (see *ante*, p. 74,) when Mr. Sumner brought forward his motion for the repeal of the Fugitive Slave Bill, he was refused a hearing ; and he obtained it only by taking advantage of the Civil and Diplomatic Appropriation Bill, and moving an amendment to it, which no parliamentary subtlety or audacity could declare to be out of order. On the presentation of petitions against the Fugitive Slave Bill, from time to time, he was met by similar checks. Meanwhile, anything for Slavery was always in order. An experience of a single day will show something of this.

On the 31st July, 1854, Mr. Seward, of New York, under instructions from the Committee on Pensions, reported a Bill, which had already passed the House of Representatives, for the relief of Betsey Nash, a poor and aged woman, whose husband had died of wounds received in the the war of 1812, and asked for its immediate consideration. This simple measure, demanded by obvious justice, was at once embarrassed by an incongruous proposition for the support of Slavery. Mr. Adams, of Mississippi, moved, as an amendment, another Bill, for the relief of Mrs. Batchelder, the widow of a person who had been killed in Boston, while aiding as a volunteer in the enforcement of the Fugitive Slave Bill. In the face of various objections this amendment was adopted. Mr. Sumner at once followed by a proposition in the following words :

"*Provided*, that the Act of Congress, approved 18th Sept. 1850, for the surrender of fugitives from service or labor, be, and the same hereby is repealed."

But this was ruled out of order, as "not germane to the Bill under consideration ;" and the two Bills, hitched together — one for a military pension, and the other for contribution to the widow of a Slave-Hunter — were put on their passage. Mr. Sumner then sprang for the floor, when a struggle ensued, which is minutely reported in the *Congressional Globe*. The careful reader will observe that, in order to cut off an effort to repeal the Fugitive Slave Bill, at least two unquestionable rules of parliamentary law were overturned.

Mr. Sumner. In pursuance of notice, I now ask leave to introduce a Bill.

Mr. Stuart. I object to it, and move to take up the River and Harbor Bill.

The Presiding Officer. The other Bill is not disposed of. The third reading of a Bill for the relief of Betsey Nash.

The Bill was then read a third time and passed.

Mr. Sumner. In pursuance of notice, I ask leave to introduce a Bill, which I now send to the table.

Mr. Stuart. Is that in order ?

Mr. Sumner. Why not ?

Mr. Benjamin. There is a pending motion of the Senator from Michigan to take up the River and Harbor Bill.

The Presiding Officer. That motion was not entertained, because the Senator from Massachusetts had and has the floor.

Mr. Stuart. I make the motion now.

The PRESIDING OFFICER. The Chair thinks it is in order to give the notice.

Mr. SUMNER. Notice has been given, and I now, in pursuance of notice, introduce the Bill. The question is on its first reading.

The PRESIDING OFFICER. The first reading of a Bill.

Mr. NORRIS. I rise to a question of order.

Mr. SUMNER. I believe I have the floor.

Mr. NORRIS. But I rise to a question of order. I submit that that is not the question. The Senator from Massachusetts has given notice that he would ask leave to introduce a Bill. He now asks that leave. If there be objection, the question must be decided by the Senate whether he shall have leave or not. Objection is made, and the Bill cannot be read.

Mr. SUMNER. Very well; the first question, then, is on granting leave, and the title of the Bill will be read.

The PRESIDING OFFICER (to the Secretary). Read the title.

The Secretary read it as follows: "A Bill to repeal the Act of Congress approved 18th September, 1850, for the surrender of fugitives from service or labor."

The PRESIDING OFFICER. The question is on granting leave to introduce the Bill.

Mr. SUMNER. And I have the floor.

The PRESIDING OFFICER. The Senator from Massachusetts is entitled to the floor.

Mr. SUMNER. I shall not occupy much time; nor shall I debate the Bill. Some time ago, Mr. President, after the presentation of the Memorial from Boston, signed by twenty-nine hundred citizens without distinction of party, I gave notice that I should, at some day thereafter, ask leave to introduce a Bill for the repeal of the Fugitive Slave Act. Desirous, however, not to proceed in that matter prematurely, I awaited the action of the Committee on the Judiciary, to which the memorial, and others of a similar character, were referred. At length an adverse report was made, and accepted by the Senate. From the time of that report down to this moment, I have sought an opportunity to introduce this Bill. Now, at last, I have it. At a former session, sir, in introducing a similar proposition, I considered it at length, in an argument which I fearlessly assert —

Mr. Gwin. I rise to a point of order. Has the Senator a right to debate the question, or say anything on it until leave be granted?

The Presiding Officer. My impression is that the question is not debatable.*

Mr. Sumner. I propose simply to explain my Bill, to make a statement, not an argument.

Mr. Gwin. I make the point of order.

The Presiding Officer. I am not aware precisely what the rule of order on the subject is; but I have the impression that the Senator cannot debate —

Mr. Sumner. The distinction is this —

Mr. Gwin. I insist upon the application of the decision of the Chair.

Mr. Mason. Mr. President, there is one rule of order that is undoubted: that when the Chair is stat-

* Nothing is clearer, under the rules of the Senate, than that Mr. Sumner was in order when, on introducing his Bill, he proceeded to state the causes for doing it.

ing a question of order, he must not be interrupted by a Senator. There is no question about that rule of order.

The PRESIDING OFFICER. The Senator did not interrupt the Chair.

Mr. SUMNER. The Chair does me justice in response to the injustice of the Senator from Virginia.

The PRESIDING OFFICER. Order, order!

Mr. MASON. The Senator is doing that very thing at this moment. I am endeavoring to sustain the authority of the Chair, which certainly has been violated.

The PRESIDING OFFICER. It is the opinion of the Chair that the debate is out of order. I am not precisely informed of what the rule is; but such is my clear impression.

Mr. WALKER. If the Senator from Massachusetts will allow me, I will say a word here.

Mr. SUMNER. Certainly.

Mr. WALKER. It is usual, upon notice being given of intention, to ask leave to introduce a Bill. The Bill is sent to the Chair, and it is taken as a matter of course that the Senator asking it has leave. But in this instance, differing from the usual practice, objection has been made to leave being granted. The necessity is imposed, then, of taking the sense of the Senate on granting leave to the Senator to introduce his Bill. That, then, becomes the question. The question for the Chair to put is, Shall the Senator have leave?

The PRESIDING OFFICER. That was the question proposed.

Mr. WALKER. Now, sir, it does seem to me that

it is proper, and that it is in order, for the Senator to address himself to the Senate, with the view of showing the propriety of granting the leave asked for. He has a right to show that there would be propriety on the part of the Senate in granting the leave. I think, therefore, as this may become a precedent in future in regard to other matters, that it should be settled with some degree of deliberation.

Mr. GWIN. Let the Chair decide the question.

The PRESIDING OFFICER. The Chair has decided that debate was not in order, in his opinion.

Mr. SUMNER. From that decision of the Chair, I most respectfully take an appeal.

The PRESIDING OFFICER. From that ruling of the Chair an appeal is taken by the Senator from Massachusetts. The question is on the appeal.

Mr. BENJAMIN. In order to put a stop to the whole debate, I move to lay the appeal on the table, That is a motion which is not debatable.

Mr. SUMNER. Is that motion in order?

The PRESIDING OFFICER. Certainly it is in order.*

Mr. WELLER. I desire to make one remark in regard to the rule.

The PRESIDING OFFICER. It is not in order now. The question must be taken without debate.

Mr. SUMNER. Allow me to state the case as it seems to me. I was on the floor, and yielded it to the Senator from Wisconsin strictly for the purpose of an explanation. When he finished I was in posses-

* The motion was clearly out of order. In the Senate an appeal from the decision of the Chair on a question of order cannot be laid on the table.

sion of the floor; and then it was that the Senator from Louisiana, on my right —

The PRESIDING OFFICER. Will the Senator from Massachusetts give leave to the Chair to explain?

Mr. SUMNER. Certainly.

The PRESIDING OFFICER. A point of order was made by the Senator from California [Mr. Gwin], that debate was not in order upon the question of granting leave; and the Chair so decided. The Senator from Massachusetts then lost the floor, as I apprehend, and he certainly did by following it up by an appeal. After that he could go no further. He lost the floor then again for a second time, and then it was that the Senator from Louisiana intervened with another motion, which is certainly in order, to lay the appeal on the table. That is not debatable. This, it seems to me, is the state of the case.

Mr. CHASE. Will the Chair allow me to make a single statement?

The PRESIDING OFFICER. Certainly.

Mr. CHASE. The Senator from Massachusetts rose and held the floor during the suggestion made to the Chair by the Senator from Wisconsin. The Chair then, after the Senator from Wisconsin had finished his suggestion, declared his opinion to be, notwithstanding the suggestion, that debate was not in order. The Senator from Massachusetts then took an appeal, and retained the floor for the purpose of addressing the Senate on that appeal. While he occupied the floor, the Senator from Louisiana rose and moved to lay the appeal upon the table. That will be borne out by the the gentlemen present.

The PRESIDING OFFICER. That is so; but the

Chair does not understand that debate was in order on the appeal. The appeal was to be decided without debate, and therefore the Senator from Massachusetts necessarily lost the floor after he took the appeal.

Mr. Bell. I would inquire whether there is not a Bill already pending for the repeal of the Fugitive Slave Law?

The Presiding Officer. I have not inquired of the Secretary; but it is my belief there is a similar Bill pending; but it was not on that ground the Chair made this ruling.

Mr. Bell. I would inquire whether there is not such a Bill pending? Did not the honorable Senator from Ohio some time ago bring in such a Bill?

Mr. Weller. I think he did.

Mr. Chase. No, sir.

Mr. Bell. Then I am mistaken.

Mr. Chase. My Bill is not on that subject.

The Presiding Officer. The question is on the motion of the Senator from Louisiana, to lay on the table the appeal taken by the Senator from Massachusetts from the decision of the Chair.

Mr. Chase. I ask if the motion of the Senator from Louisiana is in order when the Senator from Massachusetts retained the floor for the purpose of debating the appeal?

Mr. Benjamin. The Senator is not in order in renewing that question, which has already been decided by the Chair.

The Presiding Officer. If the Chair acted under an erroneous impression in supposing that debate on the appeal was not in order, when it actually is, it was the fault of the Chair, and it would not have been in order for the Senator from Louisiana to make the motion which he did make, while the Senator from Massachusetts was on the floor. But the Chair recognized the Senator from Louisiana, supposing that the Senator from Massachusetts had yielded the floor. The Senator had taken an appeal; he followed it up by no address to the Chair, indicating an intention that he intended to debate the appeal, or the Chair certainly should so far have recognized him. But the Chair would reconsider his ruling in that respect, with the consent of the Senator from Louisiana.

Mr. Bright. The Chair will permit me to suggest that I think the motion proper to be entertained now is the one proposed by the Senator from New Hampshire [Mr. Norris]. The Senator from Massachusetts presented his Bill, the Senator from New Hampshire raised the question as to whether the Senate would grant leave to introduce it; and I think the proper question to be put now is, will the Senate grant leave to introduce a Bill repealing the Fugitive Slave Law? The effect of the motion of the Senator from Louisiana would be to lay the subject on the table, from which it might be taken at any time for action. For one, I desire to give a decisive vote now, declaring that I am unwilling to legislate upon the subject, that I am satisfied with the law as it reads, and that I will not aid the Senator from Massachusetts, or any Senator in —

The Presiding Officer. The Senator from Indiana is certainly not in order.

Mr. Bright. I certainly am in order in calling the attention of the Chair to the fact that the Senator from New Hampshire —

The PRESIDING OFFICER. The Senator from Indiana is not in order.

Mr. BRIGHT. Then I will sit down and ask the Chair to state wherein I am out of order?

The PRESIDING OFFICER. In discussing a question which is not before the Senate.

Mr. BRIGHT. I claim that the motion is before the Senate. The Senator from New Hampshire raised the question immediately that —

The PRESIDING OFFICER. The Chair decides otherwise.

Mr. BRIGHT. Then I appeal from the decision of the Chair, and I state this as my point of order: that before the Bill was presented in legal parlance, the Senator from New Hampshire raised the question as to whether the Senate would grant leave, and that is the point now before the Senate.

The PRESIDING OFFICER. The Chair will state the question which he supposes to be pending. The Senator from California made a point of order that debate on the Bill proposed to be introduced by the Senator from Massachusetts, was not in order. The Chair so ruled. From that ruling the Senator from Massachusetts took an appeal. The Chair supposed that the Senator from Massachusetts had yielded the floor, and he gave the floor to the Senator from Louisiana, who moved to lay that appeal on the table. That is the question which is now pending. The Chair before suggested that if the Senator from Massachusetts had not yielded the floor, he had made a mistake in giving the floor to the Senator from Louisiana, but he did not suppose that the Senator from Massachusetts, after taking the appeal, without some indication of his intention to debate it, could continue to hold the floor, and he therefore recognized the Senator from Louisiana. The Chair is sorry if he did the Senator from Massachusetts injustice in that respect, but he did not hear him, and recognized the Senator from Louisiana.

Mr. BRIGHT. I would respectfully ask the Chair what has become of the motion submitted by the Senator from New Hampshire?

The PRESIDING OFFICER. The Chair did not understand him to submit a motion, but the Senator from California took his point of order.

Mr. BRIGHT. I wish to inquire of the Senator from New Hampshire whether he has withdrawn his motion?

The PRESIDING OFFICER. It was not entertained. It is not in his power to say whether it was withdrawn or not, for it was not entertained.

Mr. NORRIS. I think I can inform my friend from Indiana how the matter stands. The Senator from Massachusetts proposed to introduce a Bill on notice given. I raised the question that it could not be introduced without leave of the Senate, if there was objection.

Mr. SUMNER. Do I understand the Senator to say without notice given? I asked leave to introduce the Bill in pursuance of notice.

Mr. NORRIS. The Senator from Massachusetts, I have already stated, offered his Bill agreeably to previous notice.

Mr. SUMNER. Precisely.

Mr. NORRIS. The question was then raised, whether it could be received if there was objection. The question arose whether leave should be granted to the Senator from Massachusetts to introduce the Bill?

Mr. SUMNER. That is the first question.

Mr. NORRIS. The Senator from Massachusetts, upon the question of granting leave, undertook to address the Senate. He was then called to order by my friend from California, for discussing that question. The Chair sustained the objection of the Senator from California. From the decision of the Chair the Senator from Massachusetts took an appeal, and that is where the question now stands, unless the Senator from Louisiana had a right to make the motion which he did make, which was to lay the appeal on the table.

The PRESIDING OFFICER. The question is, unless the Senator from Louisiana will disembarrass the Chair by withdrawing it, on the motion of the Senator from Louisiana, to lay the appeal on the table.

Mr. SUMNER. On that motion I ask for the yeas and nays.

The yeas and nays were ordered.

Mr. FOOT. On what motion have the yeas and nays been ordered?

The PRESIDING OFFICER. On the motion of the Senator from Louisiana.

Mr. WALKER. I wish to know, before voting, what will be the effect of a vote given in the affirmative on this motion? Will it carry the Bill and the whole subject on the table?

Mr. FOOT. An affirmative vote carries the whole measure on the table.

The PRESIDING OFFICER. Yes, sir; if the motion

to lay on the table be agreed to, it carries the Bill with it.

Several SENATORS. No, no.

Mr. BENJAMIN. The question is whether, on the motion for leave to introduce the Bill, there shall be debate? The Chair has decided that there shall be no debate. Those who vote "yea" on my motion to lay the appeal of the Senator from Massachusetts on the table, will vote that there is to be no debate upon the permission to offer the Bill, and then the question will be taken upon granting leave.

Mr. WALKER. The Chair decides differently. The Chair decides, if I understand, that it will carry the Bill on the table. Then, how can we ever reach the question of leave when objection is made?

Mr. WELLER. I object to this discussion. The Chair will decide that question when it arises. It does not arise now. I insist that the Secretary shall go on and call the roll.

Mr. WALKER. Suppose some of us object to it?

Mr. WELLER. Then I object to your discussing it.

The PRESIDING OFFICER. The Chair, on reflection, thinks that the motion, if agreed to, would not have a further effect than to bring up the question of granting leave.

Mr. BRIGHT. I desire to understand the Chair. I do not wish to insist on anything that is not right, or that is not within the rules. That I insist upon having. The honorable Senator from Louisiana is right in his conclusions as to his motion, provided he had a right to make the motion; but I doubt whether he had a right to make that motion while the motion of the honorable Senator from New Hampshire was pending. I do not wish, however, to consume the time of the Senate. If the effect of the decision of the Chair is to bring us back to the question as to whether we shall receive the Bill or not, I will yield the floor.

The PRESIDING OFFICER. That is it.

Mr. BRIGHT. Very well.

Mr. SUMNER. Before the vote is taken, allow me to read a few words from the Rules and Orders, and from Jefferson's Manual.

"One day's notice, at least, shall be given of an intended motion for leave to bring in a Bill."

That is the 25th rule of the Senate, and then to that rule, in the publication which I now hold in my hand, is appended, from Jefferson's Manual, the following decisive language:

"When a member desires to bring in a Bill on any subject, *he states to the House, in general terms, the causes for doing it,* and concludes for leave to bring in a Bill entitled, &c. Leave being given, on the question, a Committee is appointed to prepare and bring in the Bill."

Now, I would simply observe, that my purpose was merely to make a statement —

Mr. BENJAMIN. I call to order.

The PRESIDING OFFICER. The Senator had presented his Bill, and was debating it afterwards. The question is now on the motion of the Senator from Louisiana, to lay the appeal on the table; and on that the yeas and nays have been ordered.

The question being taken by yeas and nays, resulted — yeas 35, nays 10; as follows:

**YEAS — Messrs. Adams, Atchinson, Bell, Benjamin, Brodhead,**

Brown, Butler, Cass, Clay, Cooper, Dawson, Dodge, of Iowa, Evans, Fitzpatrick, Geyer, Gwin, Johnson, Jones, of Iowa, Jones, of Tennessee, Mallory, Mason, Morton, Norris, Pearce, Pettit, Pratt, Rusk, Sebastian, Slidell, Stuart, Thompson, of Kentucky, Thomson, of New Jersey, Toombs, Toucey and Weller — 35.

NAYS — Messrs. Chase, Fessenden, Fish, Foot, Gillette, Rockwell, Seward, Sumner, Wade and Walker — 10.

So the appeal was ordered to lie on the table.

The PRESIDING OFFICER. The question now is on granting leave to introduce the Bill.

Mr. SUMNER. On that question I ask for the yeas and nays.

Mr. STUART. I rise to a question of order; and I think if the Chair will consider it for the moment, he will, or, at least, I hope he will, agree with me. The parliamentary law is the law under which the Senate act. Whenever there is a motion made to lay on the table a subject connected with the main subject, and it prevails, it carries the whole question with it. It is different entirely from the rule in the House of Representatives. The rules in the House vary the parliamentary law, and you may there move to lay a matter on the table, because that is the final vote, and is equivalent to rejecting it, and a motion to take it up from the table is not in order. But now the Presiding Officer will see that if this course be pursued, the Senate may grant leave to introduce this Bill, they may go on and pass it, and yet next week it will be in order for the Senator from Massachusetts to move to take up the appeal which the Senate has just laid on the table; whereas the whole subject on which his appeal rested might have been passed and sent to the other House. That surely cannot be so. The ruling of the Chair in this respect, therefore, I suggest is wrong, and the motion to lay on the table carries the whole subject with it. It is important to have the matter settled for the future practice of the Senate.

The PRESIDING OFFICER. At the first mooting of the proposition, the Chair was of that opinion; but he is perfectly satisfied now that it did not carry the whole question with it. The question was on the motion to lay the appeal on the table, and that motion was exhausted when it did lay the appeal on the table. It did not reach back to affect the question of granting leave. That is now the question before the Senate. On that the yeas and nays have been asked for by the Senator from Massachusetts.

The yeas and nays were ordered.

Mr. STUART. I will not take an appeal from the decision of the Chair, but I only wish to say that as I am satisfied I am right, I do not wish, by acquiescing in the decision of the Chair, to embarrass us when such occasions may arise again.

The question being taken by yeas and nays upon granting leave to introduce the Bill, resulted — yeas 10, nays 35; as follows:

YEAS — Messrs. Chase, Dodge, of Wisconsin, Fessenden, Foot, Gillette, Rockwell, Seward, Sumner, Wade and Walker — 10.

NAYS — Messrs. Adams, Atchison, Bell, Benjamin, Bright, Brodhead, Brown, Butler, Cass, Clay, Cooper, Dawson, Evans, Fitzpatrick, Geyer, Gwin, Johnson, Jones, of Iowa, Jones, of Tennessee, Mallory, Mason, Morton, Norris, Pearce, Pettit, Pratt, Rusk, Sebastian, Slidell, Stuart, Thompson, of Kentucky, Thomson, of New Jersey, Toombs, Toucey and Weller — 35.

So the Senate refused to grant leave to introduce the Bill.

## THE DUTIES OF MASSACHUSETTS AT THE PRESENT CRISIS.

SPEECH BEFORE THE REPUBLICAN STATE CONVENTION AT WORCESTER, 7TH SEPTEMBER, 1854.*

---

MR. PRESIDENT AND FELLOW-CITIZENS OF MASSACHUSETTS: After months of anxious, constant service in another place, away from Massachusetts, I am permitted again to stand among you, my fellow-citizens, and to draw satisfaction and strength from your generous presence. (Applause.) Life is full of changes and contrasts. From slave soil I have come to free soil. (Applause.) From the tainted breath of Slavery I have passed to this bracing air of Freedom. (Applause.) And the heated antagonism of debate, shooting forth its fiery cinders, is changed into this brimming, overflowing welcome, where I seem to lean on the great heart of our beloved Commonwealth, as it palpitates audibly in this crowded assembly. (Loud and long applause.)

Let me say at once, frankly and sincerely, that I have not come here to receive applause or to give occasion for any tokens of public regard; but simply

* This speech is copied from the newspapers of the day.

to unite with my fellow-citizens in new vows of duty. (Applause.) And yet I would not be thought insensible to the good will now swelling from so many honest bosoms. It touches me more than I can tell.

During the late session of Congress, an eminent supporter of the Nebraska Bill said to me, with great animation, in language which I give with some precision, that you may appreciate the style as well as the sentiment: "I would not go through all that you do *on this nigger question*, for all the offices and honors of the country." To which I naturally and promptly replied: "Nor would I for all the offices and honors of the country." (Laughter and long applause.) Not in such things can be found the true inducements to this warfare. For myself, if I have been able to do anything in any respect not unworthy of you, it is because I thought rather of those commanding duties which are above office and honor. (Cries of good, good, and loud applause.)

And now, on the eve of an important election in this State, we have assembled to take counsel together, in order to determine how best to perform those duties which we owe to our common country. We are to choose eleven Representatives in Congress; also, Governor, Lieutenant-Governor and members of the Legislature, which last will choose a Senator of the United States, to uphold, for five years ensuing, the principles and honor of Massachusetts. If in these elections you were to be governed merely by partialities or prejudices, whether personal or political, or merely by the exactions of party, I should have nothing to say now, except to dismiss you to your ignoble work. (That is it, good, good.) But I assume that you are ready to renounce these influences and press forward with a single regard to those duties which are now incumbent upon us in National affairs, and also in State affairs.

And here two questions occur which absorb all others. *First*, what are our political duties here in Massachusetts at the present time? and *secondly*, how, and by what agency shall they be performed? What, and how? These are the two questions of which I shall briefly speak, in their order, attempting no elaborate discussion, but simply aiming to state the case so that it may be intelligible to all who hear me.

And first, what are our duties here in Massachusetts, at the present time? In unfolding these, I need not dwell on the wrong and shame of Slavery, or on the character of the Slave Power — that Oligarchy of slaveholders — which now rules the Republic. These you understand. And yet there are two outrages fresh in your recollection, which I must not fail to expose, as natural manifestations of Slavery and the Slave Power. One is the repeal of the Prohibition of Slavery in the vast Missouri Territory, now known as Kansas and Nebraska, contrary to time-honored compact and plighted faith. The other is the seizure of Anthony Burns, on the free soil of Massachusetts, and his surrender, without judge or jury, to a Slave-hunter from Virginia, to be thrust back into perpetual bondage. (Shame! shame!) These outrages cry aloud to Heaven, and to the people of Massachusetts. (Sensation.) Their intrinsic wickedness is enhanced by the way in which they were accomplished. Of the first, I know something from personal observation; of the latter, I am informed only by public report.

It is characteristic of the Slave Power never to stick at any means supposed to be needful in carrying forward its plans; but never, on any occasion, were its assumptions so barefaced and tyrannical as in the passage of the Nebraska Bill.

This Bill was precipitated upon Congress without one word of public recommendation from the President, — without notice or discussion in any newspaper, — and without a single petition from the people. It was urged by different advocates, on two principal arguments, so opposite and inconsistent, as to slap each other in the face. (Laughter.) One being that, by the repeal of the prohibition, the territory would be absolutely open to the entry of slaveholders with their slaves; and the other being that the people there would be left to determine whether slaveholders should enter with their slaves. With some, the apology was the alleged rights of slaveholders; with others, it was the alleged rights of the people. With some, it was openly the extension of Slavery; and with others, openly the establishment of Freedom, under the guise of "popular sovereignty." Of course, the measure, thus upheld in defiance of reason, was carried through Congress, in defiance of all the securities of legislation.

It was carried, *first*, by *whipping in* to its support, through executive influence and patronage, men who acted against their own declared judgment, and the known will of their constituents; *secondly*, by *foisting out* of place, both in the Senate and House of Representatives, important business, long pending, and usurping its room; *thirdly*, by *trampling under foot* the rules of the House of Representatives, always before the safeguard of the minority; and *fourthly*, by *driving it to a close* during the present Congress, so that it might not be arrested by the indignant voice of the people. Such are some of the means by which the Nebraska Bill was carried. If the clear will of the people had not been disregarded, it could not have passed. If the Government had not nefariously interposed its influence, it could not have passed. If it had been left to its natural place in the order of business, it could not have passed. If the rules of the House and the rights of the minority had not been violated, it could not have passed. If it had been allowed to go over to another Congress, when the people might be heard, it would have been ended — all ended.

Contemporaneously with the final triumph of this outrage — on the very night of the passage of the Nebraska Bill at Washington — another scene, beginning a dismal tragedy, was enacted at Boston. In those streets where he had walked as a freeman, Anthony Burns was seized as a slave — under the base pretext that he was a criminal — imprisoned in the court-house, which was turned for the time into a fortress and barracoon — guarded by heartless hirelings, whose chief idea of liberty was the license to do wrong — (loud applause and cries of "that's it!" "that's it!" &c.) — escorted by intrusive soldiers of the United States — watched by a prostituted militia — and finally given up to a Slave-hunter by the decree of a petty

magistrate, who did not hesitate to take upon his soul the awful responsibility of dooming a fellow-man, in whom he could find no fault, to a fate worse than death. How all this was accomplished, I need not minutely relate. Suffice it to say, that in doing this deed of woe and shame, the liberties of all our citizens, white as well as black, were put in jeopardy — the Mayor of Boston was converted to a tool — (applause) — the Governor of the Commonwealth to a cipher — (long continued applause) — the laws, the precious sentiments, the religion, the pride and glory of Massachusetts were trampled in the dust, and you and I and all of us fell down while the Slave Power flourished over us. (Shame, shame, and applause.)

These things, in themselves are bad — very bad; but they are worse when regarded as the natural offspring of the Oligarchy which now sways the country. And it is this Oligarchy which, at every political hazard, we must oppose. Already its schemes of new aggrandizement are displayed. With a watchfulness that never sleeps, and an activity that never tires — with as many eyes as Argus, and as many arms as Briareus — the Slave Power asserts its perpetual supremacy; now threatening to wrest Cuba from Spain, by violent war, or hardly less violent purchase; now hankering for another slice of Mexico, in order to give new scope to Slavery; now proposing once more to open the hideous, heaven-defying slave-trade, and thus to replenish its shambles with human flesh; and now by the lips of an eminent Senator asserting an audacious claim to the whole group of the West Indies, whether held by Holland, Spain, France or England, as "our Southern Islands," while it assails the independence

of Hayti, and stretches its treacherous ambition even to the distant Valley of the Amazon.

In maintaining its power, it has applied a new test for office, very different from that of Jefferson — "Is he honest? is he capable? is he faithful to the constitution?" None of these things are asked, but simply, "Is he faithful to Slavery?" (Cries of "That's a fact.") With arrogant ostracism it excludes from every office all who cannot respond to this test. So complete and irrational has this tyranny become, that, at this moment, while I now speak, could Washington, Jefferson or Franklin, once more descend upon the earth and mingle in its affairs to bless us with their wisdom, not one of them, with his recorded opinions on Slavery, could receive a nomination for the Presidency, from a National Convention of either of the great political parties, nor, stranger still, could he be confirmed by the Senate for any political function under the Government. Had this test prevailed in earlier days, Washington could not have been made Commander-in-Chief of the American army; Jefferson could not have taken his place on the Committee to draft the Declaration of Independence; and Franklin could not have been sent to France with the commission of the infant republic, to secure the invaluable alliance of that powerful kingdom.

In view of these things, our duties are manifest. First and foremost, the Slave Power itself must be overthrown. Lord Chatham once exclaimed, in stirring language, that the time had been when he was content to bring France to her knees; now he would not stop till he had laid her on her back. Nor can we be content with less in our warfare. We must not stop till we have laid the Slave Power on its back. (Prolonged cheers.) And, fellow-citizens, permit me to say, not till then will the Free States be absolved from all political responsibility for Slavery, and relieved from that corrupt spirit of compromise which now debases, at once, their politics and their religion; nor till then will there be any repose for the country. (Immense cheering.) Indemnity for the past, and security for the future, must be our watchwords. (Applause.) But these can be obtained only when Slavery is dispossessed of its present vantage-ground, by driving it back exclusively within the limits of the States, and putting the National Government everywhere within its constitutional sphere, openly, actively and perpetually, on the side of Freedom. The consequences of this change of policy would be of incalculable and far-reaching beneficence. Not only would Freedom become national and Slavery sectional, as was intended by our fathers; but the National Government would become the mighty instrument and spokesman of Freedom, as it is now the mighty instrument and spokesman of Slavery. Its powers, its treasury, its patronage, would all be turned, in harmony with the Constitution, to promote Freedom. The Committees of Congress, where Slavery now rules, — Congress itself, and the Cabinet also, — would all be organized for Freedom. The hypocritical disguise or renunciation of Anti-Slavery sentiment would cease to be necessary for the sake of political preferment; and the Slaveholding Oligarchy, banished from the National Government, and despoiled of its ill-gotten political consequence, without ability to punish or reward, would cease to be feared, either at the North or the South, until at last the citizens of the Slave States, of whom a large portion have no interest in Slavery, would demand Emancipation; and the great work would commence. Such is the obvious course of things. To the overthrow of the Slave Power we are thus summoned by a double call, one political and the other philanthropic; first, to remove an oppressive tyranny from the National Government, and secondly, to open the gates of Emancipation in the Slave States. (Loud applause.)

But while keeping this great purpose in view, we must not forget details. The existence of Slavery any where within the National jurisdiction — in the Territories — in the District of Columbia — or on the high seas beneath the national flag, is an unconstitutional usurpation, which must be opposed. The Fugitive Slave Bill, monstrous in cruelty, as in unconstitutionality, is a usurpation, which must be opposed. The admission of new Slave States, from whatsoever quarter, from Texas or Cuba (applause), Utah or New Mexico, must be opposed. And to every scheme of Slavery, whether in Cuba, or Mexico, — on the high seas in opening the slave-trade — in the West Indies — the Valley of the Amazon, — whether accomplished or merely plotted, whether pending or in prospect, we must send forth an EVERLASTING NO! (Long contined applause.) Such is the duty of Massachusetts, without hesitation or compromise.

Thus far I have spoken of our duties in national matters; but there are other duties of pressing importance, here at home, which must not be forgotten or postponed. It is often said that "charity should begin at home." Better say, that *charity should begin*

*everywhere.* But while contending with the Slave Power on the broad field of national politics, we must not forget the duty of protecting the liberty of all who tread the soil of Massachusetts. (Immense cheering.) Early in colonial history, Massachusetts set her face against Slavery. At the head of her Bill of Rights she solemnly asserted, that all men are born free and equal; and in the same declaration, surrounded the liberties of all within her borders by the inestimable rights of trial by jury and *Habeas Corpus.* But recent events on her own soil have taught the necessity of new safeguards to these great principles, — to the end that Massachusetts may not be a vassal of South Carolina and Virginia — that the Slave-hunter may not range at will among us, and that the liberties of all may not be violated with impunity.

But I am admonished that I must not dwell longer on these things. Suffice it to say, that our duties, in National and State affairs, are identical, and may be described by the same formula: In the one case to put the National Government, in all its departments, and in the other case the State Government, in all its departments, openly, actively and perpetually, on the side of Freedom. (Loud applause.)

Having considered *what* our duties are, the question now presses upon us, *how* shall they be performed? By what agency, by what instrumentality, or in what way?

The most obvious way is by choosing men to represent us in the National Government, and also at home, who shall recognize these duties and be ever loyal to them (cheers); men who at Washington will not shrink from the conflict with Slavery, and also other men, who, at home in Massachusetts will not shrink from the same conflict when the Slave-hunter appears. (Loud applause, and cries of "good," "good.") But in the choice of men, we are driven to the organization of parties; and here the question arises, by what form of organization, or by what party, can these men be best secured? Surely not by the Democratic party, as at present constituted (laughter); though if this party were true to its name, pregnant with human rights, it would leave little to be desired. In this party there are doubtless individuals who are anxious to do all in their power against Slavery; but, indulge me in saying that, so long as they continue members of a party which upholds the Nebraska Bill, they can do very little. (Applause and laughter.) What may we expect from the Whig party? (A voice — Resolutions.) If more may be expected from the Whig party than the Democratic party, candor must attribute much of the difference to the fact that the Whigs are *out of power*, while the Democrats are *in power*. (Long continued cheers.) If the cases were reversed, and the Whigs were in power, as in 1850, I fear that, notwithstanding the ardor of individuals, and the Resolutions of Conventions — (great laughter) — made, I fear, too often merely to be broken — the party might be brought to sustain an outrage as great as the Fugitive Slave Bill! (Laughter and applause.) But without dwelling on these things, (to which I allude with diffidence, and, I trust, in no uncharitable temper, or partisan spirit,) I desire to say that no party, which calls itself *national*, according to the common acceptance of the word, — which leans upon a slaveholding wing, (cheers) or is in combination with slaveholders,— (cheers) can at this time be true to Massachusetts. (Great applause.) And the reason is obvious. It can be presented so as to cleave the most common understanding. *The essential element of such a party, whether declared or concealed, is Compromise; but our duties require all constitutional opposition to Slavery and the Slave Power, without Compromise.* ("That's it," "good," "good.") It is difficult, then, to see how we can rely upon the Whig party.

To the true-hearted, magnanimous men who are ready to place Freedom above Party, and their Country above Politicians, I appeal. (Immense cheering.) Let them leave the old parties, and blend in an organization, which, without compromise, will maintain the good cause surely to the end. Here in Massachusetts a large majority of the people concur in sentiment on Slavery; a large majority desire the overthrow of the Slave Power. It becomes them not to scatter their votes, but to unite in one firm, consistent phalanx, (applause,) whose triumph shall constitute an epoch of Freedom, not only in this Commonwealth, but throughout the land. Such an organization is now presented by this Republican Convention, which, according to the resolutions by which it is convoked, is to co-operate with the friends of Freedom in other States. (Cheers.) As *Republicans* we go forth to encounter the *Oligarchs* of Slavery. (Great applause.)

Through this organization we may most certainly secure the election of men, who, unseduced and unterrified, will uphold at Washington the principles of Freedom and who also here at home, in our own community, by example, influence and vote, will help to invigorate Massachusetts. Indeed, I might go further and say, that, by no other organization can we reasonably hope to obtain such men, unless in rare and exceptional cases.

Men are but instruments. It will not be enough merely to choose those who are loyal. Other things must be done here at home. In the first place, all the existing laws for the protection of human freedom must be rigorously enforced; (applause, and cries of "good,") and, since these have been found inadequate, new laws for this purpose, within the limits of the constitution, must be enacted. Massachusetts certainly might do well in following Vermont, which, by a special law, has placed the fugitive slave under the safeguard of trial by jury, and the writ of *habeas corpus*. But a legislature true to Freedom, will not fail in remedies. (Applause.) A simple prohibition, declaring that no person, holding the commission of Massachusetts, as a Justice of the Peace, or other magistrate, should assume to act as a Slave-hunting Commissoner, or as counsel of any Slave-hunter, under some proper penalty, would go far to render the existing Slave Bill inoperative. (Applause.) There are not many, so fond of this base trade as to continue in it when the Commonwealth has thus set upon it a legislative brand.

But besides more rigorous legislation, Public Opinion must be invoked to step forward and throw over the fugitive its protecting panoply. A Slave-hunter will then be a by-word and reproach; and all his instruments, especially every one who volunteers in this vileness, without any positive obligation of law, will naturally be regarded as a part of his pack, and share the ignominy of the chief hunter. (Laughter and cheers.) And now, from authentic example, drawn out of recent history, learn how the Slave-hunter may be palsied by contrition. I take the story from the late letters on Neapolitan affairs by the eminent English statesman, Mr. Gladstone; and he has copied it from an Italian writer. A most successful member of the Italian police, Bolza, of the hateful tribe, known as *sbirri*, whose official duties involved his own personal degradation and the loathing of others, has left a record of the acute sense which even such a man retained of his shame. "I absolutely forbid my heirs," says this penitent official, "to allow any mark of whatever kind, to be placed over the spot of my burial; much more any inscription or epitaph. I recommend my dearly beloved wife to impress upon my children the injunction, that, in soliciting any employment from the Government, they shall ask for it elsewhere than in the *executive police*, and not, unless under extraordinary circumstances, to give her consent to the marriage of any of my daughters with a member of that service." Thus testifies the Italian instrument of legal wrong. Let public opinion here in Massachusetts once put forth its Christian might, and every instrument of the Fugitive Slave Act will feel a kindred shame. (Great applause.)

But it is sometimes gravely urged, that since the Supreme Court of the United States has affirmed the constitutionality of the Fugitive Act, there only remains to us in all places, whether in public station or in private life, the duty of absolute submission. Yes, sir, that is the assumption, which you will perceive is applicable to the humblest citizen, — who holds no office and has taken no oath to support the Constitution, — as well as to the public servant, who is under the special obligations of an official oath. Now, without stopping to consider the soundness of their judgment, affirming the constitutionality of this Act, let me say that the Constitution of the United States, as I understand it, exacts no such *passive obedience.* And, in taking the oath to support the Constitution, I have sworn to support it as I understand it, and not as other men understand it. (Loud applause. When it had subsided, it was followed by three rousing cheers for Sumner.)

In adopting this rule, which was first authoritatively enunciated by Andrew Jackson, when, as President of the United States, in the face of the decisions of the Supreme Court, he asserted the unconstitutionality of the Bank, I desire to be understood as not acting hastily. Let me add, that if it needed other authority in its support, it has that also of the distinguished Cabinet by which he was then surrounded, among whom were that unsurpassed jurist, Edward Livingston, Secretary of State, and that still living exemplar of careful learning and wisdom, Roger B. Taney, then Attorney General, now Chief Justice of the United States. But beyond these, it has the unquestionable authority of Thomas Jefferson, by whom, as President of the United States, it was asserted again and again as a rule of conduct. Thus if any person at this day be disposed to deal sharply with me on account of the support which I now most conscientiously give to this rule, let him remember that his thrusts will pierce not only myself, the humblest of its supporters, but also the great fame of Andrew Jackson and of Thomas

Jefferson — patriots both of eminent life and authority, on whose Atlantean shoulders this principle of Constitutional law will ever firmly rest.

But reason here is in harmony with authority. From the necessity of the case I must swear to support the Constitution, either *as I do understand it*, or *as I do* NOT *understand it*. (Laughter.) But the absurdity of dangling on the latter horn of the dilemma, compels me to take the former — and there is a natural end of the argument. (Great laughter and cheers.) Is there a person in Congress or out of it, in the National Government or State Government, who, when this inevitable alternative is presented to him, will venture to say that he swears to support the Constitution as he does not understand it? (Laughter and applause.) The supposition is too preposterous. But let me ask gentlemen who are disposed to abandon their own understanding of the Constitution, to submit their conscience to the standard of other men, by whose understanding do they swear? Surely not by that of the President. This is not alleged. But by the understanding of the Supreme Court. In other words, to this Court, consisting at present of nine persons, is committed a power of fastening such interpretation as they see fit upon any part of the Constitution — adding to it or subtracting from it — or positively varying its requirements — actually making and unmaking the Constitution; and all good citizens must bow to their work as of equal authority with the original instrument, ratified by solemn votes of the whole people! (Great applause.) If this be so, then the oath to support the Constitution of the United States is hardly less offensive than the famous "et cetera" oath devised by

Archbishop Laud, in which the subject swore to certain specified things, with an "&c" added. Such an oath I have not taken. (Good, good.)

The power of our Supreme Court is great, and its sphere is vast; but there are limits to its power and its sphere. According to the words of the Constitution, "the judicial power shall extend to *all cases* in law and equity, arising under the Constitution, the laws of the United States, and Treaties;" but it by no means follows, that the interpretation of the Constitution which may be *incident* to the trial of these "cases" is final. Of course, the judgment in the "case" actually pending is final, as the settlement of a controversy, for weal or woe to the litigating parties; but as a *precedent* it is not final even on the Supreme Court itself. When cited afterwards it will be regarded with respect as an *interpretation of the Constitution*, and, if nothing appears against it, of controlling authority; but, at any day, in any litigation, at the trial of any "case," it will be within the unquestionable competency of the Court to review its own decision, *so far as it establishes any interpretation of the Constitution.* But if the Court itself be not constrained by its own precedents, how can the co-ordinate branches of the Government, who are respectively under oath to support the Constitution, and who, like the Court itself, may be called within their respective spheres, *incidentally* to interpret the Constitution, be constrained by them? In both instances, the power to interpret the Constitution is simply *incident* to other principal duties, as the trial of "cases," the making of laws, or the administration of Government, and it seems as plainly *incident* to a "case" of legislation or of administration, as to one of the "cases" of litigation. And on this view I shall act with entire confidence under the oath which I have taken.

For myself, let me say, that I hold judges, and especially the Supreme Court of the country, in much respect; but I am too familiar with the history of judicial proceedings to regard them with any superstitious reverence. (Sensation.) Judges are but men, and in all ages have shown a full share of human frailty. Alas! alas! the worst crimes of history have been perpetrated under their sanction. The blood of martyrs and of patriots, crying from the ground, summons them to judgment. It was a judicial tribunal which condemned Socrates to drink the fatal hemlock, and which pushed the Saviour barefoot over the pavements of Jerusalem, bending beneath his cross. It was a judicial tribunal which, against the testimony and entreaties of her father, surrendered the fair Virginia *as a slave;* which arrested the teachings of the great Apostle to the Gentiles, and sent him in bonds from Judea to Rome; which, in the name of the Old Religion, adjudged the saints and fathers of the Christian Church to death, in all its most dreadful forms; and which, afterwards, in the name of the New Religion, enforced the tortures of the Inquisition, amidst the shrieks and agonies of its victims, while it compelled Galileo to declare — in solemn denial of the great truth he had disclosed — that the earth did not move round the sun. It was a judicial tribunal which, in France, during the long reign of her monarchs, lent itself to be the instrument of every tyranny, as during the brief reign of terror it did not hesitate to stand forth the unpitying accessary of the unpitying guillotine. Ay, sir, it was a judicial tribunal in England, surrounded by all the forms of law, which sanctioned every despotic caprice of Henry the Eighth, from the unjust divorce of his queen, to the beheading of Sir Thomas More; which lighted the fires of persecution that glowed at Oxford and Smithfield, over the cinders of Latimer, Ridley and John Rogers; which, after elaborate argument, upheld the fatal tyranny of ship money against the patriot resistance of Hampden; which, in defiance of justice and humanity, sent Sidney and Russell to the block; which persistently enforced the laws of Conformity that our Puritan Fathers persistently refused to obey; and which, afterwards, with Jeffries on the bench, crimsoned the pages of English history with massacre and murder — even with the blood of innocent woman. Ay, sir, and it was a judicial tribunal in our own country, surrounded by all the forms of law, which hung witches at Salem — which affirmed the constitutionality of the Stamp Act, while it admonished "jurors and the people" to obey — and which now, in our day, has lent its sanction to the unutterable atrocity of the Fugitive Slave Bill. (Long continued applause, and three cheers for Sumner.)

Of course the judgments of courts are of binding authority upon inferior tribunals and their own executive officers, whose virtue does not prompt them to resign rather than aid in the execution of an unjust mandate. Over all citizens, whether in public or private station, they will naturally exert, *as precedents*, a commanding influence. This I admit. But no man, who is not lost to self-respect, and ready to abandon that manhood which is shown in the Heaven-directed countenance, will voluntarily aid in enforcing a judgment which, in his conscience, he believes to be wrong Surely he will not hesitate to "obey God rather than man," and calmly abide the perils which he may provoke. Not lightly, not rashly will he take the grave responsibility of open dissent; but if the occasion requires, he will not fail. Pains and penalties may be endured, but wrong must not be done. (Cheers.) "I cannot obey, but I can suffer," was the exclamation of the author of Pilgrim's Progress, when imprisoned for disobedience to an earthly statute. Better suffer injustice than do it. Better be even the poor slave, returned to bondage, than the unhappy Commissioner. (Applause and sensation.)

The whole dogma of *passive obedience* must be rejected; — in whatever guise it may assume, and under whatever *alias* it may skulk; whether in the tyrannical usurpations of king, parliament, or judicial tribunal; whether in the exploded theories of Sir Robert Filmer, or the rampant assumptions of the partisans of the Fugitive Slave Bill. The rights of the civil power are limited; there are things beyond its province; there are matters out of its control; there are cases in which the faithful citizen may say — ay, *must* say — "I will not obey." No man now responds to the words of Shakespeare, "If a king bid a man be a villain, he is bound, by the indenture of his oath, to be one." Nor will any prudent reasoner, who duly considers the rights of conscience, claim for any earthly magistrate or tribunal, howsoever styled, a power which, in this age of civilization and liberty, the loftiest monarch of a Christian throne, wearing on his brow "the round and top of sovereignty" dare not assert.

On this two-fold conclusion I rest, and do not doubt the final result. The citizen, who has sworn to support the Constitution, is constrained to support it simply as he understands it. The citizen, whose private life has kept him from assuming the obligations of the oath, may bravely set at naught the unjust mandate of a magistrate, and, in so doing, he will serve justice, though he may expose himself to stern penalties.

Fellow Citizens of Massachusetts: — Our own local history is not without encouragement. In early colonial days, the law against witchcraft, now so abhorrent to reason and conscience, was regarded as constitutional and binding, precisely as the Fugitive Slave Bill, not less abhorrent to reason and conscience, has been regarded as constitutional and binding. The Supreme Court of the Province, with able judges, whose names are entwined with our history, enforced this law at Salem, by the execution of fourteen persons as witches; precisely as petty magistrates, acting under the sanction of the Supreme Court of the United States, and also of the Supreme Court of Massachusetts, have enforced the Fugitive Act, by the reduction of two human beings to Slavery. The clergy of Massachusetts, particularly near Boston, and also Harvard College, were for the law. "Witchcraft," shouted Cotton Mather from the pulpit, "is the most nefandous high treason"— "a capital crime" — even as opposition to the Fugitive Act has been denounced as "treason." (Laughter.)

But the law against witchcraft was not triumphant long. The General Court of the Province first became penitent, and asked pardon of God for "all the errors of His servants and people in the late tragedy." Jurymen united in condemning and lamenting the delusion to which they had yielded under the decision of the judges, and acknowledged that they had brought the reproach of wrongful bloodshed on our native land. Sewall, one of the judges, whose name lives freshly in the liberty-loving character of his descendant, [Hon. S. E. Sewall,] (applause,) and who had presided at the trials, stood up in his place at church, before the congregation, and implored the prayers of the people "that the errors he had committed might not be visited by the judgments of an avenging God on his country, his family, or himself." And now, in a manuscript diary of this departed judge, may be read, on the margin against the contemporary record of these trials, in his own handwriting, words of Latin interjection and sorrow: *Vœ, vœ, vœ.* Woe! woe! woe! (Sensation.)

The parallel between the law against witchcraft, and the Fugitive Act is not yet complete. It remains for our Legislature, the successor of that original General Court, to lead the penitential march. (Laughter.) In the slave cases there have been no jurymen to recant (laughter); and it is too much, perhaps, to expect any magistrate who has sanctioned the cruelty, to imitate the magnanimity of other days by public repentance. But it is not impossible that future generations may be permitted to read, in some newly exhumed diary or letter, by one of these unhappy functionaries, words of woe not unlike those which were wrung from the soul of Sewall. (Sensation.)

And now, fellow-citizens, one word in conclusion:

Be of good cheer. ("That's it.") I know well the difficulties and responsibilities of the contest; but not on this account do I bate a jot of heart or hope. (Applause.) At this time, in our country, there is little else to tempt into public life an honest man, who wishes, by something that he has done, to leave the world better than he found it. There is little else which can afford any of those satisfactions which an honest man can covet. Nor is there any cause which so surely promises final success. There is nothing good — not a breathing of the common wind — which is not on our side. Ours, too, are those great allies described by the poet —

——— "exultations, agonies,
And love, and man's unconquerable mind."

And there are favoring circumstances peculiar to the present moment. By the passage of the Nebraska Bill, and the Boston kidnapping case, the tyranny of the Slave Power has become unmistakably manifest, while, at the same time, all compromises with Slavery are happily dissolved, so that Freedom now stands face to face with its foe. The pulpit, too, released from ill-omened silence, now thunders for Freedom, as in the olden time. (Cheers.) It belongs to Massachusetts — nurse of the men and principles which made the earliest Revolution — to vow herself anew to her ancient faith, as she lifts herself to the great struggle. Her place now, as of old, is in the van, at the head of the battle. (Sensation.) But to sustain this advanced position with proper inflexibility, three things are needed by our beloved Commonwealth, in all her departments of government — the same three things, which once in Faneuil Hall, I ventured to say were needed by every representative of the North at Washington. The first is *backbone* (applause); the second is BACKBONE (renewed applause); and the third is **BACKBONE**. (Long continued cheering, and three cheers for "backbone.") With these, Massachusetts will be respected, and felt as a positive force in the National Government (applause), while at home, on her own soil, free at last in reality as in name (applause), all her people, from the islands of Boston to Berkshire hills, and from the sands of Barnstable to the northern line, will unite in the cry:

"No slave hunt in our borders — no pirate on our strand;
No fetter on the Bay State; no slave upon her land."

# THE POSITION AND DUTIES OF THE MERCHANT, ILLUSTRATED BY THE LIFE OF GRANVILLE SHARP.

AN ADDRESS BEFORE THE MERCANTILE LIBRARY ASSOCIATION OF BOSTON, ON THE EVENING OF 15TH NOVEMBER, 1854.

---

MR. PRESIDENT, AND GENTLEMEN OF THE MERCANTILE LIBRARY ASSOCIATION:

I HAVE been honored by an invitation to deliver an address, introductory to one of the annual courses of lectures, which your Association bountifully contributes to the pastime, instruction and elevation of our community. You know, sir, something of the reluctance with which, embarrassed by other cares, I undertook this service, — yielding to a kindly and persistent pressure, which only a nature sterner than mine could resist. And now I am here to perform what I promised.

I am to address the Mercantile Library Association of Boston, numbering, according to your last report, two thousand and seventy-eight members, and possessing a library of more than fifteen thousand volumes. With so many members and so many books, yours is an institution of positive power. Two distinct features appear in its name. It is primarily an association of persons in mercantile pursuits; and it is, next, an association for the improvement of its members, particularly through books. In either particular, it is entitled to regard. But it possesses yet another feature, more interesting still, which does not appear in its name. It is an association of YOUNG MEN, with hearts yet hospitable to generous words, and with resolves not yet vanquished by the trials and temptations of life. Especially does this last consideration fill me with a deep sense at once of the privilege and responsibility to which you have summoned me. I am aware that, according to usage, the whole circle of knowledge, thought and aspiration, is open to the speaker; but as often as I have revolved the occasion in my mind — even as the Greek poet, who hoped to sing of Atreus, was brought back to the strain of love — I have been brought back to a consideration of the peculiar character of your association; and I have found myself unwilling to touch any theme which was not addressed to them especially as merchants.

I might fitly speak to you of books; and here, while undertaking to consider the principles which should govern the student in his reading, it would be pleasant to dwell on the profitable delights, better than a "shower of cent. per cent.;" on the society, better than fashion or dissipation; and on that completeness of satisfaction, outvying the possessions of wealth and power, and making "my library dukedom large enough;" all of which are found in books. But I leave this theme. I might also fitly speak to you of young men, their claims and duties. And here again, while enforcing the precious advantages of Occupation, it would be pleasant to unfold and vindicate that reverence which antiquity wisely accorded to youth, as the season of promise and hope, pregnant with an unknown

35*

future, and, therefore, to be watched with tenderness and care; to show how in every young man the uncertain measure of yet undeveloped capacities gives scope to a magnificence of anticipation beyond any reality; and to ask what must be done, that all this anticipation may not wholly die while the young man lives. But there are other things which beckon me away. Not on books, not on youth shall I speak; but on yet another topic, suggested directly by the name of your Association.

With your kind permission, I shall speak to-night on what this age requires from the mercantile profession, or rather, since nothing is justly required which is not due, what the mercantile profession owes to this age. I would show the principle by which we are to be guided in making the *account current* between the mercantile profession and Humanity, and, might I so aspire, hold up the *Looking-glass of the Good Merchant.* And, since example is better than precept, and deeds are more than words, I shall exhibit the career of a remarkable man, whose simple life, beginning as the apprentice to a linen draper, and never getting beyond a clerkship, shows what may be accomplished by faithful, humble labors, and reveals precisely those qualities, which, in this age, are needed to crown the character of a Good Merchant.

"Every man owes a debt to his profession," was a saying of Lord Bacon, repeated by his contemporary and rival Lord Coke. But this does not tell the whole truth. It restrains within the narrow circle of a profession, obligations which are broad and universal as humanity. Rather should it be said that every man owes a debt to mankind. In determining the debt of the merchant, we must first appreciate his actual position in the social system; and here let us glance at history.

At the dawn of modern times trade was unknown. There was nothing, then, like a policy of insurance, a bank, a bill of exchange or even a promissory note. The very term "chattels," so comprehensive in its present application, yet when considered in its derivation from the mediæval Latin *catalla*, cattle, reveals the narrow inventory of personal property in those days, when "two hundred sheep" were paid by a pious Countess of Anjou for a coveted volume of homilies. The places of honor and power were then occupied by men who had distinguished themselves by the sword, and were known under the various names of knight, baron, count, or — highest of all — Duke, *Dux*, the leader in war.

Under these influences the feudal system was organized, with its hierarchy of ranks, in mutual relations of dependence and protection; and society for a while rested in its shadow. The steel-clad chiefs, who enjoyed power, had a corresponding responsibility; and the mingled gallantry and gentleness of chivalry often controlled the iron hand. It was the dukes who led the forces; it was the counts or earls who placed themselves at the head of their respective counties; it was the knights who went forth to do battle with danger, in whatever form, whether from robbers or wild beasts. It was the barons at Runnymede — there was no merchant there — who extorted from King John that Magna Charta which laid the corner-stone of English and American liberty.

Meanwhile trade made its humble beginnings. But for a long time the merchant was of a despised caste, only next above the slave who was sold as a chattel. If a Jew, he was often compelled, under direful tortures, to surrender his gains; if a foreigner, he earned toleration by inordinate contributions to the public revenue; if a native, he was treated as a caitiff too mean for society, and only good enough to be taxed. In the time of Chaucer he had so far come up, that he was admitted to the promiscuous company, ranging from the knight to the miller, who undertook the merry pilgrimage from the Tabard Inn to Canterbury; but the gentle poet satirically exposes his selfish talk —

> " His resons spake he full solempnly,
> Souning alway the encrease of his winning;
> He wold the see were kept for any thing
> Betwixen Middleburgh and Orewell."

The man of trade had been so low that it took him long to rise. A London merchant, the famous Gresham, in the time of Elizabeth, founded the Royal Exchange, and a college also; but trade continued still a butt for jest and jibe. At a later day an English statute gave new security to the merchant's accounts; but the contemporaneous dramatists exhibited him to the derision of the theatre, and even the almanacs exposed his ignorant superstitions by chronicling the days supposed to be favorable or unfavorable to trade. But in the grand mutations of society, the merchant throve. His wealth increased; his influence extended, and he gradually drew into his company decayed or poverty-stricken members of feudal families, till at last in France, (I do not forget the exceptional condition of Italy,) at the close of the seventeenth century, an edict was put forth, which John Locke has preserved in the journal of his travels, "that those who merchandise, but do not use the yard, shall not lose their gentility;" (admirable discrimination!) and in England, at the close of the eighteenth century, his former degradation and growing importance were attested in the saying of Dr. Johnson, that "the English merchant is a newly-discovered species of gentleman." But this high arbiter, — bending under feudal traditions, — would not even then concede to him any merit; proclaiming that "there were no qualities in trade that should entitle a man to superiority;" "that we cannot think a fellow, by sitting all day at a desk, entitled to get above us," and, to the supposition by his faithful Boswell, that a merchant might be a man of enlarged mind, the determined moralist replied, "Why, sir, we may suppose any fictitious character; but there is nothing in trade connected with an enlarged mind."

In America feudalism never prevailed, and our Revolution severed the only cord by which we were connected with this ancient system. It was fit that the Congress, which performed this memorable act, should have for its President a merchant. It was fit that, in promulgating the Declaration of Independence, by which, in the face of kings, princes and nobles, the new era was inaugurated, the education of the counting-house should flaunt conspicuously in the broad and clerkly signature of JOHN HANCOCK. Our fathers "builded wiser than they knew;" and these things are typical of the social change then taking place. And by yet another act, fresh in your recollection, and of peculiar interest to this assembly, has our country borne the same testimony. A distinguished merchant of Boston, who has ascended through all the gradations of trade, honored always for his private virtues as well as public abilities — I may mention the name of ABBOTT LAWRENCE — has been sent to the Court of St. James as the ambassador of our Republic, and with that proud commission, higher than any patent of nobility, has taken precedence of the nobles of that ancient realm. In this circumstance I see the triumph of personal merit, but still more, the consummation of a new epoch.

Yes, sir! say what you will, this is the day of the merchant. As in the early ages, war was the great concern of society, and the very pivot of power, so is trade now; and as the feudal chiefs were the "notables" placed at the very top of their time, so are the merchants now. All things attest the change. War, which was once the universal business, is now confined to a few: once a daily terror, it is now the accident of an age. Not for adventures of the sword, but for trade do men descend upon the sea in ships, and traverse broad continents on iron pathways. Not for protection against violence, but for trade, do men come together in cities and rear the marvellous superstructure of social order. If they go abroad, or if they stay at home, it is trade that controls them, without distinction of persons. Here, at least, in our country every man is a trader. The physician trades his benevolent care; the lawyer trades his ingenious tongue; the clergyman trades his prayers. And trade summons from the quarry the choicest marble and granite to build its capacious homes, and now, in our own city, displays warehouses which outdo the baronial castle, and sales-rooms which outdo the ducal palace. With these magnificent appliances the relations of dependence and protection, which marked the early feudalism, are reproduced in the more comprehensive feudalism of trade. Even now there are European bankers who vie in power with the dukes and princes of other days, and there are traffickers everywhere, whose title comes from the ledger and not the sword, fit successors to counts, barons and knights. As the feudal chief allocated to himself and his followers the soil, which was the prize of his strong arm, so now the merchant, with a grasp more subtle and reaching, allocates to himself and followers, ranging through multitudinous degrees of dependence, all the spoils of every land, triumphantly won by trade. I would not press this parallel too far, but, at this moment, especially in our country, the merchant, more than any other character, stands in the very boots of the feudal chief. Of all pursuits or relations, his is now the most extensive and formidable, making all others its tributaries, and bending at times even the lawyer and the clergyman to be its dependent stipendiaries.

Such in our social system is the merchant; and on this precise and incontrovertible statement I found his duties. Wealth, power, and influence are not for self-indulgence merely, and just according to their extent are the obligations *to others* which they impose. If, by the rule of increase, to him that hath is given, so in the same degree new duties are superadded: nor can any man escape from their behests. If the merchant be in reality our feudal lord, he must render feudal service; if he be our modern knight, he must do knightly deeds; if he be the baron of our day, let him maintain baronial charity to the humble — ay, sir, and baronial courage against tyrannical wrong, in whatsoever form it may assume. But even if I err in attributing to him this peculiar position, I do not err in attributing to him these duties; for his influence is surely great, and he is at least a man, bound by his simple manhood to regard nothing human as foreign to his heart.

The special perils which aroused the age of chivalry have passed away. Monsters, in the form of dragons, griffins, or unicorns, no longer ravage the land. Giants have disappeared from the scene. Robbers have been dislodged from castle and forest. Godeschal the Iron-hearted, and Robin Hood, are each without descendants. In the new forms which society has assumed, touched by the potent wand of trade, there is no place for any of these. But wrong and outrage are not yet extinct. Cast out of one body, they enter straightway another, whence too they must be cast out. Alas! in our day, amidst all this teeming civilization, with the horn of Abundance at our gates, with the purse of Fortunatus in our hands, with professions of Christianity on our lips, and with the merchant installed in the high places of chivalry, there are sorrows not less poignant than those which once enkindled knightly sympathy; and there is wrong, which vies in loathsomeness with early monsters, in power with early giants, and in its existing immunity with the robbers once sheltered by castle and forest — stalking through your streets in the abused garb of law itself, and dwarfing by its hateful presence all the atrocities of another age. A wicked man is a deplorable sight; but a wicked law is worse than any wicked man, even than the wretch who steals human beings from their home in Africa; nor can its outrages be redressed by any incidental charities, perishing at night as the manna in the wilderness. Like a monster, it must be overpowered; like a robber, it must be chained; like a wild beast, it must be exterminated.

To the merchant, then — especially to the young merchant — I appeal, by the position you have won and by the power which is yours; go forth to redress these grievances, whatever they may be, whether in the sufferings of the solitary soul or audaciously organized in the likeness of law. And now, that I may not seem to hold up any impracticable standard, that the path of duty may not appear difficult, and that no young man need hesitate, even though he find himself alone, and opposed by numbers, let me present briefly, as becomes the hour, the example and special achievement of GRANVILLE SHARP, the humble Englishman, who, without wealth, fame, or power, did not hesitate to set himself against the merchants of the time, against the traditions of the English bar, against the authority of learned lawyers, and against the power of magistrates, until, by persevering effort, he compelled the highest tribunal of the land to declare the grand constitutional truth, that the slave who sets his foot on British ground becomes that instant free. His character of pure and courageous principle may be little regarded yet; but as time advances, it will become a guiding luminary. There are stars aloft, centres of other systems, in such depths of firmament that only after the lapse of ages does their light reach this small ball which we call earth.

Mr. President, do not start, I shall not tread on forbidden ground. To the occasion and to your association I shall be loyal; but let me be loyal also to myself. Thank God, the great volume of the past is always open, with its lessons of warning and example. Nor will the assembly, which now does me the honor to listen to me, be willing to imitate the pious pirates of the Carribean Seas, who daily recited the ten commandments, always omitting the injunction, "Thou shalt not steal." I know well the sensitiveness of certain consciences. This is natural. It is according to the decrees of Providence that, whosoever has been engaged in meanness or wickedness, should be pursued wherever he moves by reproving voices — speaking to him from the solitudes of nature, from the darkness of night, from the hum of the street, and from every book that he reads, like fiery tongues at Pentecost, until at last the confession of Satan himself can alone express his wretchedness:

> 'Me miserable! which way shall I fly?
> Which way I fly is hell, — *myself am hell!*'

GRANVILLE SHARP was born at Durham in 1735. His family was of great respectability and of ancient lineage. His grandfather was Archbishop of York, and the confidential chaplain and counsellor of the renowned Chancellor, Heneage Finch, Lord Nottingham. His less conspicuous father was an arch-deacon and prebendary of the church, who, out of his ecclesiastical emoluments, knew how to dispense charity, while he reared his numerous children to different pursuits. Of these Granville was the youngest son, and, though his elder brothers were educated for professional life, he was destined to trade, a portion being set apart by his father to serve as his apprentice fee in London. With this view his back was turned upon the learned languages, and his instruction was confined chiefly to writing and arithmetic; but at this time he read and enjoyed all the plays of Shakespeare, in an apple-tree of his father's orchard. When fifteen years old, he was bound as apprentice to a Quaker linen-draper in London, and at this tender age left his father's house. Of his apprenticeship he has given an interesting glimpse: —

"After I had served about three years of my apprenticeship, my master, the Quaker, died, and I was turned over to a Presbyterian, or rather, as he was more properly called, an Independent. I afterward lived some time with an Irish Papist, and also with another person, who, I believe, had no religion at all."

Although always a devoted member of the Church of England, these extraordinary experiences in early life placed him above the prejudices of sect, and inspired a rule of conduct, worthy of perpetual memory, which he presents as follows:

"It taught me to make a proper distinction between the OPINIONS of men and their PERSONS. The former I can freely condemn without presuming to judge the individuals themselves. Thus freedom of argument is preserved, as well as Christian charity, leaving personal judgment to Him to whom alone it belongs."

Only two years before the enrolment of Granville Sharp among London apprentices — that class so famous in local history — another person, kindred in benevolence and now in fame, Howard, the philanthropist, on whose career Burke has cast the illumination of his genius, finished service in the same place as apprentice to a wholesale grocer. I do not know that these two congenial natures — or yet another contemporary of lowly fortunes, John Raikes, the inventor of Sunday schools — ever encountered in the world. But they are joined in example, and the life of an apprentice, in all its humilities, seems radiant with their presence, as with heavenly light. Perhaps, among the apprentices of Boston, there may be yet a Granville Sharp, or John Howard. And just in proportion as the moral nature asserts its rightful supremacy here, will such a character be hailed as of higher worth than the products of all the mills of Lowell, backed by all the dividends and discounts of State street.

In 1758, shortly after the completion of his apprenticeship and entrance upon business, Sharp lost both his parents, and very soon thereafter abandoning trade, obtained a subordinate appointment as a supernumerary clerk in the Ordnance Office, where, after six years' service, he became simply a 'clerk in ordinary.' Meanwhile, conscientiously fulfilling this life of routine and labor, not unlike the toils of Charles Lamb at the India House, he commenced, in moments saved from business and snatched from sleep, a series of studies, which, though undervalued by his modesty, the scholar may envy. That he might better enjoy and vindicate that Book, which he reverentially accepted as the rule of life, he first studied Greek and then Hebrew, obtaining such command of both languages, as to employ them skilfully in the field of theological controversy. Music and French he studied also, and our own English tongue too, on the pronunciation of which he wrote an excellent essay.

These quiet pursuits were interrupted by an incident which belongs to the romance of truth. An unhappy African, by the name of Jonathan Strong, had been brought from Barbadoes to London, as a slave, where, after brutal outrages, at which the soul shudders, inflicted by the person who called himself master — I regret to add lawyer also — he was turned adrift on the unpitying stones of that great metropolis, lame, blind and faint, with ague and with fever, and without a home. In this plight, while staggering along in quest of medical care, he was met by the good Samaritan, Granville Sharp, who, touched by his misfortunes, bound up his wounds, gave him charitable assistance, placed him in a hospital, and watched him through a protracted illness, until at last health and strength again returned, and he was able to commence service as a freeman in a respectable home. In this condition, after the lapse of two years, he was at last recognized in the street by his old master, who at once determined to entrap him, and to hold him as a slave. By a deceitful message the victim was tempted to a public house, where he was shocked to encounter his cruel claimant, who, without delay, seized and committed him to prison. Here, again, was the good Samaritan, Granville Sharp, who lost no time in enjoining upon the keeper of the prison, at his peril, not to deliver the negro to any person whatever, and then promptly invoked the intervention of the Mayor of London. At the hearing before this magistrate, it appeared that the claimant had already undertaken, by a formal bill of sale, to convey the alleged slave to another person, who, by an agent, was in attendance to take him on board a ship bound for Jamaica. As soon as the case had been stated, the Mayor gave judgment in words worthy of imitation: "The lad," said this righteous judge, "has not stolen anything, and is not guilty of any offence, and is, therefore, at liberty to go away." The agent of the claimant, not disheartened, seized him by the arm and still claimed him as "property." Yes! even as property! Sharp, in his ignorance of legal proceedings, was for a moment perplexed, when the friendly voice of the coroner, who chanced to be near, whispered, "Charge him;" on which hint our philanthropist, turning at once to the brazen-faced claimant, said, with justifiable anger of manner: "Sir, I charge you in the name of the King, with an assault upon the person of Jonathan Strong, and all these are my witnesses!" when, to avoid immediate commitment, and the yawning cells of the jail, he let go his piratical slave-hunting grasp, "and all bowed to the Lord Mayor and came away, Jonathan following Granville Sharp, and no one daring to touch him."

But the end was not yet. By this accidental and disinterested act of humanity, Sharp was exposed at the same time to personal insult and to a suit at law. The discomfited claimant — the same lawyer who had originally abandoned the slave in the streets of London — called on him "to demand gentlemanlike satisfaction;" to which the philanthropist replied, that, as "the lawyer had studied law so many years, he should want no satisfaction that the law could give him." And he nobly redeemed his word; for he applied himself at once to his defence against the legal process instituted by the claimant for an alleged abstraction of *property*. Here begins his greatness.

It is in collision with difficulty that the sparks of genuine character appear. This simple-hearted man, now vindictively pursued, laid his case before an eminent solicitor, who, after ample consideration with learned counsel, — among whom was the celebrated Sir James Eyre, — did not hesitate to assure him that, under the British Constitution, he could not be defended against the action. An opinion given in 1729, jointly by the Attorney General and Solicitor General of the time, York and Talbot, — two great names in the English law, and each afterwards Lord Chancellor, — was adduced, declaring, under their respective signatures, that "a slave, by coming from the West Indies to Great Britain or Ireland, either with or without his master, *doth not* become free," and "that the master may legally compel him to return again to the plantations;" and Lord Mansfield, the Chief Justice, was reported as strenuously concurring in this opinion, to the odious extent of delivering up fugitive slaves to their claimants. With these authorities against him, and forsaken by his professional defenders, Sharp was not disheartened; but, though, according to his own striking language, "totally unacquainted either with the practice of the law, or the foundations of it, having never in his life opened a law book except the Bible," he was inspired to depend on himself. An unconquerable will, and those instincts which are often profounder in their teaching than any learning, were now his counsellors. For nearly two years, during which the suit was still pending, he gave himself to an intense study of the British Constitution in all its bearings upon human liberty. During these researches, he was confirmed in his original prepossessions on the question, and aroused to an undying hostility against Slavery, which he plainly saw to be without any sanction in the Constitution. "*Neither the word* SLAVES," he exclaimed, "*or anything that* *can justify the enslaving of others, can be found there, God be praised!"* * And I, too, say God be praised!

The result of these studies was embodied in a tract, "On the Injustice and Dangerous Tendency of tolerating Slavery, or even of admitting the least Claim to Private Property in the Persons of Men in England." This was submitted to his counsel, one of whom was the famous commentator, Sir William Blackstone, and, by means of numerous copies in manuscript, circulated among gentlemen of the bar, until the lawyers on the other side were actually intimidated, and the Slave-hunter, failing to bring forward his action, was mulcted in treble costs; and thus ended that persecution of our philanthropist. This important tract was printed in 1769.

Thus far it was an individual case only which had engaged his care. Another soon followed, where, through his chivalrous humanity, the intolerable wrongs of a woman kidnapped in London and transported as a slave to Barbadoes, were redressed, — so far as an earthly decree could go. Learning the infinite woes of Slavery, he was now aroused to broader efforts. Shocked by an advertisement in a London newspaper, — such as often appeared in those days — of "a black girl to be sold, of excellent temper and willing disposition," — he at once protested to the Chancellor, Lord Camden, against such things as "a notorious breach of the laws of nature, humanity and equity, and also the established law, custom and constitution of England;" and in the same year, 15th May, 1769, he solemnly appealed by letter to the Archbishop of Canterbury against the slave trade, and thus by many

* Hoare's Life of Sharp, vol. i. p. 58, cap. I.

years heralded the labors of Clarkson and Wilberforce. "I am myself convinced," he said, "that nothing can thrive which is in any way concerned in that unjust trade. I have known several instances, which are strong proofs to me of the judgments of God, even in this world, against such a destructive and iniquitous traffic." In these things he showed not only his love of justice, but his personal independence. "Although I am a *placeman*," he wrote on another occasion, "and indeed of a very inferior rank, yet I look on myself to be perfectly independent, because I have never yet been afraid to do and avow whatever I thought just and right, without the consideration of consequences to myself; for, indeed, I think it unworthy of a *man* to be afraid of the world; and it is a point with me never to conceal my sentiments on any subject whatever, not even from my superiors in office, *when there is a probability of answering any good purpose by it.*"

Still again his protecting presence was enlisted to save a fellow-man from bondage; and here it is necessary to note the new form of outrage. A poor African, Thomas Lewis, who had once been a slave, was residing quietly at Chelsea, in the neighborhood of London, when he was suddenly seized by his former master, who, with the aid of two ruffians hired for the fiendish purpose, dragged him on his back into the water, and thence into a boat lying in the Thames, in which, with his legs tied, and his mouth gagged by a stick, he was rowed down to a ship bound for Jamaica, under a commander previously engaged in the conspiracy, to be sold for a slave on his arrival in that island. But this diabolical act, though warily contrived, did not escape notice. The cries of the victim, on his way to the boat, reached the servants of a neighboring man sion, who witnessed the deadly struggle, but did not venture a rescue. Their mistress, a retired widow, mother of the eminent naturalist and traveller, Sir Joseph Banks, on learning what had passed, instantly put forth her womanly exertions. Without the hesitation of her sex, she hurried to Granville Sharp, who was now known for his knightly zeal to succor the distressed, laid before him the terrible story, and insisted upon vindicating the freedom of the stranger at her own expense. All honor to this woman! A simple warrant, first obtained by Sharp, was scouted by the captain, whose victim, bathed in tears, was already chained to the mast. The great writ of habeas corpus was next invoked; and the ship, which had contumaciously proceeded on its way, was boarded in the Downs, happily within British jurisdiction, by a faithful officer, who, in the name of the King of England, unbound the chains of the African, and took him back to freedom.

A complaint was now presented against the kidnappers, who were at once indicted by the grand jury. The cause was removed to the King's Bench, and on the 20th February, 1771, brought into court before Lord Mansfield. The defence was, that the victim was their slave, and, therefore, property to be rightfully seized. And here the question was distinctly presented, whether any such property was recognized by the British Constitution. The transcendent magistrate, who presided on the occasion, saw the magnitude of the issue, and sought to avoid its formal determination, by presenting the subordinate point, whether the claimant, supposing such property recognized, was able to prove the man to be his. The kidnappers were found "guilty;" but judgment against them was waived on the recommendation of Lord Mansfield, who, be it observed, shrank, at every stage, from any act by which Slavery in England should be annulled, and who avowed on this occasion "his hope that the question never would be finally discussed." Sharp was justly indignant at this craven conduct, which, with all gentleness of manner, but with perfect firmness, he did not hesitate to arraign as an "open contempt" of the true principles of the Constitution.

Alas! it is the natural influence of Slavery to make men hard. Gorgon-like, it turns to stone all who look upon its face except to slay it. Among the juridical magistrates of the time, Lord Mansfield was not alone. His companion in contemporary fame, Blackstone, shared the petrifaction. An early edition of his incomparable Commentaries had openly declared that a slave on coming to England became at once a freeman; but, in a subsequent edition, after the question had been practically presented by Granville Sharp, the text was pusillanimously altered to an abandonment of this great constitutional principle; and our intrepid philanthropist hung his head with shame and anxiety while the counsel for the Slave-hunters triumphantly invoked this tergiversation as a new authority against Freedom.

But the day was at hand when the great philanthropist was to be vindicated, even by the lips of the great magistrate. The Slavery Question could not be suppressed. The Chief Justice of England could not do it. Drive out nature with a pitchfork, and still she will at once return. Only a few months elapsed, when a memorable case arose, which presented the question distinctly for judgment. A negro, James Somerset, — whose name, as the starting-point of an immortal principle, will help to keep alive the appellation of the ducal house, to which it originally belonged, — was detained in irons on board a ship lying in the Thames, and bound for Jamaica. On application to Lord Mansfield, in his behalf, 3d December, 1771, supported by affidavits, a writ of habeas corpus was directed to the captain of the ship, commanding him to return the body of Somerset into court, with the cause of his detention. In course of time, though somewhat tardily, the body was produced, and, for cause of detention, it was assigned, that he was the property of Charles Stewart, Esq., *of Virginia*, who had held him in Virginia as a slave; that, when brought as such to London, he ran away from the service of his master, but was recovered, and finally delivered on board the ship to be carried to Jamaica, there to be sold as the slave and property of the *Virginia gentleman.* As no facts were in issue here, the whole cause hinged on the constitutionality of Slavery in England; and the great question which the Chief Justice had sought to avoid, and on which the Commentator had changed sides, was once again to be heard.

In order to give solemnity to the proceedings, in some degree corresponding to their importance, the cause was brought by Lord Mansfield before the King's Bench, where it was continued from time to time, according to the convenience of counsel and of the court, running even through months, and occupying different days in January, February and May, down to the 22d June, 1772, when judgment was finally delivered. During all this period, Somerset, having recognized with sureties for his appearance in court, was left at large. To Granville Sharp he had repaired at once, and by him was kindly welcomed, and effectually aided. Under his advice, counsel learned in the law were retained, and by this humble clerk, they were instructed in the grounds of defence. At his expense, too, out of his small means, the proceedings were maintained. "Money," he nobly said, "has no value but when it is well spent; and I am thoroughly convinced, that no part of my little pittance can ever be better bestowed than in an honest endeavor to crush a growing oppression, which is not only shocking to humanity, but in time must prove even dangerous to the community." On the other side, the costs were defrayed by a subscription among the merchants! Hear this, merchants of Boston, justly jealous of the good name of your calling, and hang your heads with shame!

To the glory of the English bar, the eminent counsel for the slave declined all fees for their valuable and protracted services; and here let me pause for one moment to pay them an unaffected tribute. They were five in number: Mr. Sergeant Davy, who opened the cause with the proposition "that no man at this day *is* or *can be* a slave in England;" Mr. Sergeant Glynn; Mr. Mansfield, afterward Chief Justice of the Common Pleas; Mr. Hargrave and Mr. Alleyne, each of whom was patiently heard by the court at length. The argument of Mr. Hargrave, who early volunteered his great learning in the case, is one of the masterpieces of the bar. This was his first appearance in court; but it is well that liberty on that day had such support. For all these gallant lawyers, champions of the right, there is honor ever increasing, which the soul spontaneously offers, while it turns in sorrow from the counsel, only two in number, who allowed themselves to be enlisted on the side of Slavery. I know well that in Westminster Hall there are professional usages, which happily do not prevail in our country — where every such service depends purely on *contract* — by which a barrister thinks himself contrained to assume any cause which is properly presented to him. If this service depended on contract there, as with us, the sarcasm of Ben Jonson would be strictly applicable;

> "This fellow ——————————
> For six sols more would plead against his Maker."
>
> *The Fox, Act 4th.*

But I undertake to affirm, that no usage, professional or social, can give any apology for joining the pack of the Slave-hunter. Mr. Dunning, one of the persons in this predicament, shewed that he acted against his better nature. The first words in his argument were: "It is incumbent on me to justify the detainer of the negro." Pray why incumbent on him? He was then careful to show that he did not maintain that there was an absolute property in him; and he proceeded to say, among other things, that it was his misfortune to address an audience, the greater part of which, he feared, was prejudiced the other way; that for himself, he would not be understood to intimate a wish in favor of Slavery; but that he was bound in duty to mention those arguments most useful to the claimant, so far as consistent with the truth, and he concluded with this conscience-stricken appeal: "I hope, therefore, I shall not suffer in the opinion of those whose honest passions are fired at the name of Slavery — I hope I have not transgressed my duty to humanity." Clearly the lawyer had trangressed his duty to Humanity. No man can rightfully enforce any principle which violates human nature; nor can any subtilty of dialectics, any extent of erudition, or any grandeur of intellect, sustain him. Notwithstanding the character for liberal principles which John Dunning acquired, and which breathes in his sensitive excuses — notwithstanding his double fame at once in Westminster Hall and Saint Stephen's Chapel — notwithstanding the peerage which he vainly won, "no son of his succeeding," — this odious service rendered to a Slave-hunter, calling himself a Virginia gentleman, cries in judgment against him, and will continue to cry, as time advances. (Do not start, Mr. President, I am alluding to occurrences in another hemisphere, and another century!) As well undertake a Slave-hunt in the deserts of Africa as in the streets of London. As well pursue the fugitive with the hired whip of the overseer as with the hired argument of the lawyer. As well chase him with the bay of the blood-hound, as with the tongue of the advocate. It is the lawyer's clear duty to uphold *human rights*, whether in the loftiest or the lowliest, and when he undertakes to uphold a wrong so outrageous as Slavery, his proper function is so far reversed, that he can be aptly described only in the phrase of the Roman Church, *L'Avocato del Diavolo*, The Devil's Advocate.

Passing from the counsel to the court, we find at once occasion for gratitude and sorrow. The three judges, Ashton, Willes and Ashurst, who sat at the side of Lord Mansfield, were silent throughout the whole proceedings, overawed, perhaps, by his commanding authority, so that he alone seems to be present. Of large intellect and extensive studies, running into all regions of learning; with a silver-tongued voice and an amenity of manner which gave a constant charm to his presence; with unsurpassed professional and political experience combined; the early companion of Pope and the early competitor of Pitt; having already once refused the post of Prime Minister and three times refused the post of Chancellor; he stood forth — at the period when the poor slave was brought before him — as an acknowledged light of jurisprudence, and, take him for all in all, the most finished magistrate England had then produced. But his character had one fatal defect, which is too common on the bench. He lacked *moral firmness*, which, happily, was not lacking in Granville Sharp. Still more, he was not naturally on the side of Liberty, as becomes a great judge, but always by blood and instinct on the side of prerogative and power — an offence for which he was arraigned by his contemporary, Junius, and for which posterity will hold him to strict account. But his luminous mind, prompt to perceive the force of principles, could not resist the array of arguments now marshalled for Freedom. He saw clearly that a system like Slavery could not find a home under the British Constitution, *which nowhere mentions the name of slave.* And yet he shrank from the conclusion. More than once he coquetted with the merchants, who had the case so much at heart, and twice he ignobly suggested that the claimant might avoid the decision of the great question, fraught with Freedom or Slavery to multitudes, simply by manumitting the individual slave. And when at last the case could not be arrested by any device, or be longer postponed — when judgment was inevitable — he came to the work, not warmly or generously, but in trembling obedience to the Truth which awaited to be declared.

On other occasions of a purely commercial character, his judgments were more learned and elaborate, and they were reported with more completeness and care; but no judgment of equal significance ever fell from the great Oracle. From various sources I have sought its precise import.* It is remarkable for several rules which it clearly enunciates, and which, though often assaulted, still stand as reason and as law. Of these the first was expressed in these simple words: "If the parties will have judgment, *fiat justitia, ruat cœlum;* let justice be done, whatever be the consequences." The Latin phrase, which here plays such a prominent part, though of classical stamp, cannot be traced to any classical origin, and it has even been asserted, that it was freshly coined by Lord Mansfield on this occasion, worthy of such commanding truth in such commanding phrase. But it is of older date and from another mint, though it is not too much to say, that it took its currency and authority from him. Coming from such a conservative magistrate, it is of peculiar importance.

* It is strange that there should be no single satisfactory report of this memorable judgment. That usually quoted from Howell's State Trials, vol. xx. pp. 81, 82, was copied from Lofft, a reporter generally avoided as an authority. There is another report in Hoar's Life of Sharp, pp. 89, 90; also another in Campbell's Lives of the Chief Justices, vol. ii. p. 419; and still another, and, in some respects, the best, in the Appendix to a tract published by Sharp in 1776, entitled "The Just Limitation of Slavery in the Laws of God, compared with the unbounded claims of the African Traders and British American Slaveholders." This judgment is also considered and quoted in several other contemporary tracts.

With little expansion it says openly: To every man his natural rights; justice to all, without distinction of persons, without abridgment and without compromise. Let justice be done though it drags down the pillars of the sky. Thus spoke the Chief Justice of England.

And still another rule, hardly less important or less commanding, was clearly proclaimed in these penetrating words: "I care not for the supposed *dicta* of judges, however eminent, *if they be contrary to all principle;*" or, in other language, it is in vain that you invoke great names in the law — even the names of Hardwicke and Talbot, and my own learned associate Blackstone — in behalf of an institution which defies reason and outrages justice. Mortal precedents are powerless against immortal principles. Thus again spoke the Chief Justice of England.

Braced by these rules, the next stages were logically easy. And here he uttered words which are like a buttress to Freedom. He declared that "tracing Slavery to *natural principles*, it can never be supported;" that is to say, Slavery is a violation of the great law of nature, established by God himself, and coextensive, in space and time, with the Universe. Again he proclaimed, "Slavery cannot stand on any reason, moral or political, but only by virtue of *positive law*," and he clinched his conclusion by the unquestionable statement, that "in a matter so *odious* the evidence and authority of this law must be taken strictly;" in other words, a wrong like Slavery, which finds no support in natural law or in reason, can be maintained — if at all — only by some dread mandate, from some sovereign authority, irresistibly clear and incapable of a double sense, which declares in precise and unequivocal terms, that men guilty of no crime may be held as *slaves*, and be submitted to the bargains of the market-place, the hammer of the auctioneer, and the hunt of the blood-hound. Clearly no such mandate could be shown in England. And after asserting the obvious truth, that rights cannot depend on any discrimination of color, and thus discarding the profane assumptions of race, while he quoted apt Roman authority: —

"Quamvis ille niger, quamvis tu candidus esses,"

the Chief Justice concluded, "and, therefore, let the negro be discharged." Such was this immortal judgment. I catch its last words, already resounding through the ages, with the voice of deliverance to an enslaved people.

From Westminster Hall, where he had so long been held in painful suspense, the happy freedman, with the glad tidings of his deliverance, now hurried to his guardian protector, Granville Sharp, who, though organizing and sustaining these proceedings, had been restrained by unobtrusive modesty from all appearance of attendance in court, that he might in no wise irritate the judge, unfortunately prepossessed against his endeavor. And thus closed the most remarkable constitutional battle in English history, fought by a simple clerk, once apprentice to a linen-draper, against the merchants of London, backed by the authority of great names in law, and by the most exalted magistrate of the age. Even like the stripling David, he had gone forth to the contest, with only a sling and a few smooth stones from the brook; and Goliath fell prostrate at his feet. Not merely an individual slave was emancipated, but upwards of fifteen thousand human beings — five times as many as were held in Slavery throughout New England at the adoption of the Federal Constitution — were discharged from bonds; a slave hunt was made impossible in the streets of London; and a great principle was set up which will stand forever as a Landmark of Freedom.

This triumph, which, at the time, was hailed by the friends of human happiness with exultation and delight, has been commemorated by poetry and eloquence. It prompted Cowper in his Task, to these touching verses:

> "Slaves cannot breathe in England; if their lungs
> Receive our air, that moment they are free.
> They touch our country and their shackles fall.
> That's noble, and bespeaks a nation proud
> And jealous of the blessing. Spread it then,
> And let it circulate through every vein
> Of all your Empire, that where Britain's power
> Is felt, mankind may feel her mercy too!"

It inspired Curran to a burst of eloquence which can never be forgotten:

"I speak in the spirit of British law, which makes liberty commensurate with and inseparable from British soil; which proclaims even to the stranger and the sojourner, the moment he sets his foot upon British earth, that the ground on which he treads is holy and consecrated by the genius of Universal Emancipation. No matter in what language his doom may have been pronounced; no matter what complexion, incompatible with Freedom, an Indian or African sun may have burnt upon him; no matter in what disastrous battle his liberty may have been cloven down; nor with what solemnities he may have been devoted upon the altar of Slavery; the moment he touches the sacred soil of Britain, the altar and the god sink together in the dust; his soul walks abroad in her own majesty; and he stands redeemed, regenerated and disenthralled by the irresistible genius of Universal Emancipation."

It was this triumph which lifted Brougham, in our own day, to one of those vivid utterances by which truth is flashed upon the most unwilling souls:

"Tell me not of rights — talk not of the property of the planter in his slaves. I deny the right — I acknowledge not the property. The principles, the feelings of our common nature, rise in rebellion against it. Be the appeal made to the understanding or to the heart, the sentence is the same that rejects it. In vain you tell me of laws that sanction such a claim! There is a law above all the enactments of human codes — the same throughout the world, the same in all times; it is the law written by the finger of God on the heart of man; and by that law, unchangeable and eternal, while men despise fraud, and loathe rapine and abhor blood, they will reject with indignation, the wild and guilty phantasy that man can hold property in man."

Granville Sharp did not now rest from his labors. The Humanities are not solitary. Where one is found, there will others be also. The advocate of the slave in London was naturally the advocate of liberty for all everywhere. In this spirit he signalized himself against that scandal of the English law, the hateful system of impressment, while he encountered no less a person than Dr. Johnson, whom he did not hesitate to charge "with plausible sophistry and important self-sufficiency, as if he supposed that the mere sound of words was capable of altering the nature of things;" also, against the claims of England in the controversy with her American colonies, zealously maintaining our cause in a publication, of which it is said seven thousand copies were printed in Boston; also in establishing a colony of liberated slaves at Sierra Leone, on the coast of Africa, the predecessor of our more successful Liberia; and finally, as a leader, not only against the Slave-trade, but also against Slavery in the colonies, so that he was reverentially hailed as "Father of the cause in England," and was placed at the head of the illustrious Committee by which it was conducted, though his rare modesty prevented him from actually taking the chair to which he was unanimously elected. But no modesty could check his valiant soul in conflict with wrong. At once, after the decree wrung from Lord Mansfield, he addressed Lord North, the Prime Minister, warning him in the most earnest manner to abolish immediately both the Slave-trade and Slavery itself in all the British dominions, as utterly irreconcilable with the principles of the British Constitution and the established religion of the land, and solemnly declaring that it were better for the nation, that its American possessions had never existed, or even that that they were sunk in the sea, than that Great Britain should be loaded with the horrid guilt of such abominable wickedness. With similar boldness, in an elaborate work, he arraigned the doctrine of *passive obedience* advanced now in favor of judicial tribunals, as once in favor of kings, and he openly affirmed as unquestionable truth, that every public ordinance contrary to reason, justice, natural equity, or the written word of God, must be promptly rejected. Other things, too, I might mention; but I am admonished that I must draw to a close. Pardon me if I touch yet one other shining point in his career worthy of perpetual example.

The news of the battle of Bunker Hill, which reached London at the end of July, 1775, found him at his desk, still a clerk in the Ordnance Office, and obliged by his position, to participate in the military preparations now required. But he was unwilling to be concerned, even thus distantly, in what he regarded as "that unnatural business;" and though a close attendance on his office for eighteen years, to the neglect of all other means of subsistence, had made it important to him as a livelihood, yet he resolved to sacrifice it. Out of regard to his great worth and the respect he had won, he was at first indulged with a leave of absence, but when hostilities in the Colonies had advanced beyond any prospect of speedy accommodation, then he vacated his office. This man of charity, who had lived for others, was now left without support. But he was happy in the testimony he had borne to his principles; nor was he alone. Lord Effingham, and also the eldest son of Lord Chatham, threw up their commissions in the army rather than serve on the side of injustice. And they were all clearly right. It is vain to suppose that any human ordinance, whether from King, Parliament, or Judicial Tribunal, can vary our moral responsibilities, or release us from obedience to God. And since no man can stand between us and God, it belongs to each conscience for itself to determine its final obligations, and, where pressed to an unrighteous act, — as if to slay, or what is equally bad, to enslave a fellow-man, charged with no crime, — then at every peril to disobey it. The lofty example of Granville Sharp on this occasion is not the least among the large legacies of wisdom and fidelity which he has left to mankind.

All these are especially commended to us, as citizens

of the United States, by the early and constant interest which he manifested in our country. By pen and personal intercession he vindicated our political rights, and when independence was secured, his sympathies did not abate, as witness his correspondence with Adams, Jay, Franklin, and America's earliest Abolitionist, Anthony Benezet. His name became an authority here — at the South as well as the North — and the colleges, including Brown University, Harvard University, and William and Mary's, of slaveholding Virginia, vied with each other in conferring upon him their highest academic honors. But the growing numbers of the Episcopal Church had occasion for special gratitude, only to be repaid by a loyal regard for his character and life. On the separation from the mother country they were left without any Episcopal head. To repair this deprivation, Granville Sharp, in published writings extensively circulated, proposed the election of bishops by the churches, and their subsequent consecration in England, as congenial with the usages of early Christians, and, after much correspondence and many impediments, enjoyed the satisfaction of presenting two bishops elect from America, — one of whom was the exemplary Bishop White, of Philadelphia, — to the Archbishop of Canterbury, by whom the Christian rite of laying on of hands was performed; and thus was the English Episcopacy communicated to this continent. I know not that the powerful religious denomination, which, in its infancy, he befriended, has ever sympathized with the great effort by which his name is exalted; but they should at least repel the weak imputation, — so often levelled against all who are steadfast against Slavery, — that their benefactor was "a man of one idea."

Mr. President — I have striven to keep within the open field of history and philanthropy, on neutral ground; but you would not forgive me if, on this occasion, I forbore to adduce the most interesting testimony of Granville Sharp, touching the much debated clause in our Federal Constitution, which has been stretched to the surrender of fugitive slaves. Anterior to the Constitution, even during colonial days, he wrote that any law which orders the arrest or rendition of fugitive slaves, or which, in any way, tends to deprive them of legal protection, is to be deemed "a corruption, null and void in itself;" and at a later period, in an elaborate communication to the Abolition Society of Maryland — (mark, if you please, of slaveholding Maryland) — which was printed and circulated by this society, as "the production of a great and respectable name," calculated to relieve persons "embarrassed by a conflict between their principles and the obligations imposed by unwise and, perhaps, unconstitutional laws," he exposed the utter "illegality" of Slavery and especially of "taking up slaves that had escaped from their masters." But, in a remarkable letter to Franklin, dated 10th January, 1788, — a short time after the Constitution had left the hands of the Convention, and some months before its final adoption by the people, — and which has never before been mentioned even in the thorough discussion of this question, the undaunted champion, who had not shrunk from conflict with the Chief Justice of England, openly arraigned the Federal Constitution. Here are his words: —

"Having been always zealous for the honor of free governments, I am the more sincerely grieved to see the new Federal

Constitution stained by the insertion of two most exceptionable clauses; the one in direct opposition to a most humane article, ordained by the first American Congress to be perpetually observed [referring to the sufferance of the slave trade till 1808]: and the other, in equal opposition to an express command of the Almighty, not to deliver up the servant that is escaped from his master, &c. *Both clauses, however,* (the 9th section of the 1st article and the latter part of the 2d section of the 3d article,) *are so clearly null and void by their iniquity, that it would be even a* CRIME *to regard them as law.*" *

It does not appear that Franklin ever answered this letter, in the short term of life which remained to him. But in justice to his great name, I desire to express my conviction here — of course without argument — that this patriot philosopher never attributed to the clause, — which simply provides for the surrender of fugitives "from service or labor" without the mention of *slaves*, — any such meaning as it has since been made to assume. And Granville Sharp himself, in putting upon it the interpretation he did, forgot the judgment which he had extorted from Lord Mansfield, affirming that any law out of which Slavery is derived must be construed *strictly;* and, stranger still, he forgot his own unanswerable argument, *that the word* SLAVES *is nowhere to be found in the British Constitution.* The question under the fugitive clause of our Constitution is identical with that happily settled in England.

In works and contemplations like these was the life of our philanthropist prolonged to a generous old age, cheered by the esteem of the good, informed by study,

* Hoare's Life of Sharp, Part ii. cap. 9.

and elevated by an enthusiastic faith, which always saw the world as the footstool of God; and when, at last, in 1813, bending under the burden of seventy-seven winters, he gently sank away, it was felt that a man had died in whom was the greatness of goodness. Among the mourners at his grave stood William Wilberforce; and over the earthly remains of this child of lowly beginnings were now dropped the tears of a royal duke. The portals of that great temple of honor, where are treasured England's glories, swung open at the name of England's earliest Abolitionist. A simple tablet, from the chisel of Chantry, representing an African slave on his knees in supplication, and also the lion and the lamb lying down together, with a suitable inscription, was placed in the Poet's corner of Westminster Abbey, in close companionship with those stones which bear the names of Chaucer, Spenser, Shakespeare, Milton, Dryden, Goldsmith, Gray. As the Muses themselves did not disdain to watch over the grave of one who had done well on earth, so do the poets of England now keep watch over the monument of Granville Sharp. Nor is his place in that goodly company without even poetical title. The poet is simply a *creator;* and he who was inspired to create freemen out of slaves was a poet of the loftiest style. But not in the sacred Abbey only, was our philanthropist commemorated. The city of London, the centre of those Slave-hunting merchants, over whom his great triumph was won, now gratefully claimed a part of his glory. The marble bust of England's earliest Abolitionist was installed at Guildhall, the home of metropolitan justice, pomp and hospitality, in the precise spot where once had stood the bust of Nelson, England's greatest Admiral, and beneath it was carved a simple tribute of more perennial worth than all the trophies of Trafalgar: "Granville Sharp, to whom England owes the glorious verdict of her highest court of law, that the slave who sets his foot on British ground, becomes that instant free."

Gentlemen of the Mercantile Library Association,—such was Granville Sharp; and such honors England to her hero paid. And now, if it be asked, why, in enforcing the duties of the Good Merchant, at this day, I have selected his name, the answer is prompt. It is in him that the merchant, successor to the chivalrous knight, who aims to fulfil his whole duties, may find a truer prototype than in any stunted though successful votary of trade, while the humble circumstances of his life seem to make him an easy example. In imitating him, commerce would thrive none the less; but goodness more. Business would not be checked; but it would cease to be pursued as the "one idea" of life. Wealth would still abound; but there would be also that solid virtue, never to be moved from truth, which you will admit, even without the admonition of Plato, is better than all the cunning of Dædalus, or all the treasures of Tantalus. The hardness of heart engendered by the accursed greed for gain, and by the madness of worldly ambition, would be overcome; the perverted practice, that *Policy is the best Honesty*, would be reversed; and *Merchants would be recalled, gently but irresistibly, to the great* PRACTICAL DUTIES *of this age*, and thus win the palm of true honesty, which trade alone can never bestow.

"——— Who is the Honest Man?
He who doth still and strongly good pursue,
To God, his neighbor, and himself, most true."
Herbert.

Young Merchants of Boston! I have spoken to you frankly and faithfully, trusting that you would frankly and faithfully hearken to me. And now, in the benison once bestowed upon the youthful Knight, I take my leave: "Go forth, be brave, loyal and successful."

# THE DEMANDS OF FREEDOM — REPEAL OF THE FUGITIVE SLAVE BILL.

SPEECH IN THE SENATE OF THE UNITED STATES, 23D FEBRUARY, 1855, AGAINST MR. TOUCEY'S BILL, AND FOR THE REPEAL OF THE FUGITIVE SLAVE BILL.

---

On 23d February, 1855, on motion of Mr. Toucey, of Connecticut, the Senate proceeded to the consideration of a "Bill to protect officers and other persons acting under the authority of the United States," by which it was provided that "suits commenced or pending in any State Court against any officer of the United States or other person, for or on account of any act done under any law of the United States, or under color thereof, or for or on account of any right, authority, claim or title, set up by such officer or other person, under any law of the United States," should be removed for trial to the Circuit Court of the United States. It was seen at once that under these words an attempt was made to oust the State Courts of cases arising from trespasses and damages under the Fugitive Slave Bill; and the Bill was pressed, as every thing for Slavery is always pressed, even on Friday, to the exclusion of the private claims to which that day is devoted under the rules of the Senate. A debate commenced, which was continued with much animation and feeling late into the night.

Mr. SUMNER seized this opportunity to press again his proposition to repeal the Fugitive Slave Bill. Just before the final question, he took the floor and spoke as follows:

Mr. PRESIDENT: On a former occasion, as Slavery was about to clutch one of its triumphs, I rose to make my final opposition to it at midnight. It is now the same hour. Slavery is again pressing for its accustomed victory, which I again undertake for the moment to arrest. It is hardly an accidental conjunction which thus constantly brings Slavery and midnight together.

Since eleven o'clock this forenoon we have been in our seats, detained by the dominant majority, which, in subservience to Slavery, has refused to postpone this question or to adjourn. All other things are neglected. The various public interests which, at this late stage of the session, all press for attention, are put aside. According to the usages of the Senate, Friday is dedicated to the consideration of private claims. I have been accustomed to call it our day of *justice*, and I have been glad that, since these matters are referred to us, at least one day in the week has been thus set apart. But Slavery grasps this whole day, and changes it to a day of *injustice*. By the calendar, which I now hold in my hand, it appears that, at this moment, upwards of seventy-five private Bills, with which are associated the hopes and fears of widows and orphans, and of all who come to Congress for relief, are on your table neglected, ay, sir, sacrificed to the Bill which is now urged with so much pertinacity. Like Juggernaut, the Bill is driven over prostrate victims. And here is another sacrifice to Slavery.

But I do not adequately expose the character of this Bill when I say it is a sacrifice to Slavery. It is a sacrifice to Slavery in its most odious form. Bad as Slavery may be, it is not so bad as hunting slaves. There is a seeming apology for Slavery at home, in the States where it prevails, founded on the difficulties in the position of the master and the relations of personal attachment which it sometimes excites; but every apology fails when you seek again to enslave the fugitive whom the master could not detain by duress or by kindness; and who, by courage and intelligence, under the guidance of the north star, has achieved a happy freedom. Sir, there is a wide difference between the Slaveholder and the Slave-hunter.

But the Bill before you is to aid in the chase of slaves. This is its object. This is its "being's end and aim." And this Bill, with this object, is pressed upon the Senate by the honorable Senator from Connecticut [Mr. Toucey]. Not from slave soil, but from free soil, comes this effort. A Senator from the North — a Senator from New England — lends himself to the work, and with unnatural zeal helps to bind still stronger the fetters of the slave.

Mr. Rusk (interrupting). Will the honorable Senator allow me to interrupt him?

Mr. Sumner. Certainly.

Mr. Rusk. I ask him to point out the words in this Bill where Slavery is mentioned.

Mr. Sumner. I am glad the Senator from Texas has asked the question, for it brings attention at once to the true character of this Bill. I know its language well, and also its plausible title. On its face it purports to be "a Bill to protect officers and other persons acting under the authority of the United States;" and it proceeds to provide for the transfer of certain proceedings from the State courts to the Circuit Courts of the United States. And yet, sir, by the admission of this whole debate, stretching from noon to midnight, it is a Bill to bolster up the Fugitive Slave Act.

Mr. RUSK. I have not listened to the debate, but I ask the Senator to point out in the Bill the place where Slavery is mentioned. If the Constitution and the laws appoint officers, and require them to discharge duties, will he abandon them to the mob?

Mr. SUMNER. The Senator asks me to point out any place in this Bill where "Slavery" is mentioned. Why, sir, this is quite unnecessary. I might ask the Senator to point out any place in the Constitution of the United States where "Slavery" is mentioned, or where the word "slave" can be found, and he could not do it.

Mr. RUSK. That is evading the question. I asked the Senator to point out in the Bill the clause where Slavery is mentioned. The Bill proposes to protect officers of the United States, whom you appoint, in discharging their duties. If they are to be left unprotected, repeal your law.

Mr. SUMNER. I respond to the Senator, with all my heart, "repeal your law." Yes, sir, repeal the Fugitive Act which now requires the support of supplementary legislation. Remove this ground of offence. And before I sit down, I hope to make that very motion. Meanwhile, I evade no question propounded by the honorable Senator; but I do not consider it necessary to show that "Slavery" is mentioned in the Bill. It may not be found there in name; but Slavery is the very soul of the Bill.

Mr. RUSK rose.

Mr. SUMNER. The Senator has interrupted me

several times; he may do it more; but, perhaps, he had better let me go on.

Mr. RUSK. I understand the Senator; but I make no boast of that sort.

Mr. SUMNER. Very well. At last I may be allowed to proceed. Of the Bill in question, I have little to say. Its technical character has been exposed by various Senators, and especially by my valued friend, the Senator from Ohio [Mr. Chase], who opened this debate. Suffice it to say, that it is an intrusive and offensive encroachment on State Rights, calculated to subvert the power of the States in the protection of their citizens. This consideration alone would be ample to seçure its rejection, if the attachment to State Rights, so often avowed by Senators, were not utterly lost in a stronger attachment to Slavery. But on these things, although well worthy of attention, I do not dwell. Objectionable as the Bill may be on this ground, it becomes much more so when I regard it as an effort to bolster up the Fugitive Slave Act.

Of this Act it is difficult to speak with moderation. Conceived in defiance of the Constitution, and in utter disregard of every sentiment of justice and humanity, it should be regarded as an outlaw. It may have the form of legislation, but it lacks every essential element of law. I have so often exposed its character on this floor, that I shall be brief now.

There is an argument against it which has especial importance at this moment, when the Fugitive Act is made the occasion of a new assault on State Rights. *This very Act is an assumption by Congress of power not delegated to it under the Constitution, and an infraction of rights secured to the States.* You will mark, if you please, the double aspect of this proposition, in asserting not only an assumption of power by Congress, but an infraction of State Rights. And this proposition, I venture to say, defies answer or cavil. Show me, sir, if you can, the clause, sentence or word in the Constitution, which gives to Congress any power to legislate on this subject. I challenge honorable Senators to produce it. I fearlessly assert that it cannot be done. The obligations imposed by the "fugitive" clause, *whatever they may be*, rest upon the States, and not upon Congress. I do not now undertake to say what these obligations are; but simply that, whether much or little, they rest upon the States. And this interpretation is sustained by the practice of Congress on another kindred question. The associate clause touching the "privileges of citizens" has never been made a source of power. It will be in the recollection of the Senate, that, during the last session, the Senator from Louisiana [Mr. Benjamin], in answer to a question from me, openly admitted that there were laws of the Southern States, bearing hard upon colored citizens of the North, which were unconstitutional; but when I pressed the honorable Senator with the question whether he would introduce or sustain a Bill to carry out the clause of the Constitution securing to these citizens their rights, he declined to answer.

Mr. Benjamin. I think, Mr. President, I have a right to set the record straight upon that point. I rose in the Senate on the occasion referred to, as will be perfectly well recollected by every Senator present, and put a respectful question to the Senator from Massachusetts. Instead of a reply to my question, he put a question to me, which I answered, and then I put my question. Instead of replying to that, he again put a question to me. Considering that as an absolute evasion of the question which I put to him, I declined having anything further to say in the discussion.

Mr. SUMNER. The Senator from Louisiana will pardon me if I suggest that there is an incontrovertible fact which shows that the evasion was on his part. The record testifies not only that he did not reply, but that I was cut off from replying by the efforts and votes of himself and friends. Let him consult the *Congressional Globe*, and he will find it all there. I can conceive that it might be embarrassing to him to reply, for had he declined to sustain a Bill to carry out the clause in question, it would have been awkward, at least, to vindicate the Fugitive Slave Bill, which is derived from an identical clause in the Constitution. And yet there are Senators on this floor who, careless of the flagrant inconsistency, vindicate the exercise of power by Congress under the "fugitive" clause, while their own States at home deny to Congress any power under the associate clause, on the "privileges of citizens," — assume to themselves a complete right to determine the extent of its obligations, — and ruthlessly sell into Slavery colored citizens of the North.

Mr. BUTLER (interrupting). Does the Senator allude to my State?

Mr. RUSK. No; to mine.

Mr. BUTLER. If he means South Carolina, I will reply to him.

Mr. SUMNER. I do allude to South Carolina, and also to other Southern States; but especially to South Carolina. But let me say, that if I allude to these States, it is not to bring up and array the hardships of individual instances, but simply to show the position occupied by them on a constitutional question, identical with that involved in the Fugitive Act. And now, at the risk of repetition, if I can have your attention for a brief moment, without interruption, I will endeavor to state anew this argument.

The rules of interpretation, applicable to the clause of the Constitution securing to "the citizens of each State all privileges and immunities of citizens in the several States," are equally applicable to its associate clause, forming a part of the same section, in the same article, and providing that "persons held to service or labor in one State, under the laws thereof, escaping into another, shall be delivered up, on claim of the party to whom such service or labor may be due." Of this there can be no doubt.

If one of these clauses is regarded as a compact between the States, to be carried out by them respectively, according to their interpretation of its obligations, without any intervention of Congress, then the other must be so regarded; nor can any legislative power be asserted by Congress under one clause, which is denied under the other. This proposition cannot be questioned. Now mark the consequences.

Congress, in abstaining from all exercise of power under the first clause, when required thereto, in order to protect the liberty of colored citizens, while it has assumed power under the second clause, in order to obtain the surrender of fugitive slaves, has shown an inconsistency, which becomes more monstrous when it is considered that, in the one case, the general and commanding interests of Liberty have been neglected, while in the other, the peculiar and subordinate interests of Slavery have been carefully secured; and such an exercise of power is an alarming evidence of that influence of Slavery in the National Government which has increased, is increasing, and ought to be overthrown.

Looking more precisely at these two clauses, we shall arrive at the true conclusion. According to the express words of the Constitution, in the tenth amendment, "the powers not delegated to the United States by the Constitution, nor prohibited by it to the States, are reserved to the States respectively, or to the people;" and since no powers are delegated to the United States, in the clause relating to "the privileges and immunities of citizens," or in the associate clause of the same section, relating to the surrender of "persons held to service or labor," therefore, all legislation by Congress, under either clause, must be an assumption of undelegated powers, and an infraction of rights secured to the States respectively, or to the people; and such, I have already said, is the Fugitive Slave Act.

I might go further, and, by the example of South Carolina, vindicate to Massachusetts, and every other State, the right to put such interpretation upon the "fugitive" clause as it shall think proper. The Legislature of South Carolina, in a series of resolutions, adopted in 1844, asserts the following proposition:

"*Resolved*, That free negroes and persons of color are not citizens of the United States *within the meaning of the Constitution*, which confers upon the citizens of one State the privileges and immunities of the citizens of the several States."

Here is a distinct assumption of a right to determine the *persons* to whom certain words of the Constitution are applicable. Now, nothing can be clearer than this: If South Carolina may determine for itself whether the clause relating to "the privileges and immunities of citizens" be applicable to *colored citizens* of the several States, and may solemnly deny its applicability, then may Massachusetts, and every other State, determine for itself whether the other clause relating to the surrender of "persons held to service or labor," be really applicable to *fugitive slaves*, and may solemnly deny its applicability.

Mr. President, I have said enough to show the usurpation by Congress under the "fugitive" clause of the Constitution, and to warn you against renewing this usurpation. But I have left untouched those other outrages, plentiful as words, which enter into the existing Fugitive Slave Act, among which are the denial of trial by jury; the denial of the writ of *habeas corpus*; the authorization of judgment on *ex parte* evidence, without the sanction of cross-examination; and the surrender of the great question of Human Freedom to be determined by a mere Commissioner, who, according to the requirements of the Constitution, is grossly incompetent to any such service. I have also left untouched the hateful character of this enactment, as a barefaced subversion of every principle of humanity and justice. And now, sir, we are asked to lend ourselves anew to this enormity, worthy only of indignant condemnation; we are asked to impart new life to this pretended law, this false Act of Congress, this counterfeit enactment, this monstrosity of legislation, which draws no life from the Constitution, as it clearly draws no life from that Supreme Law which is the essential fountain of life to every human law.

Sir, the Bill before you may have the sanction of Congress; and in yet other ways you may seek to sustain the Fugitive Slave Act. But it will be in vain. You undertake what no legislation can accomplish. Courts, too, may come forward, and lend it their sanction. All this, too, will be in vain. I respect the learning of judges; I reverence the virtue, more than learning, by which their lives are often adorned. But nor learning, nor virtue, when, with mistaken force, bent to this purpose, can avail. I assert confidently, sir, and ask the Senate to note my assertion, that there is no court, howsoever endowed with judicial qualities, or surrounded by public confidence, which is strong enough to lift this Act into any permanent consideration or respect. It may seem, for a moment, to accomplish the feat. Its decision may be enforced — amidst tears and agonies. A fellow-man may be reduced anew to Slavery. But all will be in vain. This Act cannot be upheld. Anything so entirely vile, so absolutely atrocious, would drag an angel down. Sir, it must drag down every court, which in an evil hour ventures to sustain it.

And yet, sir, in zeal to support this enormity, Senators have not hesitated to avow a purpose to break down the recent legislation of States, calculated to shield the liberty of their citizens. "It is difficult," says Burke, "to frame an indictment against a whole people." But here in the Senate, where are convened the jealous representatives of the States, we have heard whole States arraigned, as if already guilty of crime. The Senator from Louisiana [Mr. Benjamin], in plaintive tones has set forth the ground of proceeding, and more than one sovereign State has been summoned to judgment. It would be easy to show, by a critical inquiry, that this whole charge is without just foundation, and that all the legislation, so much condemned, is as clearly defensible under the Constitution, as it is meritorious in purpose.

Sir, the only crime of these States is, that Liberty has been placed before Slavery. Follow the charge, point by point, and this will be apparent. In securing to every person claimed as a slave the protection of trial by jury and the *habeas corpus*, they simply provide safeguards, strictly within the province of every State, and rendered necessary by the usurpation of the Fugitive Act. In securing the aid of counsel to every person claimed as a slave, they but perform a kindly duty, which no phrase or word in the Constitution can be tortured to condemn. In visiting with severe penalties every malicious effort to reduce a fellow-man to Slavery, they respond to the best feelings of the human heart. In prohibiting the use of the county jails and buildings as barracoons and slave-pens; in prohibiting all public officers, holding the commission of the State, in any capacity — whether as Chief Justice or Justice of the Peace — whether as Governor or constable — from any service as a slave-hunter; in prohibiting the *volunteer militia* of the State, in its organized form, from any such service, the States simply exercise a power under the Constitution — recognized by the Supreme Court of the United States, even while upholding Slavery in the fatal *Prigg* case — by POSITIVE PROHIBITION, to withdraw its own officers from this offensive business.

For myself, let me say that I look with no pleasure on any possibility of conflict between the State and National jurisdictions; but I trust that, if the interests of Freedom so require, the States will not hesitate. From the beginning of this controversy, I have sought, as I still seek, to awaken another influence, which, without the possibility of conflict, will be mightier than any Act of Congress and the sword of the National Government. I mean an enlightened, generous, humane, Christian public opinion, which shall blast with contempt, indignation, and abhorrence, all who, in whatever form, or under whatever name, undertake to be agents in enslaving a fellow-man. Sir, such an opinion you cannot bind or subdue. Against its subtle, pervasive influence, your legislation and the decrees of courts will be powerless. Already in Massachusetts, I am proud to believe, it begins to prevail; and the Fugitive Act will soon be there a dead letter.

Mr. President, since things are so, it were well to remove this Act from our statute book, that it may no longer exist as an occasion of ill-will and a point of conflict. Let the North be relieved from this usurpation, and the first step will be taken towards permanent harmony. The Senator from Louisiana [Mr. Benjamin] has proclaimed anew to-night what he has before declared on this floor — "that Slavery is a subject with which the Federal Government has nothing to do." I thank him for teaching the Senate that word. True, most true, sir, ours is a Government of Freedom, which has nothing to do with Slavery. This is the doctrine which I have ever maintained, and which I am happy to find recognized in form, if not in reality, by the Senator from Louisiana. The Senator then proceeded to declare that "all that the South asks is to be let alone." This request is moderate. And I say, for the North, that all we ask is to be let alone. Yes, sir, let us alone. Do not involve us in the support of Slavery. Hug the viper to your bosoms, if you perversely will, within your own States, until it stings you to a generous remorse, but do not compel us to hug it too; for this I assure you we will not do.

But the Senator from Louisiana, with these professions on his lips, proceeds to ask, doubtless with complete sincerity, but in strange forgetfulness of the history of our country: "Did we ever bring this subject into Congress?" Yes, sir, that was his inquiry, as if there had been any moment, from the earliest days of the Republic, when the supporters of Slavery had ceased to bring this subject into Congress. Almost from the beginning it has been there, through the exercise of *usurped power*, nowhere given under the Constitution, for I am glad to believe that the Constitution of my country contains no words out of which Slavery, or the power to support Slavery, can be derived; and this conclusion, I doubt not, will yet be affirmed by the courts. And yet, the honorable Senator asks: "Did we ever bring this subject into Congress?" The answer shall be plain and explicit. Sir, you brought Slavery into Congress, when, shortly after the adoption of the Constitution, you sanctioned it in the District of Columbia, within the National jurisdiction, and adopted that barbarous slave code, still extant on your statute-book, which the Senator from Connecticut [Mr. Gillette] has so eloquently exposed to-night. You brought Slavery into Congress, when at the same period you accepted the cession of territories from North Carolina and Georgia, now constituting States of the Union, with conditions in favor of Slavery, and thus began to sanction Slavery in Territories within the exclusive jurisdiction of Congress. You brought Slavery into Congress, when, at different times, you usurped a power, not given by the Constitution, over fugitive slaves, and by most offensive legislation thrust your arms into distant Northern homes. You brought Slavery into Congress, when, by express legislation, you regulated the coastwise slave trade, and thus threw the national shield over a traffic on the coast of the United States, which on the coast of Congo you justly brand as "piracy." You brought Slavery into Congress, when, from time to time, you sought to introduce new States with slaveholding Constitutions into the National Union. And, permit me to say, sir, you brought Slavery into Congress when you called upon it, as you have done even at this very session, to pay for slaves — and thus, in defiance of a cardinal principle of the Constitution, pressed the National Government to recognize property in men. And yet the Senator from Louisiana, with strange simplicity, says that the South only asks to be let alone. Sir, the honorable Senator borrows the language of the North, which, at each of these usurpations, exclaims, "Let us alone." And let me say, frankly, that peace can never prevail until you do let us alone — until this subject of Slavery is banished from Congress by the triumph of Freedom — until Slavery is driven from its usurped foothold, and Freedom is made *national* instead of *sectional* — and until the National Government is brought back to the precise position it occupied on the day that Washington took his first oath as President of the United States, when there was no Fugitive Act, and the national flag, as it floated over the national territory, within the jurisdiction of Congress, nowhere covered a single slave.

And now, sir, as an effort in the true direction of the Constitution; in the hope of beginning the divorce of the National Government from Slavery, and to remove all occasion for the proposed measure under consideration, I shall close what I have to say with a motion to repeal the Fugitive Act. Twice already, since I have had the honor of a seat on this floor, I have pressed that question to a vote, and I mean to press it again to-night. After the protracted discussion, involving the character of this enactment, such a motion seems logically to belong to this occasion, and may fitly close its proceedings.

At a former session, on introducing this proposition, I discussed it at length, in an argument, which I fearlessly assert has never been answered, and now, in this debate, I have already touched upon various objections. There are yet other things which might be urged. I might exhibit the abuses which have occurred under the Fugitive Act; the number of free persons it has doomed to Slavery; the riots it has provoked; the brutal conduct of its officers; the distress it has scattered; the derangement of business it has caused, interfering even with the administration of justice, changing court-houses into barracks and barracoons, and filling the streets with armed men, amidst which law is silent. All these things I might expose. But in these hurried moments, I forbear. Suffice it to say, that the proposition to repeal the existing Fugitive Act stands on adamantine grounds, which no debate or opposition can shake.

There are considerations belonging to the present period which give new strength to this proposition. Public Opinion, which, under a popular Goverment, makes and unmakes laws, and which for a time, was passive and acquiescent, now lifts itself everywhere in the States where the act is sought to be enforced, and demands a change. Already three States, Rhode Island, Connecticut and Michigan, by formal resolutions presented to the Senate, have concurred in this demand. The tribunals of law are joining at last with the people. The Superior Court of Cincinnati has denied the power of Congress over this subject. And now, almost while I speak, comes the solemn judgment of the Supreme Court of Wisconsin — a sovereign State of this Union made after elaborate argument, on successive occasions, before a single judge, and then before the whole bench, declaring this act to be a violation of the Constitution. In response to public opinion, broad and general, if not universal at the North, swelling alike from village and city, from the seaboard and lakes — judically attested, legislatively declared, and represented, also, by numerous petitions from good men without distinction of party — in response to this Public Opinion, as well as in obedience to my own fixed convictions, I deem it my duty not to lose this opportunity of pressing the repeal of the Fugitive Slave Act once more upon the Senate. I move, sir, to strike out all after the enacting clause in the pending Bill, and insert instead thereof these words:

"That the Act of Congress, approved September 18, 1850, usually known as the 'Fugitive Slave Act,' be, and the same hereby is repealed."

And on this motion I ask the yeas and nays.

When Mr. Sumner took his seat, he was followed by Mr. Butler of South Carolina, who put a question to him, which was the occasion of the following dialogue.

Mr. SUMNER. The Senator asks me a question, and I answer, frankly, that no temptation, no inducement, would draw me in any way to sanction the return of any man to Slavery. But then I leave to others to speak for themselves. In this respect, I speak for myself.

Mr. BUTLER. I do not rise now at all to question the right of the gentleman from Massachusetts to hold his seat, under the obligation of the Constitution of the United States, with the opinions which he has expressed; but, if I understand him, he means that, whether this law, or that law, or any other law prevails, he disregards the obligations of the Constitution of the United States.

Mr. SUMNER. Not at all. That I never said. I recognize the obligations of the Constitution.

Mr. BUTLER. But, sir, I will ask that gentleman one question: if it devolved upon him as a representative of Massachusetts, all Federal laws being put out of the way, would he recommend any law for the delivery of a Fugitive Slave under the Constitution of the United States?

Mr. SUMNER. Never.

Mr. BUTLER. I knew that. Now, sir, I have got exactly what is the truth, and what I intend shall go forth to the Southern States.

## WAGES OF SEAMEN IN CASE OF WRECK.

SPEECH IN THE SENATE OF THE UNITED STATES, 28TH FEBRUARY, 1855, ON INTRODUCING A BILL TO SECURE WAGES TO SEAMEN IN CASE OF WRECK.

---

On the 28th February, 1855, Mr. Sumner, in pursuance of previous notice, asked and obtained leave to introduce a Bill to secure wages to seamen in case of wreck, which was read twice by its title.

Mr. Sumner. — In introducing this Bill, I desire to make a brief explanation, which shall, at least, be a record of my views with regard to it.

The Bill proposes an amelioration of the existing maritime law in respect to the wages of merchant seamen, which, so far as England is concerned, has already been made by Act of Parliament, and which, in our country, can only be accomplished by Act of Congress.

By the existing maritime law, the seaman's wages depend upon a technical rule, which sometimes occasions hardships. Freight is compendiously said to be the mother of wages. In conformity with this fanciful idea, the wages are made to depend upon the earning of freight, unless the freight has been waived by agreement of the owner, or unless the voyage or freight be lost by the negligence, fraud, or misconduct of the owner or master, or be voluntarily abandoned. In case of wreck, the sailor has simply the chance of something, under the name of salvage, if the fragments of the ship saved happen to be of any value. But if the loss be total, then the sailor is without remedy. In the wrecks which occur with melancholy frequency on our churlish winter coast, this hardship adds even to the sorrows of disaster. Thus, as in a case which has actually arisen, a crew may commence service at Calcutta, may navigate the Indian Ocean, double the Cape of Good Hope, and bring their ship safely to the sight of land, and then, by the total loss of the ship and cargo, from the acknowledged perils of the sea, they may lose everything — even their right to wages — and may find themselves in a strange port, the prey of poverty. Nor can any merit, either throughout the protracted voyage, or in the hour of peril and shipwreck, prevent the operation of this technical rule.

There is also another circumstance which constrains the poor sailor. The owner may insure his ship, and also his freight, so that he may lose nothing but the premium he pays; but the sailor is not allowed to protect himself by insurance from the loss of his wages. His loss is, therefore, literally total.

Now, this technical rule, which fastens the wages of the sailor to the fortunes of the vessel, or, in other words, makes the right dependent on the successful issue of the enterprise for which he is hired, must be considered an off-shoot of the mediæval maritime law. It is not to be found in the Roman law, nor in the maritime legislation of the Eastern Empire, nor in that early compilation which goes under the name of the Rhodian law. An eminent American judge, who has shed great light upon maritime jurisprudence — I refer to the learned and able Judge Ware, of the District Court of Maine — has said, in a judicial opinion, (see *The Dawn*, Daveis's Rep. 133,) that it owes its origin to the necessities and peculiar hazards which maritime commerce was compelled to encounter in the middle ages, when to the dangers of the winds and waves were added the more formidable perils of piracy and robbery. The rule having been thus established, has been preserved in the maritime jurisprudence of Europe, when the special exigencies in which it had its birth have ceased to exist. It has outlived the circumstances and excuses of its origin; and now survives to vex, oppress and disappoint the most needy, if not the most meritorious, of all who are concerned in the business of the seas.

This hard rule survives with us, but not everywhere. The greatest commercial nation of the world has led the way in its abolition, and set an example to the United States. The Act of Parliament of 7th and 8th Victoria, chap. 112, sec. 17 (at the close) — called "the Merchant Seamen's Act" — provides that

> "In all cases of wreck or loss of the ship, every surviving seaman shall be entitled to his wages up to the period of the wreck or loss of the ship, whether such ship *shall or shall not have earned freight;* provided the seaman shall produce a certificate from the master, or chief surviving officer of the ship, to the effect that he had exerted himself to the utmost to save the ship, cargo and stores."

But the sailor was not completely protected by this provision. Experience in England showed that the cunning of agents was able to introduce into the shipping articles an agreement waiving the right to wages in case of loss, which the unthrifty sailor signed, ignorant or careless of its import. To remedy this abuse, a further Act of Parliament, of 13th and 14th Victoria, chap. 98, sec. 53 — known as "the Mercantile Marine Act" — provides that

> "No seaman shall, by reason of any agreement, forfeit his lien upon the ship, or be deprived of any remedy for the recovery of his wages, to which he would otherwise have been entitled; and every stipulation which is inconsistent with any provision of this Act, or of any other Act relating to the merchant service, and every stipulation by which any seaman consents *to abandon his right to wages in the case of the loss of the ship*, or to abandon any rights which he may have or obtain in the nature of salvage, *shall be wholly inoperative.*"

The Bill which I now introduce is grounded on the provisions quoted from the two Acts of the British Parliament, and contains two principles. *First*, that seamen shall be paid their wages down to the time of the loss of the ship, in case they serve faithfully to the last; and *secondly*, that they shall not be permitted to lose their wages through any agreement in the shipping articles.

In some details I have departed from the British Act. It has not seemed to me advisable to make the wages dependent on "the certificate from the master or chief surviving officer of the ship," but to leave the question of services open to proof in any way according to the received rules of evidence. I have, therefore, said that the wages shall be paid, "*provided* the seaman shall have exerted himself to the utmost to save the ship, cargo and stores." The reasons for this course are clear. Masters are often part owners of American ships, and thus have a personal interest adverse to the sailor. In a mood of selfishness or recklessness, they might refuse the certificate, even though well earned. Now, in constructing a protection to the sailor, it does not seem prudent to make his wages dependent upon any such quarter. Indeed, it is hardly just to take from him the right to establish his claim before the Admiralty Court, merely because an interested master refuses a certificate, when, perhaps, plenary proof might be furnished *aliunde*. Moreover, if the question were put in the control of the master, he might obtain thereby an improper influence over the minds of the crew, inducing them even to sacrifice truth in the event of any litigation between the owners and the underwriters.

There can be no harm in leaving the question of fact to be proved by competent witnesses, like every other question of fact: and the seamen should be competent witnesses for each other. A sagacious court will know how to weigh their testimony, should it come in conflict with that of the officer. It seems proper that the master, too, though a party to the suit, — as in the case of a libel against him *in personam*, or in a suit at common law, — should be competent to testify to the conduct of the libellant or plaintiff; in other words, whether he had "exerted himself to the utmost," and I have introduced into the Bill a provision accordingly.

The British Act of 7th and 8th Victoria contains another defect. It limits the wages to "every surviving seaman." I can see no good reason why the wife and children of the sailor who has perished in the forlorn hope, perhaps, in the cause of all, should be deprived of the humble wages so dearly earned by their natural protectors, and thus be compelled to feel a new deprivation added to their bereavement. In the proposed Bill there is no such limitation.

Beyond this brief statement I need not, on this occasion, add another word. Already Congress has shown a disposition to modify the rigorous maritime law in some of its provisions. In 1851, it made a change in the liability of ship owners as common carriers. But this very liability originated to a certain extent in the same principles from which is derived the liability of the seamen, if they fail to bring the ship and cargo to land. Ship owners and sailors were both treated as insurers. This was in the age of force, before the contract of insurance had spread its broad protection over commerce in every sea. The seaman should share this protection. He should be treated as not necessarily either a pirate or a coward.

In the discussions of the Senate on the proposed change in the liability of ship-owners, it was effectively urged by my immediate predecessor, a distinguished Senator from Massachusetts, the late Robert Rantoul, jr., that, if the United States failed to adopt that measure, the other maritime nations would have an advantage in the carrying trade. It is equally true that, unless we adopt the measure now proposed, Great Britain will have the advantage of us in the rate of seamen's wages; for, under her existing laws, the sailor can afford to work cheaper on board a British ship than under the American flag.

The measure now proposed is of direct importance to the two hundred thousand sailors constituting the mercantile marine of the United States. It also concerns the three millions of men constituting the mercantile marine of the civilized world, any of whom, in the vicissitudes of the sea, may find themselves in American bottoms. I commend it as a measure of enlightened philanthropy, and also of simple justice.

I ask that the Bill, having been read twice, be referred to the Committee on Commerce.

The motion was agreed to.

# THE ANTI-SLAVERY ENTERPRISE; ITS NECESSITY, PRACTICABILITY AND DIGNITY, WITH GLIMPSES AT THE SPECIAL DUTIES OF THE NORTH.

AN ADDRESS BEFORE THE PEOPLE OF NEW YORK, AT THE METROPOLITAN THEATRE, 9 MAY, 1855.

---

This address was the concluding lecture in an Anti-Slavery course in the city of New York. On the night of its delivery the Chair was occupied by the Hon. William Jay, who introduced Mr. Sumner in the following words:

"Ladies and Gentlemen: I have been requested, on the part of the Society, to perform the pleasing but unnecessary office of introducing to you the honored and well-known advocate of Justice, Humanity and Freedom, Charles Sumner. It is not for his learning and eloquence that I commend him to your respectful attention; for learning, eloquence, and even theology itself, have been prostituted in the service of an institution well described by John Wesley as the sum of all villanies. I introduce him to you as a Northern Senator on whom nature has conferred the unusual gift of a backbone — a man who, standing erect on the floor of Congress, amid creeping things from the North, with Christian fidelity denounces the stupendous wickedness of the Fugitive law and Nebraska perfidy, and in the name of Liberty, Humanity and Religion, demands the repeal of those most atrocious enactments. May the words he is about to utter be impressed on your consciences, and influence your conduct."

As soon as the applause had subsided, Mr. Sumner said:

I am not insensible, sir, to this generous applause. Pardon

me if I say, I cannot accept it for myself, but for the cause in whose behalf I am here to speak. Let me add that I am proud to be introduced on this occasion by one whose name, illustrious by a father's renown, is also illustrious by his own noble devotion to the Rights of Man.

MR. SUMNER then proceeded to give the following address:

HISTORY abounds in vicissitudes. From weakness and humility, men ascend to power and place. From defeat and disparagement, enterprises are lifted to triumph and acceptance. The martyr of to-day is gratefully enshrined on the morrow. The stone that the builders rejected is made the head of the corner. Thus it always has been, and ever will be.

Only twenty years ago, — in 1835, — the friends of the slave in our country were weak and humble, while their great Enterprise, just then showing itself, was trampled down and despised. The small companies, gathered together in the name of Freedom, were interrupted and often dispersed by riotous mobs. At Boston, a feeble association of women, called the Female Anti-Slavery Society, convened in a small room of an upper story in an obscure building, was insulted and then driven out of doors by a frantic crowd, politely termed at the time, an assemblage of "gentlemen of property and standing," which, after various deeds of violence and vileness next directed itself upon William Lloyd Garrison, — known as the determined editor of the *Liberator*, and the originator of the Anti-Slavery Enterprise in our day, — then ruthlessly tearing him away, amidst savage threats and with a halter about his neck, dragged him through the streets, until, at last, guilty only of loving liberty, if not wisely, too well, this unoffending citizen was thrust into the common jail for protection against an infuriated populace. Nor was Boston alone. Even villages, in remote rural solitude, belched forth in similar outrage; while the large towns, like Providence, New Haven, Utica, Worcester, Alton, Cincinnati, Baltimore, Philadelphia and New York, became so many fiery craters, overflowing with rage and madness. What lawless violence failed to accomplish was next urged through the forms of law. By solemn legislative acts, the Slave States called on the Free States "promptly and effectually to suppress all associations within their respective limits purporting to be Abolition Societies;" and Rhode Island, Massachusetts and New York, basely hearkened to the base proposition. The press, too, with untold power, exerted itself in this behalf, while the pulpit, the politician and the merchant, conspired to stifle discussion, until the voice of Freedom was hushed to a whisper, "alas! almost afraid to know itself."

Since then — in the lapse of a few years only — a change has taken place. Instead of those small companies, counted by tens, we have now this mighty assembly, counted by thousands; instead of an insignificant apartment, like that in Boston, the mere appendage of a printing-office, where, as in the manger itself, Truth was cradled, we have now this Metropolitan Hall, ample in proportions and central in place; instead of a profane and clamorous mob, beating at our gates, dispersing our assembly, and making one of our number the victim of its fury, we have now peace and harmony at unguarded doors, ruffled only by a generous competition to participate in this occasion; while legislatures openly declare their sympathies; villages, towns and cities vie in the new manifestation; and the press itself, with increased power, heralds, applauds and extends the prevailing influence, which, overflowing from every fountain, and pouring through every channel, at last, by the awakened voice of pulpit, politician and merchant, swells into an irrepressible cry.

Here is a great change, worthy of notice and memory, for it attests the first stage of victory. Slavery, in all its many-sided wrong, still continues; but here in this metropolis, — ay, sir, and throughout the whole North, — freedom of discussion is at length secured. And this, I say, is the first stage of victory — herald of the transcendent Future;

> "Hark! a glad voice the lonely desert cheers;
> Prepare the way! a God, a God appears!
> A God! a God! the vocal hills reply,
> The rocks proclaim th' approaching Deity." *

Nor is there anything peculiar in the trials to which our cause has been exposed. Thus in all ages has Truth been encountered. At first persecuted, gagged, silenced, crucified, she has cried out from the prison, from the torture, from the stake, from the cross, until at last her voice has been heard. And when that voice is really heard, whether in martyr cries, or in the earthquake tones of civil convulsion, or in the calmness of ordinary speech, such as I now employ, or in that still small utterance inaudible to the common ear, then is the beginning of victory! "Give me where to stand, and I will move the world," said Archimedes; and Truth asks no more than did the master of geometry.

* Pope's Messiah.

Viewed in this aspect, the present occasion rises above any ordinary course of lectures or series of political meetings. It is the inauguration of Freedom. From this time forward, her voice of warning and command cannot be silenced. The sensitive sympathies of property may, in this commercial mart, once again recognize property in man; the watchful press itself may falter or fail, but the vantage-ground of free discussion now achieved cannot be lost. On this I take my stand, and, as from the Mount of Vision, behold the whole field of our great controversy spread before me. There is no point, topic, fact, matter, reason or argument, touching the question between Slavery and Freedom, which is not now open. Of all these I might, perhaps, aptly select some one and confine myself to its development. But I should not, in this way, best satisfy the seeming requirements of the occasion. According to the invitation of your Committee, I was to make an address, introductory to the present course of lectures, but was prevented by ill-health. And now, at the close of the course, I am to say what I failed to say at its beginning. Not as caucus or as Congress can I address you; nor am I moved to undertake a political harangue or constitutional argument. Out of the occasion let me speak, and, discarding any individual topic, aim to exhibit the entire field, in all its divisions and subdivisions, with all its metes and bounds.

My subject will be THE NECESSITY, PRACTICABILITY AND DIGNITY OF THE ANTI-SLAVERY ENTERPRISE, WITH GLIMPSES AT THE SPECIAL DUTIES OF THE NORTH. By this enterprise I do not mean the efforts of any restricted circle, sect or party, but the cause of the slave, in all its forms and degrees, and under all its names, — whether inspired by the pulpit, the press, the economist or the politician, — whether in the early, persistent and comprehensive demands of Garrison, the gentler utterances of Channing, or the strictly constitutional endeavors of others now actually sharing the public councils of the country. To carry through this review, under its different heads, I shall not hesitate to meet the objections which have been urged against it, so far at least as I am aware of them. And now, as I speak to you seriously, I venture to ask your serious attention even to the end. Not easily can a public address reach that highest completeness which is found in mingling the useful and the agreeable; but I desire to say, that, in this arrangement and co-ordination of my remarks to-night, I seek to cultivate that highest courtesy of a speaker, which is found in clearness.

I. I begin with the NECESSITY of the Anti-Slavery Enterprise. In the wrong of Slavery, *as defined by existing law*, this necessity is plainly apparent; nor can any man within the sound of my voice, who listens to the authentic words of the law, hesitate in my conclusion. A wrong so grievous and unquestionable should not be allowed to continue. For the honor of human nature, and for the good of all concerned, *it should at once cease to exist.* On this simple statement, as a corner-stone, I found the necessity of the Anti-Slavery Enterprise.

I do not dwell, sir, on the many tales which come from the house of bondage; on the bitter sorrows there undergone; on the flesh, galled by the manacle or spirting blood beneath the lash; on the human form mutilated by the knife, or seared by red-hot iron; on the ferocious scent of blood-hounds in chase of human prey; on the sale of fathers and mothers, husbands and wives, brothers and sisters, little children — even infants — at the auction-block; on the practical prostration of all rights, all ties, and even all hope; on the deadly injury to morals, substituting concubinage for marriage, and changing the whole land of Slavery into a by-word of shame, only fitly pictured by the language of Dante when he called his own degraded country a House of Ill Fame; * and last of all, on the pernicious influence upon the master as well as the slave, showing itself too often, even by his own confession, in rudeness of manners and character, and especially in that blindness which renders him insensible to the wrongs he upholds, while he,

> "—— so perfect is his misery,
> Not once perceives his foul disfigurement,
> But boasts himself more comely than before." †

On these things I do not dwell, although volumes are at hand of unquestionable facts and of illustrative story, so just and happy as to vie with fact, out of which I might draw, until, like Macbeth, you had supped full of horrors.

But all these I put aside; not because I do not regard them of moment in exhibiting the true character of Slavery, but because I desire to present this argument on grounds above all controversy, impeachment,

* Purgat. — *Canto VI. Ahi serva Italia —— bordello!*

† Milton's Comus.

or suspicion, even from slave-masters themselves. Not on triumphant story, not even on indisputable facts, do I now accuse Slavery, but on its character, as revealed in its own simple definition of itself. Out of its own mouth do I condemn it. By the *law of Slavery*, man, created in the image of God, is divested of his human character, and declared to be a mere chattel. That this statement may not seem to be put forward without precise authority, I quote the law of two different States. The civil code of Louisiana thus defines a slave :

> "A slave is one who is in the power of a master to whom he belongs. The master may sell him, dispose of his person, his industry, and his labor. He can do nothing, possess nothing, nor acquire anything but what must belong to his master." — *Civil Code*, Art. 35.

The law of another polished slave State gives this definition :

> "Slaves shall be deemed, sold, taken, reputed and adjudged in law to be *chattels personal*, in the hands of their owners, and possessors, and their executors, administrators and assigns, to all intents, constructions and purposes whatsoever." — 2 *Brev. Dig*. 229. (*South Carolina.*)

And a careful writer, Judge Stroud, in a work of juridical as well as philanthropic merit, thus sums up the law :

> "The cardinal principle of Slavery — that the slave is not to be ranked among *sentient* beings, but among *things* — is an article of property — a chattel personal — obtains as undoubted law in all of these (the slave) States." — *Stroud's Laws of Slavery*, 22.

Sir, this is enough. As out of its small egg crawls forth the slimy, scaly, reptile crocodile, so out of this simple definition crawls forth the whole slimy, scaly, reptile monstrosity, by which a man is changed into a chattel, — a person is converted into a thing, — a soul is transmuted into merchandise. According to this very definition, the slave is held simply for the good of his master, to whose behests, his life, liberty and happiness are devoted, and by whom he may be bartered, leased, mortgaged, bequeathed, invoiced, shipped as cargo, stored as goods, sold on execution, knocked off at public auction, and even staked at the gaming-table on the hazard of a card or die. The slave may seem to have a wife; but he has not; for his wife belongs to his master. He may seem to have a child; but he has not; for his child belongs to his master. He may be filled with the desire of knowledge, opening to him the gates of hope on earth and in heaven; but the master may impiously close this sacred pursuit. Thus is he robbed not merely of privileges, but of himself; not merely of money and labor, but of wife and children; not merely of time and opportunity, but of every assurance of happiness; not merely of earthly hope, but of all those divine aspirations that spring from the Fountain of Light. He is not merely restrained in liberty, but totally deprived of it; not merely curtailed in rights, but absolutely stripped of them; not merely loaded with burthens, but changed into a beast of burthen; not merely bent in countenance to the earth, but sunk to the legal level of a quadruped; not merely exposed to personal cruelty, but deprived of his character as a person; not merely compelled to involuntary labor, but degraded to be a rude thing; not merely shut out from knowledge, but wrested from his place in the human family. *And all this, sir, is according to the simple law of Slavery.*

Nor is even this all. The law, by cumulative provisions, positively forbids that a slave shall be taught to read. Hear this, fellow-citizens, and confess, that no barbarism of despotism, no extravagance of tyranny, no excess of impiety can be more blasphemous or deadly. "Train up a child in the way he should go," is the lesson of sacred wisdom; but the law of Slavery boldly prohibits any such training, and dooms the child to hopeless ignorance and degradation. "Let there be light," was the Divine utterance at the very dawn of creation, — and this commandment, travelling with the ages and the hours, still speaks with the voice of God; but the law of Slavery says, "Let there be darkness."

But it is earnestly averred that slave-masters are humane, and that slaves are treated with kindness. These averments, however, I properly put aside, precisely as I have already put aside the multitudinous illustrations from the cruelty of Slavery. On the simple *letter of the law* I take my stand, and do not go beyond what is there nominated. The masses of men are not better than their laws, and, whatever may be the eminence of individual virtue, it is not reasonable to infer that the masses of slave-masters are better than the law of Slavery. And, since this law submits the slave to their irresponsible control, with power to bind and to scourge — to shut the soul from knowledge — to separate families — to unclasp the infant from a mother's breast, and the wife from a husband's arms, — it is natural to conclude that such enormities are sanctioned by them, while the brutal prohibition of instruction — by supplementary law — gives crowning evidence of their complete complicity. And this conclusion must exist unquestioned, just so long as the law exists unrepealed. Cease, then, to blazon the humanity of slave-masters. Tell me not of the lenity with which this cruel law is tempered to its unhappy subjects. Tell me not of the sympathy which overflows from the mansion of the master to the cabin of the slave. In vain you assert these instances. In vain you show that there are individuals who do not exert the wickedness of the law. The law still endures. Slavery, which it defines and upholds, continues to outrage Public Opinion, and, within the limits of our Republic, upwards of three millions of human beings, guilty only of a skin not colored like your own, are left the victims of its unrighteous, irresponsible power.

Power divorced from right is devilish; power without the check of responsibility is tyrannical; and I need not go back to the authority of Plato, when I assert, that the most complete injustice is that which is erected into the form of law. But all these things concur in Slavery. It is, then, on the testimony of slave-masters, solemnly, legislatively, judicially attested in the very law itself, that I now arraign this institution, as an outrage upon man and his Creator. And here is the necessity of the Anti-Slavery Enterprise. A wrong so transcendent, so loathsome, so direful, must be encountered *wherever it can be reached*, and the battle must be continued without truce or compromise, until the field is entirely won. Freedom and Slavery can hold no divided empire; nor can there be any true repose until Freedom is everywhere established.

To the *necessity* of the Anti-Slavery Enterprise, there are two — and only two — vital objections; one founded on the alleged distinction of race, and the other on the alleged sanction of Christianity. All other objections are of an inferior character, or are directed logically at its *practicability*. Of these two leading objections, let me briefly speak.

1. And, first, of the alleged *distinction of race*. This objection itself assumes two different forms, one founded on a prophetic malediction in the Old Testament, and the other on the professed observations of recent science. Its importance is apparent in the obvious fact, that, unless such distinction be clearly and unmistakably established, every argument by which our own freedom is vindicated, — every applause awarded to the successful rebellion of our fathers, — every indignant word ever hurled against the enslavement of our white fellow-citizens by Algerine corsairs, must plead trumpet-tongued against the deep damnation of Slavery, whether white or black.

It is said that the Africans are the posterity of Ham, the son of Noah, through Canaan, who was cursed by Noah, to be the servant of his brethren, and that this malediction has fallen upon all his descendants, including the unhappy Africans, — who are accordingly devoted by God, through unending generations, to unending bondage. Such is the favorite argument often put forth at the South, and more than once directly addressed to myself. Here, for instance, is a passage from a letter recently received; "You need not persist," says the writer, "in confounding Japheth's children with Ham's, and making both races one, and arguing on their rights as those of man broadly." And I have been seriously assured that until this objection is answered, it will be in vain to press my views upon Congress or the country. Listen now to the texts of the Old Testament which are so strangely employed :

> "And he (Noah) said, cursed be Canaan : a servant of servants shall he be unto his brethren. And he said, Blessed be the Lord God of Shem ; and Canaan shall be his servant. God shall enlarge Japheth, and he shall dwell in the tents of Shem, and Canaan shall be his servant." — *Genesis*, chap. ix. 25–27.

That is all ; and I need only read these words in order to expose the whole transpicuous humbug. But I am tempted to add, that, to justify this objection, it will be necessary to maintain at least five different propositions, as essential links in the chain of the African slave ; *first*, that, by this malediction, Canaan himself was actually changed into a *chattel*, whereas, he is simply made the servant of his brethren ; *secondly*, that not merely Canaan, but all his posterity, to the remotest generation, was so changed, whereas the language has no such extent ; *thirdly*, that the African actually belongs to the posterity of Canaan, — an ethnographical assumption absurdly difficult to establish ; *fourthly*, that each of the descendants of Shem and Japheth has a right to hold an African fellow-man as a chattel, — a proposition which finds no semblance of support ; and, *fifthly*, that every slave-master is truly descended from Shem or Japheth, — a pedigree which no anxiety or audacity can prove ! This plain analysis, which may fitly excite a smile, shows the five-fold absurdity of an attempt to found this revolting wrong on

> "Any successive title, long and dark,
> Drawn from the mouldy rolls of Noah's ark." *

The small bigotry which could find comfort in these

* Dryden's Absalom and Achitophel.

texts, has been lately exalted by the voice of science, which has undertaken to suggest that the different races of men are not derived from a single pair, but from several distinct stocks, according to their several distinct characteristics; and it has been audaciously argued that the African is so far inferior, as to lose all title to that liberty which is the birthright of the lordly white. Now I have neither time nor disposition on this occasion, to discuss the question of the unity of the races; nor is it necessary to my present purpose. It may be that the different races of men proceeded from different stocks; but there is but *one* great Human Family, in which Caucasian and African, Chinese and Indian, are all brothers, children of *one* Father, and heirs to *one* happiness, — alike on earth and in heaven. "Star-eyed science" cannot shake this everlasting truth. It may vainly exhibit peculiarities in the African, by which he is distinguishable from the Caucasian. It may, in his physical form and intellectual character, presume to find the stamp of permanent inferiority. But by no reach of learning, by no torture of fact, by no effrontery of dogma, can it show that he is not *a man*. And as a man he stands before you an unquestionable member of the Human Family, and entitled to *all the rights of man*. You can claim nothing for yourself, *as man*, which you must not accord to him. *Life, liberty and the pursuit of happiness*, — which you proudly declare to be your own inalienable, God-given rights, and to the support of which your fathers pledged their lives, fortunes and sacred honor, are his by the same immortal title that they are yours.

2. From the objection founded on the alleged distinction of race, I pass to that other founded on the

alleged *sanction of Slavery by Christianity.* And, striving to be brief, I shall not undertake to reconcile texts often quoted from the Old Testament, which, whatever may be their import, are all absorbed in the New; nor shall I stop to consider the precise interpretation of the oft-quoted phrase, *Servants, obey your masters;* nor seek to weigh any such imperfect injunction in the scales against those grand commandments, on which hang all the law and the prophets. Surely, in the example and teachings of the Saviour, who lifted up the down-trodden, who enjoined purity of life, and overflowed with tenderness even to little children, human ingenuity can find no apology for an institution which tramples on man, — which defiles woman, — and sweeps little children beneath the hammer of the auctioneer. If to any one these things seem to have the license of Christianity, it is only because they have first secured a license in his own soul. Men are prone to find in uncertain, disconnected texts, a confirmation of their own personal prejudices or preposessions. And I — who am no divine, but only a simple layman — make bold to say, that whoever finds in the Gospel any sanction of Slavery, finds there merely a reflection of himself. On a matter so irresistibly clear, authority is superfluous; but an eminent character, who as poet makes us forget his high place as philosopher, and as philosopher, makes us forget his high place as theologian, has exposed the essential antagonism between Christianity and Slavery, in a few pregnant words which you will be glad to hear, — particularly as, I believe, they have not been before introduced into this discussion. "By a principle essential to Christianity," says Coleridge, "a *person* is eternally differenced from a *thing;* so that *the idea of a Human Being necessarily excludes the idea of property in that Being.*" *

With regret, though not with astonishment, I learn that a Boston divine has sought to throw the seamless garment of Christ over this shocking wrong. But I am patient, and see clearly how vain will be his effort, when I call to mind, that, within this very century, other divines sought to throw the same seamless garment over the more shocking slave-trade; and that, among many publications, a little book, was then put forth with the name of a reverend clergyman on the title-page, to prove that "the African trade for negro slaves is consistent with the principles of humanity and revealed religion;" † and, thinking of these things, I am ready to say with Shakespeare,

> " ——— In religion,
> What damned error, but some sober brow
> Will bless it and approve it with a text?"

In the support of Slavery, it is the habit to pervert texts and to invent authority.. Even St. Paul is vouched for a wrong which his Christian life rebukes. Great stress is now laid on his example, as it appears in the epistle to Philemon, written at Rome, and sent by Onesimus, a servant. From the single chapter constituting the entire epistle, I take the following passage, in ten verses, which is strangely invoked for Slavery:

"*I beseech thee for my son Onesimus,* whom I have begotten in my bonds; which in time past was to thee unprofitable, but

* Coleridge's Dissertation introductory to the *Ency. Metrop.*

† This was by the Rev. Thomas Thompson. Boswell's Defence of the Slave-trade was kindred in character. Life of Johnson, vol. iv. p. 55.

now profitable to thee and to me; whom I have sent again; thou, therefore, receive him, that is, mine own bowels; whom I would have retained with me, that in thy stead he might have ministered unto me in the bonds of the gospel; but without thy mind would I do nothing, that thy benefit should not be as it were of necessity, but willingly. For perhaps he therefore departed for a season, that thou shouldst receive him for ever; *not now as a servant, but above a servant, a brother beloved,* specially to me, but how much more unto thee, both in the flesh and in the Lord? *If thou count me, therefore, a partner, receive him as myself.* If he hath wronged thee, or oweth thee aught, put that on mine account. I, Paul, have written it with mine own hand, I will repay it; albeit, I do not say to thee how thou owest unto me even thine own self besides." — *Epistle to Philemon,* verses 10–19.

Out of this affectionate epistle, in which St. Paul calls the converted servant, Onesimus, his *son,* precisely as in another epistle he calls Timothy his son, Slavery has been elaborately vindicated, and the great Apostle to the Gentiles has been made the very tutelary saint of the Slave-hunter. Now, without relying on minute criticism, to infer his real judgment of Slavery from his condemnation on another occasion of "men-stealers," or, according to the original text, *slave-traders,* in company with "murderers of fathers, and murderers of mothers," and without undertaking to show that the present epistle, when truly interpreted, is a protest against Slavery, and a voice for Freedom, — all of which might be done, — I content myself by calling attention to two things, apparent on its face, and in themselves an all-sufficient response. First, while it appears that Onesimus had been in some way the servant of Philemon, it does not appear that he had ever been held as a slave, much less as a *chattel;* and how gross and monstrous is the effort to derive a wrong, by which man is changed to a chattel, out of words, whether in the Constitution of our country, or in the Bible, which do not explicitly, unequivocally and exclusively define this wrong! Secondly, in charging Onesimus with this epistle to Philemon, the Apostle announces him as "not now a servant, but above a servant, a brother beloved," and he enjoins upon his correspondent the hospitality due only to a freeman, saying expressly, "If thou count me, therefore, a partner, *receive him as myself;*" ay, sir, not as slave, not even as servant, but as a brother beloved, even as the Apostle himself. Thus with apostolic pen wrote Paul to his disciple, Philemon. Beyond all doubt, in these words of gentleness, benediction and emancipation, dropping with celestial, soul-awakening power, there can be no justification for a conspiracy, which, beginning with the treachery of Iscariot, and the temptation of pieces of silver, seeks, by fraud, brutality and violence, through officers of the law armed to the teeth, like pirates, and amidst soldiers who degrade their uniform, to hurl a fellow-man back into the lash-resounding den of American Slavery; and if any one can thus pervert this beneficent example, allow me to say, that he gives too much occasion to doubt his intelligence or his sincerity.

Certainly I am right in thus stripping from Slavery the apology of Christianity, which it has tenaciously hugged; and here I leave the first part of my subject, assuming against every objection the Necessity of our Enterprise.

II. I am now brought, in the *second* place, to consider the PRACTICABILITY of the Enterprise. And here the way is easy. In showing its necessity, I have already demonstrated its practicability; for the former includes the latter, as the greater includes the less. Whatever is necessary must be practicable. By a decree which has ever been a by-word of tyranny, the Israelites were compelled to make bricks without straw; but it is not according to the ways of a benevolent Providence, that man should be constrained to do what cannot be done. Besides, the Anti-Slavery Enterprise is right; and the right is always practicable.

I know well the little faith which the world has in the triumph of principles, and I readily imagine the despair with which our object is regarded; but not on this account am I disheartened. That exuberant writer, Sir Thomas Browne, breaks into an ecstatic wish for some new difficulty in Christian belief, that his faith might have a new victory, and an eminent enthusiast went so far as to say, that he believed because it was impossible — *credo quia impossibile.* But no such exalted faith is now required. Here is no impossibility, nor is there any difficulty which will not yield to a faithful, well-directed endeavor. If to any timid soul the Enterprise seems impossible because it is too beautiful, then I say at once that it is too beautiful not to be possible.

But descending from these summits, let me show plainly the object which it seeks to accomplish, and herein you shall see and confess its complete practicability. While discountenancing all prejudice of color and every establishment of caste, the Anti-Slavery Enterprise — at least so far as I may speak for it — does not undertake to change human nature, or to force any individual into relations of life for which he is not morally, intellectually and socially adapted; nor does it necessarily assume that a race, degraded for long generations under the iron heel of bondage, can be lifted at once into all the political privileges of an American citizen. But, sir, it does confidently assume, against all question, contradiction, or assault whatever, *that every man is entitled to life, liberty, and the pursuit of happiness; and, with equal confidence, it asserts that every individual, who wears the human form, whether black or white, should at once be recognized as man.* I know not when this is done, what other trials may be in wait for the unhappy African; but this I do know, that the Anti-Slavery Enterprise will then have triumphed, and the institution of Slavery, *as defined by existing law*, will no longer shock mankind.

In this work the first essential, practical requisite is, that the question shall be openly and frankly confronted. Do not put it aside. Do not blink it out of sight. Do not dodge it. Approach it. Study it. Ponder it. Deal with it. Let it rest in the illumination of speech, conversation and the press. Let it fill the thoughts of the statesman and the prayers of the pulpit. When Slavery is thus regarded, its true character will be recognized *as a hateful assemblage of unquestionable wrongs under the sanction of existing law*, and good men will be moved at once to apply the remedy. Already even its zealots admit that its "abuses" should be removed. This is their word and not mine. Alas! alas! sir, it is these very "abuses" which constitute its component parts, without which it would not exist, even as the scourges in a bundle with the axe constituted the dread fasces of the Roman lictor. Take away these, and the whole embodied outrage will disappear. Surely that central assumption — more deadly than the axe itself — by which man is changed into a chattel, may be abandoned; and is not this practicable? The associate scourges by which that transcendent "abuse" is surrounded, may, one by one, be subtracted. The "abuse" which substitutes concubinage for marriage — the "abuse" which annuls the parental relation — the "abuse" which closes the portals of knowledge — the "abuse" which tyrannically usurps all the labor of another — now upheld by positive law, may by positive law be abolished. To say that this is not practicable, in the nineteenth century, would be a scandal upon mankind, and just in proportion as these "abuses" cease to have the sanction of law, will the institution of Slavery cease to exist. The African, whatever may then be his condition, will no longer be *the slave* over whose wrongs and sorrows the world throbs at times fiercely indignant, and at times painfully sad, while with outstretched arms, he sends forth the piteous cry, "Am I not a man and a brother?"

In pressing forward to this result, the inquiry is often presented, to what extent, if any, shall compensation be allowed to the slave-masters? Clearly, if the point be determined by *absolute justice*, not the masters but the slaves will be entitled to compensation; for it is the slaves, who, throughout weary generations, have been deprived of their toil, and all its fruits which went to enrich their masters. Besides, it seems hardly reasonable to pay for the relinquishment of those disgusting "abuses," which, in their aggregation, constitute the bundle of Slavery. Pray, sir, by what tariff, price current, or principle of equation, shall their several values be estimated? What sum shall be counted out as the proper price for the abandonment of that pretension — more indecent than the *jus primæ noctis* of the feudal age — which leaves woman, whether in the arms of master or slave, always a concubine? What bribe shall be proffered for the restoration of God-given paternal rights? What money shall be paid for taking off the padlock by which souls are fastened down in darkness? How much for a quit-claim to labor now meanly exacted by the strong from the weak? And what compensation shall be awarded for the egregious assumption, condemned by reason and abhorred by piety, which changes a man into a thing? I put these questions without undertaking to pass upon them. Shrinking instinctively from any recognition of *rights founded on wrongs*, I find myself shrinking also from any austere verdict, which shall deny the means necessary to the great consummation we seek. Our fathers, under Washington, did not hesitate by Act of Congress, to appropriate largely for the ransom of white fellow-citizens enslaved by Algerine corsairs; and, following this example, I am disposed to consider the question of compensation as one of expediency, to be determined by the exigency of the hour and the constitutional powers of the Government; though such is my desire to see the foul fiend of Slavery in flight, that I could not hesitate to build even a Bridge of Gold, if necessary, to promote his escape.

The *Practicability* of the Anti-Slavery Enterprise has been constantly questioned, often so superficially, as to be answered at once. I shall not take time to consider the allegation, founded on considerations of economy, which audaciously assumes that Slave Labor is more advantageous than Free Labor — that Slavery is more profitable than Freedom; for this is all exploded by the official tables of the census; nor that other futile argument, that the slaves are not prepared for Freedom, and, therefore, should not be precipitated into this condition, — for that is no better than the ancient Greek folly, where the anxious mother would not allow her son to go into the water until he had first learned to swim. But, as against the Necessity of the Anti-Slavery Enterprise, there were two chief objections, so, also, against its Practicability there are two; the first, founded on its alleged danger to the master, and the second, on its alleged damage to the slave himself.

1. The first objection, founded on the alleged *danger to the master*, most generally takes the extravagant form, that the slave, if released from his present condition, would cut his master's throat. Here is a blatant paradox, which can pass for reason only among those who have lost their reason. With an absurdity which finds no parallel except in the defences of Slavery, it assumes that the African, when treated justly, will show a vindictiveness which he does not exhibit when treated unjustly; that when elevated by the blessings of Freedom, he will develop an appetite for blood which he never manifested when crushed by the curse of bondage. At present, the slave sees his wife ravished from his arms — sees his infant swept away to the auction block — sees the heavenly gates of knowledge shut upon him — sees his industry and all its

fruits unjustly snatched by another — sees himself and offspring doomed to a servitude from which there is no redemption; and still his master sleeps secure. Will the master sleep less secure, when the slave no longer smarts under these revolting atrocities? I will not trifle with your intelligence, or with the quick-passing hour, by arguing this question.

But there is a lofty example, brightening the historic page, by which the seal of experience is affixed to the conclusions of reason; and you would hardly pardon me if I failed to adduce it. By virtue of a single Act of Parliament, the slaves of the British West Indies were changed at once to freedmen; and this great transition was accomplished absolutely without personal danger of any kind to the master. And yet the chance of danger there was greater far than among us. In our broad country, the slaves are overshadowed by a more than six-fold white population. Only in two States — South Carolina and Mississippi — do the slaves outnumber the whites, and there but slightly, while in the entire Slave States, the whites outnumber the slaves by many millions. But it was otherwise in the British West Indies, where the whites were overshadowed by a more than six-fold population. The slaves were 800,000, while the whites numbered only 131,000, distributed in different proportions on the different islands. And this disproportion has since increased rather than diminished, always without danger to the whites. In Jamaica, the largest of these possessions, there are now upwards of 400,000 Africans, and only 37,000 whites; in Barbadoes, the next largest possession, there are 120,000 Africans, and only 15,000 whites; in St. Lucia, 19,500 Africans, and only

600 whites; in Tobago, 14,000 Africans, and only 600 whites; in Montserrat, 6000 Africans, and only 150 whites; and in the Grenadines, upwards of 6000 Africans, and less than 50 whites. And yet in all these places, the authorities attest the good behavior of the Africans. Sir Lionel Smith, the Governor of Jamaica, in his speech to the Assembly, declared that their conduct "proves how well they deserved the boon of Freedom." Another Governor of another island dwells on the "peculiarly rare instances of the commission of grave or sanguinary crimes among the emancipated portion of these islands;" and the Queen of England, in a speech from the throne, has announced that the complete and final emancipation of the Africans had "taken place without any disturbance of public order and tranquillity." In this example I hail new confirmation of the rule that the highest safety is in doing right; and thus do I dismiss the objection founded on the alleged danger to the master.

2. And I am now brought to the second objection, founded on the alleged *damage to the slave.* It is common among the partisans of Slavery, to assert that our Enterprise has actually retarded the very cause it seeks to promote; and this paradoxical accusation, which might naturally show itself among the rank weeds of the South, is cherished here on our Northern soil, by those who anxiously look for any fig-leaf with which to cover their indifference or tergiversation.

This peculiar form of complaint is an old device, which has been instinctively employed on other occasions until it has ceased to be even plausible. Thus, throughout all times, has every good cause been encountered. The Saviour was nailed to the cross with a crown of thorns on his head, as a disturber of that peace on earth which he came to declare. The disciples, while preaching the Gospel of forgiveness and good will, were stoned as preachers of sedition and discord. The reformers, who sought to establish a higher piety and faith, were burnt at the stake as blasphemers and infidels. Patriots, in all ages, who have striven for their country's good, have been doomed to the scaffold or to exile, even as their country's enemies. And those brave Englishmen, who, at home, under the lead of Edmund Burke, even against their own country, espoused the cause of our fathers, shared the same illogical impeachment, which was touched to the quick by that orator statesman, when, after exposing its essential vice, "in attributing the ill-effect of ill-judged conduct to the arguments used to dissuade us from it," he denounced it as "very absurd, but very common in modern practice, and very wicked." Ay, sir, it is common in modern practice. In England, it has vainly renewed itself with special frequency against the Bible Societies; against the friends of education; against the patrons of vaccination; against the partisans of peace, all of whom have been openly arraigned as provoking and increasing the very evils, whether of infidelity, idleness, disease, or war, which they benignly sought to check. And to bring an instance which is precisely applicable to our own, Wilberforce, when conducting the Anti-Slavery Enterprise of England, first against the slave-trade and then against Slavery itself, was told that those efforts, by which his name is now consecrated forevermore, tended to increase the hardships of the slave, even to the extent of rivetting anew his chains. Such are the precedents for the imputation to which our Enterprise is exposed; and such, also, are the precedents by which I exhibit the fallacy of the imputation.

Sir, I do not doubt that the Enterprise has produced heat and irritation, amounting often to inflammation, among slave-masters, which, to superficial minds, may seem inconsistent with success; but which the careful observer will recognize at once as the natural and not unhealthy effort of a diseased body, to purge itself of existing impurities; and just in proportion to the malignity of the concealed poison, will be the extent of inflammation. A distemper like Slavery cannot be ejected like a splinter. It is, perhaps, too much to expect that men thus tortured should reason calmly — that patients thus suffering should comprehend the true nature of their case and kindly acknowledge the beneficent work; but not on this account can it be suspended.

In the face of this complaint, I assert that the Anti-Slavery Enterprise has already accomplished incalculable good. Even now it touches the national heart as it never before was touched, sweeping its strings with a might to draw forth emotions such as no political struggle has ever evoked. It moves the young, the middle-aged and the old. It enters the family circle, and mingles with the flame of the household hearth. It reaches the souls of mothers, wives, sisters and daughters, filling all with a new aspiration for justice on earth, and awakening not merely a sentiment against Slavery, such as prevailed with our fathers, but a deep, undying conviction of its wrong, and a determination to leave no effort unattempted for its removal. With the sympathies of all Christendom as allies, it has already encompassed the slave-masters by a *moral blockade*, invisible to the eye, but more potent than navies, from which there can be no escape except in final capitulation. Thus it has created the irresistible influence which itself constitutes the beginning of success. Already there are signs of change. In common speech, as well as in writing, among slave-masters the bondman is no longer called a *slave*, but a *servant*, — thus, by a soft substitution, concealing and condemning the true relation. Even newspapers in the land of bondage blush with indignation at the hunt of men by blood-hounds, thus protesting against an unquestionable incident of Slavery. Other signs are found in the added comfort of the slave; in the enlarged attention to his wants; in the experiments now beginning, by which the slave is enabled to share in the profits of his labor, and thus finally secure his freedom; and, above all, in the consciousness among slave-masters themselves, that they dwell now as never before under the keen observation of an ever-wakeful Public Opinion, quickened by an ever-wakeful Public Press. Nor is this all. Only lately propositions have been introduced into the Legislatures of different States, and countenanced by Governors, to mitigate the existing law of Slavery; and, almost while speaking, I have received the drafts of two different memorials, — one addressed to the Legislature of Virginia, and the other to that of North Carolina, — asking for the slave three things, which it will be monstrous to refuse, but which, if conceded, will take from Slavery its existing character; — I mean, first, the protection of the marriage relation; secondly, the protection of the parental relation; and, thirdly, the privilege of knowledge. Grant these, and the girdled Upas tree soon must die. Sir, amidst these tokens of present success, and the auguries of the future, I am not disturbed by any complaints of seeming damage. "Though it consume our own dwelling, who does not venerate fire, without which human life can hardly exist on earth," says the Hindoo proverb; and the time is even now at hand when the Anti-Slavery Enterprise, which is the very fire of Freedom, with all its incidental excesses or excitements, will be hailed with a similar regard.

III. And now, in the *third* place, the Anti-Slavery Enterprise, which I have shown to be at once necessary and practicable, is commended by its inherent DIGNITY. Here the reasons are obvious and unanswerable.

Its object is benevolent; nor is there, in the dreary annals of the Past, a single Enterprise which stands forth more clearly and indisputably entitled to this character. With unsurpassed and touching magnanimity, it seeks to benefit the lowly whom your eyes have not seen, and who are ignorant even of your labors, while it demands and receives a self-sacrifice calculated to ennoble an enterprise of even questionable merit. Its true rank is among works properly called *philanthropic* — the title of highest honor on earth. "I take goodness in this sense," says Lord Bacon in his Essays, "*the affecting of the weal of men*, which is what the Grecians call Philanthropeia — of all virtues and dignities of the mind the greatest, being the character of the Deity; and without it, man is a busy, mischievous, wretched thing, no better than a kind of vermin." Lord Bacon was right, and, perhaps, unconsciously followed a higher authority; for, when Moses asked the Lord to show unto him His glory, the Lord said, "I will make all my goodness to pass before thee." Ah! sir, Peace has trophies fairer and more perennial than any snatched from fields of blood, but among all these, the fairest and most perennial are the trophies of beneficence. Scholarship, literature, jurisprudence, art, may wear their well-deserved honors; but an Enterprise of goodness deserves, and will yet receive, a higher palm than these.

In other aspects its dignity is apparent. It concerns the cause of Human Freedom, which, from the earliest days, has been the darling of history. By all the memories of the Past; by the stories of childhood and the studies of youth; by every example of magnanimous virtue; by every aspiration for the good and true; by the fame of the martyrs swelling through all time; by the renown of patriots whose lives are landmarks of progress; by the praise lavished upon our fathers, you are summoned to this work. Unless Freedom be an illusion, and Benevolence an error, you cannot resist the appeal. But our cause is nobler even than that of our fathers, inasmuch as it is more exalted to struggle for the freedom of *others* than for our *own*.

Its practical importance at this moment gives to it an additional eminence. Whether measured by the number of beings it seeks to benefit; by the magnitude of the wrongs it hopes to relieve; by the difficulties with which it is beset; by the political relations which it affects; or by the ability and character it has enlisted, the cause of the slave now assumes proportions of grandeur which dwarf all other interests in our broad country. In its presence the machinations of politicians, the aspirations of office-seekers and the subterfuges of party, all sink below even their ordinary insignificance. For myself, sir, I can see little else at this time among us which can tempt out on to the exposed steeps of public life an honest man, who wishes, by something that he does, to leave the world better than he found it. I can see little else which can afford any of those satisfactions which an honest man should covet. Nor is there any cause which so surely promises final success;

> "Oh! a fair cause stands firm and will abide;
> Legions of angels fight upon its side!" *

It is written that in the last days there shall be scoffers, and even this Enterprise, thus philanthropic, has not escaped their aspersions. And as the objections to its Necessity were two-fold, and the objections to its Practicability two-fold, so, also, are the aspersions two-fold; — first in the form of hard words, and secondly, by personal disparagement of those who are engaged in it.

1. The *hard words* are manifold as the passions and prejudices of men; but they generally end in the imputation of "fanaticism." In such a cause, I am willing to be called "fanatic," or what you will; I care not for aspersions, nor shall I shrink before hard words, either here or elsewhere. I have learned from that great Englishman, Oliver Cromwell, that no man can be trusted "who is afraid of a paper pellet;" and I am too familiar with history not to know, that every

* Antonio and Mellida, a play by John Marston.

movement for reform, in Church or State, every endeavor for Human Liberty or Human Rights, has been thus assailed. I do not forget with what facility and frequency hard words have been employed — how that grandest character of many generations, the precursor of our own Washington, without whose example our Republic might have failed — the great William, Prince of Orange, the founder of the Dutch Republic, the United States of Holland — I do not forget how he was publicly branded as "a perjurer and a pest of society;" and, not to dwell on general instances, how the enterprise for the abolition of the slave-trade was characterized on the floor of Parliament by one eminent speaker as "mischievous," and by another as "visionary and delusive;" and how the exalted characters which it had enlisted were arraigned by still another eminent speaker — none other than that Tarleton, so conspicuous as the commander of the British horse in the southern campaigns of our Revolution, but more conspicuous in politics at home, — "as a junto of sectaries, sophists, enthusiasts and fanatics;" and also were again arraigned by no less a person than a prince of the blood, the Duke of Clarence, afterwards William IV. of England, as "either fanatics or hypocrites," in one of which classes he openly placed William Wilberforce. But impartial history, with immortal pen, has redressed these impassioned judgments; and the same impartial history will yet rejudge the impassioned judgments of this hour.

2. Hard words have been followed by *personal disparagement*, and the sneer is often launched that our Enterprise lacks the authority of names eminent in

Church and State. If this be so, the more is the pity on their account; for our cause is needed to them more than they are needed to our cause. But alas! it is only according to the example of history that it should be so. It is not the eminent in Church and State, the rich and powerful, the favorites of fortune and of place, who most promptly welcome Truth, when she heralds change in the existing order of things. It is others in poorer condition who throw open their hospitable hearts to the unattended stranger. Nay, more; it is not the dwellers amidst the glare of the world, but the humble and lowly, who most clearly discern new duties, — as the watchers, placed in the depths of a well, may observe the stars which are obscured to those who live in the effulgence of noon. Placed below the egotism and prejudice of self-interest, or of a class — below the cares and temptations of wealth or power — in the obscurity of common life, they discern the new signal, and surrender themselves unreservedly to its guidance. The Saviour knew this. He did not call upon the Priest, or Levite, or Pharisee, to follow him; but upon the humble fisherman by the sea of Galilee.

And now, sir, I present to you the Anti-Slavery Enterprise vindicated in Necessity, Practicability and Dignity, against all objections. If there be any objection which I have not answered, it is because I am not aware of its existence. It remains that I should give a practical conclusion to this whole matter, by showing, though in glimpses only, your SPECIAL DUTIES AS FREEMEN OF THE NORTH. And, thank God! at last there is a North.

Mr. President, it is not uncommon to hear persons among us at the North, confess the wrong of Slavery, and then, folding their hands in absolute listlessness, ejaculate, "What can we do about it?" Such men we encounter daily. You all know them. Among them are men in every department of human activity — who perpetually buy, build and plan — who shrink from no labor — who are daunted by no peril of commercial adventure, by no hardihood of industrial enterprise — who, reaching in their undertakings across oceans and continents, would undertake "to put a girdle about the earth in forty seconds;" and yet, disheartened, they can join in no effort against Slavery. Others there are, especially among the youthful and enthusiastic, who vainly sigh because they were not born in the age of chivalry, or at least in the days of the revolution, not thinking that in this Enterprise, there is an opportunity of lofty endeavor such as no Paladin of chivalry, or chief of the revolution enjoyed. Others there are, who freely bestow their means and time upon the distant inaccessible heathen of another hemisphere, in the islands of the sea; and yet they can do nothing to mitigate our grander heathenism here at home. While confessing that it ought to disappear from the earth, they forego, renounce and abandon all exertion against it. Others there are still, (such is human inconsistency!) who plant the tree in whose full-grown shade they can never expect to sit — who hopefully drop the acorn in the earth, trusting that the oak which it sends upward to the skies will shelter their children beneath its shade; but they will do nothing to plant or nurture the great tree of Liberty, that it may cover with its arms unborn generations of men.

Others still there are, particularly in the large cities, who content themselves by occasional contributions to the redemption of a slave. To this object they give out of ample riches, and thus seek to silence the monitions of conscience. Now, I would not discountenance any form of activity by which Human Freedom, even in a single case, may be secured. But I desire to say, that such an act — too often accompanied by a pharisaical pretension, in strange contrast with the petty performance — cannot be considered an essential aid to the Anti-Slavery Enterprise. Not in this way can any impression be made on an evil so vast as Slavery — as you will clearly see by an illustration which I shall give. The god Thor, of Scandinavian mythology — whose strength surpassed that of Hercules — was once challenged to drain a simple cup dry. He applied it to his lips, and with superhuman capacity drank, but the water did not recede even from the rim, and at last the god abandoned the effort. The failure of even his extraordinary strength was explained, when he learned that the simple cup had communicated, by an invisible connection, with the whole vast ocean behind, out of which it was perpetually supplied, and which remained absolutely unaffected by the effort. And just so will these occasions of charity, though encountered by the largest private means, be constantly renewed, for they communicate with the whole Black Sea of Slavery behind, out of which they are perpetually supplied, and which remains absolutely unaffected by the effort. Sir, private means may cope with individual necessities, but they are powerless to redress the evils of a wicked institution. Charity is limited and local; the evils of Slavery are infinite and everywhere. Besides, a wrong organized and upheld by law, can be removed only through a change of the law. Not, then, by an occasional contribution to ransom a slave can your duty be done in this great cause; but only by earnest, constant, valiant efforts against the institution — against the law — which makes slaves.

I am not insensible to the difficulties of this work. Full well I know the power of Slavery. Full well I know all its various intrenchments in the church, the politics and the prejudices of the country. Full well I know the sensitive interests of property, amounting to many hundred millions of dollars, which are said to be at stake. But these things can furnish no motive or apology for indifference, or for any folding of the hands. Surely the wrong is not less wrong because it is gigantic; the evil is not less evil because it is immeasurable; nor can the duty of perpetual warfare, with wrong, or evil, be in this instance suspended. Nay, because Slavery is powerful — because the Enterprise is difficult — therefore is the duty of all more exigent. The well-tempered soul does not yield to difficulties, but presses *onward forever* with increased resolution.

And here the question occurs, which is so often pressed in argument, or in taunt, *What have we at the North to do with Slavery?* In answer, I might content myself by saying that as members of the human family, bound together by the cords of a common manhood, there is no human wrong to which we can justly be insensible, nor is there any human sorrow which we should not seek to relieve; but I prefer to say, on this occasion, that, as citizens of the United

States, anxious for the good name, the repose and the prosperity of the Republic — that it may be a blessing and not a curse to mankind — there is nothing among all its diversified interests, under the National Constitution, with which, at this moment, we have so much to do; nor is there anything with regard to which our duties are so irresistibly clear. I do not dwell on the scandal of Slavery in the national capital — of Slavery in the national territories — of the coast-wise slave-trade on the high seas beneath the national flag, — all of which are outside of State limits, and within the exclusive jurisdiction of Congress, where you and I, sir, and every freeman of the North, are compelled to share the responsibility and help to bind the chain. To dislodge Slavery from these usurped footholds under the Constitution, and thus at once to relieve ourselves from a grievous responsibility, and to begin the great work of emancipation, were an object worthy of an exalted ambition. But before even this can be commenced, there is a great work, more than any other important and urgent, which must be consummated in the domain of national politics, and also here at home in the Free States. The National Government itself must be emancipated, so that it shall no longer wear the yoke of servitude; and Slavery in all its pretensions must be dislodged from its usurped foothold, in the Free States themselves, thus relieving ourselves from a grievous responsibility at our own door, and emancipating the North. Emancipation, even within the national jurisdiction, can be achieved only through the emancipation of the Free States, accompanied by the complete emancipation of the National Government. Ay, sir, emancipation at the

South can be reached only through the emancipation of the North. And this is my answer to the interrogatory, What have we at the North to do with Slavery?

But the answer may be made yet more irresistible, while, with mingled sorrow and shame, I portray the tyrannical power which holds us in thraldom. Notwithstanding all its excess of numbers, wealth and intelligence, the North is now the vassal of an OLIGARCHY, whose single inspiration comes from Slavery. According to the official tables of our recent census, the *slave-masters* — men, women, and children all told — are only THREE HUNDRED AND FORTY SEVEN THOUSAND; and yet this small company now dominates over the Republic, determines its national policy, disposes of its offices, and sways all to its absolute will. With a watchfulness that never sleeps, and an activity that never tires — with as many eyes as Argus, and as many arms as Briareus — the SLAVE OLIGARCHY asserts its perpetual and insatiate masterdom; now seizing a broad territory once covered by a time-honored ordinance of Freedom; now threatening to wrest Cuba from Spain by violent war, or hardly less violent purchase; now hankering for another slice of Mexico, merely to find new scope for Slavery; now proposing once more to open the hideous, heaven-defying Slave-trade, and thus to replenish its shambles with human flesh; and now, by the lips of an eminent Senator, asserting an audacious claim to the whole group of the West Indies, whether held by Holland, Spain, France, or England, as "our Southern Islands," while it assails the independence of Hayti, and stretches its treacherous ambition even to the distant valley of the Amazon.

In maintaining its power, the Slave Oligarchy has applied a new test for office, very different from that of Jefferson; "Is he honest? is he capable? is he faithful to the Constitution?" These things are all forgotten now in the controlling question, "Is he faithful to Slavery?" With arrogant ostracism it excludes from every national office all who cannot respond to this test. So complete and irrational has this tyranny become, that, at this moment, while I now speak, could Washington, Jefferson, or Franklin, once more descend from their spheres above, to mingle in our affairs and bless us with their wisdom, not one of them, with his recorded, *unretracted* opinions on Slavery, could receive a nomination for the Presidency from a National Convention of either of the late great political parties; nor, stranger still, could either of these sainted patriots, whose names alone open a perpetual fountain of gratitude in all your hearts, be confirmed by the Senate of the United States for any political function whatever under the National Government — not even for the office of Postmaster. What I now say, amidst your natural astonishment, I have more than once uttered from my seat in the Senate, and no man there has made answer, for no man, who has sat in its secret sessions and there learned the test which is practically applied, could make answer; and I ask you to accept this statement as my testimony derived from the experience which has been my lot. Yes, fellow-citizens, had this test prevailed in the earlier days, Washington — first in war, first in peace, first in the hearts of his countrymen — could not have been created Generalissimo of the American forces; Jefferson could not have taken his place on the Committee to draft the Declaration of Independence; and Franklin could not have gone forth to France, with the commission of the infant Republic, to secure the invaluable alliance of that ancient kingdom.

And this giant strength is used with a giant heartlessness. By a cruel enactment, which has no source in the Constitution — which defies justice — which tramples on humanity — and which rebels against God, the Free States are made the hunting-ground for slaves, and you, and I, and all good citizens, are summoned to join in the loathsome and abhorred work. Your hearts and judgments, swift to feel and to condemn, will not require me to expose here the abomination of the Fugitive Slave Bill or its utter unconstitutionality. Elsewhere I have done this, and never been answered. Nor will you expect that an enactment, so entirely devoid of all just sanction, should be called by the sacred name of *law*. History still repeats the language in which our fathers persevered, when they denounced the last emanation of British tyranny which heralded the Revolution, as the Boston Port *Bill*, and I am content with this precedent. I have said that if any man finds in the Gospel any support of Slavery, it is because Slavery is already in himself; so do I now say, if any man finds in the Constitution of our country any support of the Fugitive Slave Bill, it is because that Bill is already in himself. One of our ancient masters — Aristotle, I think — tells us that every man has a beast in his bosom; but the Northern citizen, who has the Fugitive Slave Bill there, has worse than a beast — a devil! And yet in this Bill — more even than in the ostracism at which you rebel — does the Slave Oligarchy stand confessed; heartless, grasping, tyrannical; careless of humanity, right, or the Constitution; wanting that foundation of justice which is the essential base of every civilized community; stuck together only by confederacy in spoliation; and constituting in itself a *magnum latrocinium;* while it degrades the Free States to the condition of a slave plantation, under the lash of a vulgar, despised and revolting overseer.

Surely, fellow-citizens, without hesitation or postponement you will insist that this Oligarchy shall be overthrown; and here is the foremost among the special duties of the North, now required for the honor of the republic, for our own defence, and in obedience to God. Urging this comprehensive duty, I ought to have hours rather than minutes before me; but, in a few words, you shall see its comprehensive importance. Prostrate the Slave Oligarchy — and the wickedness of the Fugitive Slave Bill will be expelled from the statute book. Prostrate the Slave Oligarchy — and Slavery will cease at once in the national capital. Prostrate the Slave Oligarchy — and liberty will become the universal law of all the national territories. Prostrate the Slave Oligarchy — and the Slave-trade will no longer skulk along our coasts, beneath the national flag. Prostrate the Slave Oligarchy — and the national government will be at length divorced from Slavery. Prostrate the Slave Oligarchy — and the national policy will be exchanged from Slavery to Freedom. Prostrate the Slave Oligarchy — and the North will no longer be the vassal of the South.

Prostrate the Slave Oligarchy — and the North will be admitted to its just share in the trusts and honors of the Republic. Prostrate the Slave Oligarchy — and you will possess the master-key to unlock the whole house of bondage. Prostrate the Slave Oligarchy — and the gates of emancipation will be open at the South.

But, without waiting for this consummation, there is another special duty to be done here at home, on our own soil, which must be made free in reality, as in name. And here I shall speak frankly, though not without a proper sense of the responsibility of my words. I know that I cannot address you entirely as a private citizen; but I shall say nothing here, which I have not said elsewhere, and which I shall not be proud to vindicate everywhere. "A lie," it has been declared, "should be trampled out and extinguished forever," and surely you will do nothing less with a tyrannical and wicked enactment. The Fugitive Slave Bill, while it continues unrepealed, must be made a dead letter; not by violence; not by any unconstitutional activity or intervention; not even by hasty conflict between jurisdictions; but by an aroused Public Opinion, which, in its irresistible might, shall blast with contempt, indignation and abhorrence, all who consent to be its agents. Thus did our fathers blast all who became the agents of the Stamp Act; and surely their motive was small compared with ours. The Slave-hunter who drags his victim from Africa is loathed as a monster; but I defy any acuteness of reason to indicate the moral difference between his act, and that of the Slave-hunter who drags his victim from our Northern free soil. A few puny persons, calling themselves the Congress of the United States, with the titles of Representatives and Senators, cannot turn wrong into right — cannot change a man into a thing — cannot reverse the irreversible law of God — cannot make him wicked who hunts a slave on the burning sands of Congo or Guinea, and make him virtuous who hunts a slave in the colder streets of Boston or New York. Nor can any acuteness of reason distinguish between the bill of sale from the kidnapper, by which the unhappy African was originally transferred in Congo or Guinea, and the certificate of the Commissioner, by which, when once again in Freedom, he was reduced anew to bondage. The acts are kindred, and should share a kindred condemnation.

One man's virtue becomes a standard of excellence for all; and there is now in Boston, a simple citizen, whose example may be a lesson to Commissioners, Marshals, Magistrates; while it fills all with the beauty of a generous act. I refer to Mr. Hayes, who resigned his place in the city police rather than take any part in the pack of the Slave-hunter. He is now the door-keeper of the public edifice which has been honored this winter by the triumphant lectures on Slavery Better be a door-keeper in the house of the Lord than a dweller in the tents of the ungodly. For myself, let me say, that I can imagine no office, no salary, no consideration, which I would not gladly forego, rather than become in any way an agent for the enslavement of my brother-man. Where, for me, would be comfort or solace after such a work! In dreams and waking hours, in solitude and in the street, in the study of the open book and in conversation with the world, —

wherever I turned, there my victim would stare me in the face; while from the distant rice-fields and sugar plantations of the South, his cries beneath the vindictive lash, his moans at the thought of liberty once his, now, alas! ravished away, would pursue me, repeating the tale of his fearful doom, and sounding — forever sounding — in my ears, "Thou art the man." Mr. President, may no such terrible voice fall on your soul or mine!

Yes, sir, here our duty is plain and paramount. While the Slave Oligarchy, through its unrepealed Slave Bill, undertakes to enslave our free soil, we can only turn for protection to a Public Opinion, worthy of a humane, just and religious people, which shall keep perpetual guard over the liberties of all within our borders; nay more, which, like the flaming sword of the cherubim at the gates of Paradise, turning on every side, shall prevent any Slave-hunter from ever setting foot on our sacred soil. Elsewhere he may pursue his human prey; he may employ his congenial blood-hounds, and exult in his successful game. But into these domains of Freedom he must not come. And this Public Opinon, with Freedom as its watchword, must proclaim not only the overthrow of the Slave Bill, but also the overthrow of the Slave Oligarchy behind, — the two pressing duties of the North, essential to our own emancipation; and believe me, sir, while they remain undone, nothing is done.

Mr. President, far already have I trespassed upon your generous patience; but there are other things which still press for utterance. Something would I say of the arguments by which our Enterprise is commended; something also of the appeal it makes to men of every condition; and something also of union, as a vital necessity among all who love Freedom.

I know not if our work can be soon accomplished. I know not, sir, if you or I can live to see in our Republic the vows of the Fathers at length fulfilled, as the last fetter falls from the limbs of the last slave. But one thing I do know, beyond all doubt or question, that this Enterprise must go on — that in its irresistible current, it will sweep schools, colleges, churches, the intelligence, the conscience, and the religious aspirations of the land, while all, who stand in its way or speak evil of it, are laying up for their children, if not for themselves, days of sorrow and shame. Better to strive in this cause, even unsuccessfully, than never to strive at all.

There is no weapon in the celestial armory of truth; there is no sweet influence from the skies; there is no generous word that ever dropped from human lips, which may not be employed. Ours, too, is the argument alike of the Conservative and the Reformer, for our cause stands on the truest conservatism and the truest reform. It seeks the conservation of Freedom itself and of its kindred historic principles; it seeks also the reform of Slavery and of the kindred tyranny by which it is upheld. Religion, morals, justice, economy, the Constitution, may each and all be invoked; and one person is touched by one argument while another person is touched by another. You do not forget how Christopher Columbus won Isabella of Spain to his enterprise of discovery. He first presented to her the temptation of extending her dominions; but she hearkened not. He next promised to her the dazzling wealth of the Indies; and still she hearkened not. But when at last was pictured to her pious imagination the poor heathen with souls to be saved, then the youthful Queen poured her royal jewels into the lap of the Genoese adventurer, and, at her expense, that small fleet was sent forth, which gave to Spain and to mankind a New World.

As in this Enterprise, there is a place for every argument, so also is there a place for every man. Even as on the broad shield of Achilles, sculptured by divine art, was wrought every form of human activity; so in this cause, which is the very shield of Freedom, whatever man can do by deed or speech, may find its place. One may act in one way, and another in another way; but all must act. Providence is felt through individuals; the dropping of water wears away the rock; and no man can be so humble or poor as to be excused from this work, while to all the happy in genius, fortune or fame, it makes a special appeal. Here is room for the strengh of Luther, and the sweetness of Melancthon; for the wisdom of age, and the ardor of youth; for the judgment of the statesman, and the eloquence of the orator; for the grace of the scholar, and the aspiration of the poet; for the learning of the professor, and the skill of the lawyer; for the exhortation of the preacher, and the persuasion of the press; for the various energy of the citizen, and the abounding sympathy of woman.

And still one thing more is needed, without which Liberty-loving men, and even their arguments, will fail in power — even as without charity all graces of knowledge, speech and faith are said to profit nothing. I mean that *Unity of Spirit* — in itself a fountain of strength — which, filling the people of the North, shall make them tread under foot past antipathies, decayed dissensions, and those irritating names which now exist only as the tattered ensigns of ancient strife. It is right to be taught by the enemy; and with their example before us and their power brandished in our very faces, we cannot hesitate. With them Slavery is made the main-spring of political life, and the absorbing centre of political activity; with them all differences are swallowed up by this *one idea*, as all other rods were swallowed up by the rod of Aaron; with them all unite to keep the national government under the control of slave-masters; and surely we should not do less for Freedom than they do for Slavery. *We too must be united.* Among us at last mutual criticism, crimination, and feud, must give place to mutual sympathy, trust and alliance. Face to face against the SLAVE OLIGARCHY must be rallied the UNITED MASSES of the North, in compact political association — planted on the everlasting base of justice — knit together by the instincts of a common danger, and by the holy sympathies of humanity — enkindled by a love of Freedom, not only for themselves, but for others — determined to enfranchise the national government from degrading thraldom — and constituting the BACKBONE PARTY, powerful in numbers, wealth, and intelligence, but more powerful still in an inspiring cause. Let this be done, and victory will be ours.

## THE SLAVE OLIGARCHY AND ITS USURPATIONS — THE OUTRAGES IN KANSAS — THE DIFFERENT POLITICAL PARTIES — THE REPUBLICAN PARTY.

SPEECH ON THE EVENING OF 2D NOVEMBER, 1855, AT FANEUIL HALL, BOSTON.

FELLOW-CITIZENS OF BOSTON: Are you for Freedom or are you for Slavery? This is the question which you are to answer at the coming election. Above all other questions, whether national or local, it now lifts itself directly in the path of every voter, and calls for a plain and honest reply. There it is. It cannot be avoided. It cannot be banished away. It cannot be silenced. Forever sounding in our ears, it has a mood for every hour — stirring us at times as with the blast of a trumpet — then visiting us in solemn tones, like the bell which calls to prayer — and then again awaking us to unmistakable duty, like the same bell, when at midnight it summons all to stay the raging conflagration.

And yet, there are persons among us who seek to put this great question aside. Some clamor for financial reform, and hold up a tax-bill; others clamor for a modification of the elective franchise, and they hold up the Pope; some speak in the name of old parties, calling themselves Democrats or Whigs; others in the name of a new party, which shall be nameless at present. Surely the people of Massachusetts will not be diverted from the true issue — involving Freedom for broad territories and Freedom for themselves — by holding up a tax-bill or by holding up the Pope. The people of Massachusetts are intelligent and humane. They are not bulls to be turned aside by shaking in their eyes a bit of red cloth; nor are they whales to be stopped by a tub. The pertinacious and exclusive advocacy with which, at this crisis of Freedom, humbler matters and even personal aspirations have been pressed, in disregard of a sacred cause, finds a prototype in an effort of selfishness, which, occurring at the very crisis of our Revolution, was chastised by the humor and eloquence of Patrick Henry. The story is familiar. Our small army, contending for Freedom, was reduced to the depths of distress: exposed, almost naked, to the rigors of a winter sky, and marking the frozen ground with the blood of shoeless feet. "Where is the man," said Patrick Henry, "who would not have thrown open his fields, his barns, his cellars, the doors of his house, the portals of his breast, to receive the meanest soldier in that little famished band? Where is the man? There he stands; but whether the heart of an American beats in his bosom, you are to judge?" It was to John Hook that he pointed, who was then pressing a vexatious claim for supplies taken for the use of these starving troops. "What notes of discord do I hear?" exclaimed the orator, "They are the notes of John Hook, hoarsely brawling through the patriot camp, *Beef! Beef! Beef!*" And now, among us, the selfishness of John Hook is renewed, and politicians disturb the hour, as they hoarsely brawl their petty claims through our patriot camp. But above all these is heard the great question, which will not be postponed, Are you for Freedom, or are you for Slavery? "Under which king, Bezonian, speak or die!" Are you for Freedom, with its priceless blessings, or are you for Slavery, with its countless wrongs and woes? Are you for God, or are you for the Devil?

Fellow-citizens, I speak plainly; nor can words exhibiting the enormity of Slavery be too plain, whether it be regarded simply in the legislative and judicial decisions by which it is upheld, or in the unquestionable facts by which its character is revealed. It has been my fortune latterly to see Slavery face to face in its own home, in the Slave States; and I take this early opportunity to offer my testimony to the open barbarism which it sanctions. I have seen a human being knocked off at auction on the steps of a court house, and as the sale went on, compelled to open his mouth and show his teeth, like a horse; I have been detained in a stage-coach, that our driver might, in the phrase of the country, "help lick a nigger;" and I have been constrained, at a public table, to witness the revolting spectacle of a poor slave, yet a child, almost felled to the floor by a blow on the head from a clenched fist. Such incidents were not calculated to shake my original convictions. The distant slaveholder, who, in generous solicitude for that truth which makes for Freedom, feared that, like a certain Doctor of Divinity, I might, under the influence of personal kindness, be hastily swayed from these convictions, may be assured that I saw nothing to change them in one tittle, but to confirm them; while I was entirely satisfied that here in Massachusetts, where all read, the true character of Slavery is better known than in the Slave States themselves, where ignorance and prejudice close the avenues of knowledge.

And now, grateful for the attention with which you honor me, I venture to hope that you are assembled honestly to hear the truth; not to gratify prejudice, to appease personal antipathies, or to indulge a morbid appetite for excitement; but with candor and your best discrimination, to weigh facts and arguments in order to determine the course of duty. I address myself particularly to the friends of Freedom — the Republicans — on whose invitation I appear to-night, but I make bold to ask you of other parties, who now listen, to divest yourselves for the time, of partisan constraint — to forget for the moment that you are Whigs or Democrats, or how you are called, and to remember only that you are *men*, with hearts to feel, with heads to understand, and with consciences to guide. Then only will you be in a condition to receive the truth. "If men are not aware of the probable bias of party over them, then they are so much the more likely to be blindly governed by it." Such is the wise remark of Wilberforce; and I fear that among us there are too many who are unconsciously governed by such bias. There are men, who, while professing candor, yet show that the bitterness of party has entered into their whole character and lives, as the bitterness of the soil in Sardinia is said to appear even in its honey.

At this election we do not choose a President of the United States, or member of Congress; but a Governor, Lieutenant Governor, Attorney General, and other State officers. To a superficial observer, the occasion seems to be rather local than national; it seems to belong to State affairs rather than Federal — to Massachusetts rather than to the Union. And yet, such are our relations to the Union — such is the solidarity of these confederate States — so are we all knit together as a Plural Unit, that the great question which now disturbs and overshadows the whole country, becomes at once national and local, addressing itself alike to the whole Republic and to each constituent part. Freedom in Kansas, and our own Freedom here at home, are both assailed. They must be defended. There are honorable responsibilities belonging to Massachusetts, as an early and constant vindicator of Freedom, which she cannot renounce. "If the trumpet give an uncertain sound, who shall prepare himself for the battle?" The distant emigrant — the whole country — awaits the voice of our beloved Commonwealth in answer to the question, Are you for Freedom or are you for Slavery? So transcendent, so exclusive, so all-absorbing at the present juncture is this question, that it is vain to speak of the position of candidates on other things. To be doubtful on this is to be wrong; and to be wrong on this is to be wholly wrong. Passing strange it is that here in Massachusetts, in this nineteenth century, we should be constrained to put this question. Passing strange, that when it is put, there should be any hesitation to answer it, by voice and vote, in such way as to speak the loudest for Freedom.

A plain recital will show the urgency of this question. At the period of the Declaration of Independence, upwards of half a million colored persons were held as chattels in the United States. These unhappy people were originally stolen from Africa, or were the children of those who had been stolen, and, though distributed throughout the whole country, were to be found chiefly in the Southern States. The Slavery to which they were reduced was simply a continuation of the violence by which they had been originally robbed of their rights, and was of course as indefensible. The fathers of the Republic, leaders of the war of Independence, were struck with the inconsistency of an appeal for their own liberties while holding in bondage fellow-men, only "guilty of a skin not colored like their own." The same conviction animated the hearts of the people, whether at the North or South. Out of ample illustrations, I select one which specially reveals this conviction, and possesses a local interest in this community. It is a deed of manumission, made after our struggles had begun, and preserved in the Probate records of the County of Suffolk. Here it is:

"Know all men by these presents, that I, JONATHAN JACKSON, of Newburyport, in the county of Essex, gentleman, *in consideration of the impropriety I feel, and have long felt in beholding any person in constant bondage — more especially at a time when my country is so warmly contending for the liberty every man ought to enjoy* — and having sometime since promised my negro man, POMP, that I would give him his freedom, and in further consideration of five shillings, paid me by said POMP, I do hereby liberate, manumit, and set him free; and I do hereby remise and release unto said POMP, all demands of whatever nature I have against said POMP.

"In witness whereof, I have hereunto set my hand and seal, this nineteenth June, 1776.

"JONATHAN JACKSON. [Seal.]

"*Witness*, Mary Coburn, William Noyes."

Such was the general spirit. Public opinion found

free vent in every channel. By the literature of the time — by the voice of the Church, and by the solemn judgment of the College, Slavery was condemned, while all the grandest names of our history were arrayed openly against it. Of these I might dwell on many; but I am always pleased to mention an illustrious triumvirate from whose concurring testimony there can be no appeal. There was Washington, who at one time declared that "it was among his first wishes to see some plan adopted by which Slavery might be abolished by law," and then at another, that to this end, "his suffrage should not be wanting." There also was Jefferson, who by early and precocious efforts for "total emancipation," placed himself foremost among the Abolitionists of the land — perpetually denouncing Slavery — exposing the pernicious influences upon the master, as well as the Slave — declaring that the love of justice and the love of country pleaded equally for the Slave, and that "the abolition of domestic Slavery was the greatest object of desire." There also was the venerable patriot, Benjamin Franklin, who did not hesitate to liken the American master of black Slaves to the Algerine corsair with his white Slaves, and who, as President of the earliest Abolition Society — the same of which Passmore Williamson is now the honored Secretary — by solemn petition, called upon Congress "to step to the very verge of the power vested in it to *discourage* every species of traffic in the persons of our fellow-men." Thus completely, by this triumvirate of Freedom, was Slavery condemned, and the power of the Government invoked against it.

By such men, and in such spirit, was the National

Constitution framed. The emphatic words of the Declaration of Independence, which our country took upon its lips as baptismal vows, when it claimed a place among the nations of the earth, were not forgotten. The preamble to the Constitution renews them, when it declares the object of the people of the United States to be, among other things, "to establish justice, to promote the *general* welfare, and to secure the blessings of liberty to ourselves and posterity." Thus, according to undeniable words, the Constitution was ordained, not to establish, secure or sanction Slavery — not to promote the special interest of slave-masters, bound together in oligarchical combination — not to make Slavery national in any way, form or manner; but to "establish justice," which condemns Slavery — "to promote the general welfare," which repudiates every Oligarchy — and "to secure the blessings of Liberty," in whose presence human bondage must cease. Early in the Convention, Gouverneur Morris broke forth in the language of an Abolitionist: "He never would concur in upholding domestic Slavery. It was a nefarious institution. It was the curse of Heaven." In another mood, and with mild juridical phrase, Mr. Madison, himself a slaveholder, "thought it wrong to admit in the Constitution the idea of property in man." The discreditable words, *Slave* and *Slavery*, were not allowed to find a place in the instrument, while a clause was subsequently added by way of amendment, — and, therefore, according to the rules of interpretation, particularly revealing the sentiments of the founders, — which is calculated, like the Declaration of Independence, if practically applied, to carry Freedom everywhere within the sphere of its influence.

It was specifically declared that "no person shall be deprived of life, *liberty* or property, *without due process of law*," that is, without due presentment, indictment or other formal judical proceedings. Here is an express guard of personal Liberty, and a prohibition of Slavery everywhere within the national jurisdiction.

In this spirit was the National Constitution adopted. In this spirit the National Government was first organized under Washington. And here there is a fact of peculiar significance, well worthy of perpetual memory. At the time this great chief took his first oath to support the Constitution of the United States, *the National Ensign nowhere within the National Territory covered a single slave.* On the sea, an execrable piracy, the trade in slaves, was still, to the national scandal, tolerated beneath the national flag. In the States, as a sectional institution, beneath the shelter of local laws, Slavery, unhappily, found a home. But in the only territories at this time belonging to the Nation — the broad region of the North West — it had already, by the Ordinance of Freedom, been made impossible, even before the adoption of the Constitution. The District of Columbia, with its Fated Dowry, had not yet been acquired.

The original policy of the Republic, begun under the Confederation, and recognized at the initiation of the new Government, is clear and unmistakable. Compendiously expressed, it was *non-intervention by Congress with Slavery in the States, and its prohibition in all the national domain;* and also, as a corollary from this policy, the complete ascendency of the principle of Freedom in the National Government. Thus were reconciled all discordant feelings on this subject.

Slave-masters were left at home in their respective States, without any intervention from Congress to hug Slavery until it stung them to contrition, while the great mass opposed to this wrong were properly exempted from any responsibility for it in the national domain, and the National Government was placed indubitably on the side of Freedom.

Most true it is — beyond all question — that our Constitution was framed by the lovers of Human Rights; that it was animated by their divine spirit; that the institution of Slavery was regarded by them with aversion, so that, though covertly alluded to, it was not named in the instrument; that, according to the debates in the Convention, they refused to give it any "sanction" or "to admit into the Constitution the idea of property in man," while they looked forward to the certain day when it would be obliterated from the land. Surely, fellow-citizens, they did not contemplate any Oligarchical combination, constituting a mighty Propaganda, such as we now witness, to uphold and extend it; nor can any person put his finger on any clause, phrase or word, which sanctions any such Propaganda; and, in making this assertion, I challenge criticism and reply.

But the original policy of the Government did not long prevail. The generous sentiments, which filled the early patriots, giving to them historic grandeur, and which stamped upon the Republic, as upon the coin which it circulated, the very image and superscription of LIBERTY, gradually lost their power. The blessings of Freedom being already secured to themselves, the freemen of the land became indifferent to the Freedom of others. They ceased to think of the

Slaves. The slave-masters availed themselves of this indifference, and, though few in number, compared with the non-slave-masters, even in the Slave States, they have, under the influence of an imagined self-interest, by the skilful tactics of party, and especially by an unhesitating, persevering union among themselves — swaying by turns both the great political parties — succeeded, through a long succession of years, in obtaining the mastery of the National Government, bending it to their purposes — compelling it to do their will, and imposing upon it a policy offensive to Freedom, and directly opposed to the sentiments of its founders; while on the forehead of the Republic, once beaming with Liberty, they have stamped the image and superscription of SLAVERY.

The actual number of slaveholders in the country was for a long time unknown, and, on this account, was naturally exaggerated. It was often represented to be very great. On one occasion, a distinguished Representative from Massachusetts, whose name will be ever cherished for his devotion to Human Rights, the Hon. Horace Mann, was rudely interrupted on the floor of Congress by a member from Alabama, who averred that the number of slaveholders was as many as three millions. At that time, there was no official document by which this assumption could be corrected. But at last we have it. The late census, taken in 1850, shows that the whole number of this peculiar class — embracing men, women and children, all told, who are so unfortunate as to hold slaves — was only three hundred and forty-seven thousand; and, of this number, the larger part are small slaveholders, leaving only ninety-two thousand persons as the owners of the great mass of slaves, and as the substantial representatives of this class. And yet, this small company — sometimes called the Slave Power, or Black Power, better called the Slave Oligarchy — now dominates over the Republic, determines its national policy, disposes of its offices, and sways all to its absolute will. Yes, fellow-citizens, it is an Oligarchy — odious beyond precedent; heartless, grasping, tyrannical; careless of humanity, right or the Constitution; wanting that foundation of justice which is the essential base of every civilized community; stuck together only by confederacy in spoliation; and constituting in itself a *magnum latrocinium;* while it degrades the Free States to the condition of a slave plantation, under the lash of a vulgar, despised and revolting overseer.

There is nothing in the National Government which the Slave Oligarchy does not appropriate. It entered into and possessed both the old political parties, Whig and Democrat — as witness their servile resolutions at Baltimore — making them one in subserviency, though double in form; and renewing in them the mystery of the Siamese twins, which, though separate in body and different in name, were constrained, by an unnatural ligament, to a community of exertion. It now holds the keys of every office, from that of President down to the humblest Postmaster, compelling all to do its bidding. It organizes the Cabinet. It directs the Army and Navy. It manages every department of public business. It presides over the census. It controls the Smithsonian Institution, founded by the generous charity of a foreigner, to promote the interests of knowledge. It subsidizes the national press, alike in the national capital and in the remotest village of the North. It sits in the chair of the President of the Senate, and also in the chair of the Speaker of the House. It arranges the Committees of both bodies, placing at their head only the servitors of Slavery, and excluding therefrom the friends of Freedom, though entitled to such places by their character and the States they represent; and thus it controls the legislation of the country.

In maintaining its power, the Slave Oligarchy has applied a test for office, very different from that of Jefferson, "Is he honest? Is he capable? Is he faithful to the Constitution?" These things are all forgotten now in the single question, "Is he faithful to Slavery?" With arrogant ostracism it excludes from every national office all who cannot respond to this test. So complete and irrational has this tyranny become, that at this moment, while I now speak, could Washington, or Jefferson, or Franklin, once more descend from their spheres above, to mingle in our affairs and bless us with their wisdom, not one of them, with his recorded, *unretracted* opinions on Slavery could receive a nomination for the Presidency from either of the political parties calling themselves *national;* nor, stranger still, could either of these sainted patriots, whose names alone open a perpetual fountain of gratitude in all your hearts, be confirmed by the Senate of the United States for any political function whatever, not even for the office of Postmaster. What I now say, amidst your natural astonishment, I have often said before in addressing the people, and more than once uttered from my seat in the Senate, and no man there has made answer, for no man who has sat in its secret sessions, and there learned the test which is practically applied, could make answer; and I ask you to accept this statement as my testimony, derived from the experience of four years which has been my lot under the commission which I have received from our honored Commonwealth. Yes, fellow-citizens, had this test prevailed in the earlier days, Washington — first in war, first in peace, first in the hearts of his countrymen — could not have been created generalissimo of the American forces; Jefferson could not have taken his place on the Committee to draft the Declaration of Independence; and Franklin could not have gone forth to France, with the commission of the infant Republic, to secure the invaluable alliance of that ancient kingdom.

All tyranny, like murder, is foul at the best; but this is most foul, strange and unnatural, when it is considered that the States, which are the home of the Slave Oligarchy, are far inferior to the Free States in population, wealth, education, schools, churches, libraries, manufactures and resources of all kinds. By the last census, there was in the Free States a solid population of freemen, amounting to upwards of thirteen millions, while in the Slave States, there was a like population of only six millions. In other respects, important to civilization, the disparity was as great. And yet, from the beginning, they have taken to themselves the lion's share among the honors and trusts of the Republic. But, without exposing the game of political "sweepstakes," which the Slave Oligarchy has perpetually played — interesting as it would be — I prefer to hold up for one moment the assumptions, aggressions and usurpations by which, in defiance of the Constitution, it has made Slavery national, when it is, in reality, sectional. Here is a brief catalogue :

Early in this century, when the District of Columbia was finally occupied as the National Capitol, the Slave Oligarchy succeeded, in defiance of the spirit of the Constitution, and even of the express letter of one of its amendments, in securing for Slavery, within the District, the countenance of the National Government. Until then, Slavery had existed nowhere on the land within the reach and exclusive jurisdiction of this Government.

The Slave Oligarchy next secured for Slavery another recognition under the National Government, in the broad territory of Louisiana, purchased from France.

The Slave Oligarchy next placed Slavery again under the sanction of the National Government, in the territory of Florida, purchased from Spain.

The Slave Oligarchy, waxing powerful, was able, after a severe struggle, to dictate terms to the National Government, in the Missouri Compromise, compelling it to receive that State into the Union with a slaveholding Constitution.

The Slave Oligarchy instigated and carried on a most expensive war in Florida, mainly to recover fugitive slaves, thus degrading the army of the United States to be Slave-hunters.

The Slave Oligarchy wrested from Mexico the Province of Texas, and, triumphing over all opposition, finally secured its admission into the Union, with a Constitution making Slavery perpetual.

The Slave Oligarchy plunged the country in war with Mexico, in order to gain new lands for Slavery.

The Slave Oligarchy, with the meanness, as well as the insolence of tyranny, has compelled the National Government to abstain from acknowledging the neighbor republic of Hayti, where slaves have become freemen, and established an independent nation.

The Slave Oligarchy has compelled the National Government to stoop ignobly before the British Queen, to secure compensation for slaves, who, in the exercise of the natural rights of man, had asserted and achieved their freedom on the Atlantic Ocean, and afterwards sought shelter in Bermuda.

The Slave Oligarchy has compelled the National Government to seek to negotiate treaties for the surrender of fugitive slaves, thus making our Republic assert abroad, in foreign lands, property in human flesh.

The Slave Oligarchy has joined in declaring the foreign slave-trade *piracy*, but insists on the coastwise slave-trade, under the auspices of the National Government.

The Slave Oligarchy for several years rejected the petitions to Congress adverse to Slavery, thus, in order to shield this wrong, practically denying the right of petition.

The Slave Oligarchy, in defiance of the privileges secured under the Constitution of the United States, imprisons the free colored citizens of Massachusetts, and sometimes sells them into bondage.

The Slave Oligarchy insulted and exiled from Charleston and New Orleans, the honored representatives of Massachusetts, who were sent to those places with the commission of the Commonwealth, in order to throw the shield of the Constitution over her colored citizens.

The Slave Oligarchy has, by the pen of Mr. Calhoun, as Secretary of State, in formal despatches, made the Republic stand before the nations of the earth as the vindicator of Slavery.

The Slave Oligarchy has put forth the hideous effrontery that Slavery can go to all newly acquired territories, and enjoy the protection of the National Flag.

The Slave Oligarchy has imposed upon the country an Act of Congress, for the recovery of fugitive slaves, revolting in its mandates, and many times unconstitutional; especially on two grounds, *first*, as a usurpation by Congress of powers not granted by the Constitution, and an infraction of rights secured to the States; and *secondly*, as a denial of Trial by Jury, in a question of Personal Liberty, and a suit at common law.

The Slave Oligarchy, in defiance of the declared desires of the Fathers to limit and discourage Slavery, has successively introduced into the Union, Kentucky, Tennessee, Alabama, Mississippi, Louisiana, Missouri, Arkansas and Texas, as slave-holding States, thus, at each stage, fortifying its political power, and making the National Government give new sanction to Slavery.

Such, fellow-citizens, are some of the assumptions, aggressions and usurpations of the Slave Oligarchy! By such steps, the National Government has been perverted from its original purposes, its character changed, and its powers all surrendered to Slavery. Surely, no patriot soul can listen to this recital, without confessing that our first political duty is, at all hazards and without compromise, to oppose this Oligarchy, to dislodge it from the National Government, and to bring the administration back to that character which it enjoyed when first organized under Washington, himself an Abolitionist, and surrounded by Abolitionists, while the whole country, by its Church, its Colleges, its Literature, and all its best voices, was united against Slavery, and the National Flag nowhere within the national territory covered a single slave.

Fellow-citizens, I have said enough to stir you; but this humiliating tale is not yet finished. An Oligarchy seeking to maintain an outrage like Slavery, and drawing its inspirations from this fountain of wickedness, is naturally base, false and heedless of justice. It is vain to expect that men, who have screwed themselves to become the propagandists of this enormity, will be constrained by any compromise, compact, bargain or plighted faith. As the less is contained in the greater, so there is no vileness of dishonesty, no denial of human rights, that is not plainly involved in the support of an enormity, which begins by changing man, created in the image of God, into a chattel, and sweeps little children away to the auction-block. A power which Heaven never gave, can be maintained only by means which Heaven can never sanction. And this conclusion of reason is confirmed by late experience; and here I approach the special question under which the country now shakes from side to side. The protracted struggle of 1820, known as the Missouri Question, ended with the admission of Missouri as a slaveholding State, and the prohibition of Slavery in all the remaining territory, West of the Mississippi and North of 36° 30′. Here was a solemn act of legislation, called at the time a compromise, a covenant, a compact, first brought forward by the Slave Oligarchy — vindicated by it in debate — finally sanctioned by its votes, also upheld at the time by a slaveholding President, James Monroe, and his cabinet — of whom a majority were slaveholders, including Mr. Calhoun himself — and made the condition of the admission of Missouri — without which that State could not have been received into the Union. Suddenly, during the last year — without any notice in the public press or the prayer of a single petition — after an acquiescence of thirty-three years, and the irreclaimable possession by the Slave Oligarchy of its special share in the provisions of this Compromise — in violation of every obligation of honor, compact and good neighborhood — and in contemptuous disregard of the out-gushing sentiments of an aroused North, this time-honored Prohibition, in itself a Landmark of Freedom, was overturned, and the vast region, now known as Kansas and Nebraska, was opened to Slavery; and this was done under the disgraceful lead of Northern politicians, and with the undisguised complicity of a Northern President, forgetful of Freedom, forgetful also of his reiterated pledges, that during his administration the repose of the country should receive no shock.

And all this was perpetrated under pretences of popular rights. Freedom was betrayed by a kiss. In defiance of an uninterrupted prescription down to our day — early sustained at the South as well as the North — leaning at once on Jefferson and Washington — sanctioned by all the authoritative names of our history, and beginning with the great Ordinance by which Slavery was prohibited in the North West — it was pretended that the people of the United States, who are the proprietors of the national domain, and who, according to the Constitution, may "make all needful rules and regulations" for its government, nevertheless were not its sovereigns — that they had no power to interdict Slavery there; but that this eminent dominion resided in the few settlers, called squatters, whom chance or a desire to better their fortunes, first hurried into these places. To this precarious handful, sprinkled over immense spaces, it was left, without any constraint from Congress, to decide, whether into these vast, unsettled lands, as into the veins of an infant, should be poured the festering poison of Slavery destined, as time advances, to show itself in cancers and leprous disease, or whether they should be filled with all the glowing life of Freedom. And this great power, transferred from Congress to these few settlers, was hailed by the new-fangled name of *Squatter Sovereignty.*

It was fit that the original outrage perpretrated under such pretences, should be followed by other outrages perpetrated in defiance of these pretences. In the race of emigration, the freedom-loving freemen of the North promised to obtain the ascendency, and in the exercise of the conceded sovereignty of the settlers, to prohibit Slavery. The Slave Oligarchy was aroused to other efforts. Of course it stuck at nothing. On the day of election when this vaunted popular sovereignty was first invoked, hirelings from Missouri, having no home in the territory, entered it in bands of fifties and hundreds, and assuming an electoral franchise to which they had no claim, trampled under foot the Constitution and laws. Violently, ruthlessly the polls were possessed by these invaders. The same Northern President, who did not shrink from unblushing complicity in the original outrage, now assumed another complicity. Though prompt to lavish the Treasury, the Army and the Navy of the Republic in hunting a single slave through the streets of Boston, he could see the Constitution and laws, which he was sworn to protect, and those popular rights which he had affected to promote, all struck down in Kansas, and then give new scope to these invaders by the removal of the faithful Governor, — who had become obnoxious to the Slave Oligarchy because he would not become its tool, — and the substitution of another, who vindicated the dishonest choice by making haste, on his first arrival there, to embrace the partisans of Slavery. The legislature, which was constituted by the overthrow of the electoral franchise, proceeded to overthrow every safeguard of Freedom. At one swoop it adopted all the legislation of Missouri, including its Slave Code; by another act it imposed unprecedented conditions upon the exercise of the electoral franchise, and by still another act it denounced the *punishment of death* no less than five times against as many different forms of interference with the alleged property in human flesh, while all who only write or speak against Slavery are adjudged to be felons. Yes, fellow-citizens, should any person there presume to print or circulate the speech in which I now express my abhorrence of Slavery, and deny its constitutional existence anywhere within the national jurisdiction, he would become liable under this act as a felon. And this overthrow of all popular rights is done in the name of Popular Sovereignty. Surely its authors follow well the example of the earliest Squatter Sovereign — none other than Satan — who, stealing into Eden, was there discovered, by the celestial angels, just beginning his work; as Milton tells us,

> "—— him there they found
> *Squat* like a toad, close at the ear of Eve."

Would you know the secret of this unprecedented endeavor, beginning with the repeal of the Prohibition of Slavery down to the latest atrocity? The answer is at hand. It is not merely to provide new markets for Slaves, or even to guard Slavery in Missouri, but to build another Slave State, and thus, by the presence of two additional slaveholding Senators, to give increased preponderance to the Slave Oligarchy in the National Government. As men are murdered for the sake of their money, so is this territory blasted in peace and prosperity, in order to wrest its political influence to the side of Slavery.

But a single usurpation is not enough to employ the rapacious energies of our Oligarchy. At this moment, while the country is pained by the heartless conspiracy against Freedom in Kansas, we are startled by another effort, which contemplates, not merely the political subjugation of the National Government, but the actual introduction of Slavery into the Free States. The vaunt has been made, that slaves will yet be counted in the sacred shadow of the monument on Bunker Hill, and more than one step has been taken towards this effrontery. A person of Virginia has asserted his right to hold slaves in New York on the way to Texas; and this claim is still pending before the highest judicial tribunal of the land. A similar claim has been asserted in Pennsylvania, and thus far been sustained by the court. A blameless citizen, who — in obedience to his generous impulses and in harmony with the received law — merely gave notice to a person held as a slave in a Free State, that she was in reality free, has been thrust into jail, and now, after the lapse of months, still languishes there, the victim of this pretension; while, — that no excess might be wanting in the madness of this tyranny — the great writ of Habeas Corpus, proudly known as the writ of deliverance, has been made the instrument of his imprisonment. Outrage treads upon outrage, and great rights pass away to perish. Alas! the needful tool for such work is too easily found in places low and high — in the alleys and cellars of Boston — on the bench of the judge — in the chair of the President. But it is the power behind which I arraign. The Slave Oligarchy does it; the Slave Oligarchy does it all.

To the prostration of this Oligarchy you are bound by a three-fold cord of duty; *first*, as you would secure Freedom for yourselves; *secondly*, as you would uphold Freedom in distant Kansas; and *thirdly*, as you would preserve the Union in its early strength and integrity. The people of Kansas are, many of them, from Massachusetts — bone of our bone, flesh of our flesh; but as fellow-citizens under the Constitution, they are bound to us by ties which we cannot disown. Nay, more; by the subtle cord which connects this embryo settlement with the Republic, they are made a part of us. The outrage which touches them touches us. What galls them galls us. The fetter which binds the slave in Kansas binds every citizen in Massachusetts. Thus are we prompted to their rescue, not only to save them, but also to save ourselves. The tyranny which now treads them down, has already trampled on us, and only awaits an opportunity to do it again. In its complete overthrow is the only way of safety. Indeed, this must be done before anything else can be done. In vain you seek economy in the Government — improvement of rivers and harbors — or dignity and peace in our foreign relations, while this power holds the national purse and the national sword. Prostrate the Slave Oligarchy, and the door will be wide open for all generous reforms. Oh! the imagination loses itself in the vain endeavor to picture the good that will be then accomplished. Prostrate the Slave Oligarchy, and Liberty will become the universal law of all the national territories; Slavery will cease at once in the national capital; the slave-trade will no longer skulk along our coasts beneath the national flag; and the wickedness of the Fugitive Slave Bill will be driven from the statute book. Prostrate the Slave Oligarchy, and the national Government will be at length divorced from Slavery and the national policy will be changed from Slavery to Freedom. Prostrate the Slave Oligarchy, and the North will no longer be the vassal of the South. Prostrate the Slave Oligarchy, and the North will be admitted to its just share in the trusts and honors of the Republic. Prostrate the Slave Oligarchy, and you will possess the master-key with which to unlock the whole house of bondage. Prostrate the Slave Oligarchy, and the gates of emancipation will be open at the South.

To this work, fellow-citizens, you are now summoned. By your votes you are to declare, not merely your predilection for men, but your devotion to principles. Men are erring and mortal. Principles are steadfast and immortal. Forgetting all other things — especially forgetting men — you are to cast your votes so as best to promote Freedom.

But in the choice of men we are driven to the organization of parties; and here occurs the practical question on which hinges our immediate duty, by what political party can our desire be accomplished? There are individuals in all the parties, even the Democratic, who hate Slavery, and say so; but a political party cannot be judged by the private opinions of some of its members. Something else, more solid and tangible, must appear. The party that we select to bear the burden and honor of our great controversy, must be adapted to the work. It must be a perfect machine. Wedded to Freedom, for better or for worse, and cleaving to it with a grasp never to be unloosed, it must be clear, open and unequivocal in its declarations, and must admit no other question to divert its energies. It must be all in Freedom, and, like Cæsar's wife, it must be above suspicion. But besides this character which it must sustain in Massachusetts, it must be prepared to take its place in close phalanx with the united masses of the North, now organizing through all the Free States, *junctæque umbone phalanges*, for the protection of Freedom, and the overthrow of the Slave Oligarchy.

Bearing these conditions in mind, there are three parties which we may dismiss, one by one, as they pass in review. Men do not gather grapes from thorns, nor figs from thistles; nor do they expect patriotism from Benedict Arnold. A party which sustains the tyrannies and perfidies of the Slave Oligarchy, and is represented by the President, through whom has come so much of all our woe, need not occupy our time; and such is the Democratic party. If there be within the sound of my voice a single person, who, professing sympathy with Freedom, still votes with this party, to him I would say: The name of Democrat is a tower of strength; let it not be a bulwark of Slavery; for the sake of a name do not sacrifice a thing; for the sake of party do not surrender Freedom.

According to a familar rule, handed down from distant antiquity, we are to say nothing but good of the dead. How, then, shall I speak of the late powerful Whig party — by whose giant contests the whole country was once upheaved — but which has now ceased to exist, except as the shadow of a name? Here, in Massachusetts, a few who do not yet know that it is dead, have met together and proffered their old allegiance. They are the Rip Van Winkles of our politics. This respectable character, falling asleep in the mountains, drowsed undisturbed throughout the whole war of the Revolution, and, then returnimg to his native village, ignorant of all that had passed, proposed to drink the health of King George. But our Whigs are less tolerant and urbane than this awakened Dutchman. In petulant and irrational assumptions they are like the unfortunate judge, who, being aroused from his slumbers on the bench, by a sudden crash of thunder, exclaimed, "Mr. Crier, stop the noise in Court." The thunder would not be hushed; nor will the voice of Freedom, now reverberating throughout the land.

Some there are among these who openly espouse the part of Slavery, while others, by their indifference, place themselves in the same unhappy company. If their position at this moment were of sufficient importance to justify grave remark, they should be exhibited as kindred in spirit and isolation to the Tories of our Revolution, or, at least, as the Bourbons of Massachusetts — always claiming everything, learning nothing, forgetting nothing, and at last condemned by an aroused people for their disloyalty to Freedom. Let no person who truly loves Freedom join this company, tempted by its name, its music, and its banners.

There is still another party, which claims your votes, but permit me to say, at this crisis, with small pretence. I am at a loss to determine the name by which it may be properly called. It is sometimes known as the Know Nothing party; sometimes as the American party; but it cannot be entitled to these designations — if they be of any value — for it does not claim to belong to the organization, which first assumed and still retains them. It is an isolated combination, peculiar to Massachusetts, which, while professing certain political sentiments, is bound together by the support of one of the candidates for Governor. At this moment, this is its controlling idea. It is, therefore, a *personal party*, and I trust that I shall not be considered as departing from that courtesy which is with me a law, if I say that, in the absence of any appropriate name, expressive of principles, it may properly take its designation from the candidate it supports.

Of course, such a party wants the first essential condition of the organization which we seek. It is a *personal party*, whose controlling idea is a predilection for a man and not a principle. Whatever may be the private sentiments of some of its members, clearly it is not a party wedded to Freedom, for better and for worse, and cleaving to it with a grasp never to be unloosed. While professing opposition to Slavery, it also arraigns Catholics and foreigners, and allows the question of their privileges to disturb its energies. It is not all in Freedom; nor is it, like Cæsar's wife, above suspicion. Besides, even as a party of Freedom, it is powerless from its isolation; for it stands by itself, and is in no way associated with that great phalanx now rallying throughout the North. In this condition should it continue to exist, it will, in the coming Presidential contest, from natural affinity lapse back into the American party of the country which is ranged on the side of Slavery. Of course, as a separate party, it is necessarily short-lived. Cut off from the main body, it may still show a brief vitality, as the head of a turtle still bites for some days after it is severed from the neck: but it can have no permanent existence. Surely this is not the party of Freedom which we seek.

But the incompetency of this party, as the organ of our cause, is enhanced by the uncongenial secrecy in which it had its origin and yet shrouds itself. For myself, let me say that, on the floor of the Senate I have striven, by vote and speech, in conjunction with my distinguished friend Mr. CHASE, for the limitation of the secret sessions of that body, under shelter of which so much of the business of the nation is transacted, and I have there presented the example of that ancient Roman, — who bade his architect so to construct his house that his guests and all that they did might be seen by the world, — as a fit model for American institutions. What I have urged there, I now urge here. But the special aims which this party proposes, seem to be in harmony with the darkness in which it begins. Even if justifiable, on any grounds of public policy, they should not be associated with our cause; but I am unwilling to allude to them without expressing my frank dissent.

It is proposed to attaint men for their religion and also for their birth. If this object can prevail, vain are the triumphs of Civil Freedom in its many hard-fought fields; vain is that religious toleration which we all profess. The fires of Smithfield, the tortures of the Inquisition, the proscriptions of non-conformists, may all be revived. It was mainly to escape these outrages, dictated by a dominant religious sect, that our country was early settled, in one place by Quakers, who set at naught all forms; in another, by Puritans, who disowned bishops; in another, by Episcopalians, who take their name from bishops; and in yet another, by Catholics, who look to the Pope as their Spiritual Father. Slowly among the struggling sects was evolved the great idea of the Equality of all men before the law without regard to religious belief; nor can any party now organize a proscription merely for religious belief, without calling in question this unquestionable principle.

But Catholics are mostly foreigners, and, on this account, are condemned. Let us see if there be any reason in this; and here indulge me with one word on foreigners.

With the ancient Greeks, a foreigner was a *barbarian*,

and with the ancient Romans, he was an *enemy*. In early modern times, the austerity of this judgment was relaxed; but, under the influence of feudalism, the different sovereignties. whether provinces or nations, were kept in a condition of isolation, from which they have been gradually passing until now, when provinces are merged into nations, and nations are giving signs that they too will yet commingle into one. In our country another example is already displayed. From all nations people commingle here. As in ancient Corinth, by the accidental fusion of all metals, accumulated in the sacred temples, a peculiar metal was produced, better than any individual metal, even silver or gold; so, perhaps, in tho arrangements of Providence, by the fusion of all races here, there may be a better race than any individual race, even Saxon or Celt. Originally settled from England, the Republic has been strengthened and enriched by generous contributions of population from Scotland, Ireland, Switzerland, Sweden, France and Germany; and the cry is still they come. At no time since the discovery of the New World, has the army of emigrants pressed so strongly in this direction. Nearly half a million are annually landed on our shores. The manner in which they shall be received is one of the problems of our national policy.

All will admit that any influence which they may bring, hostile to our institutions — calculated to substitute priestcraft for religion and bigotry for Christianity — must be deprecated and opposed. All will admit, too, that there must be some assurance of their purpose to become not merely consumers of the fruits of our soil, but useful, loyal and permanent members of our community, upholders of the general welfare. With this simple explanation, I am not disposed to place any check upon the welcome to foreigners. There are our broad lands, stretching towards the setting sun; let them come and take them. Ourselves the children of the Pilgrims of a former generation, let us not turn from the Pilgrims of the present. Let the home, founded by our emigrant fathers, continue open in its many mansions to the emigrants of to-day.

The history of our country, in its humblest as well as most exalted spheres, testifies to the merits of foreigners. Their strong arms have helped furrow our broad territory with canals, and stretch in every direction the iron rail. They have filled our workshops, navigated our ships, and even tilled our fields. Go where you will, among the hardy sons of toil on land or sea, and there you will find industrious and faithful foreigners bending their muscles to the work. At the bar and in the high places of commerce, you will find them. Enter the retreats of learning, and there you will find them too, shedding upon our country the glory of science. Nor can any reflection be cast upon foreigners, claiming hospitality now, which will not glance at once upon the distinguished living and the illustrious dead — upon the Irish Montgomery, who perished for us at the gates of Quebec — upon Pulaski the Pole, who perished for us at Savannah — upon De Kalb and Steuben, the generous Germans, who aided our weakness by their military experience — upon Paul Jones, the Scotchman, who lent his unsurpassed courage to the infant thunders of our navy — also upon those great European liberators, Kosciusko of Poland, and Lafayette of France, each of whom paid his earliest vows to Liberty in our cause. Nor should this list be confined to military characters, so long as we gratefully cherish the name of Alexander Hamilton, who was born in the West Indies, and the name of Albert Gallatin, who was born in Switzerland, and never, to the close of his octogenarian career, lost the French accent of his boyhood — both of whom rendered civic services which may be commemorated among the victories of peace.

Nor is the experience of our Republic peculiar. Where is the country or power which must not inscribe the names of foreigners on its historic scroll? It was Christopher Columbus, of Genoa, who disclosed to Spain the New World; it was Magellan, of Portugal, sailing in the service of Spain, who first pressed with adventurous keel through those distant Southern straits which now bear his name, and opened the way to the vast Pacific sea; and it was Cabot, the Venetian, who first conducted English enterprise to this North American continent. As in the triumphs of discovery, so, also, in other fields have foreigners excelled, while serving States to which they were bound by no tie of birth. The Dutch Grotius — author of the sublime work, "The Laws of Peace and War" — an exile from his own country — became the Ambassador of Sweden, and, in our own day, the Italian Pozzo di Borgo, turning his back upon his own country, has reached the most exalted diplomatic trusts in the jealous service of Russia. In the list of monarchs on the throne of England, not one has been more truly English than the Dutch William. In Holland, no ruler has equalled in renown the German William, Prince of Orange. In Russia, the German Catharine II. takes a place among the most commanding sovereigns. And who of the Swedish monarchs was a better Swede than Bernadotte, the Frenchman; and what Frenchman was ever filled with aspirations for France more than the Italian Napoleon Bonaparte?

But I pass from these things, which have occupied me too long. A party, which, beginning in secrecy, interferes with religious belief, and founds a discrimination on the accident of birth, is not the party for us.

It was the sentiment of that great Apostle of Freedom, Benjamin Franklin, uttered during the trials of the Revolution, that, "Where Liberty is, there is my country." In similar strain, I would say, "Where Liberty is, there is my party." Such an organization is now happily constituted here in Massachusetts, and in all the Free States, under the name of the REPUBLICAN PARTY.

In assuming our place as a distinct party, we simply give form and direction, in harmony with the usage and genius of popular governments, to a movement which stirs the whole country, and does not find an adequate and constant organ in either of the other existing parties. The early opposition to Slavery was simply a sentiment, out-gushing from the hearts of the sensitive and humane. In the lapse of time, it became a determined principle, inspiring larger numbers, and showing itself first in an organized endeavor to resist the annexation of slaveholding Texas; next, to prohibit Slavery in newly acquired territories: and now, alarmed by the overthrow of all rights in Kansas, and the domination of the Slave Oligarchy throughout the

Republic, it breaks forth in a stronger effort, a wider union, and a deeper channel inspiring yet larger numbers and firmer resolves, while opposite quarters contribute to its power — even as the fountain, first outgushing from the weeping sides of its pure mountain home, trickles in the rill, leaps in the torrent, and flows in the river, till at last, swollen with accumulated waters, it presses onward, forever onward, in irresistible beneficent current, fertilizing and uniting the spaces which it traverses, washing the feet of cities, and wooing states to repose upon its banks.

Parties are the natural expression of a strong public sentiment, which seeks vent. As old controversies subside, the parties by which they have been conducted must yield to others which represent the actual life of the times. In obedience to this law, political parties in France and England — the only countries where these are known — have undergone mutations with time. In France, under the royalty of Louis Phillippe, the small band of *republicans*, feeble at first in numbers, and represented in the Legislature by a few persons only, but strong in principles and purpose, rallied together and at length prevailed over the old parties, until all were equally subverted by Louis Napoleon, and their place supplied by the enforced unity of despotism. In England, the most brilliant popular triumph of her history — the repeal of the monopoly of the corn laws — was finally carried, by means of a newly-formed, but wide-spread political organization, which combined men of all the old parties, Whigs, Tories, and Radicals, and put forward the single idea of opposition to the corn laws, as its end and aim. In the spirit of these examples the friends of Freedom, in well compacted ranks, now unite to uphold their cherished principles, and by combined efforts, according to the course of parties, to urge them upon the Government and the country.

Our party has its origin in the exigencies of the hour. Vowing ourselves against Slavery wherever it exists, whether enforced by the Russian knout, the Turkish bastinado, or the lash of the Carolina planter, we do not seek to interfere with it at Petersburg, Constantinople, or Charleston; nor does any such grave duty rest upon us. Our political duties are properly limited by our political responsibilities; and we are in no just sense responsible for the local law or usage by which human bondage in these places is upheld. But wherever we are responsible for the wrong, there our duty begins. The object to which, as a party, we are pledged, is all contained in the acceptance of the issue which the Slave Oligarchy tenders. To its repeal of the Missouri Compromise, and its imperious demand that Kansas shall be surrendered to Slavery, we reply, that Freedom shall be made the universal law of all the national domain, without compromise, and that hereafter no Slave State shall be admitted into the Union. To its tyrannical assumption of supremacy in the National Government, we reply that the Slave Oligarchy shall be overthrown. Such is the practical purpose of the Republican Party.

It is to uphold and advance this cause, that we have come together, leaving the parties to which we have been respectively attached. Now, in the course of human events, it becomes our duty to dissolve the political bands which bound us to the old organizations, and to assume a separate existence. Our Declaration of Independence has been made. Let us, in the spirit of our Fathers, pledge ourselves to sustain it with our lives, our fortunes and our sacred honor. In thus associating and harmonizing from opposite quarters, in order to promote a common cause, we have learned to forget former differences, and to appreciate the motives of each other. We have learned how trivial are the matters on which we may disagree, compared with the Great Issue on which we all agree. Old prejudices have vanished. Even the rancors of political antagonism have been changed and dissolved, as in a potent alembic, by the natural irresistible affinities of Freedom. In our union we have ceased to wear the badges of either of the old organizations. We have become a new party, distinct, independent, permanent, under a new name, with Liberty as our watchword, and our flag inscribed, "By this sign conquer."

Our object is reasonable, consistent with the Constitution, and required by just self-defence. And yet it is assailed from opposite quarters, and by various objections.

It is even objected, that the Republican Party is actually *injurious* to the very cause we seek to promote, and this paradoxical accusation, which might naturally show itself among the rank weeds of the South, is cherished here on our Free Soil by those who anxiously look for any fig-leaf with which to cover their indifference or tergiversation. This peculiar form of complaint is an old device which has been instinctively employed on other occasions, until it has ceased to be even plausible. Thus, throughout all time, has every good cause been encountered. Even Wilberforce, when pressing the abolition of the slave trade, was told that those efforts by which his name is now consecrated for evermore, tended to retard the cause he sought to promote, even to the extent of riveting anew the chains of the slave; and, mentioning this great example, I may dismiss the objection to the contempt it deserves.

With more pertinacity it is objected, that ours is a *sectional* party, and the significant words of Washington are quoted to warn the country against "geographical" questions. This is a mere bugbear, with which to disturb timid nerves. It is a part of the intolerable usurpation of the Slave Oligarchy, that the sectional institution of Slavery is exalted to be national in its character, so that a National Whig is simply a Slavery Whig, and a National Democrat is simply a Slavery Democrat. According to the true interpretation of the Constitution, Freedom and not Slavery is national, while Slavery and not Freedom is sectional. Now, if the Republican party proposed any measures calculated to operate exclusively upon any "geographical" section, or if it sought to direct the powers of Congress upon Slavery in the States, then, perhaps, it might be obnoxious to this charge; but as it simply acts against Slavery under the National jurisdiction, and seeks to dislodge the Slave Oligarchy from their usurped control of the National Government, it is absurd to say that it is sectional. Our aim is in no respect sectional, but in every respect national. It is in no respect against the South, but against the Evil Spirit at the South, which has perverted our national politics. As well might it be said that Washington, and Jefferson and Franklin were sectional and against the South. To all who are really against *sectionalism*, I would say, what sectionalism so direful as that of Slavery? To all who profess to be against *isms*, I would say, what *ism* so wretched as the *ism* of Slavery? If you are in earnest, join the National party of Freedom.

Again, it is objected that the Republican party is *against the Union*, and we are reminded of the priceless blessings which come from this fountain. Here is another bugbear. With us the Union is not the object of mere lip service, but it is cherished in simple sincerity, as the aged Lear was loved by his only faithful daughter, "according to her bond, nor more nor less." Our party does nothing against the Union, but everything for it. It strives to guard those great principles which the Union was established to secure, and thus to keep it ever worthy of our love. It seeks to overthrow that baleful Oligarchy, under which the Union has been changed from a vessel of honor to a vessel of dishonor. In this patriot work it will persevere, regardless of menace from any quarter. Not that I love the Union less but Freedom more, do I now, in pleading this great cause, insist that Freedom, at all hazards, shall be preserved. God forbid, that for the sake of the Union, we should sacrifice the very things for which the Union was made.

And yet again, it is objected that ours is a party of a *single idea*. This is a phrase, and nothing more. The party may not recognize certain measures of public policy, deemed by some of special importance; but it does what is better, and what other parties fail to do. It acknowledges that beneficent principle, which, like the great central light, vivifies all, and without which all is dark and sterile. The moving cause and the animating soul of our party, is the idea of Freedom. But this idea is manifold in character and influence. It is the idea of the Declaration of Independence. It is the great idea of the founders of the Republic. It is the idea which combined our Fathers on the heights of Bunker Hill; which carried Washington through a seven years' war; which inspired Lafayette; which touched with coals of fire the lips of Adams, Otis, and Patrick Henry. Ours is an idea, which is at least noble and elevating; it is an idea which draws in its train virtue, goodness and all the charities of life, all that makes earth a home of improvement and happiness —

> "Her track, where'er the goddess roves,
> Glory pursues, and generous shame,
> The unconquerable mind and Freedom's holy flame."

Thus do all objections disappear, even as the mists of morning before the sun, rejoicing like a strong man to run his race. The Republican party stands vindicated in every particular. It only remains that I should press the question with which I begun — "Are you for Freedom, or are you for Slavery?" As it is right to be taught by the enemy, let us derive instruction from the Oligarchy we oppose. The three hundred and forty-seven thousand slave masters are always united. Hence their strength. Like arrows in a quiver, they cannot be broken. The friends of Freedom have thus far been divided. They, too, must be united. In the crisis before us, it becomes you all to forget ancient feuds, and those names which have been the signal of strife. There is no occasion to remember anything but our duties. When the fire-bell rings at midnight, we do not ask if it be Whigs or Democrats, Protestants or Catholics, natives or foreigners, who join our efforts to extinguish the flames; nor do we ask any such question in selecting our leader then. Men of all parties, Whigs and Democrats, or however named, let me call upon you to come forward and join in a common cause. Do not hesitate. When Freedom is in danger, all who are not for her are against her. The penalty of indifference, in such a cause, is akin to the penalty of opposition; as is well pictured by the great Italian poet, when, among the saddest on the banks of Acheron — rending the air with outcries of torment, shrieks of anger and smiting of hands — he finds the troop of dreary souls who had been ciphers only in the great conflicts of life:

> "Mingled with whom, of their disgrace the proof,
> Are the vile angels, who did not rebel,
> Nor kept their faith to God, *but stood aloof.*"

Come forth, then, from the old organizations; let us range together. Come forth, all who have stood aloof from parties; here is an opportunity for action. You who place principles above men! come forward. All who feel in any way the wrong of Slavery, take your stand! Join us, ye lovers of Truth, of Justice, of Humanity! And let me call especially upon the young. You are the natural guardians of Liberty. In your firm resolves and generous souls she will find her surest protection. The young man who is not willing to serve in her cause — to suffer, if need be, for her — gives little promise of those qualities which secure an honorable age.

FELLOW-CITIZENS: We found now a new party.

Its corner-stone is Freedom. Its broad, all-sustaining arches are Truth, Justice, and Humanity. Like the ancient Roman Capitol, at once a Temple and a Citadel, it shall be the fit shrine for the genius of American Institutions.

www.ingramcontent.com/pod-product-compliance
Lightning Source LLC
LaVergne TN
LVHW021233110826
845150LV00002B/319